KT-549-292

Partners in Protest

Partners in Protest

Life with Canon Collins

DIANA COLLINS

London
Victor Gollancz Ltd
1992

First published in Great Britain 1992
by Victor Gollancz Ltd
14 Henrietta Street, London WC2E 8QJ

© Diana Collins 1992

The right of Diana Collins to be identified as
author of this work has been asserted by her in
accordance with the Copyright, Designs and
Patents Act 1988

A catalogue record for this book
is available from the British Library

ISBN 0 575–04823–9

Typeset at The Spartan Press Ltd, Lymington, Hampshire
Printed and bound by Butler & Tanner Ltd, Frome, Somerset

To past and present members of
The Fellowship of the Transfiguration,
past and present members of
The Council of Christian Action;
and to all the many, many people
who have supported the work
and made it possible.

Contents

Acknowledgements

THERE are so many people I should like to thank that I hardly know where to begin. The list of people who have talked and written to me about John would fill more than a page. Considerations of length have not allowed me to quote all I would have wished from them, but all they have told me has helped me to create a lively picture of John in the days before I knew him.

For John's earliest days, I have to thank his surviving sister Margaret Todd. She has a remarkably clear memory, and from her I have learned a great deal about the Collins family, and the childhood life of the four children.

Among those who have read the MS and made helpful and encouraging comments, I thank Sir John Verney, Jacquetta Priestley, Nadir Dinshaw, and my nearly blind aunt, Eve Bingham, who listened patiently and helpfully as I read aloud each completed chapter.

I cannot sufficiently thank my heroic friend Val Robinson who has typed the MS for me, and has made helpful suggestions and comments as we went along. She wrestled with my awful handwriting, and then again with all the cuts, alterations and rewritings recommended by my helpful editor Elfreda Powell.

Immense gratitude to Eric James, director of Christian Action, and to Jane Spurr, his secretary, who have undertaken the index, and to Val Robinson and Maggie Bishop for help with proof-reading. I am much relieved not to have to face these two demanding tasks.

Mill House
March 1992

Foreword
by Bishop Trevor Huddleston CR

To have been asked by the author to write a foreword for this book is an honour and a privilege, but it is also something more. I believe that this is exactly the moment for a biography of Canon John Collins and that, as I hope to show, his wife Diana is the only person who has the ability and the understanding to do justice to the subject. That may seem an exaggerated claim. I do not think so. My reasons for making it are two-fold, and in fact are spelt out in the title: *Partners in Protest. Life with Canon Collins*. The book is an historical biography of John and at the same time a deeply moving autobiography of Diana. The result is an enthralling account of a partnership in marriage which not only survived for over forty years and was immeasurably deepened in the process, but which, because it was a *true* partnership, enabled the many gifts of John and Diana to be used creatively in a great cause. And this is precisely the moment when the story should be told. It is a moment in the history of humanity when choices of immense importance confront the nations of the world. All these choices, whether we look east or west, north or south, involve the *resolution of conflict*, consensus or confrontation, a new world order or global devastation.

For me, reading every page of this book slowly and carefully was literally a revelation not just of the achievements, against great odds, of John and Diana over forty years, but of the power of protest when it is the result of total commitment and dedication to the cause of Truth. I put it that way for I believe that protest is not what it may sometimes appear to be: a negative reaction to traditional values or to the institutions which embody them; a kind of petulance, like that of the adolescent seeking his own identity and rebelling against his parents whilst still dependent on them; a shout or a scream designed to shatter complacency but which cannot be much more than diversion. Although I had known John and Diana for half my life (I was born seven years after John and four years before Diana), I realised as I read this book how little I had really known

about the well-spring of commitment that drove them forward and had
such consequences for Church and state and society itself. Their protest
was a protest against injustice. Thank God for it! It produced Christian
Action, the Campaign for Nuclear Disarmament, the International
Defence and Aid Fund for Southern Africa, and stirred into effective
participation thousands – perhaps millions – of individuals who had
felt that their contribution to peace and justice on earth was too
insignificant to change anything. I know from personal experience how
easy it is to think that way until some form of solidarity in a righteous
cause becomes possible and, in the end, effective.

As this book reveals, the childhood and adolescence of John and Diana
had, each in its own way, a foreshadowing of what was to come. But
only with hindsight could that be recognised. I think that it is for this
reason that, most unusually, biography and autobiography have been
so perfectly blended. There is a fine example of this when, as a canon of
St Paul's in 1949, John published a small book and called it *A Theology of
Christian Action*, based upon three lectures he had given in Lichfield
Cathedral. In it he defined what he meant by Christian Action: 'Its
emphasis is upon action, but its roots are in faith and worship
– theology therefore is fundamentally important'. The movement had
and must have 'sound theological justification'. He described his book
as 'merely an *hors d'oeuvre* to a proper theology'. But, as Diana says, 'the
major theological treatise never followed – *action overwhelmed us . . .*'
From time to time John would say that he was 'really an academic at
heart'. I questioned this; if it were true he could, after all, have remained
in Oxford (as dean of Oriel). 'You have the academic ability,' I said, 'but
not the temperament. I have the temperament without the comparable
ability.' And Diana sums up: 'Certainly John put a great deal of thought
into Christian Action and its related causes but it was good feeling that
fuelled it and him; it was his sympathetic heart that led, and occasionally
misled, him. "The seat of knowledge," wrote Hazlitt, "is in the head; of
wisdom in the heart. We are sure to judge wrong, if we do not *feel right.*"
The point about John was that he did "feel right"; he had, as his RAF
colleague Joseph Blades said, "*a passion for justice*".' I have quoted this
passage at length – and I could have quoted many others to illustrate my
point – because it seems to me to epitomise so perfectly the theme of the
whole book and the real meaning of that partnership in protest that it
describes.

It is not, however, the purpose of a foreword to be a précis of the
book itself and it would spoil the enjoyment of the reader if I were to
use it in that way. My purpose is to point to the significance of this

biography/autobiography for this moment, ten years after John's death, when so much in the turbulence of world events is proving his life and actions so profoundly important. I suppose that is the purpose of all historical writing, for history is never simply a chronicle of the past: it is always a challenge to contemporary thought for the future. It is an instrument of change which, if it is disregarded, can lead to national and international disaster. It is often disregarded by our politicians. Of course John's career from the moment when he won a scholarship to Cambridge and achieved a good first class in the theological tripos seemed certain to lead to an academic career. In fact it did so far more rapidly than is usual for, after only one very short curacy he returned to Cambridge as chaplain of his old college, Sidney Sussex, determined to read for a PhD and become a creative theologian. That determination – or ambition – was real and entirely in keeping with his pastoral vocation; it led directly to other important work in the training of men for the ministry, and indirectly from Cambridge to Oxford via St Paul's Cathedral and to the outbreak of war and marriage to Diana in 1939.

It was when he joined the RAF as a chaplain and was posted in the late autumn of 1941 to Yatesbury, reputed to be the worst run and most unpopular camp in RAF Technical Training Command, that the greatest challenge and most important development in John's vocation occurred. Indeed, without it, there would have been no Christian Action, no CND, and no International Defence and Aid Fund for Southern Africa. For it was there, in that bleak and dismal training camp, with no centre of worship and no inducement to create one that John's true pastoral and prophetic ministry came to life. The chapters on the Fellowship of the Transfiguration which, against all the odds, he founded are in many respects the most important in this book. The 'FT' runs like Blake's 'golden string' from that moment to the end of the story. 'I give you the end of a golden string / Only wind it into a ball / It will bring you in at Heaven's gate / Built in Jerusalem's wall.' For it was the response of individuals caught up in the chaos of war, in the years of conflict and boredom in camps and outposts and, when war was over, in a painful return to 'civvy street' that gave John the vision of a *new* spirituality. It was to be a spirituality based upon the kind of church that existed in the first years of Christianity – small 'cells' scattered across a pagan, persecuting, Roman Empire, with no status, no access to the corridors of power, only the realisation that 'we could do nothing of value except by the grace of God and the power of the Holy Spirit working in us . . .'

A new spirituality? Not really, because it was the spirituality that had 'turned the world upside down' in the first place that had to be recovered for the Church and for the world in the second half of the twentieth century.

This book, with its fascinatingly detailed study of Christian Action and what it led to for the future of our world, should be compulsory reading for all sectors of our Western society today. It is a book that knows how to distinguish between facile optimism and hope.

One day, I have no doubt, a blue plaque will be placed on the wall of 2 Amen Court recording, for posterity, the fact that 'John and Diana Collins lived here and together, through Christian Action and its offspring, helped to light the candle of hope in a grey and darkening world'.

Bishop Trevor Huddleston CR
May 1992

Prologue – An End and a Beginning

JOHN and I were married in 1939 on 21 October. This was the most important event in my life. But days before the wedding, I had had a sudden panic. Late at night, alone in my small bedroom, I had begun to wonder, to fear, what I was about to do. I looked around my room: there were my books, the table at which I worked and scribbled, outside were fields and trees and the wide sweep of the Stour estuary; it was here that I had dreamed and thought and wondered about my future: it was me. Though I had often rebelled against my home and my family, they were security and love, experienced and familiar. Could I really commit myself for ever to this man? I knew that it would have to be for ever. We had known each other for a year, but did I really know him? Was I ready to lead his life, rather than my own, tentative and dilettante as mine was?

Although I seemed unable to avoid getting tangled up with the clergy, if anyone had asked me if I wanted to become the wife of a clergyman I would have answered emphatically 'No'.

Next morning confidence returned and never left me. Custom decreed that bride and groom must not spend the night before their wedding under the same roof, so John had been packed off to stay with nearby relatives. But we were allowed to meet, and John came to tea. As soon as I saw him I knew that all was well. Tall, dark and handsome as the fortune-tellers say, an Anglican priest, fellow of an Oxford college, he appeared conventional and traditional, but he had an inner spirit that would keep shaking and breaking through all those conventional constraints. He was so often laughing and surrounded by laughter. 'But he's not a bit like a clergyman,' people said, 'he's so human'. This was John, my safe haven, how could I ever have doubted that I wanted to share the rest of my life with him? And then my grandmother brought out her best Rockingham tea service which I had never before been allowed even to touch.

Outside it was grey and raining, but my young brother had bicycled all over the countryside – petrol was already on wartime rationing – and had collected armfuls of autumn leaves, scarlet hips, dusky haws and a mass of spindle-berries. These last seemed to fill the church with their softly glowing pink heads, and startling flashes of orange-seed.

We were married by B. K. Cunningham, principal of Westcott House theological college, where John had been a student and then vice-principal. B. K. was assisted by John's close friend and some-time pupil Mervyn Stockwood, who met me with cheering words at the church door. Now it was John, encased in forbidding clerical morning dress, who appeared sweating and nervous, was it nerves or emotion or both? But I was glad and wholehearted, nothing less than those tremendous promises could do justice to all that I felt for John.

We had studied the marriage service together, and it was I who insisted on the old 1662 version with its robust down-to-earth language. We looked at the three 'objects' for which marriage was supposedly ordained. 'As a remedy against fornication': far too negative; I would have been happily prepared for fornication before we were married, but John was firm, the rule must be kept. 'Children': that was fine, we were going to have six, three boys and three girls, we had already chosen their names. 'Mutual help society and comfort that the one ought to have of the other': that was exactly what I wanted to give and hoped to receive. And I wanted John to say 'with my body I thee worship', rather than the tepid updated 1928 version, 'with my body I thee honour'. Honour sounded cool and distant, I had no wish to be honoured, but 'worship', that suggested the warmth and comfort of the body I loved and longed for.

As for that matter of promising to obey my husband, I knew that John would never ask me to do anything to which I strongly objected. Now, in my less innocent and more feminist old age, I would happily make those promises again, but I would not repeat 'obey'. It is bad for men to imagine that they have any right to command obedience.

John might have liked a more musical service than our little Suffolk village choir and organist could provide, but I was content with it all. I still remember B. K. Cunningham's words, and his comments on John as a man with 'great gifts of scholarship, and no small gift of leadership'. I wondered about that at the time, now I know that B. K. got it the wrong way round.

Borne aloft as I was, it all seemed dreamlike, and unreal, as did the lunchtime reception in the large Tudor house which had been my mother's and grandmother's home. I saw it all through a haze of happiness, love and champagne, and the hesitant autumn sun that obligingly appeared to lighten our way.

Then, at last, we were alone in a slow, heavily blacked-out train, and after a number of changes we arrived at Moreton-in-Marsh in the Cotswolds, where a car was waiting to take us to the Lygon Arms at Broadway. John was a magnet for anything that could buzz and bite and sting, and, *en route*, he collected several fleas, which settled in most awkward places upon his appetising flesh. We spent a great part of our first night with cakes of damp soap, trying to trap those elusive little wretches.

So 1939 was for us an end and a beginning. It was an end, too, for the kind of world in which John and I had grown up. It had taken us time, in John's case quite a long time, to find each other; we had each made false starts. We had had difficulties, some painful, before we finally reached the altar, and now we had to find each other at a different and deeper level, a lifetime's occupation.

'Love consists in this that two Solitudes protect and touch and greet each other.'

1

A Flowering Meadow

I am running through a meadow, proud of how fast I can run. The meadow is all wild flowers and grasses; they seem very tall since I am still small. There are moon daisies, buttercups, dandelions, young red sorrel, and masses of tiny wild flowers; the grasses stroke my bare legs and arms delightfully. The wind is blowing in my face, and rippling the grass. It must be early summer, before the hay harvest. Skylarks and blackbirds are in full song, I can hear wood pigeons crooning, and swifts and swallows are diving after insects. It must be early evening, since the sun is low, throwing dark blue shadows and shining with a particularly rich and golden light. And it must be a Sunday evening, for the sound of church bells is carried clearly over the waters of the river.

And I am running to the river, the magical, mysterious river, the Stour estuary, which is now at high tide, a huge two-mile stretch of the bluest of deep blue sea-water. I love the river passionately, and the meadow, and the wind in my face. I feel what I can only describe as an ecstasy of physical joy. This is an enchanted place, Stutton and Stutton Hall, the home of my mother's parents. The grown-ups, my mother, my grandmother and an aunt or two are walking behind. My brother David, my playmate, rival and later my closest friend, is somewhere behind as well; he is eighteen months younger than I am, and cannot yet run as fast. In this bright little fragment of faraway childhood lives much that gave me such an idyllic entry into this strange and fascinating world.

At my back is the emotional security of the people I love, and the people who love me, and will continue to love me however outrageous my behaviour. I adore my grandmother, a central figure in my young life. I am her first grandchild, and never can there have been a more devoted nor a more consistently indulgent grandmother. And there is my mother, who is beautiful and generally indulgent as well, and certainly there is her younger sister, Aunt Tilly, our favourite aunt, always ready to play games, to take us birds'-nesting or butterfly-chasing.

We walk through parkland to the river, and just above the shore we enter the wild and exciting Grove. Here, in springtime, we pick primroses and bluebells and listen to the nightingales, and, if we are lucky, find their nests among the brambles and nettles, along with the nests of so many other wild birds. In summer there are delectable picnics, and in autumn we come to gather blackberries and mush-rooms. This pastoral scene is so familiar, and roots me to the land in which my mother's family – the Fisons – have lived for several generations.

But there is another aspect to the river. Twice in twenty-four hours, salt water from the North Sea flows slowly up and covers the grey-green mud flats. Then the water retreats way out to sea, leaving the mud flats to hungry sea and marsh birds, with only a thin ribbon of a channel in the middle, and the sea is the way to adventure and exploration. On clear days, when we look down to Harwich, we can see the ships returning from and departing to strange and faraway places. A part of me wants to stay for ever in the earthly paradise that I know and love, but another part longs to follow the tides to the sea, to embark on the great ships and to explore the unknown world beyond.

The church bells are still ringing through that golden evening. Religion, the Church of England, is always there in our lives. It is not just a formal and conventional religion such as is required of the owners of the 'big houses' in a village community. My grandmother is the daughter of an Essex clergyman, and religion is the basis and mainspring of her life. My mother too is religious, and Bible stories old and new are our familiar reading. At this early age I am happy with all this. Our butler's thirteen-year-old daughter escorts David and myself to Sunday school; we like her very much, and we love her father Mr Vinall. Sunday school is not bad, the rector's wife reads to us, there are other children to play with, and sometimes we get sweets.

At night we say prayers with Mother or Grandmother, and sometimes we sing a hymn. 'All things bright and beautiful' and 'Now the day is over' are my favourites, giving me a comforting feeling of security when the lights are turned out and the bedroom is full of faintly menacing shadows. I am afraid, however, that the reiterated petition to 'make Diana a good girl' seems to meet with little or no response. I go fairly willingly to church with my grandmother, many of the words sound like poetry to which I am soon addicted. Occasionally there is something interesting in the sermons, and I enjoy the hymns, though sadly I am totally lacking in any musical talent. Best of all I enjoy 'helping' my grandmother decorate the church for the festivals, Christmas, Easter, Whitsun and Harvest Thanksgiving.

One important figure is missing from this early picture, and that is our young father. He seems almost godlike to us. Handsome, fair-haired and tall, he is splendidly athletic and good at every game, he turns somersaults with us, does handstands, climbs trees and teaches us swimming and tennis and cricket. He is a wonderful bedtime storyteller. Some of his stories are about India, for that is where he and his elder brother and three younger sisters spent their early childhoods; but there are fairies and witches and giants at the bottom of the garden too: it is all exciting, and sometimes very funny.

Not all memories of childhood can be happy and golden. We had to have nannies. They seemed to follow in quick succession, arriving with tales of their previous charges, all boringly well-behaved, and leaving after a few months declaring that we were the naughtiest children they had ever known. One of my aunts used to say that after each departure I would jump up and down chanting gleefully 'Another one done for! Hurrah! Another one gone!'

I did not love my nannies. I found their rules and their regimes unbearably restricting. Life with them was worst in my parents' London home in Putney, far from the freedom of Stutton. We were taken for walks on Putney Heath and because we were supposed to be a little lady and a little gentleman, we had to wear hats and gloves and walk sedately – no climbing trees or fishing in muddy ponds for tiddlers. How we envied ragged urchins with their jam jars and their sticks with bits of string and a bent safety-pin on the end.

Back at home our parents made us a sandpit in the garden, but nannies would not allow us to use water with the sand in case we got ourselves and our clothes wet and dirty. We used to stand by this pit, haunted by thoughts of the river shore at Stutton, vainly trying to summon up enough spit to make this London sand just the smallest bit damp.

Perhaps my aversion to nannies stemmed from an experience when I was about five years old. I had been a bridesmaid to my mother's brother Clavering who was marrying Evelyn Bland. For the first year of their marriage they rented a house in Stutton village, and there we all went for a summer holiday.

Every morning after breakfast, the grown-ups drove off to compete in various tennis tournaments, and David and I were left alone with the nanny of the moment. As soon as the grown-ups had departed, Nanny

took me upstairs, pulled down my knickers, put me across her knees
and gave me a severe spanking. The spanking was hard enough to
make me cry, but what I chiefly remember is my outraged sense of
injustice: I knew I had done nothing wrong. The spankings were
regularly administered even after I had made special efforts to be
obedient and well-behaved.

I protested vehemently, I said I would tell my mother, but Nanny
replied that she would tell my mother what a naughty little girl I was,
and I would get more and more severe spankings. In spite of my brave
words, I was frightened, nannies had power, and grown-ups had a
way of lining up together. In the end, I did tell my mother, and this
particular nanny departed. That was my first encounter with injustice.

Sunshine and shadow, but I was fortunate, it is the sunlight that
illumines so many of my earliest memories.

2

Stutton Hall

M Y grandfather, James Fison, had bought Stutton Hall and the surrounding estate in 1887, soon after his marriage to Lucy Nash. The house, which in some form or other dates back to the sixteenth century, was in a state of neglect and disrepair. James, with considerable knowledge and taste, set about its restoration; he planted woods and parkland, and together he and Lucy laid out the gardens. In a little flourish of grandeur peacocks were later introduced, and finding their brilliant tail-feathers was a special delight for my brother and me.

The Fisons had been around in East Anglia for many years, as farmers, as millers, and, when milling became unprofitable, they turned to the chemical fertiliser industry. They really cared about the conservation and improvement of the land, and were knowledgeable and enthusiastic about all its wildlife.

In those first years life flourished in all directions. Fison children arrived in quick succession – Lorimer, Madeleine, Clavering, Vere (my mother), Sylvia, known as Tilly because she found the letter 'S' unmanageable, and John. There is no doubt that my grandparents were devoted to each other, and in those years before the First World War this must have seemed an ideal family growing up in ideal conditions. While James was respected in the locality as a good landlord and employer, and a responsible JP, his wife, Lucy, visited and cared for the poorer families in the village; 'Lady Bountiful' yes, except that she never condescended. A 'do-gooder' yes, all those roles that are now regarded in progressive circles with a kind of contempt. But in those days, who else was there to help those in need? My grandmother took the Christian imperative of charitable giving very seriously. During the First World War she kept in touch with every man from the village who was serving abroad, and at Christmas each one received a parcel of good things, while my grandfather ensured that their families at home were cared for.

There must have been some social and personal insecurity lurking inside my grandfather. The Fisons were rising through the complex levels of the English middle classes, but some of the older county families still thought them faintly parvenus. I am told that James used to ride into his Ipswich office by circuitous back routes so that, should he meet anyone he knew, it would look as if he were exercising one of his hunters, rather than making his way to the sordid business of trade.

In contrast to the Fisons, my father's family, the Elliots, were adventurers, soldiers, diplomats, professional people, empire builders and protectors. The Elliots were more secure in their social position than the Fisons. One of my Elliot forebears was a Dr John Lettsom, who began life as a Quaker, and when quite young inherited substantial estates in the West Indies. This was some time before slavery was legally abolished, but his first action upon entering into his inheritance was to free all his slaves.

My paternal grandfather was a doctor in the Indian Medical Service, and his father had also worked in India. So it was that the Elliot children, Grenfell, Ian (my father), Hazel, Heather and Evangeline, the baby, therefore known as 'Bobby', spent their earliest years in India. They seem never to have had a settled home in England, and when the time came for them to be sent home to boarding schools, they spent their holidays with relatives. Money was always in short supply.

My father was clever, hard-working and ambitious. He won a scholarship to Rugby, and another to Christ Church, Oxford. There he met two young Fisons, Lorimer and Clavering, and soon he and his two sisters Hazel and Heather, along with other Oxford friends, were invited to Stutton Hall to take part in tennis, cricket and swimming in the summer, shooting and hockey in the winter, and various social activities. In the Fison family there was a great deal of badinage, teasing, dressing-up, charades and amateur theatricals. Ian, always highly susceptible to feminine charms, fell in love with Vere, the prettiest of the Fison daughters, and she with him, while Lorimer and Hazel began to take an interest in each other.

What a period of promise this was for my father: after two years at Oxford he had a first in Classical Honour Mods, and was on his way to a cricket blue; he was in love with the most wonderful girl in the world, who felt the same about him. Then, in 1914, the world that he and his young friends knew fell apart for ever.

Immediately after the declaration of war, Lorimer, Clavering and my father enlisted in the Suffolk Regiment, and as soon as he was old enough, John joined them. The girls went off to train as nurses, and to drive ambulances. The boys fought continuously in France.

By 1915, Ian and Vere were both twenty-one, so they were allowed to become formally engaged. They were married in July 1916 and I was born at Stutton Hall in August 1917. Lorimer and Hazel were married in March 1917.

The boys had survived almost three years of one of the most – if not the most – appalling wars in history. But in the end they joined so many millions in physical suffering and grief. In November 1917, only three months after his marriage, Lorimer died of pneumonia, after being badly gassed. Lorie was the much-loved heir, the pride of his parents, a decorated war hero, a leader of men, and respected in the village. Lorie's death devastated the family. Both Clavering and John were severely wounded. My father too was wounded, and my brother and I used to be fascinated by the scar on his side, and the knowledge that he still carried bits of German shrapnel inside him.

After demobilisation my father had to find a job and a home. He had been destined for the Civil Service, but he needed to earn money rather quickly, so he moved into the world of business, and became a junior executive in the iron and steel firm of Guest, Keen and Nettlefold.

Soon my parents, and I with them, settled in Putney. In March 1919 my mother, already six months pregnant, caught the virulent Spanish 'flu. With only a sister-in-law in the house a tiny baby boy arrived unexpectedly, to be followed to everyone's amazement by another tiny boy. The younger twin, John Lettsom, only lived for a week, but the elder, David, was wrapped in cotton-wool, put in a basket on top of the kitchen stove and, miraculously, survived.

I never remember being jealous of David. I don't think it occurred to me that anyone could prefer him to me! Of course, later on, nannies much preferred him to me, but as I didn't think much of nannies, that didn't bother me. I felt secure in the uncritical love of my grandmother and of my father; my mother too was loving and fair to us both; I never remember seeing her angry or ill-tempered. But I think she had a special feeling for David after his precarious beginning. He grew into an exceptionally attractive little boy, affectionate, loving and gener-ous, and though when roused he had quite a violent temper, he was normally gentle and easy, and altogether a much nicer character than I was.

Though I was not jealous of David, I was envious of his masculinity. I longed desperately to be a boy: boys had all the fun, were allowed to do exciting things, whereas girls, it seemed, were condemned to marriage and domesticity. And David was much more domesticated than I was. He was an industrious little boy, content to sit at home making rugs and kettle-holders, and trying his hand at knitting. He weeded and dead-headed for our grandmother, while I ran about admiring the flowers. On blackberrying expeditions he would settle down and methodically pick basket after basket full of berries; I picked very unmethodically with frequent breaks for climbing trees or looking for wild flowers. I wanted to be a soldier or an explorer, I refused to wear my girl's clothes and struggled into David's trousers, I refused to answer to my own name, and insisted on being called by a boy's name – I fancied Richard, because of Richard Coeur-de-Lion, or Edward, because of the Black Prince. I hated dolls.

David and I fought a good deal, often violently. We were both highly competitive, and in any game we each wanted to be the winner, so that led to accusations of cheating, indignant denials, personal abuse, fists and tears. It took us a very long time to learn to be good losers. But we were happy companions in crime, such as collecting great handfuls of caterpillars and stuffing them into the grown-ups' beds, and we collaborated in our two major activities, collecting birds' eggs, and collecting butterflies and moths. There were strict rules about birds'-nesting: never take more than one egg, if there was only one you had to leave it. To cause a bird to desert its nest was a dreadful disgrace. Going out at night after moths was really exciting. We smeared the barks of trees with a mixture of sugar and beer, and then crept out with torches to capture the inebriated insects – I hope that, at least, they died a happy death.

Back in London we had to be content with collecting cigarette cards, unfortunately in competition and therefore accompanied by quarrels. Life improved somewhat when we grew older and were allowed to take our scooters out into our street – 'So long as you don't go near the main road'. Obedience didn't figure very high in my priorities, but I knew that if this injunction were disobeyed I would lose my scooter. I introduced the game of 'Last Across' which we played with the children next door. We would watch for the approach of a car or a van, and see who dared wait the longest before dashing across in front of it; I got rather good at this. Twice I ran away from home, not because I was unhappy or wanted to leave permanently, I just wanted some unsupervised exploration on my own. The upset when I returned seemed unreasonable.

Granny was always ready to read aloud; I loved all tales of adventure and romance, fairy stories; Charles Kingsley's *The Heroes* impressed and excited me. I loved history as presented in *Our Island Story*, and I had *The Secret Garden* read to me so often that I knew most of it by heart. Soon, when I looked at it on my own, I found that the letters fell into place and formed words, and when I looked at books that I knew less well, the letters continued to fall into place, and that was how I learned to read. I did have my own secret garden that I had discovered in the woods, and which I cleared and tended devotedly. I suspect that everyone knew about it, but I pretended that they didn't.

And then there was poetry. I had it read to me, and, as soon as I was able, I read as much as I could find to myself. Before I could really write I made up rhymes in my head, and again as soon as I was able, I scribbled away.

On one visit to Stutton, I was told that I had to be particularly well-behaved, because a princess was coming to stay. I imagined some radiant creature out of a fairy story, crowned with gold and silver, sparkling with jewels, but reality cheated me badly. An ordinary lady arrived, not nearly as good-looking as my mother or my grand-mother. Much more important and interesting was the priest who had brought the princess to Stutton, Father Vernon Johnson. He had been a great influence on my Uncle Lorimer, and was an old family friend. He dressed in the strangest of clothes, and was dark and handsome. He had a charismatic quality that, even at that early age, created in me a powerful and lasting impression. He and the princess spent long hours in earnest conversation, walking in the garden and along by the river, but though I often hung hopefully around, I could never quite catch what they were saying.

Years later I discovered that Vernon had been deeply in love with my mother – all the young men seemed to have been in love with her at one time or another. She was apparently by no means immune to Vernon's charms, and they almost became engaged. But then my father appeared and swept all before him.

Vernon finally left the Anglican Church and became a Roman Catholic priest. Many years later when John and I were living in Oxford, and Vernon was chaplain to the Roman Catholic under-graduates, I invited him to tea. Before he left, he shyly produced a white silk scarf. 'Your mother gave me this,' he said. 'I keep it with me always; I kiss it when I go to bed.' And he added, 'Ian was so attractive as a young man, you couldn't refuse him anything.'

After Vernon and the princess's visit I went through a religious phase and began to consider the possibility of becoming a heroic missionary among savage tribes. But my religious enthusiasm abated, and doesn't seem to have had much effect on my behaviour. I was growing strong, and becoming more and more aggressive. I enjoyed fighting, especially boys. 'Fancy not daring to fight a girl,' I taunted, jumping threateningly around one of my victims; he was quite big, I never went for anyone smaller than myself. In the ensuing fracas I upset the boy's bicycle, and the groceries in his basket were smashed. The boy burst into tears. The upshot was that the shop manager and the boy came to see my parents. Of course they paid for everything, and my pocket-money was stopped for months. It was explained to me that this was a boy from a very poor home who was earning a little money to help his widowed mother, and having lost his groceries he was afraid that he might lose his job. I felt dreadfully ashamed.

I fear to think what I might have become had I not had such an extended and loving family. An aunt told me later, 'You were such a naughty little girl, Diana, such a dreadfully naughty child, but I did love you so much.' David and I – particularly I – were naughty children, but we did have a kind of code of honour which we more or less observed. You didn't tell lies, you didn't cheat, you didn't tell tales, and if challenged, you owned up rather than let anyone else take the blame.

When I was seven years old, and David six and a half, our lives began to change. Our mother had been ill, and was told that she ought not to winter in England. So for the next two winters, the family, including our grandmother and a nanny, were transported to the Alps. Our father came and went according to the dictates of his work. David and I were delighted by this change of scene, and revelled in the snow and the skiing. Our mother spent much of her time lying out on her balcony in the sun, treatment then prescribed for any lung complaint, though now considered almost lethal.

For the winter of 1926–1927 we did not go abroad. Instead the family moved to Hindhead where the air was thought to be especially healthy, and David and I were sent to a small local dame school.

By February our mother was in a nearby nursing home, and on most afternoons we were taken to have tea with her. One warm spring-like day we arrived to find her dressed and sitting out of bed. The window was open, and sunlight streamed in, bringing the astringency of pine trees and the honey scent of flowering gorse; all seemed wonderfully hopeful and life-giving.

Next day it was cold and raining, and we went again with our grandmother to the nursing home. We hurried up the stairs and along the passage to Mummy's room. She was back in bed, a doctor and two nurses were standing by the bed pumping oxygen into her lungs; she was breathing with difficulty in quick gasps, and her face was twisted and drawn, her eyes, normally bright with happiness and laughter, were now full of pain. She tried to speak to us but the effort was too great and we were hurried away.

Soon after this David and I both developed acute tonsillitis with high temperatures, so we saw nothing of each other and little of the rest of the family. Then came an evening that I remember as vividly as if it happened yesterday. The house seemed strangely quiet, only Nanny and Cook sitting below in the kitchen and talking in low voices. I was still running a temperature and confined to bed, but, against all rules, I climbed out and crept halfway down the stairs to listen. A bell rang, and Nanny went to the front door. I heard a man's voice, Uncle Vernon's voice.

'They are all up at the nursing home,' Nanny said, and he left immediately.

'I only hope he gets there in time,' she said to Cook. Miserable and frightened, I crept shivering back to bed. Of course I couldn't sleep, and after what seemed like hours the family returned and came silently upstairs. I didn't see my father, but Aunt Tilly was crying softly. Granny was quiet and calm; I think I must have been sleeping in her room.

'How is Mummy?' I asked desperately.

'She is very, very ill,' was all they said, but I knew it wasn't the truth.

Next morning I climbed into Granny's bed, and she told me that Mummy had died. What she actually said was: 'Jesus has taken your darling Mummy to live with himself'. And I think that was what she truly believed – I never saw her cry. As for me, I was overwhelmed, stunned by an inconceivable and unbelievable fact: I would never, never see my mother again.

After breakfast my father came and sat on my bed and wept, terrible heart-breaking sobs. I had never seen grown-ups cry, I didn't know they did. I thought only naughty children cried and now this young god of my childhood had become a broken man. I stroked his hair and tried to comfort him. I thought that as soon as I was old enough, I would look after him and make a home for him. I thought that I would love him and take care of him for ever.

3

Learning

A period of change and upheaval followed my mother's death. David and I were separated, he to board at a small preparatory school, I to stay briefly at our little dame school. In spite of our fights and squabbles, we hated having to be long apart.

Then we learned that Aunt Tilly was to be married, and since her husband to be (whom we knew as Uncle Hugh) was a coffee farmer, he would take her away to live in Kenya. 'You can't marry him,' I protested with nine-year-old tact. 'He's an old man.' (Hugh must have been around thirty-five.)

There was another shadow over our young lives, a big black cloud. Granny was going to leave Stutton Hall, and it would pass into the hands of strangers. We were only slightly consoled by being told that a new house was to be built on the estate, and we were to live there with Granny. We inspected the site – it was called Stony Field. It had a fine view of our river, and in the ditch that ran along one side we found three nightingales' nests beautifully decorated with oak leaves. It was next to an interesting farmyard, and beyond this, at Crepping Hall, another estate house, lived Uncle Clav and Aunt Evelyn, and their baby daughter Elizabeth.

The new house was built, mistakenly like a miniature Stutton Hall – not an architectural success. It was called Little Hall. I remember being mystified, when we finally moved in, by the fact that while two bathrooms were provided for us in the front of the house, in the back quarters where three living-in maids were to be accommodated, there was no bathroom, only a kind of household sink for washing. But outside, in that unpromising field of stones, Granny's love and green fingers worked their accustomed magic, and she created another blossoming garden.

Life assumed a pattern. I was sent to board and do lessons with a boy and girl of suitable ages living with their widowed mother and a resident governess. It was a thoroughly English country life, full of pet animals, ponies and hunting, and we drove around the countryside in a pony trap. Everyone was kind to me, I was neither happy nor unhappy, just adrift. Holidays were spent at Little Hall with Granny. These were made happier by the nearness of Uncle Clav and Aunt Evelyn and their ever-open and welcoming house. Clav always made us laugh, and we loved him for that. Evelyn had a marvellous understanding of children of all ages, and was endlessly patient. Although intensely home-loving, she was also a county councillor, and chaired numerous committees. There were Quakers in her family background, including Elizabeth Fry, the prison reformer, and Evelyn accepted without question the obligations of privilege and affluence. Like all my family, she was firmly Conservative, but she had an independent mind, and at a local level her views were progressive.

Our father visited us as often as he could. He wanted to give us everything, and with Granny's permission, he built us a hard tennis court and a squash court. The public-school mystique and worship of games pervaded our lives; it seemed more important to be good at games than to be clever, especially if you were a girl – men were not supposed to like clever women. Our mother had, in fact, been clever, though rather poorly educated, but she was a brilliant tennis player. Before the war she had won the All England Junior Singles Tournament, and in 1923 she got into the quarter finals of the Women's Singles at Wimbledon – but those were the days when sport was genuinely amateur.

David and I enjoyed and were good at games, but I soon found the mystique comic and boring. At one stage, my devoted father bought me a pony, and hired a groom to look after it, while I went through a young girl's passionate – though in my case temporary – addiction to horses. Poor Daddy, he could not have done more for us during those difficult times.

One year a large field just below the Little Hall garden was planted with clover, and by the summer holidays there were acres and acres of this sweet-smelling crop. Why are there so few fields of clover now? What do our vitamin-enriched, hormone-injected cattle eat in the winter? This field was a haven for nectar-hungry butterflies, and in this especially glorious summer, it was a year for migrant Clouded Yellows. They came in hundreds, in every shade from pale lemon to dusky ochre, and their markings were often rare and interesting. Our grandmother then discovered that the new bishop of St Edmundsbury and Ipswich was a keen entomologist, so she invited him to lunch to try his luck in our field. He was a little on the portly side. David and I raced about and caught numbers of rare and beautiful specimens; the bishop, unable to run very fast, caught rather few. But when we went back for tea we found that Granny proposed to give most of our splendid catch to the bishop. When he slipped away to wash we protested with vigour, but for once, indeed for the only time that I can remember, Granny stood firm, and we had to part with our precious specimens. That little episode really put me off bishops.

I was at last sent to a girl's boarding-school. It was a good school, with a progressive headmistress and an emphasis on the arts; it should have suited me. But the daily routine was inevitably monotonous, and boarding-schools have to be restrictive, so I soon found that it was much more fun to break the rules than to obey them.

For the Christmas holidays of 1930, our father announced that we were to go to Switzerland for a skiing holiday. We went with a boy and girl roughly our own ages, a married couple, and a young woman called Madeline Maclachlan. Madeline was particularly kind to David and me; she was very good-looking, always smartly dressed, and managed to combine an air of sophistication with a natural, straightforward approach to life. David and I took to her. On New Year's Eve we were allowed – for the first time – to stay up to welcome in 1931. After the traditional and emotional singing of 'Auld Lang Syne', our father, who must have been nerving himself up to this for the whole evening, told us that he was going to marry Madeline. For reasons which I certainly didn't understand at the time, I went to bed and cried all night.

David and I grew very fond of our stepmother; she was fun; she had a sense of humour, and she was a good friend to us. She could hardly, however, have been more different from our Stutton relatives. Her parents lived in Buenos Aires, where she had spent most of her life, though she had been briefly to a convent school in England. She was entirely urban: the country was there, not to be enjoyed for its own sake, but for sport; real life, social life was to be lived in the city. She seemed to have no background of public or charitable work, such as we saw at Stutton. And she was a Roman Catholic. For all her apparent worldliness, she was devout and disciplined, however difficult the circumstances, she never missed Mass on a Sunday. But none of this was likely to endear her to our Stutton relatives; for them Rome was still 'the scarlet woman'.

Our father went off to the Argentine to be married, and David and I returned to school. By this time, I was in revolt against all authority. I had become an atheist, and thought rather well of myself for having discarded the religious shackles of my upbringing. Once back at school a demon seemed to get into me. I aspired to become the naughtiest girl in the school. Looking back it all seems extraordinarily innocent, no drugs, no drink, no sex – I knew nothing of that. It was just breaking bounds, going on buses, going to cinemas, the odd cigarette, midnight feasts. I had friends who accompanied me on these escapades, but somehow I was always the one who got the blame.

I fell in love, really in love, with the games mistress. She took an interest, probably too much of an interest, in me. We read poetry together, and sometimes she kissed me. She encouraged me in my tentative forays into the worlds of music and art. Since I was ignorant of the facts of life, lesbianism would have been incomprehensible to me; my love was pure, idealistic and poetic. The games mistress did me no harm, and I owe her one important debt: 'Diana,' she said one day, 'after you leave school you really ought to go to Oxford'. I had never thought of such a thing, no girls I knew went to Oxford, they went to dances, came out, did a season, got married. But that little seed took root, germinated and shaped my life.

By the spring term of 1931 I had proved too disruptive for the school, and was asked to leave. The games mistress left too and, though we corresponded for a while, I never saw her again. My father was away honeymooning in South America, so my long-suffering grandmother had to come to take me back to Little Hall. I never had a word of reproach from her. Perhaps she understood me better than I understood myself.

Another school had to be found for me in a hurry, this time a more conventional school run by the Church Education Corporation. Here, after a rocky start, I eventually calmed down. Life for David and me became outwardly more settled. As well as our country home, we now had a home in London, where we could stay with our father and Madeline, and soon the birth of a baby sister, to be followed by baby brothers, was pure joy; we had always wanted brothers and sisters. We were taken for holidays abroad with Daddy and Madeline, in the summer to Le Zoute, a kind of poor-man's Le Touquet, on the Belgian coast, and for the occasional skiing holiday in the winter. David had moved on to Rugby with a scholarship, and superficially we were leading a privileged and a not unhappy life.

But David and I had troubles, and the normal troubles of adolescence were compounded by the circumstances of our lives. We loved, and would always love, the country, but we had outgrown our loving grandmother. Our grandmother's attitude to life was simple and

Victorian, her religious faith was based upon a literal acceptance of the Bible, her general outlook was narrow and prejudiced, and to her, we were still the little children who had to be cared for and fussed over. We chafed at her gentle fussing, we rebelled against church-going, we suffered from the total lack of mental stimulus, we were often rude and petulant, and then felt guilty and unhappy. For Granny spent her days pottering about on innumerable ploys and arrangements, all of which had in view one object only, our pleasure and our well-being; it was her delight to slave for us, indeed she lived for us, and young and thoughtless as we were, we took it all for granted.

Life with our father and stepmother was certainly more interesting, but still we did not want to lead their kind of life, and we did not want to live all the time in London. To Madeline the small, closed, provincial circle of Stutton life was incomprehensible; she thought them all narrow-minded, dull, dowdy and unappreciative of our father. And as she thought, she spoke, she was a very open and honest, if unimaginative person. She criticised all our Stutton relatives in a way we found distressing and disturbing; we were aware of a widening gulf between our father and Stutton, and we suffered from an uncomfortable clash of loyalties.

As we grew older, David and I grew closer. The quarrels of childhood were left behind, and we began to feel that if we didn't belong anywhere that we knew, at least we knew that we belonged together. David and I had a great deal of fun together, but it was with him too that I was able to share my most serious thoughts and feelings. Physically and materially we accepted and enjoyed all that our lives offered. Joy is a mode of being that has little to do with happiness. On spring mornings, summer evenings, at night under the stars, I knew moments of intense joy. But while it is possible to live in the valleys and meadows of happiness, it is not possible to remain for ever on the heights of joy; and David and I had other and deeper needs.

From my east-facing bedroom at Little Hall I could look down the river and see the moving lights of Harwich. I could listen to the shivering whispering aspen tree outside, and catch the small bird and animal noises of the darkness; and here night after night I tried to discover myself. I read avidly – the Romantic poets – the Georgians – the War poets. I read and reread Robert Bridges' anthology *The Spirit of Man*, and I was elated at discovering so much I recognised in Blake. I felt in myself a deep, unexplained hunger, for beauty, for meaning, for love of a different order from the human loves that I knew and cherished; it was to this hunger that the poets spoke.

I began to think again about religion. Along with a belief in God, I had jettisoned anything to do with the institutional Church, and at first this had seemed a glorious liberation. I had thrown away all literal interpretations of the Bible, and the Christian creeds, without comprehending any of their symbolic and mythological significance. But many of the writers and poets whom I revered spoke of religion, some of them directly of Christianity. I could not fail to be moved by the extraordinary figure of Christ, though certainly not by the 'gentle Jesus meek and mild' of my childhood. I was moved by the beauty of his teaching, and though I found what little I understood about redemption rather horrible, I recognised intuitively the dramatic and poetic necessity of the crucifixion and the resurrection. And some of the best people I knew and read about were Christians. A little grain of humility began to disturb some of the arrogance of my youthful certainties.

But still I could find no connection, no bridge between my vague but real desires, my joy in nature and poetry, and the institutional Church. Those lonely night hours sometimes seemed to be the most real, in some ways the most important part of my life.

I wanted to find out about this life that was opening up before me, and obscurely I felt that I was committed to some kind of 'spiritual' search. It was poetry that hinted at, pointed to, a state of being, a paradise perhaps, not of moral good, but of the imagination; it contained, as I did myself, a wild, anarchic element – here were no rules, only a conviction of 'the holiness of the heart's affections', a belief that 'what the imagination seizes as beauty must be truth'. But the way of the Church was full of rules and incomprehensible dogmas, and the love that it preached seemed strangely limited. In all this confusion the question of my confirmation arose. I did not want to be, did not think I should be, confirmed. I had long talks with my headmistress who was understanding, and prepared to support me if I felt that I must finally refuse. My father took me for a Sunday morning walk; this was standard practice whenever he had anything serious to say to David or me. He spoke of the crucifixion; in worldly terms the greatest possible failure, in spiritual terms the greatest triumph; he made it clear that he believed in the spiritual triumph. Coming from a man who seemed dedicated to the pursuit and admiration of every kind of worldly success, this was an interesting surprise; I was impressed. And then there was my ever-dear, ever-loving grandmother, and surely I had already grieved her enough. So I agreed to be confirmed. Although it meant little to me at the time, I am glad that I took that decision.

Much of all this I shared with David. He was less rebellious than I was,

but he too was a searcher. We began to go to the theatre together, and
to try to discover a little about classical music. David was much more
genuinely musical than I was. At home there had been no music in our
lives, no art either, and virtually no literature, certainly no discussion
of books, except of the ones that were not considered suitable reading
for the young, and which, of course, we immediately made strenuous
efforts to find and to read. So with some small help from our respective
schools, David and I had to discover our culture for ourselves.

At this stage in our lives we were nothing if not high-minded, not to
say priggish. We passed censorious judgements upon our elders, we
thought they led superficial social lives, we were well on the way to
becoming moral and intellectual snobs, while strongly condemning
the social snobbery of our families. We wanted our own lives to have
purpose and meaning, a vocational element, something different –
more worthwhile – than the lives we saw around us.

We were not unmindful of what was happening in the world, and
we began to question the Conservatism of our family. During my last
year at school, a German university professor, a friend of the
headmistress, stayed a night or two at the school. She was half Jewish
and was on her way to America, since she had been forced to leave her
academic post in Berlin. She was allowed to speak to the sixth form,
and she told us, with tears, what was happening to the Jews in
Germany. When I got home I spoke of my horror; yes, they said, it was
all very deplorable, but I must understand that Hitler had to be
supported, since a strong Germany was a bulwark against the worse
menace of Communism. I was deeply shocked by this, I never forgot
it. It opened my eyes to a great deal, including the latent, probably
barely conscious anti-Semitism that I began to detect around me; it
made me think about politics in a much more serious and ethical way.

My school career ended head-girl, captain of games, a string of good
public examination results, and a secured entrance to Lady Margaret
Hall, Oxford. For once, I was a satisfactory child. My father was
proud, my stepmother thought me very peculiar to want to go on
studying when I might have been 'having a good time', while my
Stutton relatives were dubious. Oxford was all very well for men who
had to go out into the world, but frailer girls might be exposed to all
kinds of bad and subversive influences. Had not the young men just
voted in the Union against fighting for King and Country? Oxford
was not desirable, especially for me. Judging by my past record, I
might well prove all too susceptible to the bad and the subversive.

♦ 4 ♦

Experiencing and Playing

I had for several years reconciled myself to the fact that I could not be otherwise than I was – a girl; in this I might even find some advantages. David's future was already planned: four years reading Classics and Greats at Oxford, and then into the expanding Fison fertiliser business of which Clavering Fison was chairman. My future, unless I married, was gloriously open. And boys were beginning to become objects of interest in themselves. Girls at school had provided information of a rather garbled kind about the facts of life. I thought it all sounded horrible. However, poets and novelists suggested something different, and I felt that they were the more reliable guides. I did at first imagine that any young man who kissed me would, almost automatically, propose marriage, but experience rapidly dispelled that illusion.

I was to have a year off before going up to Oxford, so I was despatched to Paris to be 'finished'; that meant learning a little French and acquiring some kind of cultural polish. I loved it – whole new worlds opened to me, picture galleries and exhibitions, opera-going, sight-seeing of all kinds, lectures on French literature and history at the Sorbonne. I heard Chaliapin sing Boris Godunov, and, perhaps strangely enough, I was swept off my feet, dazed for several days, by the music of Wagner's *Parsifal*. There was an attractive idea that after Christmas I should continue the 'finishing' process in Florence. But this was now late 1935, and on 3 October Italian troops had invaded Abyssinia. My father judged that the international situation was too threatening to allow me to go to Italy, and since he was, by then, in a position of some eminence in the international business world, I had to accept that perhaps he did know best.

So what was to be done with me? The idea of a London season began to surface. I don't know why I accepted, even wanted, to do this. Was it some idea of the illusory 'good time' that seemed to be the aim of so many of the girls with whom I was vaguely friendly? I was certainly

avid for 'experience', as much and as wide as possible. I have always
believed that – within limits – I should try anything for myself before
passing judgement upon it.

Madeline had done her best to smarten up David and me, and fit us
for social life. She did tell me in her honest, forthright manner that her
first reaction on seeing me aged thirteen was, 'We shall never get this
off our hands'. As one of my various mentors had also told me that I
was the ugliest child she had ever seen, I had no great confidence in my
personal charms. As a child I was very shy and detested children's
parties, and this persisted throughout my teens. I never had any
capacity for 'small talk', so would usually, on social occasions, remain
dumb. Aunt Evelyn had tried to coach me in the niceties of upper-
middle-class mores, how you spoke, what you called or didn't call
things, all the little idiocies that have been sent up by Nancy Mitford.
But I was not an apt pupil, I thought it all ridiculous and nearly always
got it wrong. Altogether poor material for a London season.

However, the experience might help me to acquire that desirable
quality, 'poise', something evidently essential to success in life.
Preparations for the season were set in train. I had for some time
yearned for a black dress, it seemed the acme of the sophistication and
seductiveness to which young girls aspired. But no, I was told, I was
much too young, it would look ridiculous. Then King George V died,
and three months of Court mourning were declared. I got my black
dress. In succeeding years I have hardly ever worn black.

I enjoyed quite a lot of the season's festivities, all the tinsel, glitter
and glamour of dinner parties and dances in fine surroundings, smart
and sometimes beautiful clothes, the big social occasions, champagne,
strawberries and flowers all the way. I enjoyed the dance that my father
generously gave for me, for then I could invite my own friends, and
there was never any likelihood of my being without a partner.

I look back on that period in my life with amazement. What was this
season all about? So much money, so much luxury poured out upon all
those young – and often silly – girls? All those dances and appearances
at Ascot, the Derby, Eton and Harrow, culminating I suppose in the
meaningless formality of presentation to the reigning monarch – poor
man. In my year we were presented to an unbelievably miserable and
bored-looking Edward VIII. We were all, at least in theory, strictly
chaperoned. That duty fell to my young, good-looking stepmother,
and I only hope she got some fun out of it all. There were lists,
competitive lists, that you had to be 'on', in order to secure the desired
invitations. If by any chance you were seen in a public place, or even in

a taxi alone with a young man, or, perish the thought, entering a man's flat, you were promptly – or so we were told – struck off any list, and received no more invitations. I had one or two close shaves. Short of getting engaged to some wealthy young peer – a most improbable eventuality – the height of social ambition seemed to be to appear in the pages of *The Tatler* – I never managed that. But any idea that the object of all this expensive charade was to find suitable husbands for all those young girls was much misplaced. The majority of young men who got on to the 'lists' and came to the dinner parties and dances were not in search of wives, they were in search of splendid free meals and entertainment.

Those months in London had not, for me, been entirely arid. Earlier in the year, at a dance in Oxford, I had met a serious and attractive young man. Ronald Lunt had recently left Oxford with a first in Greats, and was teaching in London, before deciding whether or not to be ordained as an Anglican priest. He was as interested as I was in poetry, literature and the theatre, and we saw quite a lot of each other. I don't know how seriously my father took this friendship, it was already considerably more than just a friendship, but he encouraged it. Here was a thoroughly presentable and respectable young man who could be relied upon to do his rather wild daughter no harm.

Towards the end of the season after a series of late nights, I set off one Saturday afternoon to drive to Stutton in the little second-hand car which my father had given me. I got sleepier and sleepier, and finally dropped off at the wheel. The next thing I knew was that I had knocked a man off his bicycle, a workman cycling home with his tools. Mercifully his injuries were not serious. But I was charged with careless driving. I felt very upset and ashamed; I would have sold my car and forfeited my allowance, to send money to the man I had injured, but this was not allowed: it might suggest admission of guilt. My father arranged for me to be defended by the AA so that I did not even have to appear in court. I don't know what untruths were told on my behalf, but I was acquitted. This made me feel even worse. I experienced a great revulsion against my privileged, extravagant, indulged and indulgent life.

But now I was quite unwell. Eventually appendicitis was diagnosed, and I had my appendix removed by an exceedingly incompetent surgeon. After that I was judged to be too frail to go up to Oxford. I did not resist. Aunt Tilly was at home for the summer and suggested that I should return with her and Hugh to Kenya for six months. It took little to persuade me – Oxford could wait for another year.

★

Travel by ship was as romantic, if not as heroically adventurous, as from childhood I had hoped it would be. The seas were calm and sunlit. Flying fish, moonlight and phosphorus on the sea, sunsets and sunrises, new harbours, new countries: all was fresh and marvellous; I wanted to see everything. I found a boyfriend, or perhaps I should say that he found me. Donald was a district officer in what was then the mandated territory of Tanganyika. He talked about his work among the Africans for whom he had respect and sympathy. I found this fascinating, and was filled with admiration for the British colonial administration. Donald had no doubt that his job was to assist the Africans in every way he could towards the running of their own independent country.

At Port Said the ship docked for a day or two; at night, Donald and I walked hand in hand along a jetty; the soft air was full of wonderfully exotic scents, and alongside, numbers of Arab dhows were moored, their immensely tall masts rocking rhythmically against a sky of stars more brilliant than any I had ever seen. Romance, I felt, could go no further. But it might have gone further; some of the passengers wanted to make up a party to sail up the Nile, visit some of the pyramids and rejoin the ship at Suez. I was wild to go, and Donald was eager to escort me. But alas, it was not to be. Donald and I were not immune to the stirrings of the flesh, and Tilly had discovered us in my cabin in a somewhat compromising position, so she refused to let me go. ('How ridiculous of me,' she was to say when, years later, I teased her about this.)

I said goodbye to Donald, and prepared for new adventures. Hugh's coffee farm was at Kiambu, about fifteen miles outside Nairobi and high in the desirable White Highlands. An avenue of flame-trees led up to the bungalow, and I was almost dazzled by the brilliant colours of the birds and flowers that filled the garden. We lived and ate on the verandah and looked across hundreds of miles of coffee plantations, banana trees, feathery wattles and blue-grey eucalyptus. At breakfast, if there was not too much early morning mist, we gazed further over the great open plains to Mount Kenya, emerging resplendent with its everlasting crown of snow.

I fell in love with the extraordinary beauty of Africa, with its wildness and emptiness and endless space. Those were the days before tourism and game parks, and the wild animals were still around us. In the evenings we could drive up to the edge of the Great Rift Valley and look down on vast herds of buck and zebra, and smile at ungainly giraffe feeding peacefully off flat-topped thorn trees. Nights were full of strange noises and dawn brought a sour-sweet African smell, fresh earth mixed with something heavy and sensual, sweat and blood and the dung of wild beasts.

I was immediately interested in the Africans and their customs, and tried to learn all that I could about them. In the evenings I was aware of throbbing, rhythmic drum-beats mixed with the acrid smell of hundreds of little fires. Africans, with their glowing ebony skins, seemed so much a part of that land of red earth as did the orange, purple, gold and crimson of the native cloth worn by the women. It was only the tall, pale Europeans who rode and strode about the country who looked out of place.

I would have liked to be able to talk to the Africans, but it was not usual to employ educated and English-speaking Africans, and above all, I was told, you should avoid the Christian converts: they were nearly always dishonest. It was assumed that the servants understood no English, but as I looked at their faces I often wondered about this. In fact, I very much hoped that they were not able to understand some of the things that were said. I could not help contrasting the way some of the settlers talked with all that my friend Donald had told me of his work in Tanganyika. Tilly and Hugh never spoke disparagingly about the Africans; in fact Hugh, as I discovered later, was much respected by both black and white, and had a reputation for consistent justice and fair judgement. Warm-hearted Tilly ran an extremely popular clinic on the farm, and was constantly besieged by dozens of wide-eyed children with real and imaginary ailments.

There were plenty of spare young men around – soldiers, farmers and government servants, and not too many girls. I rode, played tennis, picnicked and occasionally danced and got mildly entangled with a young farmer; but it was Africa itself that had my heart. Sometimes we went on safaris; the best was a long camping expedition made round the lower slopes of Mount Kenya. Early in the morning we drove past Lake Nakuru, the home of thousands of rose-coloured flamingos, and stopped for lunch on the north-facing slope of the mountain.

While African servants were preparing food for us I climbed on to the roof of the car and gazed over thousands of miles of empty land, desert and semi-desert, far away to the dim blue mountains of Somalia and Abyssinia. I was lost, absorbed into that infinity of space and distance, my chattering little ego annihilated. Thought, sensation, emotion annihilated. Time itself was no more. And even when time returned there was a sensation of peace, integration, oneness and a renewed spiritual – I can find no other word – vigour. It seemed an experience of profound significance, but of what? A kind of creative nothingness, or at least nothing that I could articulate. That feeling has remained with me, and occasionally I have known again that extraordinary enlargement of spirit that can be experienced among the beauties and immensities of the natural world.

Although I enjoyed my time in Kenya, I was glad to go home, other more interesting possibilities beckoned. So, armed with several books, I went to Germany to read and learn something of the language, which I am afraid I completely failed to do. Frau Burger von Duhn was a widow who had fallen on difficult times, so in her house in Heidelberg she took in foreign students, and tried to teach them a little German. It was a pleasant house and garden, some way up on the steep banks of the river Neckar and facing the university and the old castle.

On my first evening we all went over the river to a students' dance in the castle. A tall young German came up, bowed politely, and asked me in slightly American English to dance; we spent the rest of the evening together. The next day Karl called with a bunch of flowers, the next day he called again, and the next, and we began to spend our free time together. Karl was an intelligent young man who had spent two years in America studying law and politics on a scholarship. He was a Nazi sympathiser, and we argued about politics. I spoke about the Jews, and he skirted around that subject, saying that there was no anti-Semitism in Heidelberg, and certainly I never saw any, though I have no doubt it was there. Karl had a cause, the resurrection of a defeated and humiliated country; he was a patriot, he believed in and wanted to serve his country. I fear that he may have been typical of many potentially decent but dreadfully misled young people, and it is so fatally easy to mislead the young, many of whom long to immerse themselves in a cause, preferably one demanding a degree of nobility and self-sacrifice.

In the end Karl and I gave up arguing about politics, turned to literature, and just enjoyed ourselves. We sat in little cafés along the Neckar drinking a kind of white wine fruit cup; I shall always associate the heavy, sweet scent of lime blossom with that dreamy summer in Heidelberg. Sometimes we walked for whole days through those marvellous pine forests, stopping at small inns, and the sun seemed always to be shining, the evenings were warm and voluptuous, and Karl was a pleasant, intelligent companion.

Frau Burger von Duhn took me aside, and gave me a little homily about the dangers of losing my 'one precious treasure'. Another English girl had lost her 'precious treasure', and had had to be hurriedly married to the young man responsible. I listened dutifully, but I was beginning to feel that my 'one precious treasure' was more of a burden and I might be well rid of it. I really wanted, physically wanted, to sleep with Karl, but something held me back, certainly not fears of a possible pregnancy. Karl assured me that he would see that that was not possible, and I trusted him, he was a decent young man who never pushed me further than I wanted to go. I was fond of Karl, but I was not in love with him, and I cherished the conviction that the act of sex should only be for love – and luckily for me, it always was.

My visit to Germany, my talks with Karl and others, and the evident fear among older Germans who had been through the First World War, convinced me that the Nazis were bent on war. Already in the minds of young men war was glorious, the greatness of a country was the greatness of the conqueror, the greatness of military might. There would be one aggression after another until conflict was inevitable.

By the late summer and early autumn, David and I were settled at Little Hall, solemnly determined to prepare ourselves for Oxford. David had grown into a fine-looking man. He was tall and broad-shouldered. He had his mother's wide-set hazel eyes, though, as she had been nicknamed 'cat's-eyes', hers must have been greener. As small children David and I were platinum blonds, 'Angles' though not 'angels'; David's hair had darkened, but it still had golden lights when the sun caught it. When serious his thoughtful face expressed a kind of gentle strength. But more often he was laughing, joking and teasing. David was generous, affectionate and wholeheartedly enthusiastic in everything that he did. He was certainly a high-flyer; his exuberance and bounciness might have been mistaken for conceit, but in fact they concealed a measure of insecurity and uncertainty about himself. But he carried within him much bright promise of leadership, of courage and of love. He was about to follow in our father's footsteps to Christ Church, and because of my two years' travelling and playing about, he and I would go to university together. We slipped back into our old companionship, but deeper now, for we had both matured, and were more interesting to ourselves and to each other. The magic of our childhood was still there, all around us; the weather was perfect and Granny pottered happily about in her garden; for now, to her at least, we were no longer troublesome teenagers, but young adults able, at last, to express our love for her with some care and consideration. We had tennis and swimming and long walks by the river, and Stutton Hall was once more open to us. It had been let on a long lease and when this expired Clav and Evelyn with their two young daughters had decided to move back into the family home.

Every day when the morning mists had cleared we took our books into the garden, though I don't remember that we ever reached the targets we had set for ourselves, it was all too delectable and we had too much to say to each other. Chiefly we talked of Oxford, and of all we meant to do there. For us it seemed a city of dreams, a place where all our vague longings and searchings might be canalised and directed. David was deep in Classics, and I remember long discussions about Plato; he enjoyed his work, but felt that Honour Mods would be a bit of a grind, though he hoped he just might achieve a First in Greats. And somehow or other he hoped to manage a cricket blue as well. My ambitions were vague, but equally rose-coloured, and now at least my life had direction and purpose, and I was happily embarked upon a course of English language and literature.

We talked a little of politics. In his last year at school, David had gone for a week to South Wales to live with the family of an unemployed miner, and he returned filled with indignation at social injustice: 'Why should we have so much and they so little?' In the years to come he hoped that he might be able to do something about this. We even discussed seriously whether we ought not to give up the small private incomes that we had inherited from our mother. As we were not yet twenty-one there was, fortunately, nothing we could do about that.

Of course, we talked of war. We were both influenced by Dick Shepherd's Peace Pledge Union, we had read *The Merchants of Death* and were horrified by the international arms trade. Our father was now commercial director of the British Iron and Steel Federation, and president of the International Scrap Convention and we challenged him, suggesting that if Britain, the European powers and the USA were to stop exporting iron and steel as well as scrap to Japan, that might halt her aggression against China. He agreed that might be so, but implied that we, naïvely, understood neither the demands of international business, nor of international politics. But perhaps in our innocent idealism we were not after all so wrong.

Vernon paid us one of his periodic visits. We loved talking to him, he spoke a lot about our mother and made us feel close to her, and of course, he talked about religion, and our questing and questioning young minds could not fail to respond to his charismatic personality, and to his high seriousness and dedication. To the distress of our grandmother, and perhaps unscrupulously, he tried to convert us to

Roman Catholicism. Vernon was persuasive, though David was more inclined than I was to be persuaded.

So we dreamed dreams and gazed, wondering and hopeful, at the mysteries of life and death. It was a truly golden autumn; before so many storms both national and personal, it was a period of halcyon calm.

Et in Arcadia ego.

Oxford was no disappointment. Lady Margaret Hall is a particularly pleasant college, with a large garden bounded by the river. I was happy in my work, and I made friends who have remained so for the rest of my life. David was equally happy and absorbed in university life, and since he had a large set of rooms overlooking Christ Church meadows, and could call on the resources of an excellent college kitchen, we were able to entertain our friends together.

In the idealistic days at Little Hall we had resolved that we would steer clear of emotional entanglements so that we could enjoy everything that Oxford had to offer. This was a resolution that David managed to keep better than I did. Ronald Lunt reappeared rather more seriously in my life. He had been to stay at Stutton, and during the Christmas vacation I went to stay with his parents. He was by now at Westcott House, Cambridge, having taken the decision to be ordained, and then continue his career as a teacher – schoolmasters in orders were not then uncommon. By the late spring of 1938 Ronald and I became unofficially engaged. Our respective families seemed happy with our relationship. We agreed that once Ronald was settled in his career, and I had taken my degree, we would get married.

At the beginning of the summer term Ronald appeared in Oxford and said that he wanted to take me to meet a friend who had just become dean of Oriel. This was John Collins, newly arrived from Cambridge where he had been vice-principal of Westcott House, and had tutored Ronald in the New Testament and in theology. John had a friend from Cambridge days due to spend the weekend with him, and he wanted to give a small dinner party. But John knew no girls in Oxford, could Ronald help? Ronald obligingly produced me. John thought that I would pass, so I was invited to a dinner party in his rooms in Oriel. I don't remember much about the evening, I think I found it dull.

Meanwhile Ronald was getting cold feet about our engagement. He began to feel that he was too young, too unsettled for such a firm commitment; marriage might result in a conflict between his wife and

his work, and he was very seriously committed to a vocation as a
Christian teacher. He dithered about, but it was increasingly clear that
he really wanted to get out of the engagement. I was unhappy about
this, and since John knew Ronald well, and was an older and more
experienced man, I thought I would seek his advice. I got in touch with
him, and he invited me to dinner.

John had a car, so he drove me out of Oxford to Shillingford Bridge,
to a hotel on the river. We had a pleasant dinner, I talked a lot, and John
gave me what, I suppose, was good advice. There was a warm,
reassuring quality about his personality which made him accessible,
and easy to talk to. He was a good and sympathetic listener. Though he
wore glasses, I was aware of his friendly but penetrating brown eyes.
Some years later, his old friend Yvonne Cooper said to me, 'John looks
at every woman as if she were the only woman in the world'. I didn't
feel that, but I was certainly conscious of his gaze. I think that look of
John's was often – of course, not always – more pastoral than
romantic.

After dinner we moved to the hotel lounge and sat on a sofa drinking
coffee. Quite suddenly an extraordinary conviction took hold of me,
almost as if some inner voice said, 'This is the kind of man I want to
marry'. I did not feel 'I'm in love with this man, this is *the* man in my
life'; with another part of me I still thought that I wanted to marry
Ronald. Nothing was said or done that could signal any particular
interest that John and I might have in each other. This was more like a
kind of presentiment, fate knocking on the door, and I wasn't at all sure
that it was the kind of fate that I wanted. I had a vague apprehension of
trouble.

John drove me back to Lady Margaret Hall and we said goodnight
politely. He suggested that we might meet again at some unspecified
date to see how things were going with Ronald and me. I went to bed
in some bewilderment. I knew hardly anything about this man, we had
met socially twice, and this was the first time that we had been alone
together, and while I had talked volubly about myself, he had told me
nothing at all about himself. I wondered about this stranger who had
disturbed me so suddenly and unexpectedly; I wondered where he
came from, and what kind of a person he was.

A Different Childhood

I N 1909, when John was four, he was given a walking stick for
his birthday; he was inordinately proud of this status symbol,
and stumped about announcing: 'I'm Lewis John Jacky Gentleman
Collins'.

In that male-dominated, hierarchical society, his position was now
established – never mind his two elder sisters, nor even his brother,
that powerful and admired figure who mysteriously seemed to come
and go in the family circle, he, John, was a man. Some two years later,
a visiting relative enquired, 'Well, Jacky, what do you want to be when
you grow up?' 'I want to be a clergyman with a face like Mr Long', was
the unexpected answer. Mr Long was the curate at All Saints church,
Hawkhurst, and was responsible for the Sunday afternoon children's
service, dutifully attended by four little Collinses. They also had to
attend Matins with their parents and sometimes Evensong as well;
they were spared Sunday school, since in Hawkhurst society this was
considered unsuitable and unnecessary for the children of middle-class
families.

John was a happy child, born with an easy temperament, he was well
contented with his home and his family, and with his idea of his future;
his sister remembers him as being always remarkably good-tempered.

John's parents, Arthur and Hannah Collins, had married in 1899,
and children arrived quickly, Edward (Ted) in 1900, Margaret in
1901, Dorothy, 1903, and John (Jacky), 1905. John's paternal grandfather, son of a Sussex yeoman farmer, had married one of his family's
servants, an uneducated woman who belonged to a narrow and
fanatical religious sect. Their son Arthur was a bright lad with a fine
voice and a good musical ear and, despite his mother, he was soon
singing solos in the local Anglican church choir. One Easter a visitor
with influential connections with Westminster Abbey listened to this
young songster. He was so impressed by the quality of his singing, and
by the boy generally, that he approached the parents and proposed

that, at no cost to themselves, their son should join the Abbey choir and go as a boarder to the Westminster Under School which reserved places for budding choristers. But to Arthur's ignorant mother London was a wicked city, a breeding ground of every possible evil and corruption. She adamantly refused to part with her boy. So Arthur continued at the local state school, and left at the age of fourteen. By the time he met John's mother, Hannah Priscilla (Annie) Edwards, he was managing a grocer's shop in Tonbridge.

It was the maternal grandparents, Lewis and Elizabeth Edwards, who played such a great and influential part in the lives of the Collins family, and John grew to love and admire his grandfather almost more than any other person. Lewis was born in Shropshire, but was half Welsh. He was sent to Shrewsbury public school, and was doing well until his father suddenly died. So at the age of fourteen Lewis had to leave school and prepare to earn his living as apprentice to a firm of builders. While working in Manchester, Lewis met Elizabeth Hancock, and they were married in 1870. There was something inside this masterful young wife that drove her to curious acts of self-assertion. Lewis found lodgings for them both, only to find on his return from work that his bride was gone, leaving a note to say that she had found better lodgings elsewhere, and that he was to come and join her. This pattern was repeated throughout her life, to the considerable embarrassment of her family; they would be shown to a table in a restaurant, or to a pew in some strange church, but as soon as they were all comfortably settled, Grandma would insist on moving everyone to a different table or pew.

Lewis and Elizabeth's only child, Hannah Priscilla (Annie) was born in 1872, and soon afterwards Lewis developed a bad lung infection. His doctor advised him to leave the cold damp air of Manchester, still thick with fumes from 'dark, Satanic mills', and move to a warmer and cleaner climate in the south of England. So it was that the Edwardses settled in Hawkhurst, Kent, where Lewis bought land and set up his own building and contracting business.

Lewis was a passionate believer in education; he was determined that his daughter, and later his grandchildren, should have the advantages of the kind of education that had, in his own case, been so abruptly terminated. At whatever cost or sacrifice the children, girls as well as boys, were all to be privately and properly educated, and Hawkhurst boasted several good schools.

Annie Edwards did well at school, and under her father's direction acquired the accomplishments considered necessary for young ladies: she sang and played the piano, learned to draw, dance and play tennis, and she was encouraged to read widely. She also developed a talent for mathematics, and when she left school, she began to help her father in his office, and eventually took over the accounting and book-keeping. The business flourished, and Lewis Edwards soon established an excellent reputation for undeviating honesty and integrity, and for the high quality and fine craftsmanship of his work. He was active and respected in the whole life of the community, but, at heart, Lewis was no business man. He would never charge more than five per cent profit on labour and material. 'Whether it means bankruptcy or not, five per cent is a more than adequate return on any man's capital – to charge more is exploitation,' he was heard to say. He was also absentminded: he had been known to put his umbrella into a taxi, and then walk home. He was slow in sending out bills, and sometimes forgot them altogether. While Elizabeth managed the home with true, if rather domineering, north country efficiency, Lewis was much relieved when his Annie came to help him manage the business.

But then Annie insisted on marrying Arthur Collins. Her departure was a real blow, the accounts got more and more behind, the paperwork muddled – Annie could no longer help her father, she already had one baby, and another was on the way: what was to be done? Whatever Lewis may have thought of his son-in-law, he recognised his ability, so he suggested that Arthur should join the firm as business manager.

This arrangement made everybody happy. Some three or four hundred yards down the hill from his builder's yard, Lewis had built a house for himself and his wife; he called it 'Carchafan', a Welsh word meaning a safe and secure place. He then turned his attention to the Collins family, and built them a fine new house, Holly Grove, about 150 yards up the hill, and next to the builder's yard.

John's birth was difficult and dangerous for mother and son; when his grandmother saw the pathetic scrawny little baby she thought that it might almost be better if he were not to survive. But Elizabeth was not the woman to sit by and let things happen. She organised her daughter away for a convalescent holiday, and herself took the baby to Carchafan. She even bought her own cow so that the baby could have fresh milk. He flourished; grew rounder and rounder and fatter and fatter, and ended up almost spherical. When Annie returned from her convalescence she hardly recognised her son.

Holly Grove had a large garden, and Arthur was a keen gardener. Each child was given a plot, and there was a prize for the best kept, invariably won by industrious little John. The builder's yard next door was a magnet for the children, who spent long hours in the carpenter's shop, pestering the friendly workmen with questions. All his life John enjoyed finding out about the workings of various trades and professions.

John had a special relationship with his sister Margaret. He was instinctively drawn to people with gifts of imagination, both literary and musical, and sister Margaret was clever and imaginative: 'She always had her nose in a book'. It was Margaret who invented the imaginary world of Bearland, where stuffed toys led an exciting life, and in which John lived enthralled. He had two bears, one head of the Bearland church, the other chief of the army.

John was a timid child, and until his last years at school felt overshadowed by his elder brother, Ted, who was brought up by his grandmother at Carchafan. Ted as head of the family thought it was up to him to make a man of John, and was inclined to bully him, but Margaret always rushed fearlessly to his defence. John never betrayed the slightest envy of the immensely preferential treatment meted out to Ted by Grandma Edwards; that was how the world was, boys were more important than girls, older brothers were more important than younger ones; John was still a long way away from being any kind of a rebel.

Meanwhile the family business expanded sufficiently for Grandpa Edwards to buy a car; he was one of the first people in Hawkhurst to own one of these new-fangled machines. He never learned to drive it himself, but Arthur soon mastered the driving and the mechanism, and the children took turns in accompanying him on his business rounds. They were not in much danger, since their father thought it unwise to exceed twenty-five miles per hour.

Arthur had thrown himself into the business with enthusiasm; through reading and observation, he had made himself an expert on the restoration and conversion of old houses, and of the Kentish oast houses, and this was a highly profitable side of the business. He chafed against the five per cent rule; left to himself, he would have followed common practice and added fifteen per cent to the bills, but nothing would shake Lewis, who could perhaps be obstinate as well as principled. Arthur would also have liked more responsibility; he felt that, given his head, he could manage things better than his father-in-law. But Arthur had a weakness of which Lewis was well aware, and that weakness was drink. He spent long hours in the local pubs which were a kind of refuge from himself, as well as from the problems of his life.

Inevitably the drinking got worse over the years. Sometimes the children would rush out to greet their father on his return from work, only to find him collapsed on the doorstep. Annie was often frightened; she took to concealing the cut-throat razor-blades and kitchen knives under the children's pillows at night, which perplexed and frightened the children. She was afraid that Arthur might harm himself: when drunk he sometimes spoke of suicide, but she knew, that whatever his state, he would never harm his children.

Drinking made Arthur an erratic father. When sober he was loving, generous and indulgent; he enjoyed taking his family out on expeditions; he helped his wife in the home, and took a keen interest in the children's development. At other times he was irascible and authoritarian, and John especially would be a target for random spankings, Ted being conveniently out of reach at Carchafan.

Matters finally came to a crisis after the First World War, and some time in 1924 Arthur came back one night in such a state that his wife sent for the family doctor. He came and put Arthur to bed with a sedative, and the next day he came round and put the fear of death, God, damnation and everything else into him. Arthur gave up drinking from that day. The withdrawal symptoms must have been terrible, but he stuck to it. It was at this period that Lewis, at the age of seventy-seven, finally handed over full responsibility for the business to his son-in-law.

Arthur did become rather sanctimonious and priggish on the subject of alcohol, but the better side of his nature was released. He devoted himself to his wife, taking her out with him, taking her away for holidays, giving her, at last, a really happy life. But all too soon, in 1926, at the early age of fifty-three, Annie died. Towards the end of her life she said to John, 'You know, in spite of everything, I never stopped loving your father'.

6

John's Schooldays

JOHN was a naïve and unsuspicious child; he never quite lost this innocent naïveté in spite of the trouble into which it sometimes led him. He believed what people told him, however improbable their information might seem. He could never understand why members of his family should think it funny to tell him things that they knew to be untrue, and when grown-ups did so, this was even more incomprehensible, since they were the ones who made such a fuss about children always speaking the truth.

Tudor Hall, the local boys' prep school, was near enough for John and Ted to be day boys. John was an easy target for the teasing and tall stories with which new boys were customarily greeted. Mild bullying was considered character-building, preparing boys to become builders and defenders of Empire, and John got his share. He accepted it stoically, as he accepted beatings, and he subscribed to current schoolboy ethic, didn't sneak, and was not thought to be soft or cowardly. Happily, Mr Long was the school chaplain.

He saw more of Mr Long at All Saints church as well, for John was now a member of the choir. He soon became head choirboy and soloist; a position of eminence which he much enjoyed. Music and singing were a regular part of Collins family life, evenings of song-singing with Annie at the piano, as well as regular hymn-singing on Sundays. The three older children were each given private piano lessons, but, by the time it came to John, money was scarce, and the outbreak of the First World War put an end to any extras.

When John – aged nine – first heard about the war, he asked what field it was going to be fought on, and his teasing family assured him that it would be where they all played, on the big field behind Carchafan. Even John must have realised rather quickly that he was being taken for a ride. And soon the soldiers came marching through the village, and people came out to greet them with bowls of plums and cherries and other seasonal fruits.

'Back by Christmas,' the men shouted cheerfully.

It was not long before numbers of Grandpa's younger workmen, John's friends and heroes, were also marching away, and all too many of these never marched back again. The war years were lean years for everyone, lean years for Grandpa's business and lean years for the family. John remembered being perpetually hungry; towards the end, there just never seemed enough to eat, and he and his young friends, defying the local farmers, crept out into the fields at dusk and early morning to catch rabbits which they could skin and cook for themselves.

Somehow or other the Collins children were kept at school, and the fees were paid, and in September, 1918, John followed his brother to Cranbrook. Now that they were at a public school together Ted became John's confidant and helper. It was Ted who rescued him from the attentions of a homosexual master, from the undeserved, if mild, beatings followed by sweets and cakes and soft drinks. John was sexually uninstructed but he knew something was wrong, so he told his brother who went straight to the headmaster, and the master in question left at once.

During his second year at Cranbrook, John was confirmed; paradoxically this both strengthened his intention to become a priest, and stirred doubts and questionings. The religion he had been brought up on was clear-cut, based upon a literal fundamentalist interpretation of the Bible and a devotion to Cranmer's prayer-book. John described the services to which he was accustomed as 'the cold, very cold worship of a respectable Anglicanism that steers a dull middle course between high and low extremes of churchmanship; no emotional nonsense about it; no popish practices on the one hand and no vulgar evangelical fervour on the other'.

As for politics, John's family was Conservative to the core as was mine. Even Liberals, supported as they were by Free Churchmen, were thought to be unpatriotic and destructive of the British way of life, and as for Socialists, they were envious, evil and anti-Christian. Just as my uncle, Clavering Fison, would employ no union members, so John's kindly and Christian grandfather regarded as dangerous agitators any persons who tried to persuade his own workmen to join a trade union.

The Anglican prayer-book, and in particular the catechism, as John saw it in later years, seemed to have been drawn up expressly to support law and order, and to inculcate obedience and subservience to all forms of authority. Considering the turbulent days in which the prayer-book was compiled that is hardly surprising, but in the relative social calm of Edwardian England, it had become a middle-class charter, designed to support the *status quo*, and well suited to the 'Tory party at prayer'. As far as orthodox Anglicans were concerned, there was to be no dangerous mixing of religion and politics, the social order had been ordained by God.

John took his confirmation seriously. All instruction was based on the catechism, 'A hard and robust morality for individuals', John called it. In addition, all candidates had one private session with the headmaster. This was exclusively devoted to SIN, and in particular to the fearful and damning consequences of any form of sexual sin; as much guilt and fear as possible was to be instilled into these adolescent boys as they approached the problems and pressures of manhood. Sexual sin certainly took precedence over failures to heed those other injunctions such as loving your neighbour, hurting nobody by word or deed, being true and just in all your dealings, and bearing no malice nor hatred in your heart.

John found all this uninspiring, but he was still emotionally bound to his family, and he accepted what was handed down to him. His incipient doubts were intellectual, a questioning of literal interpretations of the Bible, and of the absolute authority of some Church dogmas.

Meanwhile school life was going well. John was a keen Rugger player and managed, at different times, to break both his collar-bone and his nose. He successfully captained the school Shooting VIII at Bisley, and became house prefect, captain of his house, school prefect and captain of the school. But his most enthusiastic activity was the OTC – the Corps. He was sergeant-major and enjoyed marching at the head of his company swinging the sergeant-major's baton. On the parade ground, he shouted commands in such a stentorian voice that he ended up completely hoarse; this powerful and carrying voice of his was much used in later years, in the service of some less orthodox activities. As head-boy, John was known as a strict disciplinarian. One old boy who suffered under him wrote: 'I remember him as a boy who saw clearly that there was a lot wrong with the world, that he proposed to do something about it, and that there was no reason why he shouldn't start at once on the nearest available material i.e. his juniors, and in consequence, to us small toads beneath the harrow of his reforming zeal, he was occasionally a rather forbidding, but nevertheless very human figure.'

John's account of this was that when he became head-boy he found that the school had got thoroughly slack, that some of the older boys and prefects were idle and a bit corrupt, so he decided to carry out a reformation. In his military enthusiasm he managed to lick the Corps into such good shape that, at its annual summer camp, Cranbrook came second in the inter-public schools competition for the most efficient company, and beat Eton into third place.

Underneath all this square-bashing was John's deeper side. One of the school matrons remembered him as a boy with a hatred of injustice, and one always ready to champion the underdog; she was not at all surprised to read about his later career. And there was his closest friend, Wyatt Joyce, who remained a friend for life. Wyatt, son of the local doctor, was talented, musical and imaginative. Together he and John read novels, plays and poetry, and listened to as much classical music as they could. The war had made the recruitment of adequate staff at Cranbrook almost impossible, and when John arrived in the sixth form there was virtually no one equipped to teach him. John was a reasonably good mathematician, and it was assumed that mathematics was the subject he should study at university, but, because he had no proper teacher, he was given innumerable free periods during which he was expected to study on his own. Instead, with Wyatt as his companion, John read widely, and later he felt that this was a valuable period in his life, and one that helped considerably to broaden his mind and his outlook.

During his last year at school, John fell romantically and idealistically in love. All his romantic, sexual and religious longings were transmuted, perhaps sublimated would be the modern word, and projected on to an idealised image of beauty and purity, longed for and yet untouchable. The object of his devotion, as well as being attractive, was a religious girl, and an ardent Anglo-Catholic, so as John fell head over heels in love, so he fell head over heels into Anglo-Catholicism. His family, when he announced his conversion, were appalled. Anglo-Catholicism could all too easily lead into the clutches of the Roman Catholic Church. They were alarmed too when they found John getting up early nearly every morning to attend a daily Eucharist with his beloved, but his wise grandfather counselled that the boy should be left alone. This experience was for John something of a liberation. Anglo-Catholic ritual and practices were sacramental and symbolic, imbued with drama and mystery, and touched with an apprehension of the numinous. John was drawn too to the powerful Anglo-Catholic theology of the Church and especially of the priesthood that he hoped to enter, and devotion to the Virgin Mary, combined with the practice of confession, seemed an acceptable means of lightening the load of sexual frustration with its accompanying guilt, that had been instilled into him by his upbringing and his confirmation.

John's ethereal love, unrooted in the realities of ordinary human nature, soon died a natural death, and the time came in 1924 when he had to sit the entrance examination for Cambridge. At Sidney Sussex, the college of his choice, he had to write the examination, and though he had tried rather desperately to patch up his mathematics, his papers were not of a very high standard. However, the Master of the College, the Reverend A. Weekes, understood that John intended to be ordained, and seems to have taken a fancy to him; by a combination of cheek and charm John managed to talk him into giving him a mathematical sizarship. The money from this would not be enough to support him fully, so, on the strength of his intended ordination, he succeeded in squeezing a supplementary grant out of the Canterbury diocese. Financially, if not emotionally, John was now ready for the larger world.

7

'José' Collins: Cambridge

JOHN went off to Sidney Sussex in good spirits, all the more buoyant because Wyatt Joyce, with a history exhibition to his credit, was going with him. For his first two years, John led a relaxed and carefree life. He entered energetically into college activities, played tennis and Rugger and took up rowing. There was the play-reading society with Wyatt, there were evenings of bridge and of talk, outings to pubs, cinemas, the theatre and an occasional concert, and there was the Conservative Association of which he was a member. John was, by nature, friendly and gregarious, 'a lively, cheerful and extrovert person, the kind of person at the sight of whom one's own spirits rose a little'.

'He acquired a reputation for sowing a wild oat or two,' someone else wrote. These 'wild oats' were not, by modern standards, particularly wild, they were mostly to do with pub-crawling, and a few drunken sprees. On one or two occasions, John's drinking companions, some of whom had cars, collected girls and drove off to suitably secluded spots, but when John found that rather too much was expected of him, he retreated as gracefully as he could.

John's friends nicknamed him 'José' – José Collins was the – female – star of *Maid of the Mountains*, a popular, long-running musical comedy; she was something of a public idol. I am assured that 'José' stuck only because John's name was Collins, it was no reflection on his sexual preferences. However, he was undeniably attractive to men as well as to women; until he finally got married, he did suffer occasionally from the attentions of homosexuals. In later years, perceptive friends remarked upon the feminine qualities in his make-up, characteristics that made him especially intuitive and sympathetic. But in spite of 'José', there was never any real doubt about John's sexual orientation; he remained innocent, somewhat diffident in his approach to women, and genuinely surprised by the effects of his own powers of attraction.

One result of his happy, sociable life was that when the time came for the first part of the Mathematical Tripos, John managed only an inglorious third, and was threatened with the loss of his sizarship. Things improved as soon as he switched to theology. Mathematics had been a mistake, and one that John regretted; he felt that his academic education had been too narrow; he would have been better equipped with some knowledge of history or philosophy. But theology soon absorbed him, extended his horizons, and gave rise to new and exciting ideas and questions.

John's cheerful lifestyle, well lubricated with beer and other alcoholic drinks, also meant that money disappeared rather too quickly. Throughout his life he was generous in ensuring adequate and pleasurable supplies of alcohol, and at college he certainly contributed more than his share to the lubrication. So when the Long Vac arrived there were no jaunts to the Continent, only the necessity to earn money by tutoring a rather dull youth.

In John's final year at Sidney Sussex, his way of life changed dramatically. Charles O'Dwyer, a fellow undergraduate, ordinand and friend, describes this: 'John took himself firmly in hand, he became a strict teetotaller, set himself a firm rule of life in which study, training for games and social activities all had their proper places. Inwardly he was a new man, outwardly he was still the same good mixer, interested in his fellow men, and ready to discuss any topic with them. Little was said by anyone about his new rule of life, but the change was widely noted, and he was highly respected for it.'

Part of this change could have been attributed to the approach of finals, and to the influence of John's tutor, B. T. D. Smith, an Anglo-Catholic priest and a brilliant New Testament scholar. This was a period of Anglo-Catholic revival, a socially conscious and forward-looking movement, and Sidney Sussex was an Anglo-Catholic college. John had arrived as a moderate, not particularly instructed Anglo-Catholic. During his first two years, his religious belief and practice had descended quite a long way from the emotional heights to which his first love had borne him. But towards the end of John's second year, Father Vernon Johnson, still an Anglican priest, conducted a mission to Cambridge University, and on one Sunday evening he preached in the Sidney Sussex College chapel. 1926 was being celebrated in Church circles as the 700th anniversary of the death of Francis of Assisi, and Vernon was a member of the Anglican order of Franciscans. In his monk's brown habit, with his fine ascetic face, and his eloquent sincerity, Vernon must have seemed a romantic and compelling figure. He captured, inspired and held the young men, and no one was more impressed by him than John. This was 'the conscious beginning of [his] spiritual life'. He went to talk to Vernon after the sermon, and was advised by him to go and see Wilfred Knox, who became for some years his confessor and spiritual director.

Wilfred lived in Cambridge, in a house belonging to the Oratory of the Good Shepherd, a peculiarly Anglican order. Its members were bound by rules of celibacy, poverty and a rather loose form of obedience. They pooled resources, and were particularly devoted to scholarship and study, 'the labour of the mind'; they did not normally live together under one roof. Wilfred was a lovable eccentric and a fine scholar, as brilliant as his more celebrated younger brother, Ronald, who had by then defected to Rome. Wilfred was also a Socialist and a member of the Labour party. He had seen acute poverty in his father's Manchester diocese, and in the East End of London, and it never ceased to distress and haunt him. He deplored the identification of the Church with middle-class respectability, he called it 'an unholy alliance . . . that has led to the deadness of English religion'. For himself he resolved never to live on more than £100 a year, and implored all Anglican clergy to do the same, a plea, need it be said, that fell upon very deaf ears.

John remained a Conservative. In the General Strike of 1926 he went off, though with some misgivings, to join the middle-class strike-breakers, and was enrolled briefly as a special constable. John, unlike Wilfred, had not as yet seen real poverty face to face. But this holy, attractive man sowed many seeds in John's mind and heart; 'the seeds in silence slept', but, in later years, they yielded some remarkable, if unorthodox, fruits.

It was in October 1926 that John's mother died of kidney failure. Grandpa Edwards had died in 1923 and was much missed in the family circle. But Annie's early death was a sharper and deeper grief, and John was very much shaken by it. As she lay dying and half delirious, Annie kept murmuring snatches of quotation from the New Testament; almost her last coherent words were, 'Children love one another'. John never forgot this.

John settled down to his year of discipline and serious study, and in the summer of 1929, his hard work was rewarded with a good first class in the Theological Tripos, and he went on to win the Carus Greek Testament prize. His position as a potential scholar and theologian was now established, and he moved down the road to Westcott House Theological College, for a year's course of training for the priesthood.

Westcott House was small, with around thirty-five students and a senior staff of three; the young men's lives were not ruled, but they were regulated, and they moved together in one direction towards one predestined end. This produced something of a hothouse atmosphere, one in which intense friendships, homosexual in feeling though not in practice, could and did spring up, and, as one extreme provokes its opposite, intense dislikes could also flourish, though these would be virtuously concealed. The remarkable personality of B. K. Cunningham held this mixed bag together. He encouraged variety and believed firmly in the inclusiveness, the unity in diversity, of the Anglican Church, something quite different from a broad and fuzzy churchmanship. B. K. was careful to see that his students represented all theological and liturgical persuasions from high Anglo-Catholic to extreme evangelical. He would never allow one brand of churchmanship to dominate the house, he prohibited all Church papers, and arranged for a different form of liturgy to be conducted every day, and, since no one knew in advance what had been laid on, no one had an excuse for absenting himself from a form of service that he disliked or of which he disapproved – all of which was good training in Anglican tolerance.

B. K. was sometimes called 'the best-loved man in the Church of England'; he was also, according to Archbishop Garbett of York, one of the two most influential. B. K. was neither a scholar nor a theologian, he was a wise, understanding and deeply pastoral priest. Perhaps this is a little surprising in view of his early and progressive deafness, but, as physical handicaps often stimulate compensatory skills, his very deafness may well have helped to develop his exceptionally intuitive and sympathetic understanding of so many different personalities. B. K. revolted against the professional priest, 'Let the order of growth', he said, 'be first that which is natural, afterwards that which is spiritual,' and 'Please do not begin by building the priest, begin with the man . . .' 'He made us human,' said one of his students. B. K. had a childlike – not childish – quality, he remained at heart something of a good public-school boy; he believed in the moral value of cricket, and always referred to his students, all grown men in their early twenties, as his 'boys'.

At Westcott John was remembered by his fellows for his 'friendly nature and general enthusiasm' and also as 'one of the few real scholars in the house'. He impressed by his strong views, and his vigorous and trenchant manner of expressing them. John found much that was helpful and sympathetic in the training at Westcott House, but there was one aspect of it that he disliked. It was the middle- and upper-class ethos of the Anglican Church that B. K. really liked, and in which he felt at home. He was never easy with 'boys' who did not come from public schools; he would refer to them as the 'weaker brethren', and urge the others to be 'nice' to them; he believed that it was men of what he called 'the better type' who should be encouraged to seek ordination; he was, in short, a snob.

John was sympathetic to theological liberalism, but he was also not altogether happy with the hothouse atmosphere of Westcott. He had many friends in Cambridge, so he would frequently escape in the evenings after hall, just managing to get back in time for Compline at 10 p.m. 'He probably went on a pub-crawl,' wrote one of his contemporaries.

In his critical work on the texts of the New Testament, John wrestled thoughtfully with the contradictions and inaccuracies in the Gospel stories, and with the doubtful datings and attributions of the Pastoral Epistles. Somehow he felt that the validity, the authentication of his faith must be elsewhere. John was no doubting Thomas: emotionally and spiritually he believed in the revelation of God in Jesus Christ, he wanted to lead, and to help others to lead, what he saw as a Christian life, and he was convinced of his vocation to the priesthood. It was the intellectual foundations and the intellectual presentation of his faith with which he had difficulties. But with the help of his supervisors, honest and often devout men, he was able to reconcile his scholarship and his faith in a way that did not seem to destroy his intellectual integrity. He even managed with the help of what he later described as 'the intellectual tricks so beloved of theologians' to come to terms with the thirty-nine articles as set out in the *Book of Common Prayer*, to which, on ordination, he would be required to swear a solemn assent.

In 1928, Vernon Johnson, causing considerable conturbation among the Anglo-Catholics, finally joined the Roman Catholic Church. There was a very brief period when John felt that he too must seriously consider for himself the claims of that powerful church. Perhaps he was affected by a desire for certainty and authority such as had driven Vernon. John never lost his affection for the gentle Franciscans, but it was to the Jesuit order that he felt more drawn, if he were going to take such an enormous and decisive step, he might as well do it wholeheart-edly. The Jesuits were more suited to John's intellectual and combative temperament; they went out into the world after years of rigorous and disciplined theological training; they were not afraid to use some of the weapons of the world, they confronted it intellectually and politically, they were often skilled diplomats; military metaphors became them – they were the soldiers of the Lord, out to conquer the world for Jesus. John just wondered for a, perhaps emotional, moment, whether his vocation might not be in that direction. But the tolerant, comprehensive ethos of Westcott House, Catholic as well as Protestant, and John's own critical faculties quickly reasserted themselves. Perhaps, too, he was helped by Wilfred Knox.

So John left Westcott House with renewed conviction, and in eager anticipation of his ministry. On 23 December, 1928, he was ordained deacon by Archbishop Cosmo Gordon Lang, in Canterbury Cathedral.

◆ 8 ◆

The Curate

JOHN's ordination, unlike his confirmation, was a high point in his experience; for those few days, his great expectations seemed about to be greatly fulfilled. From his youth John had known Canterbury Cathedral. As a small boy, he had prayed that he might become Archbishop of Canterbury, not through ambition for power and glory, but because, in his innocence, he believed that men rose through the hierarchy of the Church according to the growth and measure of their personal holiness, so the Archbishop of Canterbury must be the holiest man of all. He was prepared to be impressed, and was impressed by Cosmo Gordon Lang, Primate of All England. He was impressed by the retreat conducted by the archbishop, by his brilliant address on moral and pastoral theology, and by his personal approach to each individual ordinand.

At the ordination service it was customary to choose one outstand- ing young man to read the Gospel, and this choice fell upon John. Privilege and joy were his feelings, as, in that marvellously beautiful and historic setting, he rose to read to a large congregation that included his family and friends, as well as the vicar to whom he had been assigned as a curate. John's sense of dedication was so powerful that he was not disturbed by some of the questions that he was required to answer – such as: 'Do you unfeignedly believe all the Canonical Scriptures of the Old and New Testaments?' and: 'Will you reverently obey your Ordinary and other chief Ministers of the Church, and them to whom the charge and government over you is committed, following with a glad mind and will their godly admonitions?'

Whitstable, where John was to serve his curacy, was a relatively prosperous mainly middle-class parish. John liked his vicar and tried hard to fulfil the duties that were expected of him: pastoral and sick visiting, work in youth clubs and other Church organisations, conducting of the regular and of the occasional services. He found a friendly landlady who looked after him for the princely sum of two

pounds a week, and now that he was earning a regular stipend, he
bought himself a gramophone, and began to build up his collection of
classical records.

'I remember,' wrote Dr Raymond Whitney, 'that his tall and
handsome appearance caused quite a flutter among the unmarried
ladies in the congregation – and perhaps among the married ones too.'
Dr Whitney also remembered a flutter of another kind, always referred
to as 'the Kruschen Salts sermon'. A high-powered advertising
campaign was under way for these salts. If you took them every
morning, just enough to cover an old-fashioned sixpence, you were
supposed to be freed from constipation for ever, and to experience a
state of mental and physical euphoria known as 'the Kruschen feeling'.
John, searching for an illustration to some point that he was trying to
make in a sermon, referred to 'the Kruschen feeling'. This was
considered dreadfully improper, it quite shocked all the elderly ladies
of the congregation, and even the good-natured vicar had to speak
rather sharply to his curate. It was all a very long way from
Cambridge, and from John's scholarly and theological preoccupations. He was particularly nonplussed by one of his pastoral problems.
He was sent by his vicar to minister to a poor bedridden old lady who
was suffering from a stomach cancer; she remained at home, looked
after by her devoted, unmarried daughter. Both mother and daughter
were regular communicants, and when the old lady died, the daughter
asked that John might conduct the funeral service. A few days later
John went to visit the daughter and found her hysterically inconsol-
able. At last it all came out: 'I stayed behind after the funeral,' she
sobbed, 'and saw them shovelling all that earth over the coffin. How
will my mum get out of her grave when the trumpet sounds for the
resurrection?' Many years later, John wrote: 'The hopes and expectations with which I began at Whitstable, quickly changed into
questionings and doubts. What was wrong?' No doubt there were
many things wrong; first, in John himself in the innocence of his
expectations, and perhaps in a streak of arrogance that inclined him to
feel that, given the chance, he could run things better than his vicar. He
must, too, have suffered from a lack of intellectual stimulus and
companionship, and in his solitary lodgings, he felt lonely. He
discovered, too, that the Church ministered not to the whole parish,
but to a small, inner circle of churchgoers, and, except on special civic
occasions such as Armistice Day, or the installation of a new Mayor, it
was irrelevant to the real life of the town. Attendance at his first and last
ruridecanal conference confirmed John's experience of constraint

and unreality. After long and rather wearisome formalities, he intervened to ask whether the conference might not debate and question the Church's whole approach to the real problems of modern life, only to be told firmly by the rural dean that this matter could not be discussed, since it was not on the agenda.

The Church did much good ambulance work among the sick, the poor and the troubled, and it ministered unobtrusively to the needs of the small Anglican community. Everything went along well enough, but nothing seemed to take off, there were no sparks of Pentecostal fire. Whitstable went along well enough too in its small provincial way. But John chafed and wondered, enmeshed in what Wilfred Knox had called 'the unholy alliance of the Church with middle-class respectability'.

As often as he could, John got away to visit old friends in Cambridge, and sometimes, it must be said, he got away when he should not. But soon a more delightful distraction appeared; he was introduced to a girl. They played tennis together, went swimming, went to dances and other social events, they began to spend time together and began to grow fond of each other. Joan was a thoroughly nice, normal healthy girl, with a particularly good figure, and the affair developed. This time it was an affair well grounded in normal, healthy sex. John was always grateful to Joan; she helped to release him from much of the inhibition and associated guilt that had been implanted in him by his upbringing and his training. Theirs was an enjoyable emotional and physical relationship; together he and Joan ventured some way down that beguiling sexual path without going too dangerously far.

Of course, the parish noticed what was going on, and many people would have been happy for this nice young curate to marry and settle down in Whitstable. Young clergy are in a difficult position, whatever they do, however they spend their leisure, this is bound to be noticed and to be the subject of speculation and gossip. John had been trained to believe that he should marry the girl, probably the first girl, who physically attracted him. So before too long, John and Joan were unofficially engaged.

It would hardly have been possible to marry on a curate's meagre pay, and Joan's parents would certainly not have allowed it. Those were the days of long engagements, when young men were not expected to marry until they were in a position to provide a home and to support a wife. But in addition to these considerations there came, quite soon, the possibility of a change in John's prospects.

At Sidney Sussex, a chaplain was to be appointed for the first time, and John received a letter offering him the post at a salary of £175 a year plus rooms and dinner in hall. Calculations about money never played much part in John's decisions, but before accepting the offer he had to get permission from the Archbishop of Canterbury; this was obtained grudgingly. The College wanted John in October, so that he could begin his work by getting to know the 1929 intake of freshmen. But the archbishop dug in his heels, John must remain at Whitstable, and complete his year of curacy, only then could he return to Cambridge.

John felt in no mood to accept the archbishop's 'godly admonitions with a glad mind and will', he thought the decision to keep him at Whitstable was stupid; he stayed rebelliously, and got more and more entangled with Joan.

9

Return to Cambridge

JOHN returned to Cambridge full of hope and resolution. As well as his normal duties, the Master, Dr Weekes, wanted John to make friends among the undergraduates, keep his ear to the ground, and if there were any serious problems among the young men, any instance of injustice, anything beyond John's own competence, then he should bring it to his attention.

John was also determined to return seriously to his academic work. He would read for a PhD and work for another university prize. He talked to his old tutor B. T. D. Smith, who advised him to make a further study of continental theologians, the Germans and possibly the French as well. John resolved to learn German, he arranged for lessons, and planned a vacation visit to stay with a German family. There was, naturally, an element of personal ambition in all this academic activity, though it is hardly surprising that he was attracted by the possibility of an academic career. But John had sincere and rather more worthy ambitions. He had studied enough Biblical criticism – higher criticism, lower criticism, and form criticism – to realise, along with a number of thoughtful Christians, that something in the nature of a crisis was developing in Christian belief. The Christian Churches in Britain and on the Continent were fighting what looked like a rearguard action in the face of scientific advance, and of rigorous analytical study of Christian records and dogmas. There were good Christian men who wondered seriously whether the days of a supernatural religion tied to a dogmatic system were not over. These were men of faith, but they wanted to restate their faith in a manner that the world could continue to accept. But for centuries the Roman Catholic Church and, in different ways, the post-Reformation Protestant Churches, had insisted that faith and belief had to be identical; perhaps another way of putting it would be that faith was only valid when expressed in dogmatic formulations acceptable to the Church. The Athanasian creed has influenced Church attitudes throughout the ages: it opens with the words:

1. Whosoever will be saved: before all things it is necessary that he hold the Catholick Faith.
2. Which Faith except everyone do keep whole and undefiled: without doubt he shall perish everlastingly.

Although the brilliant and paradoxical formulations that follow can hardly be called simple, the position advanced is clear enough, and the conclusion underlines it:

41. They that have done good shall go into life everlasting, and they that have done evil into everlasting fire.
42. This is the Catholick Faith: which except a man believe faithfully, he cannot be saved.

The Anglican prayer-book of 1662 prints this creed. The 1928 prayer-book also prints the creed, but says that verses 2 and 42 *may* be dropped – a typically Anglican compromise between the traditionalists and the modernists.

How to combine intellectual honesty and still remain within the Catholic tradition; how to present a religion that combines both historical and mythological elements: these were the problems that faced John and his theological contemporaries. In all his academic studies, he was searching for clues that might lead to some reconciliation between his heart and his active mind. He still hoped to become a true defender of the faith, but a faith so expressed as to make it intellectually respectable.

Meanwhile, John followed B. T. D. Smith's advice, and tackled the German theologians, whose scholarly researches were undermining any possible fundamentalist approach to the New Testament. John was no linguist, but he struggled with the language, and paid his visit to Germany. He found it all heavy going. It was not only a question of linguistics, but also of theology. He was dissatisfied with the conclusions of most of the writers that he studied. He turned his attention to the Roman Catholic Modernists and became especially interested in M. Loisy who had been excommunicated for his radical views. John resolved to concentrate on improving his French so that he could visit M. Loisy and talk to him in person.

He soon had a wide circle of friends among the young men, not only among those who were preparing for ordination. He enjoyed the seductions of Cambridge life both in and out of the college. Sidney Sussex was noted for the excellence of its high table; so from discriminating between different brews of beer, John progressed to a discriminating appreciation of fine wines. Since this was a high church college, Fridays were supposed to be days of relative abstinence, no meat allowed, but the master chef was so cunning in his production of a variety of fish dishes, that Friday became the most popular evening for dining in hall. And there were the famous College Feasts, for which the fellows went into 'training' for at least a week beforehand. They must have needed that to prepare for fourteen courses with accompanying wines. 'You only had small portions for each course,' John assured me, but my latent East Anglian puritanism did receive something of a shock at accounts of these almost 'Roman' orgies.

Feasts and the high table apart, John led a dutiful and disciplined life as college chaplain. There was not much he could do about chapel services, which were in the hands of three senior fellows; he played his part, his sermons were thought interesting and his manner of conducting services was appreciated; but he would have liked more independence. He made a point of befriending people who seemed lonely and at odds with life, and this got him into trouble. He also, through no fault of his own, incurred the displeasure of B. T. D. Smith, the senior tutor. Several of the young men found this tutor difficult, and his supervisions perfunctory; he was not much interested in students outside his own Anglo-Catholic circle, and in his lectures he appeared to be moving towards a somewhat arid agnosticism. To the undergraduates John was refreshing; they enjoyed his openness and his practical approach. He was an enthusiast, he expressed his views on theology or politics with fervour and passion. Sometimes with rather too much passion.

Meanwhile John was worried about one of the undergraduates. This young man was suffering from an acute sense of injustice, and the more John looked into his case, the more convinced he became that this student was, indeed, being treated unfairly by the senior tutor. John was inclined to rush in where other more cautious or more self-interested characters might have feared to tread, and sometimes his active sympathy with those in trouble could cloud his judgement. But this time he felt there was a real case, he decided to take the master at his word, to refer to him. But the approach was badly received, John was given to understand that anything that might result in criticism of a senior member of the governing body was definitely not in his brief. B. T. D. Smith was already suspicious of his young protégé and disliked John's popularity among the undergraduates. John began to realise that this was the end of any hope of a college fellowship; he felt badly let down, and disappointed by this set-back to his bright academic prospects. He had come up against the hypocritical, frequently dishonest aspect of authority, always liable to close ranks against anyone – however principled – who appears to threaten their continuing hold on power, and always, of course, able to justify such dishonesty and such action with arguments of expediency. John, rather sadly, decided that he would have to seek employment elsewhere.

More than fifty years later, James Fisher, one of the theological students who found B. T. D. Smith's tutorials uninspiring, preached at John's funeral service, and reflected upon the young chaplain in those far-off days at Sidney Sussex:

'I recall him in his rooms tending his gramophone, trying to persuade us of the beauties of Brahms and César Franck; or arguing, discussing, wagging an admonitory finger, laughing, playing bridge. He made a good chaplain, one who seemed to offer to anyone who would accept it a good-humoured, real, but undemanding friendship and, if needed, practical help. He was particularly sensitive – and then it seemed to me slightly odd in him – to the misfits, those who seemed ill at ease and resentful of college and university life. It was, I think, through taking their part when Authority leaned on them, that for the first time as a priest, he came up against "the Institution". In particular, he faced that sad feature of institutions which persuades good men to protect their institution by acting unjustly towards some individual and then concealing the fact. That is a feature of life which most of us come to accept and live with. John always resented, and very often fought it; and because he was not without a combative streak usually fought with spirit and energy. But to us not in authority he was always friendly, ready to take trouble; and remained so, even when we acted foolishly, or childishly or in a way likely to damage himself.'

10

Minor Canon at St Paul's

WHILE John was wondering what to do with himself, he saw that St Paul's needed a new minor canon. In ecclesiastical terms this would be promotion; minor canons were appointed to fulfil various administrative functions in the cathedral, but mainly for the ability to sing the services – daily Matins and Evensong, at least four services on Sundays, and several special services throughout the year. They had to sing with one of the most prestigious of cathedral choirs, consisting of thirty boy choristers who were educated free in the cathedral choir school, and of eighteen professional men. John's musical education had been sketchy, but as chaplain, he had enjoyed singing services in the college chapel, and he remembered his childhood visit to the great edifice of St Paul's.

John set off for the audition carrying with him a short secular song with which he hoped to impress the selectors. He felt rather nervous: the other applicants appeared much better qualified, some had been minor canons elsewhere, and they had come prepared to sing serious ecclesiastical compositions. John answered several questions, and then, sweating profusely, he sang his song. Singing in St Paul's is particularly difficult because of the echo to which tempo has to be carefully adjusted. He was then required to strike, unaccompanied, a single and difficult note; he had a moment of panic, when suddenly, out of the air, came a gentle hum, and he knew that it was the note that he needed. He was offered the minor canonry.

Later, John learned that it was Douglas Hopkins, the sub-organist, who had seen his distress, and had hummed the required note. Douglas became a good friend, and coached John in the ways of singing in St Paul's. And Dean Inge had briefed the musicians, he did not want just another 'singing bird', and if this fellow Collins could sing at all he was the one to be appointed. Inge positively disliked musical services, he was a Cambridge man himself, and had been impressed by John's scholastic record, and by the fact that he had won the Carus Greek Testament prize, something that Inge had failed to win.

Up at the top of Ludgate Hill as you move round to the right of the cathedral, small lanes with suitably ecclesiastical names lead off the main road. Creed Lane, Godliman Street, and in between these an even smaller one, Dean's Court, which takes you to the eighteenth-century mansion erected for such eminent churchmen as deans of St Paul's. Here John presented himself and was met and welcomed by Mrs Inge. She took him upstairs to the bedroom he was to occupy until the house allocated to him was ready. As soon as he had washed and unpacked, she said, the dean wished to see him. Dutifully John appeared, and was shown into the study for his first encounter with the 'gloomy dean'. As well as a reputation for general pessimism, Inge was known for his barbed witticisms, and the sharpness of his tongue; he did not suffer fools gladly. He and John exchanged a few pleasantries, and the conversation languished. After a year spent with B. K. Cunningham, John was accustomed to deafness, and Inge was nearly as deaf as B. K. John sensed that he was tired, conventional politenesses would have bored him, and this was not the occasion, nor was Inge in the mood for serious talk. They sat in silence for some twenty to thirty minutes, until the bell rang for them to retire upstairs and dress for dinner. John was slightly worried by this encounter, but soon after he came downstairs Mrs Inge appeared.

'Oh Mr Collins,' she said happily. 'You are a *great* success with the dean.'

John's visit passed off well. Inge thought that, as a priest, he and his family should live simply, that is to say, they kept no manservant and had only three living-in maids. There might have been a grain of self-interest in this laudable attitude, since Mrs Inge was a fanatically economical housekeeper, and managed to persuade a somewhat unwilling John to accompany her round the local markets so that he could carry home her bargains and avoid the delivery charge.

John had several discussions with Inge, and soon found a very different person beneath the dean's public image. He was shy but kindly, he liked intelligent conversation, and had no time for small talk; he put a high value on friendship, and he proved a good friend to John. Inge had been a classical scholar at Eton, and later a professor of theology at Cambridge, he was widely read and interested in politics, and in contemporary social problems; he seemed happy to discuss theological and philosophical questions with this younger man, and treated him as an intellectual equal. While John admired the honesty and clarity of Inge's thinking, he was attracted by an element of mischief in him, a gadfly instinct that made him want to sting and shock complacency, ignorance and prejudice. Inge's public sallies provoked predictable responses: he had many admirers, but there were others who thought him a danger to Church and State, and he received his share of 'hate' mail. He was fond of quoting one example from a lady who wrote, 'I am praying for your death; I have been very successful on two former occasions.'

Inge was a modernist, and was interested in Loisy, though he thought that the Frenchman's iconoclasm had gone too far. 'Christianity', Inge wrote in his diary, 'must cease to depend on belief in miraculous interventions in the order of nature,' but he added, 'I question the wisdom of such utterances from the pulpit.' He was well aware of the dilemmas facing liberal churchmen; his advice was that while clergy ought not to conceal their real opinions, their duty was 'to say what they do, not what they do not believe'. He encouraged John to pursue his studies, and suggested that he might find a lectureship at King's College.

As soon as his house at No. 7 Amen Court was ready, John moved to the other side of Ludgate Hill. Here, another small road, Ave Maria Lane, leads off the main hill, and a little way along on the left is a smaller lane, Amen Corner, that takes you into Amen Court. On your left as you enter is the stout wall of the Stationers Hall, and on your right a row of eighteenth-century houses, that are the residences of the three Crown canons. These are not, of course, as large or as grand as the deanery, their once red bricks have been darkened by years of exposure to London grime, but they form a fine and harmonious whole. Particularly pleasing are their doorways, approached by stone steps flanked with elegantly curved iron railings that support a lantern and two old lamp extinguishers. The end of the Court has a high wall obscured by trees, and incorporates vestigial remains of a Roman wall. Now, at the back of the canons' houses, you are in the heart of the Court, a sizeable area of grass, flowerbeds and trees, with a tough old mulberry in the middle, and along the far side a row of Victorian houses for the minor canons and the cathedral organist. These, in their unostentatious way, are also fine houses and blend happily into the atmosphere of the Court. Completing the rectangle is another Victorian house with rooms extending over an archway beneath which you may return to Ave Maria Lane. This is, or was then, a home for the archdeacons of London, who also serve as cathedral canons. Ecclesiastical hierarchy is meticulously observed and carefully displayed, so this house is larger and more decorated than those of the minor canons, and it seals off that end of the Court, effectively enclosing it from the outside world.

In this quiet, miniature cathedral close, John's house was in the corner, near the archdeaconry. He viewed it with some trepidation; by modern standards it was large, probably cold in winter, and he was expected to decorate, heat and furnish it out of his depleted financial resources. A Cambridge friend helpfully introduced him to Houston Wallace, an accountant who wanted somewhere to live near his work with a City firm. John and Houston had dinner together and went to a 'leg-show'; they decided that they liked each other, could live happily in the same house, and share the housekeeping expenses. They engaged Mrs Moore, a handsome, cheerful widow as cook-housekeeper. This all proved a good arrangement.

It cannot be said that the residents of Amen Court lived entirely in love and charity with one another. Soon after John's arrival, Mrs X came to call, mainly it appeared to warn him against Mrs Y, 'a very dangerous woman'. A few days later Mrs Y arrived to warn him that he must be very careful what he said in front of Mrs X, since she was known as a dangerous and malicious gossip. As for the Crown canons in their eighteenth-century glory, they looked down upon the archdeacon, a nice enough chap, 'a hand-shaking man', as one described him, but whereas they had been commissioned by the reigning monarch, he had only been appointed by the Bishop of London, and they suspected him of being a bishop's spy – over the years, relations between bishops and deans had been, to say the least, uneasy.

In John's time, it was the senior canon, Alexander, who presided over Amen Court; he lived at No. 2. Alexander had been a bright and scholarly young priest, the youngest ever to be appointed to a canonry of St Paul's. He was now the chapter treasurer, and managed the cathedral finances, and this combined with his strong personality made him a powerful and influential figure. He and the dean cordially disliked each other: when Inge had to account for the absence of the senior canon at some function he said, 'Canon Alexander sends his apologies, Saturday night is his bath night.' Alexander thought Inge was a mountebank, Inge thought Alexander a stick-in-the-mud old reactionary. Alexander's passion was the cathedral, about which he knew more than anyone else; his home life was sad, he and his wife had no children, and she was a pathetic and embarrassing alcoholic.

Life in Amen Court and at St Paul's was formal – John had to buy himself clerical morning dress and top hat, the costume in which all cathedral clergy had to appear on Sundays. 'Makes us all look like a bevy of undertakers,' John commented. Minor canons were expected to be similarly attired whenever they went to call on canons or other senior church dignitaries. Inge thought Amen Court dreadfully stuffy, 'A little Cranford set down in the middle of London'. Life went on beneath a stifling cloak of respectability, but human frailties and passions would keep threatening to tear it apart; there were minor scandals and small human tragedies, but little beacons of warmth and kindness were lighted, and John helped to light some of these.

Everyone was interested in the new minor canon, and John was aware of net curtains being twitched aside as the ladies of Amen Court watched his comings and goings. They did not quite know what to make of him, he seemed nice enough, he was reputed to hold advanced views, so was the dean, but then nobody much approved of the dean. Mr Collins had introduced a stranger into the Court, a layman unconnected in any way with St Pauls, so they preferred not to notice him. Houston was never invited into any other house in the Court, and the only person who was friendly to him as well as to John was Douglas Hopkins. After a few months, John and Houston gave a sherry party; such a thing had never before happened in Amen Court. Later this modern young cleric bought a motor-car, another startling innovation, and he was sometimes seen about not in clerical dress and without even a dog-collar. Then Mr Collins and his friend were seen to entertain ladies, clearly young, unmarried ladies – nothing really wrong, of course, but a young clergyman could not be too careful.

John was unperturbed by all this. When he noticed it he was mildly amused, and he went on organising his life. He was appointed a priest-in-ordinary to King George V, one of the 'perks' of minor canons of St Paul's, he was engaged to lecture at King's College, and he found an excellent French teacher. He worked hard at his duties as a minor canon; the musicians had made no mistake in his appointment, he had a fine baritone voice, and an excellent ear. 'He was always reliable,' said Douglas Hopkins. 'He never sang out of tune, his diction was good, and he never showed off.' The music of St Paul's became, for John, a life-long delight, and so conditioned was he to the pure voices of the young choristers that, with rare exceptions, he grew almost to dislike the female voice. He took trouble over his speaking voice as well. In those days there was no mechanism of sound amplification, but John was determined to be heard along the whole 515 feet of the cathedral. He took himself off to be trained in voice production, and learned to throw his voice so that he became one of the

few preachers to be consistently audible, and the quality of his voice
made it a pleasure to listen to him.

John grew to love St Paul's, and his love and knowledge were fed by
a growing friendship with Canon Alexander, who sensed in this
young man a potential devotee like himself. 'You can't play around
with St Paul's,' he said to John. 'People come here and think they'll try
this or that new-fangled thing, but those great stones are greater than
any of them. St Paul's doesn't respond to stunts.'

11

Alfred Loisy

A s soon as John thought that his French was sufficiently fluent, he arranged his first visit to the excommunicated priest and scholar, Alfred Loisy, who was living in retirement at Montier-en-Der, a small village in northern France. Loisy had been accused of abandoning the Christian faith altogether, of reducing it to an absurdity – a fiction based upon the subjective imaginings of Peter; he was supposed to have denied the divinity of Christ and the transcendence of God. It was questioned whether he even believed in God, and his views on the resurrection were hard to understand and far from orthodox.

Loisy was already seventy-five years old, but his mind was as acute and fresh as ever. John was immediately captivated by him. He found something greatly appealing in this distinguished old man, living so simply in a small country cottage, devotedly tending his garden and his livestock in the manner of his peasant forebears, still writing, studying, praying, truly a man of faith. John admired 'the sparkle and wit of his conversation; the extent of his knowledge, the width of his vision and the sincerity of his convictions' and agreed with the views of an old friend of Loisy, Maud Petre, who wrote 'morally it was a life of utter purity, integrity; unworldly, unambitious; direct and truthful'. Unquestionably a good man, but could he still be called a Christian?

Loisy had repudiated both the obscurantist dogmatism of the Roman Catholic Church, and the efforts of liberal Protestants to discover 'the Jesus of history', to 'demythologise' the New Testament and to anchor the Christian faith upon the few reliable facts that could be painstakingly dredged up from a study of history and of historical documents. Loisy was as radical a critic as any – perhaps more radical – but he believed that this kind of criticism would, in the end, prove a sterile exercise, both it and Roman dogmatism would succeed only in robbing Christianity of its spiritual content and of its evangelical power. Loisy never denied the historical existence of Jesus of Nazareth, but he insisted that the New Testament documents must be seen as the products of faith and not its cause, just as the creeds were interpretations of the original religious experience. This did not make either the documents or the creeds untrue, but they could not be judged only by accepted methods of historical research, their validity lay in their witness to spiritual reality.

Loisy assured John that he had never denied the existence of God either in his thinking or in his writing, nor did he deny what he called 'Le tout rapport de Jésus Christ envers la Divinité'. Of God he wrote, 'He is before everything else a mystery that transcends us. And to claim to express in human language the last word about him is, in effect, to blaspheme him . . . Absolute truth is not revealed.' 'God is more real than we are,' he said, but he could not regard him as what he called 'Le Grand Individu' and he added 'I forbid myself to define God'.

'Perhaps,' commented Alec Vidler, 'his agnosticism had more reverence in it and even more faith, than the confident dogmatism of those who condemned him'. Loisy drew a clear distinction between the formulas of belief, such as those that his own Church sought to impose upon its members, and the life of faith. Of the latter he held an exalted view. 'What is religious faith?' he wrote in a passage underlined by John. 'Essentially nothing else than the whole mind, reason, imagination and will putting forth their combined energy to break a way through the natural forms of existence and escape from the mechanism which seems inexorably to govern the destinies of things.'

Loisy discerned this faith in all religions, even in the most primitive, though he believed Christianity to be its highest and truest expression. Even about this he could be agnostic. 'Faith outlives under new forms of religion, the religions that are dead', and towards the end of his life he did not consider it impossible that the forms of the Roman Catholic Church might also die. But the faith that could not die was for him a mystical belief in humanity and its future.

The crucial point of faith, and one that John was most eager to discuss with Loisy, was the resurrection. While Loisy did not believe that a purely historical proof of the resurrection was possible, he insisted that we must look at the experience of Peter and of the other disciples. Here was a group of apparently quite ordinary men who could hardly have made a worse showing at the moment of crisis. Their leader Peter denied that he had ever had anything to do with Jesus, and they all ran away and hid in terror. Yet within a short time, these men and their friends were transformed, the secular and religious powers held no more fears for them and their preaching changed the world. What had happened to effect this extraordinary transformation which exposed them to persecution, imprisonment and death? Whatever experiences they may have had individually and together, and however those experiences may be explained, the result was an unshakeable belief in the resurrection, the continuing life of Christ in the world, in which they could continue to share. This faith, and its effects on the lives not only of the first Christians, but on succeeding generations of men and women, does not constitute historical proof, but is a witness to spiritual reality, and to the dynamism that such reality creates.

In reply to John's questioning Loisy said, 'How do we account for Peter's faith that after the Crucifixion Jesus was alive? Can we account for his faith, for what happened to him as a result of it, and for the life of the Apostolic Church in any other way than to assume that he was correct in his belief? . . . The proof of the Resurrection must lie, not in assessment of the historicity of the records, but in an assessment of the validity of Peter's faith.' There is a subtlety in Loisy's approach that makes it difficult to commend his views to those who want, or perhaps psychologically need, an authoritative dogma by which to live, and who are confused by the idea that the truth of a myth or a symbol does not become less true if it is not identical with, or related to, a truth of scientific fact.

Loisy accepted that the religious faith that grew from the life and death of Jesus of Nazareth created its own myth, but he was opposed to those who would try to banish the whole story into the realm of myth. 'And yet it is true,' he said, 'that Jesus has lived a myth, and that a myth has borne him to the summit of history'. This may sound too extreme and complex a paradox, but Loisy distinguished between what he saw as artificial and self-made myths – often the work of theologians – and the genuine religious myth that grew spontaneously out of an experience of faith – this latter myth, centred on faith in the resurrection of Christ, Loisy believed to be profoundly true. Loisy disclaimed any systematic theology, he distrusted systems. He preferred that in his writings 'there should be only fragments of truth'.

It was in these 'fragments of truth' that John found so much interest, and a stimulus that led him in the new directions towards which he had been groping. He was in complete agreement with Loisy that what was needed was 'to renew theology from top to bottom, and substitute the religious for the dogmatic spirit'. Loisy was a mystic, but, for him, mysticism had to come down to earth and find its expression – one might say its incarnation – in life.

John continued to visit and to correspond with Loisy until the outbreak of war. He began to contribute articles to learned theological journals trying to explain and defend Loisy's views. But it was not ideas alone that fired John, it was personal relationships and their influence upon him that were the real catalysts, and his friendship with Loisy was one of the most formative in his life. 'I had not realised before,' John wrote, 'that Christianity stands or falls at the existential level . . . questions of faith can be assessed only by reference to their effects in human experience. Where faith is concerned, the proof of the pudding is in the eating.'

It is not an exaggeration to say that, in some form or other, the rest of John's ministry was devoted to an attempt to work out, in his own life and in society, the implications of the ideas and insights that he absorbed during this period.

12

Goodbye to St Paul's

WHEN John accepted the minor canonry one or two perceptive friends had warned him that St Paul's might prove a soul-destroying place. But John was still searching for his personal role as a man and as a priest. There was much at St Paul's that he enjoyed, his duties in the cathedral, his new friends and his social life, his nature was innocent and happy; he was not plagued by guilt.

John's most enduring and influential friendship was with his French teacher, Yvonne Cooper, and her husband Harold, a master at Dulwich College. Harold was as English as Yvonne was French: he equable and philosophical, she volatile and emotional, up in the air one minute, plunged in gloom the next; while Harold chuckled with quiet humour, Yvonne sparkled with Gallic wit: she was a superb raconteur. When Harold first took his bride to stay with his East Anglian family, a screen was provided in their bedroom behind which Yvonne was expected to undress; she was so incensed that she promptly threw it down the stairs. They were a perfect union of opposites, and gave John a vision of a deeply satisfying and happy marriage. The Coopers were involuntarily childless, but were entirely content in their mutual companionship. However, their joint affection for John was such that he was soon treated as a son of the house.

John now seemed well on the way to the top. He moved among men high in the ecclesiastical establishment, and he was winning golden opinions in influential places – and in humbler places too. Among virgers, choirmen, and the 300-strong contingent of artisans and craftsmen who kept the fabric of the building in repair. Some would bring their personal problems to him; they found a good and tolerant listener, someone who talked to them sympathetically and was refreshingly free from ecclesiastical jargon. It was not long after John had settled in No. 7 that the Conservative politics he had inherited from his family began seriously to be disturbed. Beggars have always haunted Amen Court, believing rightly or wrongly that the clergy are 'a soft touch'. But the mass unemployment of the 1930s produced something different – numbers of desperate men who had walked all the way from the depressed areas, from the north, from as far away as Scotland, from the Midlands, from South Wales, all in search of work, anything to save their families from near-starvation. 'How could a social and economic system which put men in so undignified a position and into such misery be anything but contrary to the will of God revealed in the life and teachings of Christ?' John said. He went to talk to the Salvation Army who ran hostels for the homeless. He made an arrangement whereby he would telephone through the names of men who had come looking for work, direct them to the Army who would then supply them with chits for bed, morning and evening food, and sometimes with much-needed cash; they would send in monthly bills to John. For a time this worked well, but the bills began to mount, and seemed far bigger than was warranted by the numbers of men John tried to help. Enquiries led to the discovery that one of the beggars was an out-of-work actor who had learned to mimic John's voice so accurately that the Army officials were deceived, and the actor got a nice rake-off from the men that he recommended, in John's name, to various hostels.

Of course, John realised that his little bit of personal charity was the smallest of drops in an ocean of misery; more and more he felt that the Church ought to be concerned not just with individual suffering, but with the system that allowed such suffering to develop.

Partly through his contact with Loisy, John had developed a European view of the Church's need to be involved with politics. He was never remotely attracted by Communism, he could not accept a purely material basis for human life, and did not believe in the possibility or desirability of any materialist Utopia. But he did not fall into the opposite trap of regarding Fascism and Nazism as bulwarks against Communism as many at that time did. John had a horror of Fascism; he had been sympathetic to the early peace movements, but after the Nazis came to power in Germany, he supported Winston Churchill, one of the few politicians who consistently warned of the dangers to come.

When John looked back on this period in his life he felt that it had been too easy and worldly. He was capable of periods of self-discipline and mild austerity, he went fairly regularly on retreats, but London life provided plenty of worldly pleasure, and John enjoyed theatres, concerts and dinner and bridge with friends. He was naturally and generously hospitable, and was happy to be able to entertain at 7 Amen

Court. But the time came when household bills began to rise rather steeply. Mrs Moore had explanations about rising prices, but one day the chief superintendent of the local police force arrived. 'Are you aware,' he asked, 'that one of my policemen spent last night in your house?'

John and Houston were not aware; they had noticed that the police seemed more than usually assiduous in patrolling Amen Court, and they had assumed that this was due to the increased number of beggars, but, not at all, it was due to Mrs Moore's all-embracing hospitality. She had to leave forthwith, an event and its cause not unnoticed by the residents of Amen Court.

There were other troubles in this life of a young bachelor priest. John's ministry at Buckingham Palace seemed satisfactory, he took the services well, and the King did not seem displeased by his sermons; seven minutes for preference, John had been instructed, and never, never more than ten, the King would not stand for that. One Sunday morning John was due to celebrate the eight o'clock Communion service at the Palace, but the evening before he had been out, to a party, and he overslept. Houston, unfortunately, was away for the weekend, and there were less than twenty minutes for John to dress, shave, collect his robes and get to the Palace on time, he knew he could never do it. In a panic he telephoned and said that he had a bad attack of diarrhoea, and dared not venture out. Palace officials expressed suitable solicitude, and said they would find another celebrant. Unfortunately for John, they found another minor canon, all dressed and ready.

John got up slowly, and began to prepare some breakfast for himself, but the news had spread round Amen Court, and the good ladies were much concerned about young Mr Collins with nobody to look after him. They telephoned anxiously, and the wife of one of the minor canons, a rather masterful lady, arrived on the doorstep.

'No, no,' she said. 'You mustn't eat *anything* for at least twenty-four hours; that would be fatal; I have brought you some very good medicine.' John viewed the medicine with extreme distaste, but he had to swallow a large dose. 'I shall come back and make sure you are all right,' promised his ministering angel. 'You ought to have another dose in a few hours' time, I shall look in after church.' She was as good as her word, and since John did not want to appear to have recovered too quickly, he had to swallow another dose. John had something of a phobia about constipation, he felt his intestines turning to concrete, so to counteract the effect of the medicine he took a large dose of a powerful aperient. By the end of the day, he felt really ill.

John survived this unfortunate lapse and its uncomfortable penalty, but then a little cloud blew up over his relationship with Canon Alexander. St Paul's has an attraction for neurotic and psychologically disturbed persons, and an unnamed woman started writing John a series of obscene letters. They became more and more unpleasant and, at one stage, she accused him of being the father of her illegitimate child. She never gave any address and the postmark varied. John needed advice so he went to consult Canon Alexander, who suggested that he put the matter in the hands of the police. He then looked seriously at John and said: 'You know, Collins, there's no smoke without fire'.

Fortunately for John the woman in question, for no apparent reason, switched her attentions to Canon Alexander, and accused *him* of fathering any number of illegitimate children. She was finally tracked down and taken to what we now call a psychiatric hospital.

Full and active as John's life was, he felt an emotional void. Now that he was well paid and had a house of his own he was in a position to marry. At first he had told Houston that their arrangement might have to be temporary, as he was engaged; he still felt himself committed to Joan. But as they were separated the affair died a natural death, and although he no longer wished to marry her, he missed her. He liked feminine company, he enjoyed talking to women, and they to him. On one of his periodic visits to Cambridge, he ran into Helen, a girl he had known when he was at Sidney Sussex, and she at Newnham. Helen was now working in London, and sharing a flat with friends. John invited her out to dinner, and they began to meet regularly. John had always liked Helen, they had intellectual and cultural tastes in common, a mild intimacy developed, and they decided to get married. John bought a ring, and the engagement was announced in *The Times*, everything was respectable and above board. It seemed so suitable, but somehow the magic was missing. Helen was suffering a rebound from an unhappy affair with a married man, and when it came to the point, she was not at all certain that she could face life as the wife of a clergyman. So, by mutual consent, the engagement was broken off. Helen realised that John was depressed by this, and that he missed their weekly dinners; she suggested he should take Frances, one of her flatmates, out instead. This proved a good counter-attraction, Frances was not an intellectual, but she was a talented pianist, and was studying at the Royal College of Music; she was relaxed, happy-go-lucky and sexually attractive; John became very fond of her.

There were domestic complications at No. 7 Amen Court. Houston Wallace was away, and it looked as if John would have, temporarily, to move out of his house. His professor at King's College, Dr Maurice Relton, urged him to stay at his home. John knew and had visited the family, he enjoyed theological discussion with Relton, and he enjoyed hearing Mrs Relton play the piano – she had sometimes taken the trouble to learn pieces by his favourite composers. Friends, aware of John's susceptibilities, counselled caution. Mrs Relton had been a widow, and had brought three unmarried daughters to her second marriage. But John was not inclined to listen to cautionary advice, he liked the Reltons, and he went off, trusting and confident.

Only one daughter S. was at home, a girl John already knew. As the evenings were rather staid and formal he got into the habit of taking S. out, and was kindly encouraged by her mother and stepfather. When the young people returned, the older generation would have gone to bed, the drawing room looked inviting with shaded lights, and a tray with a decanter full of whisky, and other drinks, and an invitation to John to help himself to anything he fancied. John was sufficiently alert to be careful about his behaviour; he felt over-enveloped in kindness, and was relieved when the time came to return to Amen Court. On his last evening, he took S. out to a cinema, and on the way back, nearing the end of the taxi-ride, he gave her a goodnight, goodbye kiss – a thanks for making his two weeks' visit pleasant.

Next morning John arrived down to breakfast, packed and ready, to be greeted by Mrs Relton who smothered him in an enthusiastic embrace.

'We are so happy,' she said, 'that you and S. are going to be married – Daddy has sent an announcement to *The Times*.' John was so taken aback that he hardly knew what to say. He began to try to explain that it was all a great mistake, much too premature, but his protestations were swept aside. Uncharacteristically, he hesitated, they had all been so kind to him; Relton was his professor, and he didn't wish to humiliate S. in front of her mother and stepfather. He could find no words to explain the situation, he would go back to No. 7 and then sort things out. But, of course, every hour, let alone every day, that he procrastinated it became more and more difficult to act. He liked S., she was not unattractive, it would be a suitable marriage. S. was much more suitable than Joan, or Helen or Frances, none of whom really wanted to marry a clergyman. S. was a religious girl, she would make a good wife, perhaps it would work, people were known to fall in love after marriage as well as before, and perhaps somehow he had raised false expectations. So John dithered. He had, since his teens, been subject to migraines, and one day, in the middle of a lecture, he was hit by the worst migraine he had ever experienced, flashing lights before his eyes, and a frightening inability to speak properly – if words came at all, they came in a dreadful jumble. 'Gentlemen, I am unwell,' he managed to stammer out, and then collapsed. This episode alarmed John so much that he decided to see a doctor. He was recommended to a Dr Hadfield who was also a psychiatrist, a wise and sympathetic man, and a practising Christian. He needed only a very short consultation.

'There is certainly nothing serious the matter with you,' Hadfield said. 'But you must break off this ridiculous engagement at once.' The doctor had only told John what, in his heart, he already knew, but he had given him the necessary spur to action. John arranged to see S. and tried to persuade her to break the engagement. She wept and refused. John could not bear seeing a woman cry, feebly he suggested that she think it over, and they would meet in two days' time; he did try to make clear that he could not go through with the marriage. After two days, S. had been stiffened by Mummy and Daddy, and she again refused to break the engagement.

John communicated with *The Times*, and paid for an announcement to the effect that the marriage would not now take place. The next day he went to see Relton. The professor was sitting with his head in his hands.

'Why did you do it?' he almost sobbed. John began to try to explain. Relton lifted his head. 'Are you impotent?' he demanded. 'I haven't had occasion to discover,' John replied, and the interview became increasingly acrimonious. It ended with Relton's angry words, 'I'll break you for this'.

John left, relieved, but distressed; he would have to resign his lectureship at King's, he felt badly about S. who had probably become genuinely fond of him, and although Relton's threat had been made in the heat of the moment, he was a man of influence in the ecclesiastical and academic worlds. Worse was to follow. That evening the newspapers all carried banner headlines and photographs: 'Priest-in-ordinary to the King breaks engagement'. And in the manner of investigative journalists, they had ferreted out information about two former engagements and had written up the story in a customary salacious and sensational manner. What an irresponsible, unreliable and heartless young man this must be! Those were the days when it was almost a crime for a man to break an engagement, and subject a poor innocent girl to public shame. Men could be, and sometimes were, sued for breach of promise, and could be made to pay both damages and legal costs.

John went to see the dean, and told him the whole story. Inge listened quietly. 'Well, Collins,' he said. 'You've been a fool, but we're all fools at some time or other in our lives.' For various reasons Inge disliked Relton, and was annoyed by his behaviour, and his threat to John's future. 'If you feel you should have to go,' he said, 'I'll do my best to help you get another job'. And he added, 'I hear the dean of Peterhouse is retiring, that might suit you.'

John was not appointed fellow and dean of Peterhouse College, Cambridge, in spite of powerful support from Inge. He wondered about the influence of Professor Relton, but he also wondered about his own credentials. His friends and others whose opinions he respected assured him that he should pursue an academic career, so John assumed that that was what he had to do. But it was not enough to lecture and publish articles, he needed to produce something more substantial, he ought to organise his ideas into a book. A literary friend, Ashley Sampson, was editing the Christian Challenge series, and when he approached John for a contribution, this seemed an obvious answer. He agreed to write a book to be called *The New Testament Problem*.

Apart from this constructive enterprise, the pattern of John's life at St Paul's seemed to be breaking up. Houston Wallace's mother had died, and Houston felt that he must leave to share the family home with his unmarried sister. Frances, into whose pleasant arms John might well have fallen, had got married rather suddenly, and was preparing to live somewhere up in the north. And Inge was leaving St Paul's. B. K. Cunningham was always remarkably well informed about matters ecclesiastical, and he liked to keep a distant eye on the progress of his 'boys'; now he needed a new vice-principal. He wrote to John suggesting that he might like to fill the vacancy.

John was very ready to consider this offer. Materially it would mean considerable sacrifice; as a minor canon, with his outside posts and activities, he was earning around £1,000 a year, and, at that pre-inflationary period, this was very good pay for a young man. B. K. could offer a salary of only £250 a year plus keep, and John would have, of course, to give up his house. But it did not take him long to make up his mind to accept; with luck he might soon be on the University Board of Divinity's list of recognised lecturers, and he would have time to write. When he needed a more domestic atmosphere, Harold and Yvonne Cooper would always welcome him to their home in Dulwich.

Inge retired before John left for Cambridge, and the cathedral awaited the appointment of a new dean. All assumed that this would be Canon Alexander, and Alexander himself had been assured that it was almost a foregone conclusion. But then it was announced that Dr

W. R. Matthews, dean of Exeter, was to be the next dean of St Paul's. Alexander's disappointment was deep and bitter. He never reconciled himself to the gentle and scholarly Walter Matthews and continued to do as he pleased in the cathedral, sometimes, as chapter treasurer, countermanding instructions given by the dean.

When John went to say goodbye to Alexander, the old man pointed to his desk and said sorrowfully, 'That drawer contains all my plans for St Paul's, nobody will ever see them now'. John was thankful to escape from so much unhappiness.

13

Vice-principal of Westcott House

B.K.'s intuition about John was correct; he was to spend three happy and valuable years at Westcott House from 1934 to 1937. Many of those ordained during this time thought that it was Westcott's greatest period. B. K. was still in his prime, John was there as a theologian to stimulate the young men's minds, and widen their horizons, and the chaplain, Gerald Hawker, was a saintly, ascetic and spiritual man, ready to be helpful in matters of prayer and devotion. B. K.'s hearing had inevitably deteriorated, he had a somewhat unreliable box as a mechanical amplifier, so John had to spend quite a lot of time interpreting, and acting as B. K.'s ears, and, as he worked more closely with him, he became as attached to him as were nearly all those who passed through Westcott House. But John did rebel against B. K.'s snobbery and games-worship, and disliked some of his typical comments on the new student intake . . .

Gerald Ellison – Rowing Blue – First Class.
Mervyn Stockwood – No good at games – Not much.

True, Gerald Ellison rose to become Bishop of London, in spite of having difficulties with examinations, but it is Mervyn who, as Bishop of Southwark, has had a far greater and an enduring influence upon the Church.

Several students have commented on how difficult it must have been for John to work in the tremendously popular shadow of B. K. but he faced the problem well. John's rooms were open, and those with whom he was temperamentally compatible gravitated to them. He would dispense sherry before dinner, an innovation at Westcott; some were delighted, and others a little shocked. He treated all the students as friends and equals, and his rooms echoed with laughter. As was his nature, John took special notice of those who seemed misfits, and of those who did not come from public schools. Anyone B. K. found difficult he would hand over to John.

As well as his sherry parties, John used to take groups of ordinands out to local pubs, on river picnics, and expeditions further afield. One student remembers being invited to a Saturday evening meal at a pub in Exning, near Newmarket. There they were joined by one of the 'regulars', a stable boy who told them that though Mr Collins was not a betting man, he was a very good friend of his. In fact, John *was* becoming something of a betting man, he was interested in the lives of the stable boys, and used to visit them at Newmarket, and listen to their problems, and, with advice from the ground, he began to study form, and opened a modest account with Ladbrokes under the code-name of 'Final Word'.

John was a man of the world to his students, indeed a rather worldly person. Some found his natural unecclesiastical approach helpful, especially those who were a little uncertain about their vocations, while others were intimidated or disapproving.

Some were stimulated by John's lectures and tutorials, others were alarmed by his radical views. Ronald Lunt spoke of him as 'a person putting a keen, accurate mathematical mind to work on demolishing the credentials of the faith one had come to Cambridge to learn. His course of lectures on Acts pointed out the inconsistencies and tore the book to shreds as a writing of history. I rather feared this sceptic . . . I did not expect in an ordination course at Cambridge to be taught that large slices of the New Testament were bogus or phoney.'

On Christmas Eve, 1936 B. K. wrote to John thanking him for his help and loyalty, and added perspicaciously, 'I consider you are one of those people (they are generally the best) for whom the angels and the devils have a fairly even tug-of-war, the lowest and the highest, so near to one another, it is the more credit that, in your case, the highest (by God's grace) win. And yet, more wonderfully so, because you do not *appear* (N.B. only appear) to find much help on the more specifically devotional side (quiet time, intercessions etc.). Indeed I sometimes wonder what the younger folk make of it! that you penetrate through the initial barrier it is bound to create in their minds is to the credit of both you and them.'

By the end of 1936, in a scramble to meet the appointed deadline, John completed *The New Testament Problem*. One of the disadvantages of living too happily in the present is that deadlines seem a long way off until they suddenly bear down upon you, and then there are long night sittings, smoking too many cigarettes, and drinking too many cups of black coffee, in order to get the sermon, article, or, in this case, the book, finished on time. I am no theologian, and I do not know how this book would stand up to modern scholarship. It seems to me to give a clear, and, to the layman, easily understood sketch of the making of the New Testament. All along John stresses the importance of the exercise of the imagination in trying to understand the environment, the outlook, and the problems of Christians in the first and second centuries.

The influence of Loisy is evident on every page, though John did not go all the way with his mentor. John took his stand on the living reality of the resurrection, and he concluded his book with a quotation from Robert Bridges' 'Testament of Beauty':

> So it was when Jesus came in his gentleness
> with his divine compassion and great Gospel of Peace,
> men hail'd him WORD OF GOD, and in the title of Christ
> crown'd him with love beyond all earth-names of renown.
> For He, wandering unarm'd save by the Spirit's flame,
> in few years with few friends founded a world-empire
> wider than Alexander's and more enduring;
> since from his death it took its everlasting life.
> HIS kingdom is God's kingdom, and his holy temple
> not in Athens or Rome but in the heart of man.

That, perhaps, expresses John's faith better than any theological formulation.

While John was trying to broaden the theological ideas of his students, and to suggest to them that it was possible to question, without losing, their Christian faith, he was also encouraging them to look out into the world beyond Cambridge and beyond the Church. Several of them remarked on his evident concern with social issues and with questions of war and peace.

John's closest friend at this period was probably Mervyn Stockwood. 'If ever a master owed more to his pupil than the pupil to his master, I was that man,' John was to say later. Mervyn, for all his ability, was not a very rewarding pupil, he was not really interested in theology. And he was one of the few who realised that theology was unlikely to remain John's chief interest either.

John and Mervyn made the transition from the Tory to the Labour party more or less together. Soon after John's arrival at Westcott, one of the young men, son of a Welsh Nonconformist minister, invited him to stay for a week at Porth in South Wales. Here, for the first time in his life, John saw real poverty and deprivation face to face. He was shocked by the squalor and ugliness, and particularly by the hopelessness and despair of the unemployed men and their wives. 'I realised,' he wrote, 'once and for all what a humbug the establishment is, and how feeble and at fault is the Church in its social and political witness.'

Mervyn was ordained while John was still vice-principal, and went off to his first parish in Bristol. Very soon John went to visit him, and once again he saw the realities of poverty and slum life. By that time, Mervyn was a member of the Labour party, and, convinced of the necessity of making Christianity relevant to political and social life, he was engaged, at this local level, in doing just that. John was enormously impressed. 'It is certainly to him,' he wrote, 'more than to anybody else, that I owe my first attempts to relate the Gospel to social and political matters.' Mervyn also introduced John to the sitting member of parliament, Sir Stafford Cripps, and later, to Victor Gollancz. Both these men were to have an enormous influence upon John's thinking and upon his life.

Internationally everything was becoming more and more menacing. John still visited Alfred Loisy regularly, and watched Europe through Loisy's eyes. Like him he was shocked by the ease and speed with which the Vatican, in return for very minor concessions, had accommodated itself to both the Fascist and Nazi governments. But the worst shock, and one that perhaps more than anything turned John against the Tory policy of appeasement, was the Italian invasion of Abyssinia in 1935, and the fact that Cardinal Pacelli, later Pope Pius XII, blessed the departing troops, assuring them that they were carrying Christianity and civilisation into darkest Africa. What of course they were actually carrying, among other modern weapons, was mustard gas to be sprayed on defenceless Ethiopians. The whole sorry saga of appeasement, which was supported by the Archbishop of Canterbury, and the overwhelming majority of the Anglican bishops, roused John to a ferment of indignation.

Of course, Christians had to try to be peacemakers. Shortly before John left St Paul's, Dick Shepherd had been appointed a canon. Like so many, John had succumbed, though not uncritically, to Dick's enormous personal charm and sincerity, but he could not embrace his wholehearted pacifism.

As always, a great deal of thinking and discussing around theology and politics was going on in Cambridge. John spent time with Wilfred Knox and Alec Vidler, who was then living at the Oratory. Alec was a fine scholar and writer, and an attractive, humorous personality; he was much concerned with trying to relate Christianity to the modern world and its seemingly intractable problems, and he, as well as Wilfred, was a member of the Labour party; their concerns were increasingly John's concerns. John was also thinking more and more about a 'living Christian fellowship', and wondering where it was to be found.

There was talk going on in progressive Christian circles, about taking a leaf out of the Communists' book, and creating small Christian cells throughout the country, which it was hoped might leaven the larger and increasingly secular lump. Alec evolved an idea which he labelled 'Koinonia'. This was to be in Alec's words 'An unofficial or secret fellowship of youngish Christians who would help one another to work out an authentically Christian understanding of what was taking place in the world, and to discuss what we ought to be doing about it'. John was very fond of Alec, and, at first, was enthusiastic about 'Koinonia', he took part eagerly in the preliminary discussions. But in the end he found it too theoretical; he was beginning to look for action.

It was Philip Wheeldon who said that, though conscientious and painstaking as vice-principal, John did not seem entirely at ease, 'deep down he was searching for some kind of release from the "smallness of Westcott"'. This became increasingly true, and when he heard that the dean of Oriel College, Oxford was leaving, he decided to apply for the post. Largely on the strength of '*The New Testament Problem*' by which Professor Grensted was particularly impressed, John got the job. He was appointed fellow, chaplain and dean of Oriel College. Oxford had given him the academic post which his own university had denied him.

John left Westcott House at the end of 1937, and on Christmas Eve, B. K. wrote him a characteristically affectionate and encouraging letter:

'You will not want me to try to say all I owe to you these years at the House; but I *am* grateful beyond words. You with all your gifts social and deeper than social, could have made life very difficult for me, and on the contrary you were ever loyal and helpful. I much doubt whether had I been in your place and with your gifts, I could have done likewise with no desire to exalt self . . . May you be as helpful to others at Oriel as you have been to your generation at Westcott House.'

14

The Course of True Love . . .

WHENEVER John embarked on any new work he threw himself into it wholeheartedly, tackling everything with energy and enthusiasm. First of all, he got to know the undergraduates with his customary dispensation of sherry, not universally approved even at Oriel. The role of chaplain was more rewarding than that of dean, responsible for discipline; but since the normal climbing-in route for those out later than lock-up was via the coal-shed just below the dean's sitting-room window, John could not altogether avoid gating or fining the offenders.

John is remembered there as a 'lively and vigorous' addition to the High Table, and, of course, as a 'bon viveur' he was horrified to learn that Oriel's once excellent wine cellar had been disposed of by two puritanical Nonconformist fellows. He was also remembered for his strong political views, and as being 'very argumentative'. But however much people disagreed with him, he was still liked.

There were three unresolved strands in John's life and personality. His emotional and sexual life was still a question-mark; he wanted and needed to get married. There was his official life, and with it the ambition natural to an able young man of whom many people spoke well, and who had risen rapidly in his chosen career. But, deeper than these, was the question of his own contribution to the life of the Church, the expression of his personal religious experience and belief.

John was still interested in one of his Cambridge girlfriends, but, in 1936, Frances and her husband, David, had come south to live at Seer Green, near Beaconsfield. While still at Cambridge, John had begun to visit them there, but from Oxford, Seer Green was much more accessible, and John was able to escape from the all-male life at Oriel to what had always been an incipiently romantic relationship. An added attraction was that David was an experienced mountaineer; he took John to North Wales, and initiated him into rock-climbing, and John resolved to spend time in the Alps, tackling those beckoning, challenging peaks.

Meanwhile, I resolved to resist too many of the pleasures of summer in Oxford, and to devote myself to my studies. Work and college life were widening my horizons. My closest friend at that time was the senior scholar of our year, with whom I was lucky enough to share tutorials. Daphne had a brilliant mind, and like so many gifted people, she had an abundance of gifts, artistic and musical, as well as literary. She was far better educated than I was, and had read much more widely, she introduced me to many modern poets and to my first encounter with Jung in a fascinating study by Maud Bodkin, *Archetypal Patterns in Poetry*. Daphne came from a background very different from my conventional English upbringing; her father was Burmese, a distinguished scholar, and her mother was English. I imagined that I had broken away from the prejudices and limitations of my family, but I soon learned better. Daphne and I discussed everything under the sun – poetry, philosophy, religion – that was still a problem to me, and to Daphne, who had a partly Buddhist inheritance; and, of course, we pursued that ever-elusive 'meaning of life'. But as well as all our high-minded reading and talking we had a great deal of fun.

In spite of my muddled emotional life, I could not fail to enjoy the summer in Oxford. That beady-eyed lady, Jane Austen, makes Mr Bennet observe of his daughter, Jane, 'Next to being married, a girl likes to be crossed in love a little now and then. It is something to think of, and gives her a sort of distinction among her companions.' Distinction or not, my friends were sympathetic and supportive during my problems with Ronald, and some of them too were in various stages of love, requited and unrequited.

At the end of term, there was to be a Commemoration Ball at Christ Church, and my father had volunteered to take a party of ten, allowing David and me to choose the guests. Before our troubles, I had invited Ronald to come as my partner, and David had secured an attractive, if rather lightweight, girlfriend. We wanted our stepmother and father to enjoy themselves as well, so we thought we should invite my father's old college friend and brother-in-law, Uncle Clav, and his wife Evelyn, and an Oxford couple, Wilfred and Marjorie House, friends of the Fisons, who had been particularly kind and hospitable to David and me. Wilfred was a fellow of New College, and though younger than my father had been at Rugby with him, and his wife was a beautiful woman, with whom susceptible undergraduates were liable to fall in love. Looking back, I think this did show rather nice sentiments on the part of David and me. But it was now awkward for me; I wrote to Ronald offering him an escape, but he replied that, if I didn't mind, he would still like to come to the dance.

A Commem. Ball is immeasurably more romantic and more real than any of those extravagant, superficial social dances of the London season. Ronald and I decided that we would enjoy what was to be our final, at all intimate, meeting; we would pretend that our relationship still existed, as to a certain extent it did. So we succumbed to a perfect English June night – dancing to sentimental tunes – champagne flowing – fairy lights in the college gardens – the warm air scented with roses and lime-blossom. David's rooms for sitting-out, and perhaps for more than just sitting. There was also a Commem. Ball at the next-door college, Oriel, and to this John had invited Frances, her David must have been away. At some stage in that long night, Ronald and I were drinking with them in John's rooms, and we agreed to meet for breakfast.

Daybreak found Ronald and me – I don't remember how we got there – in a meadow by the river. It was filled with buttercups, grasses and flowers lightly hung with dew, and, as the sun rose, it became a magical golden carpet, with a scattering of sparkles and tiny rainbows, and here, stolidly stared at by a few cows, Ronald and I, a little sadly, a little regretfully, said goodbye to each other. We have, in the conventional cliché, remained good friends.

I suppose we all got out to Seer Green in John's car; no sign of Frances's husband, and the atmosphere of the past night did seem to have affected her and John, especially John. 'That's a dangerous situation,' Ronald said to me before we separated. I too had observed it with mixed feelings; I liked Frances, but that made it look more dangerous. I gathered that her David, as well as being a mountaineer, was also a yachtsman, and that John had accepted an invitation for the immediate summer vacation, to sail with him and Frances to Norway, and explore the fjords. I thought poorly of this idea, assuring myself that this was due to my concern for the reputation of a priest, whom I regarded as an avuncular friend.

I must have written to John to tell him of my final break with Ronald, because I got a letter back by return of post. What a lot of letters we all wrote in those days, how impatiently we waited for the postman, and how eagerly we scanned letters from male friends for clues to their feelings! There was a recognised progression in the

Right Diana with her brother David, 1924

Left Diana, Grandmother and
David at Clavières, 1925

Below The Collins family:
John, Ted, Dorothy and
Margaret at Holly Grove,
Hawkhurst, 1906

Left John at Cambridge

Below The wedding at Stutton in October 1939

openings. 'Dear Diana' replaced 'Dear Miss Elliot'; 'My dear Diana' was a little step, as was 'Diana dear'; with 'My very dear Diana', and then 'Diana, my very dear', things were warming up well, and when it got to 'Dearest' or 'My dearest', we were getting quite hot; after 'My very dearest', further steps are left to the reader's imagination. This slow, step-by-step progress was enormously exciting to us.

The first letter from John that I still possess, dated 29 June, began 'Diana, my dear', and that was certainly interesting. Most of it was commiseration over my break with Ronald, but he did write: 'I can, too, speak of my affection for you; ordinarily, I believe, friendships should grow slowly; but with us there has been that unusual element which has enabled us to become friends and to share affection in a very short time.' Had I really been 'sharing affection'? I thought I was a tragedy queen. John also wrote: 'I'm not going to Norway with Frances and David. That bare statement will probably tell you a great deal in a very few words.'

So John went off to spend a summer walking and climbing in the Alps with Harold and Yvonne, and I went to nurse my broken heart in good works. I volunteered to spend a fortnight working in the East End of London at the Kennington settlement that was run and supported by Lady Margaret Hall. This, for me, was an equivalent of John's and my brother David's visits to South Wales. For the first time in my sheltered and privileged life, I saw real poverty and deprivation, and I was as shocked as they had been.

John and I continued to correspond sporadically, and his letters seemed to indicate something of a 'warming-up' process. By the time we returned to Oxford for the autumn term, I had got over any regret that I might have felt for Ronald, I looked forward to my work, I looked forward to seeing my friends, male and female, and I looked forward with interest and some excitement to meeting John again.

Oxford in October 1938 appeared more beautiful than ever, perhaps by contrast, because we returned under the dark shadow of the Munich agreement. Relief at the fact that, for the moment, we were not to be involved in war mingled with shame and apprehension. Everyone was talking, arguing, forecasting. John was appalled by Munich; although moving steadily left, as far as international affairs were concerned, he was still a Churchill man. He had no confidence in 'peace in our time' – the twenty-year non-aggression pact was worthless, and as for 'peace with honour', that was quite simply 'appeasement with shame'. These views were not well received in the Oriel Senior Common Room; he was known as 'fire-eating John'.

For David and me, Munich was a moral shock. We had grown up convinced that war and preparations for war were the ultimate evils. How often in my bedroom had I read and reread the poems of Wilfred Owen and other war poets. And now we were faced with this appalling clash of evils. 'Righteousness and Peace' faced each other as enemies. What genuinely distressed young men, like my brother David, was not so much fear of death as a feeling that they might die taking part in something intrinsically evil. Only the dedicated few seriously considered conscientious objection for themselves. David's first action on returning to Christ Church was to join the Oxford University Training Corps, which meant that he would be liable to be called up immediately on the outbreak of war: rather unrealistically, he joined the cavalry, but those in charge did not seem to have any more realistic suggestions.

Meanwhile, as best we could in that uneasy period, we got on with our engrossing personal lives. John invited me to another dinner party in his rooms, where I looked suspiciously at a beautiful dark-haired girl, called Francesca, who was a 'cellist, John's favourite musical instrument. I invited John to tea in my modest room in L.M.H. I took enormous trouble over the preparations, I decided to wear my cherished black dress, I wished to create an impression of sophistication – how foolish can one be at the age of twenty-one! However, the occasion seemed to have been a success, and John wrote me what was clearly a love letter. Within a day or two he asked me out to dinner at the Mitre Hotel, then the best restaurant in Oxford and just across the High Street, about three or four minutes' walk from Oriel. After dinner we would go back to John's rooms and play some of his gramophone records; he wished to introduce me to Brahms, his favourite composer.

It was the slow movement of the 2nd Piano Concerto that was our undoing, we kissed each other for the first time, and John told me that he loved me. After that, things didn't go quite as I expected. I looked forward to a romantic friendship that might, or might not, develop into something more serious; but John made it quite clear that he was not interested in anything like that, this was to be all or nothing; he wanted, even demanded, a total commitment; otherwise we would have to part. I returned to Lady Margaret Hall in an emotional turmoil.

I was alarmed by this total commitment. Once again I had a vague intimation of possible trouble ahead, but I was powerfully attracted by this dark, vigorous, determined man, about whom I still knew rather little. I held out for two or three days, but I could not face the 'nothing';

in my heart I knew that it was the 'all' that I wanted with John. I capitulated; I rang him up, and said I would like to come and see him.

I walked up the staircase and into John's room and said, 'I do love you, John'.

John said, 'This is the most wonderful moment of my life, and I don't know what to say'.

I didn't know what else to say either, but lovers have a language that is other than words. It was 1 November, All Saints' Day. That afternoon we walked by the river, a faintly misted blue and gold autumn day, the glowing end of St Luke's little summer. In the evening we dined at the Mitre with a bottle of wine.

Then I came down to earth. The following morning at nine, I had a tutorial, for which I was required to produce an essay. It was not begun, not even thought about. Rather fearfully, I went to see my tutor; she, wise woman, had seen students in a similar condition, she recognised the symptoms, and she let me off my essay. Years later at a college Gaudy, in the course of a brilliant speech, she remarked that the college motto, 'Souvent me souviens', might more aptly read, 'Souvent monsieur vient'.

That evening John wrote to me: 'I want to shout from the house tops that I'm happy and you're wonderful . . . Goodness gracious me . . . we must keep our feet firmly on the earth . . . I feel rather like a ginger-beer bottle, shaken, and whose stopper has been loosened.' I had similar feelings, and our feet were nowhere near the earth.

We saw each other every day, we spoke on the telephone, we wrote to each other daily; the respective college messengers must have got fed up pedalling backwards and forwards on their bicycles between Oriel and L.M.H. In the afternoons we walked together – round Christ Church meadows, where a kingfisher darted along the river bank in front of us – through Magdalen College, and along Addison's Walk, beneath a colonnade of gold and brown beech trees – up the tow-path to Iffley. 'Our spirits grew as we went side by side.' At Iffley we stood together in that perfect little Norman church, enveloped in a silence so profound and peaceful, yet so pregnant with mystery and with our own passionate feelings. In the evenings we had dinner and wine at the Mitre, and then back to John's rooms for music, and a little, necessarily restrained, love-making. We didn't think about future problems, when or how we could get married; the world beyond was going horribly, threateningly mad, but we were intoxicated by love, we lived only in that marvellous present. Oxford was

> A place to stand and love in for a while,
> With darkness and the death-hour surrounding it.

This state of affairs went on for two weeks; then an icy wind blew bitingly from the east. Wilfred and Marjorie House had obviously been deputed by my Uncle Clavering to keep an eye on me. Whenever John and I crossed the High, he, always protective, was accustomed to take my hand; we were observed. It was improper, undignified, simply not done, for the dean of a college to be seen *in public* hand in hand with a female undergraduate. Alarm bells began to ring; investigations were set afoot.

There were men in Oxford who had been at Cambridge with John, one in particular had known him well. This was a priest with whom John had been friendly, but with whom he had fallen out politically, when this man became an admirer of Mussolini and his Fascists. So what did Wilfred's enquiries reveal? Nothing very encouraging. John's family background was far from satisfactory, definitely lower middle class – he was a clever chap, rather fond of alcohol, and a bit of a woman-chaser. The Relton affair could have been instanced, and from Relton's point of view. It was even believed that John was 'carrying on' with a married woman; had he not invited her *alone* to the Oriel Commem., and they had spent time alone together in his rooms; what could *that* mean? 'Malice', observed one of the Oriel dons, 'is like charity, it hopeth all things and believeth all things'.

My uncle came on a visit, and the storm broke over me. I couldn't possibly marry this man; I must understand how dreadful it would be for any children we might have, they couldn't expect to be received anywhere respectable. My uncle wrote me a letter saying that he felt sure that, when I married, I would want to be able to come with my husband to Stutton Hall, the implication being that with someone like John, that would be impossible. My unfortunate brother was dragged in, and told that he must explain to John that he could not possibly contemplate marriage with me.

I was devastated, these were people whom I had loved and trusted; in spite of my rebelliousness they were part of my security. It was much worse for John, he was the one who was insulted and humiliated. And our innocent, radiant love seemed suddenly sullied by the falsity and false values of the world in which we had to live.

On 14 November John wrote to me:

'I had thought, at the age of 33, to have had my fill of surprises! And I had boasted of being unshockable – hubris indeed! . . . My reactions are varying from one extreme to another . . . Completely shattered would be but a mild description of one extreme . . . David was very sweet, but the seed of doubt has been sown, and one more growing friendship has been endangered by the heavy tread of human insensitivity. Yes, I felt terribly sorry for David; he so hated his doubt, and, himself entirely sensitive, he disliked a great deal having to talk about a subject he would wish had never been raised. And yet the iron had been forced into his soul. And his friendship I would cherish, for, in the little while that I have known him, I have learned to like him tremendously.

'But thank goodness for a telephone conversation with Ronald. It was a tonic. He made me laugh; and in that laugh I refound my sense of proportion and my self-respect. And it was a pleasure to find him so completely astonished at the turn of events. With his mingling of seriousness and flippancy he cheered me a lot; "How beastly" and "How incredibly funny"; those were the texts of his conversation. Strange indeed, is the play of life that we three are writing'. John went on to speak of the marvellous and permanent reality of our love, but he had been sufficiently shaken to write:

'Marriage? Yes, perhaps, that may now be impossible; the future may disclose to us barriers which the present has permanently set up . . . but our love, of the present and the past, because it is a true love, will be eternally – for love is not of time . . . But enough, I am nearer to weeping than all else – not for self-pity, but for love . . .'

I too had been 'completely shattered'; the possibility of cutting myself off from my family was inexpressibly painful, but I was not going to lose John, I was going to marry him. I was already beginning to understand something of the worth and goodness of the man I loved. The family objections had been presented to us in purely social terms, and they seemed ridiculous. I grew angry: all this absurd carry-on was likely to drive me in directions very different from any that my relatives might approve.

I stood firm, and on 16 November John was writing to me: 'Today has been marvellous – and from the moment I saw you at the station till our hands parted just now, the cup of my happiness has been overflowing, and your letter this morning made me quite ridiculously happy.'

So the college messengers continued pedalling backwards and forwards between Oriel and L.M.H. and we continued to end up, extravagantly, at the Mitre, enjoying our dinners and bottles of wine.

The next hurdle to be negotiated was my father. He took a more detached attitude. I think he was annoyed by the rather hysterical reaction from Stutton. My marriage was, after all, primarily his concern, and he did realise that this was something serious. He took John out to lunch at his club – not for John a very happy or easy occasion. First of all, John's family: John was particularly upset by my father's, 'And I suppose your mother was just a country girl?' But then another, and in some ways, more serious objection surfaced – money.

When John went to Westcott House, he had cheerfully accepted a large cut in income, but he had not entirely adjusted his easy and generous way of living; the result was an overdraft of around £500. Nowadays, you are thought peculiar if you do not borrow to the limit of your credit, but in 1938 overdrafts were viewed with disapproval, evidence of irresponsible, if not dissolute, living and £500 was then a lot of money. Poor John: in some ways this distressed him more than all the other nonsense, since, in this, he did feel himself to be culpable.

My father was, however, impressed by John, and especially by what he saw as his brilliant career, but, of course, he didn't want me to *marry* him, he had quite other ideas about my future. He had not particularly wanted me to marry Ronald, the old Etonian, son of a bishop, but I don't think that he had ever seriously thought that I would. Now he thought up a plan. We were to be subjected to a test, 'I shall take her round the world with me,' he said. 'And, if after that, she is still determined to marry you, we will see about it.'

'You can ask her,' said John bravely, 'but she won't come'. John reported the interview to me, but said nothing about my father's proposal, and when it was put to me, I of course rejected it. My father was surprised, and, I think, a little hurt.

My father was an emotional and passionate man, he could display great charm, and also violent temper, he was susceptible to women and they to him, and as a child and teenager I adored him. Through all our disagreements and battles I loved him. He was a devoted father, all his little goslings were magnificent swans to him, but he did want to dictate and to organise our lives as he thought best. John reckoned that my father was his only real rival.

So there were John and I: we loved each other, we were going to get married – but when? And a nasty little worm had wriggled its way into our relationship. Money worries can be trouble-makers. Looking back, I think they drove me into little meannesses and anxieties that I much regret. And I began to look more critically at John's friends, and hated myself for doing so.

At Cambridge and in London, John had mixed easily with every kind of person; he could and did 'walk with kings nor lose the common touch'. He was as happy and natural with the stable boys at Newmarket, as with any of his well-born public-school friends. As one of my friends observed, 'John is a completely classless person'. He valued people for themselves and for what they were, without any of the artificial tags that society likes to put upon them. So John's friends were of all kinds and classes, and later of all colours.

I took John to Little Hall, and my grandmother was charmed by his natural courtesy. She thought it was a lovely idea for me to marry a clergyman, though my other relatives thought, perhaps not without reason, that I would make a most unsuitable clerical wife. John was a success with all the women in my family, even my Aunt Evelyn, who had very much annoyed me by saying, 'Really, Diana, you can't marry anybody called "John Collins",' now said that she liked him.

Of course, I took John to the river – my river. It was a cold December, frost and snow had arrived early and the day was grey and foggy. We walked by the marshes and along the river shore. The tide was going out leaving the mud flats – the best time for watching the birds that rush to feed as the salt water withdraws. And that day there were literally hundreds of sea birds. There was, too, and unusually, a huge gathering of coots – they looked so absurd in their dark suits, their heads so neatly patched with white – whiter than Persil can ever wash – plop-plopping around in the mud with frantic energy. We watched them delightedly, and as we watched we were one as we had been one on our Oxford river walks, and in the Iffley church. Here was reality; doubts and problems were false phantoms from an unreal world. And so, as lovers do, we collected our never-to-be-forgotten tokens of happiness, kingfishers, comical coots, and later those bright pink spindle-berries.

I returned to London and to a subtle propaganda – 'the contagion of the world's slow stain' continued its insidious attack. My stepmother had taken easily to John. Though she admired money and success, she was not a snob, and just thought I would be miserable married to a priest, and needed rescuing from a terrible mistake. 'You'll have such a dull life,' she said, 'It really won't suit you at all. Madeline Mellor's sister is buried away in a country parish, and is *miserable*.' And my father was still not pleased. 'You haven't met the right man yet,' he pronounced.

So John and I had problems, and sometimes disagreements; we had lovers' quarrels too, always quickly resolved. I could be just as argumentative as John. We walked up a hill in Richmond Park pursuing some ridiculous discussion about money, and at the top we parted for ever, but, by the time we got to the bottom, we were together again for ever.

After one disagreement John wrote penitently, though he had no need for penitence: 'Remember, beloved, it has not been particularly easy for me the last two weeks; and my pride has had to be forcibly pushed aside on several occasions. If I had not been in love with you (and so, as David says, have lost my full critical faculties!) my pride would most certainly (and rightly) have triumphed. But being in love alters the whole situation.' I don't know how John stood it all, especially as occasionally, and only by one or two men, he was rudely cold-shouldered; he bore it throughout with dignity and with charity.

Despite the air of disapproval that still hung over us, we had some wonderful times together. We were not yet completely at one, since sexual fulfilment was denied to us, and the sexual pressures were increasingly powerful and urgent. John and I were trapped, trapped by his profession and position, as well as by the mores of our time, trapped by my youth and uncompleted education, trapped and frustrated, but not unhappy.

John took me to Dulwich to be introduced to Harold and Yvonne Cooper. He had delayed this meeting, saying, with an unaccustomed touch of bitterness, 'You'll think they aren't suitable'. Yvonne had taken enormous trouble – her dinner-table was decorated with slim white candles and white scented jonquils, the food was superb.

I was delighted by Harold and Yvonne, and they, luckily, took to me. It was an evening of celebration for another foursome friendship.

Back at Oxford, it was not easy to remain immersed in academic study, as the international situation went, as John had feared, from bad to worse. We tried, rather unsuccessfully, to carry out a regime of financial economy. John sold his car, and cancelled his proposed summer holiday.

We were not allowed to become officially engaged. I suppose we might have taken this into our own hands, but I did not wish to provoke any further family troubles – better to allow them to get used to the idea that we were going to marry, come what may, and they could not prise us apart. John bought me a ring, a beautiful blue sapphire in a diamond setting, and, later in the summer, I began to wear it defiantly. We went to the Merton Commem. Ball, and so nearly slipped over the permitted sexual edge, and we had a magical evening with *The Marriage of Figaro* at Glyndebourne. But the pressures and frustrations were beginning to get us down; John developed back trouble and lumbago, and I was afflicted by a revolting plague of boils.

Meanwhile, the worst political prophecies were being fulfilled; the Nazi-Soviet Pact was like a bombshell, followed all too soon by the German invasion of Poland, and by 3 September we were at war with Germany. The advent of war changed all our futures. David knew that he must leave Oxford to join the Army; he had passed Classical Honour Mods with – slightly to his disappointment – a good second, he was captain of the university squash team, and cricket was going well; he was the same age as our father had been on the outbreak of the First World War. As for John and me, we knew that we must marry as soon as possible.

On 10 September I telephoned John to say that family opposition had collapsed, and we could marry as soon as it could be arranged. Our engagement was announced in *The Times*, and wedding preparations were begun. The war had forced everyone to face the basic facts of life and death, and all those unreal barriers that had been erected against and between John and me dissolved away; no doubt, too, my father remembered 1914.

Nobody suggested to me that it might be possible to marry, to live with my husband, and still complete my degree. There had never been married undergraduates at L.M.H. Had I thought this a possibility, I might well have considered it seriously. With John still at Oriel there would have been no practical problems. As it was, I believed that I had to leave L.M.H., and David and I went sadly together to dismantle our college rooms.

The wedding was to be at Stutton – there might be air raids on London. Clav and Evelyn were generously co-operative; it was hard to imagine that they had been so unwilling to accept John into the family. The reception would be at Stutton Hall, and their seven-year-old daughter Gay would be our only bridesmaid. Aunt Tilly was luckily at home, and took the arrangements into her enthusiastic and capable hands.

And so, at last, on 21 October 1939, John and I were married.

15

Married Life

AFTER five days' honeymoon in the Cotswolds, we returned to Oxford. Wilfred and Marjorie House, anxious to hold out an olive branch, invited us to stay with them until we could find somewhere to live. We were much too happy to refuse, and with their help, we soon found reasonable lodgings. It was a strange period – an unreal 'phoney' war, an unreal job for John, students leaving, a future in question, and for me a time of waiting, not the normal 'nesting', home-making beginning of a marriage. But at last we were living and sleeping together. We had decided to take no precautions, we wanted no artificial barriers to our love-making – perhaps, too, this was an instinctive affirmation of life, in the face of imminent death and destruction. So before long, to our personal delight, I became pregnant, and that transformed the waiting into something creative, though there were friends and relatives who thought us very irresponsible.

After term, we went to stay with the Inges who had retired to Wallingford. I was intimidated by Inge, who was, by then, very deaf, but he and John could still communicate, and both he and Mrs Inge were kind and welcoming to me. It was already cold outside, and inside there was economy with heat, and, true to form, there was economy with food. John and I had to make several visits to the village to stock up with chocolate and biscuits.

One morning, Mrs Inge took me aside and said: 'Now, my dear, I would like to talk to you about being the wife of a clergyman.' I was, at that stage, serious and starry-eyed about being a clerical wife, so I was eagerly expectant.

'The first and most important thing for a clergyman's wife to understand about,' said Mrs Inge, 'is precedence'. I couldn't imagine what she meant, but it really was all to do with who should go through doors first or last, who should sit where at table, who should be presented to whom and how. I was incredulous, but the talk, for which I thanked her politely and hypocritically, never got much above that level.

A little later, she gave another 'talk' which I attended. This was to her assembled domestic helpers, and a few press-ganged villagers. It was a warning against the dangerous influence of some wicked people who were out to make everybody discontented, to upset the good and established order of society, and to overthrow the Christian religion. Communism was not explicitly mentioned, though that was clearly what it was, and I expect it included Socialism and the Labour party; they too were on the 'black', or rather the 'red' list. The assembled company listened deferentially, but with very little apparent comprehension.

We then went to London, and John said that he would like to take me to see his old friend, Canon Alexander. So we arrived for tea at No. 2 Amen Court. We were shown into the large ground-floor room at the back of the house, that served as Alexander's dining and living room. A very old man was sitting by a wretched little gas fire; it was cold and dark. Of course, there was a heavy black-out, but it was made much worse by walls covered with dark, ancient wallpaper, and paintwork all a dismal brown. The whole place made a terrible impression on me, and even tea and toasted teacakes were no help, because, in the early stages of pregnancy, tea made me feel sick. We then found our way over to the cathedral, which, I am ashamed to say, I had never yet visited. Here again everything was inevitably dark and cold; it seemed forbidding, hostile, almost evil, I shivered internally and externally. 'I don't think I could bear it if you were ever appointed here,' I said. 'I don't think that's very likely,' said John.

In spite of the distractions of courtship, marriage and the war, John had continued studying and writing; he had powers of concentration that I admired and lacked. He had managed to complete a long chapter on the New Testament for a book called *The Priest as Student*. In recommending a possible approach, he suggests, interestingly, that students might begin with the first chapters of Acts, as representing an early and theologically undeveloped preaching, and continue by relating parts of Acts to relevant Epistles, as different problems, moral and theological, arose in the young Christian communities, and finally students should turn to the Gospels. 'If we first see the Gospel *in action*,' he wrote, 'we shall better be able to understand the Gospel'.

In 1939, Alec Vidler had left Cambridge to become warden of St Deiniol's Library at Hawarden, near Chester. At the same time, he took over the editorship of *Theology*. John was delighted when Alec invited him to become a member of the advisory board; he was in sympathy with Alec's ideas about broadening the journal, and relating the best of contemporary theology to contemporary problems and developments both cultural and social. John contributed articles and reviews to *Theology*, and went regularly to stay at Hawarden.

John enjoyed Alec's wry humour, and found his gloom and doom about the Church, society and the future of civilisation generally a good balance to his own impetuous and hopeful temperament. 'Koinonia' was eventually submerged in something called 'The Moot', which brought together supposedly concerned and progressive thinkers within and on the fringes of the Church; when John was able to get away to Hawarden he took part in these discussions.

Soon after the outbreak of war, John had written to B. K. Cunningham, asking advice as to whether he should volunteer as a forces chaplain. B. K., as always, was in touch with the top, this time with the chaplains-in-chief of the three armed services, and the information was that they had more than enough regulars and volunteers, and in any case, B. K. thought that service life would be a waste of John's talents. So John stayed at Oriel, and I read poetry, dreamed, wandered among the buttercup meadows, and became more and more placid and cow-like.

When you are in love, you imagine that you radiate a glow of charity for all the world. John and I did tell each other that we wanted our marriage to be outward- as well as inward-looking, we had big and naïve ideas about what we would do for the world. But, in that first year, I was deeply self-absorbed. So happily concerned was I with John and our coming child, that I failed to notice or understand what was happening to my brother. Men were, apparently, not yet needed in the Army, so David found himself some local coaching and teaching, but a severe emotional crisis was building up inside him; he felt unwanted, useless and adrift, having to face the war and his own possible death, yet feeling no life and security within himself; he developed bad back trouble, and became generally ill. He had emerged from a love affair with a woman old enough to be his mother – a classic case – but with David it went deep, a search for the mother he had lost before he knew her. Perhaps too I and our companionship had been an anchor for him, now partially removed by my marriage – that at least was something suggested by a long and emotional letter that he wrote me. As soon as David finally managed to get into the Army, as a recruit in the Welsh Guards, he became his old humorous, bouncy self, and developed into an enthusiastic and first-rate soldier; but by then there was a deeper, stronger and more integrated person within.

It was early summer, the Whitsun weekend, when John and I, with two friends, drove out of Oxford for a picnic on the Berkshire downs. We found a grassy slope surrounded by blossoming hawthorns, the sun shone with a benign glory, and the only sound was a cascade of song from nesting larks; the war seemed impossibly far away. But the war, in fact, was alarmingly near, nothing phoney about it now: Norway, Denmark, Holland, Belgium, all fallen before the Nazi armies, the French defences breached, the Channel ports under threat. John, remembering conversations with M. Loisy, predicted the imminent collapse of France, a statement received with incredulity by our two friends. But within a very short time it happened, and on 22 June Marshal Pétain signed an armistice – John acquired a reputation for exceptional sagacity.

Back at Oriel, we hung on the radio for news and followed the evacuation of British troops from Dunkirk. Although this signalled a crushing military defeat, it somehow seemed like a victory for British courage and tenacity, as an armada of small rescue ships set sail across the Channel, such brave little Davids facing so hideous a Goliath. John found it more and more impossible to concentrate upon a projected academic treatise on the Acts of the Apostles, and junior fellows were now disappearing along with the undergraduates. There seemed nothing left to do, but to volunteer as a chaplain. The Air Force C-in-C captured John's imagination by talking of 'standing on the tarmac, seeing the boys off on their missions, welcoming back those who return, and comforting the families of those who don't.' John joined the RAF.

Soon Britain itself appeared to be in imminent danger of invasion, and some arrangement had to be made for me and for our baby. American universities had offered safe refuge to wives and children of Oxford fellows, but I had no intention of leaving. Stutton was clearly a danger zone, and my father and family had gone to America where he was to try to organise vital supplies of iron and steel. But my mother's elder sister, Madeleine, lived with her three children in Bedford; she had a large garden well-stocked with fruit and vegetables, for like all the Fisons she was a keen and expert gardener. My grandmother was already there, but there was still one large double bedroom and a smaller adjoining room that were not in use. So Madeleine wrote suggesting that we might like to be her evacuees.

John's first posting was to Cardington, the training centre for Barrage

Balloon Command; not the most glamorous of RAF stations, and far from any active fighters or bombers. It was a huge place, and served as the main reception centre for thousands of young conscripts who now joined the RAF. For John and me it was providential; it was situated on the other side of Bedford from my aunt's house, but near enough, and as soon as he had settled in as chaplain, he would be able to live out with me.

We had the use of a small car belonging to my father, and at the beginning of July, I drove John, dressed up in his new squadron-leader's uniform, to Cardington. The great iron gates opened, and I watched him walk through alone, looking so small, and so absurdly out of place. Then the gates closed, as if for ever, on some vast, drab prison-house.

I felt more than strange, I was beginning to feel rather ill. During our uncertain and changing life, toxaemia had been developing unnoticed in my kidneys. Within a week our longed for son, Jeremy, was still-born. Nowadays there is much more understanding of the feelings of parents of still-born children. Mothers are allowed to see and hold their babies, something I longed to do. The attitude of the Church, at that time, was horrible, unbaptised babies could not have a Christian burial, and their little graves must remain unmarked. I shall never forget John's face when he first came to see me, he was struggling so hard not to weep, that was something men were not supposed to do. John got some comfort from the Roman Catholic padre who told him that, in cases of still-birth, a priest would immediately baptise the baby, and he or she would be given a Christian burial. So John baptised Jeremy and together we buried him in the local cemetery; we put up a small white cross with his name and date of birth, and planted forget-me-nots on his grave. Burying Jeremy was a comfort to us both, he had meant much in our lives, he could not just be discarded. It was a hard, sad time, but John and I were together, and sometimes shared grief can bring you even closer to each other than shared delight.

Churchill's speeches – J. B. Priestley's postscripts – the Battle of Britain. Those who lived through it all must remain grateful. It was an experience of comradeship, of mutual concern and helpfulness; throughout the war you could walk through the blacked-out streets of London, and all you needed to fear were the enemy bombers. The courage and unselfishness of a majority of people in the face of danger and disaster is well known, but it is good to have seen it at first hand.

At Cardington, John was wondering what a chaplain could possibly do beyond taking compulsory church parades, and trying to organise some marginal welfare. The young recruits seldom stayed more than two or three weeks, and were a bewildered lot being rushed through the confusing and often incomprehensible basics of service life. It was, for both of us, a frustrating period, and would have been worse, if John had not luckily run into James Fisher in a Bedford bookshop. James was chaplain at Bedford School and lived with his wife Joan in the town. They were our life-savers, and became our life-long friends.

In late autumn, John got some leave, and we went for a mountain holiday in North Wales. It was a happy two weeks, we walked, climbed mountains and made love. But back at Bedford, I became increasingly frustrated. I had found myself a part-time teaching job, but it did not absorb me; I longed to be alone with John. Eventually I persuaded him that for the sake of our marriage, we must live on our own, so we found a flat in the town. More intellectual companionship entered our lives, and there were interesting meetings and discussions.

On the camp, John was now in charge and was beginning to enliven the chaplain's department. He decided to organise a mission, and invited Bryan Green, an experienced evangelist, and Brother Charles from the Anglican Franciscans. It certainly created considerable interest, and numbers of people came voluntarily to listen. However, the chaplain's department, in its extraordinary lack of wisdom, almost immediately after the mission, posted John away, allowing no possible follow-up to the work that had been begun. So in the late autumn of 1941, he arrived at Yatesbury, a large training station for radar and radio operators, and reputed to be the worst run and most unpopular camp in Technical Training Command.

16

Yatesbury and the Fellowship of the Transfiguration

WHEN John left for Yatesbury I returned to Stutton Hall. My grandmother, already showing signs of approaching senility, had been reinstated, with suitable carers, at Little Hall, and I was glad to be near her. And whenever David had leave he wanted to spend it at Stutton. Clav and Evelyn welcomed me into their already full household and were not too deterred by the fact that I was pregnant – again.

It would be hard to imagine anywhere that appeared more bleak and forbidding than Yatesbury when John arrived on a cold, wet November day. The camp was large, line after monotonous line of mud-coloured huts, set down on top of the bare Wiltshire downs; everything rigid, uniform and ugly; it was isolated from the outside world, and public transport was minimal. Round about were connected establishments – flying schools and technical and radar schools where strictly secret work was carried on. There was also a large hospital dealing with physical and mental casualties. In these dismal surroundings lived and worked 5,000–6,000 RAF and WAAF personnel; most of the men were training as wireless operators, air gunners, radar operators, and many of them went on to become air crew; there were the lecturers and technical staff there to train them. The WAAF also worked on the technical side, some of them as lecturers and technicians, others were employed in clerical duties, administration, signals, transport, technical drawing, as well as the more obvious duties such as catering, tailoring, and work in the hospital; later in the war they also trained as mechanics.

In the camp there was corruption and inefficiency right from the top. 'A real racket,' John wrote to me. 'It really is a scandalous place, and shocks even me which shows that it must be pretty bad . . . a rotten dump officered by duds. The rotten influence from the top spreads right through, and saps the morale and vitality of the place.' There was not much joy to be had from Church life either; it seemed as

dull and lacking in vitality and morale as the rest of the camp. The only
bright hope was in the second padre, Evelyn Dunford, and he and John
rapidly became friends. The Roman Catholics and other denominations (ODs) each had their own padre, and any form of proselytising
or poaching was strictly forbidden. But the padres did all meet for
convivial chats and elevenses in the Anglican chaplain's office, and
co-operated on the camp where they could.

Religious services apart, the padres were regarded as extra welfare
officers. They had to address the new intakes and distribute comforts –
socks, scarves, balaclavas knitted by numerous patriotic ladies; there
were pastoral problems, people needing help and advice, and there was
the hospital to be visited. As far as possible the padres tried to lighten
the tedium of off-duty hours by organising brains trusts, discussion
groups and various forms of entertainment. It was a regular and
disciplined life; a daily Eucharist at seven a.m., Matins at nine in the
church or the chaplain's office; for John a half-hour study of his Greek
New Testament, and in the evenings a regular Evensong. There was
work in the church office, there were confirmation classes; there was
plenty to do, but John was aware that throughout the camp the Church
'cut no ice'.

Immediately after Christmas I went on a visit to Yatesbury and on
Sunday morning went with John to the church parade service. This
was held in a large, draughty marquee that accommodated about a
thousand people. It was cold inside, outside it was bitter, sleeting in
an icy wind. The men had already had to endure an inspection parade
and were in no mood for worship. There were whistles and catcalls
throughout the service, and after about ten minutes the next contingent of sufferers was lined up outside, so the service was punctuated as
well by the bellowing of NCOs and the stamping of heavy boots. We
learned later that some of these disaffected characters used to smuggle
in packs of cards, arrange themselves at the back of the marquee, and
pass the time of compulsory 'worship' with games of poker. Once the
men had been herded in, the duty officer and all NCOs above the rank
of corporal quickly disappeared.

John disliked compulsion for himself, and was not prepared to have
it inflicted on others in the name of religion. He was determined to get
compulsory church parades abolished. It was a long struggle, but John
succeeded by refusing, in the end, to take any more services unless
NCOs, officers, and the CO himself were also compelled to attend.
That settled the matter. John was soon involved in another battle on
behalf of the WAAF who manned the bar and were made to stay up

late and clear up afterwards. Proposals that the bar should close at
eleven p.m. made John very unpopular with some senior officers,
and after a row, he was threatened with court-martial, but, again,
he won his point.

Voluntary church congregations grew steadily. The young trainees had to be intelligent and well educated, a majority came from
local grammar schools. John's lucid and scholarly sermons stimulated the young Christians, and they wanted to discuss the questions
that he raised. So John started a regular 'teach-in' followed by questions and answers.

A secular discussion group was also the chaplain's responsibility.
Here John found active left-wingers, and a fair proportion of Communists. The Church appeared to them to have nothing to say to
their search for means of abolishing unemployment, poverty and
war. To John these serious and committed young people presented
an urgent challenge.

John decided he must go for a retreat, and try to sort out his
ideas. He went to Hawarden, where he could read and meditate in
quiet, and talk to Alec Vidler and his interesting visitors. A night
spent in Bristol with Mervyn Stockwood completed this stimulating
and refreshing week. John returned determined that he and his
fellow chaplains must go straight ahead with the formation of a
Christian cell in the camp. On the question of religion and politics,
John's mind was not so clear. In Jewish religion there was no separation between the secular and the religious, the Mosaic law is full
of social as well as of personal obligations; the Old Testament
prophets constantly reminded the people of both of these, nor did
the prophets hesitate to pronounce judgement upon the nation or
to confront authority. They attacked kings and rulers fearlessly
whenever they were seen to have transgressed the laws of God;
priests were constantly embroiled in politics. This was the tradition
that Jesus inherited.

'I'm definitely in a state of groping for a solution to this great
question of the right action for Christians in regard to social obligations,' John wrote to me. He was clear that Christians must try to
tackle economic, political and social questions.

John discussed his idea of a cell with his two Anglican colleagues,
Evelyn Dunford and Eric Johnson. They agreed that something
different was needed from the inward-looking, self-consciously 'religious' church fellowships to be found in many parishes. This cell
must be a group of committed and dynamic men and women,

prepared to impregnate the whole camp with the reality and power of the living Gospel.

For a number of weeks the idea of a cell was announced at church services. Then John called a meeting for further discussion to which around forty people came. They wanted the cell to be formed immediately, but John sent them away urging them to think and pray seriously about the nature of such a commitment. Twenty people came to a second meeting, and again John sent them away. Sixteen people came to a third meeting, and the Christian cell was born.

A day or two later, on 4 June, John wrote to me: 'An inspiration came to me this morning. I've decided to try to get an autumn programme of speakers for the camp on the subject of Christianity and the Social Gospel. I'm going to ask Temple [recently appointed Archbishop of Canterbury] to give the opening talk.' John's ambitions and exciting plans were made easier to fulfil because Yatesbury had a new and sympathetic CO. Although a Roman Catholic, he was interested in John's ideas, and impressed by the liveliness of the Anglican Church. The Anglicans were given their own room for meetings and activities. John himself was to have the use of a shorthand typist, and permission was given for the new Christian 'cell' to organise a communal breakfast to follow the Sung Eucharist on Sunday mornings. This 'Parish Communion' that John introduced at Yatesbury was something relatively new in Christian worship, though now it can be found in churches throughout the land.

For the past few months, a tempting proposition had been dangled before John and me. A group of masters and governors had asked John to allow his name to be put forward for the vacant headmastership of Harrow School. Now another candidate was appointed. John wrote to me: 'So our dream was only a dream . . . but I do not lose my real hope that sooner or later we shall be called upon to do a big work together for the advancement of those things in which we believe. My chief disappointment is that we shall not yet have our home together and our united work.'

That was my disappointment too, but otherwise I don't remember feeling particularly let down. At Yatesbury John was poised to embark upon one of the most important and influential pieces of work in his career. And I was poised for the imminent birth of our child. In order to relieve pressure on Stutton Hall, I had decided to return to Aunt Madeleine in Bedford, and there go into a nursing home for this event. German bombers no longer dared to appear over Britain in daylight, and by night they had been driven away from the major cities; now they were beginning to turn their unwelcome night-time attentions to 'softer' and lightly defended targets such as Canterbury, Bath, and among others, inoffensive little Bedford. So it was that on 19 July, shortly before midnight, Andrew David made his appearance in the middle of a rather nasty air raid, but with that safely over, I, too, was fully and happily occupied.

The Christian cell was an experiment for John as well as for those who might join. Within it there was to be neither rank nor seniority; all, padres included, were called by Christian names, something unheard of in the regular service. John really disliked having to wear uniform, and, whenever possible, he put on his cassock; he thought it absurd for chaplains to be called squadron-leaders, but he did recognise advantages attached to their officer-status: they were able to frustrate the occasional bullying practised by warrant officers and NCOs.

There was plenty to do cleaning, decorating and furnishing the new room. Then it had to be equipped with books, records, games, an old piano, and a record-player built by two of the technical chaps. Helpers were needed for the growing congregations, and for the communal breakfast, food had to be fetched from the NAAFI, then cleared away and everything washed up and cleaned. There was never any lack of volunteers for practical work, but John was concerned with the inner spiritual life of the group. They decided to call themselves the Fellowship of the Transfiguration, and to meet for a weekly 'chapter' meeting, when John would give them a little 'natter'. The heart of the Fellowship, the real spiritual power-house was always, John insisted, the Sunday Eucharist. They were soon ready to constitute themselves formally with Harry Gray, a wireless instructor on the permanent camp staff, as president, Alan Marsh as treasurer, and a small committee. Together a Rule of Life, to be voluntarily undertaken, was worked out and accepted. At first, the Rule followed an ecclesiastical pattern, daily prayer and Bible reading, regular attendance at the Eucharist on Sundays, and on special weekdays, self-examination, alms-giving and work for the Church. Living and sleeping in crowded huts as most of them did, it required courage to persevere with prayer and Bible reading, there were plenty of sceptics and scoffers. But once committed, the Fellowship members did persevere, and sometimes those who came to mock eventually stayed to pray. Soon, under John's guidance, further rules were added 'to try to make the social, economic and political implications of the Gospel effective in local, national and international affairs'. All this cheerful activity aroused interest and curiosity and attracted increasing numbers. For many of them it must have seemed a welcome change, a refuge from the dreariness of camp life. 'From my first week at Yatesbury,' wrote Tom Robson, 'the wooden Church and accompanying rooms were like a haven for me. In environment, in atmosphere and in friendship, this small oasis within the crudeness, harshness and officialdom of the surrounding camp, resembled the home I had left behind.'

The Fellowship stretched John's pastoral gifts to the full; he had to deal with many personal problems. But it was not only to Church people that the chaplains ministered. John studied King's Regulations, and developed a serpent subtlety in getting round them. Rules of life, those guards against human frailty, were to be kept, but administrative and secular rules, necessary, of course, but so often in conflict with justice, compassion and commonsense, these were to be skilfully circumvented in the interests of any higher good. This was a talent that John improved and used throughout his ministry; it did not endear him to authority.

John was happy with the growing influence of the Fellowship throughout the camp, but he was still looking to the wider world beyond. He wanted the young trainees to feel that they were fighting, not only to defeat the abominations of Nazi Germany, but for the vision of a fairer and better world, based upon Christian principles of justice, freedom and compassion. So he set to work on the series of talks on the social implications of the Christian Gospel. 'If you begin by catching a big fish, you are more likely to be able to lure the lesser fish into your net,' so John wrote first to Archbishop Temple, inviting him to open the series by speaking on the 'Tradition of the Christian Church in Social Teaching'. To his delight, Temple accepted. Then it was just a question of finding suitable dates for, among others, Sir Richard Acland ('The Christian and Politics'), Dr Hewlett Johnson, Dean of Canterbury ('The Christian and Communism'), The Moderator of the Free Church Federal Council, Barbara Ward, a distinguished Roman Catholic, and the Bishop of Bristol. John tried hard to balance his team, and endeavoured, unsuccessfully to secure Lord Halifax on the Conservative side. He found left-wing speakers more eager to talk to the troops than the conservatively inclined. Finally his speakers were in place.

A last-minute crisis threatened to scupper the whole series. The C-in-C Technical Training Command took fright, fearing that Temple might preach Socialism. He tried to get the invitation withdrawn; John indignantly refused. A meeting of RAF top brass, air marshals and air vice-marshals assembled at Reading, and John went to do battle. After two and a half hours of argument, another air marshal, chief of personnel, was summoned from London to adjudicate; luckily he supported John. Of course, news of the drama leaked out, so Temple was assured of a full house. The next most successful talk was that of the dean of Canterbury. 'What an actor,' John said. 'And what a vain man!' But he gave a brilliant and entertaining performance, and since nobody knew much about Russia, and Russian soldiers were dying heroically, the dean was listened to with deference and enthusiasm. Like the Webbs, he had 'seen the future' at first hand and brought back a glowing report; it was assumed by many that he knew what he was talking about, and he somehow managed to charm even the doubters and critics. But the realities of war were never far away. Bombs fell around Yatesbury. The dangerously long hours that trainees were forced to spend in the air were the subject of some of John's strongest protests. In one form or another, death was never far from anyone's consciousness; that perhaps helped to deepen apprehension of spiritual realities. 'We were young, we were eager, we needed spiritual leadership, and that is what we got. Many of us were bound for operational flying, and for me certainly that spiritual basis proved essential when I reached the "sharp end".' So wrote the poet John Allison.

John's next idea of a representative from each of the Allied governments to speak on how they saw the future seemed interesting and harmless. The authorities appeared benign until they realised that a Russian spokesman must be included in the series; then alarm bells began to ring. John had anticipated possible trouble, he was aware of the spreading fear that he and his speakers might be intent on promoting left-wing propaganda, so by the time he was summoned once again to the Air Ministry, M. Maisky, the Russian ambassador, had been invited and had accepted. Every possible pressure was exerted to make John withdraw the invitation. This he refused to do. Maisky's visit remained uncertain until the last minute. The day before he was due, a message arrived to say that he was ill; a diplomatic illness John wondered? A new date was found and John was asked to come to London to accompany the ambassador on the drive to Yatesbury. Punctually he arrived at the Russian Embassy, to be told that Maisky had been summoned to an interview with Churchill, and it was uncertain whether he would be ready to leave on time. He did return, half an hour later and, within another quarter of an hour, they were on the road. 'I've seldom been more scared in a car,' John wrote. 'The

Russian driver gave me good grounds for believing in the reckless courage of the Soviet fighting men and women.'

There was, of course, a full house, over one thousand people in the audience. But John was not happy with the talk nor with its reception. It was a clever speech, 'evasive' and not informative, and Maisky was a past master at getting round awkward questions. There was plenty of cheering and shouting, mostly, John thought, rather hysterical. 'They hardly clapped at all when Maisky spoke of the tremendous courage of the Russian people. But as soon as he spoke of their method of government, and of the abolition of the landowners, there was a shout which raised the roof. And for the rest of the talk, Maisky had only to pause for a moment to take breath in order for there to be another burst of clapping, shouting and whistling. It made me realise what we are in for after the war if there is no strong reformist action taken by the Government.'

The rest of the talks went off satisfactorily. The one that gave John most personal pleasure was that by André Philipe, De Gaulle's Minister of the Interior and of Labour. He had a good command of English, and was a brilliant and amusing speaker, as well as being a highly principled man, but De Gaulle and the Free French were not popular with Churchill and his government, so this was not likely to help John's growing reputation as a trouble-maker. John never made calculations about such matters, and his real happiness lay in inviting his old friend Yvonne Cooper to stay in the camp for the occasion.

On Easter morning the WAAF produced a large hard-boiled egg for their Padre John, on one side was painted the face of Joe Stalin, on the other a hammer and sickle. And once again John was summoned to Reading, and was told that any future speakers must first be vetted by the C-in-C Technical Command. Opposition, for John, was a spur. Obstructions, obstacles, difficulties: these were challenges that demanded only more determined action, and where questions of injustice were concerned he showed bulldog tenacity. So he continued planning another series of talks for the autumn, as well as a few interesting hors d'oeuvres. He wanted to encourage the young men and women to think seriously about the great problems of the post-war world.

All this planning involved visits to London to meet and pin down prospective speakers. Sometimes John was able to slip away for a night with me, and he could fit in meetings with friends. He was seeing more and more of Victor Gollancz, and this influential friendship was developing happily. John joined the Left Book Club, and occasionally, at Victor's invitation, wrote for the *Left News*. Serving officers were not, by King's Regulations, allowed to write to the Press, but since senior RAF officers were unlikely to read the *Left News*, John's articles passed unnoticed. Publications from the Left Book Club found their way into the camp, but when John recommended them to anyone, he was careful to point out that they were likely to be one-sided; other and opposing views ought to be taken into account. He tried to persuade Victor to give one of the Yatesbury talks, but Victor was going through a physical and emotional crisis, he had to refuse all speaking engagements, except for those concerned with the rescue of as many Jews as possible from the Nazi holocaust. It was in this campaign that John became involved early in 1943.

The dreadful reality of the extermination camps was not widely known until Allied armies entered them, too late for most of the sufferers. Some of the atrocities were, however, documented in horrifying detail in a pamphlet written by Victor, and it included practical suggestions for action by the British and Allied governments. This John sold and distributed in the camp. He also prepared a petition on the subject to be sent to the Home Secretary, and secured 700 signatures, including that of the CO. When some of the senior officers accused John of subversion, the CO became alarmed, and John was in trouble again. He did not intend to give up, he would go to the Archbishops of Canterbury and York who had spoken strongly in support of efforts to rescue the Jews. But this time he managed to persuade the air marshal responsible for technical training, and he carried on successfully with his petition. The British government, to its shame, did nothing.

Injustice to individuals always stirred John to action. He was approached by a man trained, but still at Yatesbury, having been three times turned down after being recommended for a commission. Because he had a Czech wife this man, John discovered, was on an MI5 list of potential enemy agents. Investigations proved that there were no possible grounds for considering him a danger to British security. John tried to get the case reopened, and when his efforts failed, he wrote privately to Herbert Morrison, the Home Secretary, something forbidden by King's Regulations. John pleaded professional and pastoral duty, but was nevertheless again threatened with court martial. This hung over him for about a month, and was then quietly dropped. The man got his commission.

There were times when John was 'browned off' and depressed. 'How I do dislike this stupid racket,' he wrote to me. 'How anyone could desire to be a regular officer I cannot imagine. The narrow-mindedness and bigotry and stupidity are beyond belief. I shall be delighted to get clear of the Chaplain's Department . . . There are times when I wonder that my soul has survived such squalor of spirit.' It would be hard to imagine anyone more temperamentally unsuited to service life than John!

John was extremely critical of the chaplain's department, and wrote to the Archbishop of Canterbury, enclosing a memorandum of suggested reforms. Temple replied: 'I consider you are quite right in regarding it as rather shocking that the Church of England has submitted to arrangements which make the Chaplain's Department something so completely separated from the general life of the Church and of Episcopal supervision. The result has been in fact a surrender of Church principles.'

At the beginning of September John went for a night to Canterbury for further discussion with the archbishop. In the palace, he found himself sleeping in the same room that he had occupied on the night before his ordination. He couldn't help thinking and wondering about his career in the Church: would he continue to climb the ecclesiastical ladder, or would his life's work lead in quite another direction? The archbishop was charming, encouraged John in his rebellion and promised to do something about the chaplain's department. They talked late into the night, discussing the state of the Church and of the world, and John's own work and future. 'He thinks I ought not to be posted overseas, and that I should return to Oxford as soon as the European part of the war is over – he added significantly (I think) "for a short while"'. John's depressions never lasted long, he loved the Fellowship, and they loved him. 'I wish you could share with me the wonderful spiritual work there is to do on this camp,' he wrote, 'you would then also share with me in its benefits, it really is an inspiration, in spite of many difficulties and disappointments and battles, to see in actual fact, evidence of the working of the Spirit . . . I cannot imagine a happier life than that of a priest.'

The Fellowship continued to grow, and the workload became heavier. 'It's a constant struggle trying to keep things going, for no sooner do we get hold of someone than he is posted away.' By the middle of August there were about a hundred posted members, and John kept up a personal correspondence with each one. I have fifteen letters to write, he would say, or thirty, or forty, and once there were fifty on his desk. I don't know how he managed it, since nearly every day he wrote to me, and still, he commented, the chaplain-in-chief doesn't think it necessary for chaplains to have secretaries. John also began writing pastoral letters to posted members, for Christmas, Easter and the Feast of the Transfiguration. But such was the pull of the Fellowship, that posted members would often give up their precious forty-eight hours leave to return to Yatesbury to take part again in the activities and the worship.

The next list of speakers was passed by the authorities; they couldn't very well object to the Foreign Secretary, Anthony Eden, the Deputy Prime Minister, Clement Attlee, the Duke of Devonshire for the Colonial Office, Sir Stafford Cripps, Minister of Aircraft Production, and Sir William Beveridge, though they might have preferred not to have Cripps and Beveridge stirring up the men. Eden remained uncertain; he did not think it worthwhile coming unless he was guaranteed an audience of at least a thousand and the Press were allowed. Attlee made no pre-conditions, he didn't mind a small audience, only hoped it would be serious and interested, and he didn't want the Press; he would speak on the democratic ideal after the war. Eden called off at the last minute, Attlee came. He told his secretary that he had thoroughly enjoyed himself and thought it all most worthwhile.

Sir William Beveridge's lecture was as successful as Sir Stafford Cripps's had been. Beveridge agreed that his welfare scheme could perfectly well be worked in a capitalist society, though he told John privately that he feared that the present government or one like it would not in fact implement the scheme fully. But he told his audience to read the white paper carefully and consider it, before attacking the government. Very fair, John thought, since Beveridge, as an old-fashioned Liberal, very much disliked the government.

Christmas was always a good time for the Fellowship. 'It was so wonderful and special that no one wanted to go home,' said Joyce Holmes. This year, 1944, there was talk of a Nativity play and a performance of the Brahms Requiem at Christmas. Then John had one of his ambitious ideas. Why not a Passion Play at Easter, with choruses from the Requiem? This was accepted with enthusiasm, and John approached Dorothy Sayers to ask if they might adapt part of her radio drama *The Man Born to be King*. She was sceptical, but agreed. An RAF volunteer who had been a professional actor and producer did the adaptation, and took on the production. For the rest, the forty-one actors were amateurs. John insisted that this was to be an act of devotion, not a theatrical performance, there were to be no credits on the posters, and no names attached to the cast list. Every kind of obstacle arose, and was somehow overcome. Each rehearsal was preceded by prayer, ending with a corporate communion on the morning of the first performance. Easter proved impossible, but they were able to put on four performances on successive nights leading up to Whit Sunday.

The play was quite extraordinarily impressive. Nobody who saw it was unaffected by it, and many came more than once. Dorothy Sayers came on the first night and was delighted. She had supper with the cast afterwards. 'I told your padre you bloody well couldn't do it,' she said, 'and you bloody well have done it.' I managed a night off and came with Sir Stafford and Lady Cripps. Stafford was so moved, that he begged to be excused from the customary drinks in the officers' mess, as he did not wish to dilute or mar such an experience.

John was now exhausted. His old enemy, migraine, began to build up and he suffered unpleasant spells of dizziness. After some home leave, he returned to Yatesbury ready to embark on further projects. But at the beginning of July a communication from the chaplain's office announced that from 18 July the Reverend (Squadron-Leader) L. J. Collins RAFVR was posted to Bomber Command HQ at High Wycombe.

17

My Personal War

FOR four years of war I was not with John. In the post-war years we discussed this, and wondered about the rightness of the decision to remain apart. In nearly every letter that John wrote he said how much he missed me, and how he longed for the time when we could live and work together, and I wrote the same to him. But John felt that a chaplain's most valuable work was in the evenings and at weekends, nor were the men allowed to live out with their wives.

Outwardly John's life at Yatesbury was, as he sometimes complained, 'a dull routine', but inwardly it was brimming with vitality and movement; an aspiring academic developing into a man of Christian activity. In this his crucially formative period, I could share only from a distance, and that made our post-war readjustment the more difficult. Later on, we agreed that our separation had perhaps been a mistake.

So there was I at Stutton Hall cocooned in kindness and comfort. There was plenty for everyone to do, a full household, and helpers inside and outside disappearing into war-work. My aunt Evelyn's soldier brother Captain John Bland and family had all found refuge there, as had John's soldier-servant George and his family. For some mysterious military reason, John and George were able to spend every weekend at Stutton, since their battalion of the Scots Guards was supposedly guarding the Tower of London. By the end of 1942 there were three small but demanding additions to the party, Andrew Collins, James Bland, and Margaret Ross. We were lucky in having Mrs Kirkman, a splendid Yorkshire cook, and my old childhood friend Mr Vinall the butler. Other helpers came and went, except for Gwennie the kitchen-maid who never quite learned to read, in spite of my efforts to teach her.

So I helped in the house and the garden; of course, I much preferred the garden. Indoors there were no mechanical aids, no Hoovers, no washing-machines, and Aunt Evelyn believed in standards – maintaining them. Rooms must be cleaned daily, and 'turned out' once a week, and in springtime there was a positive orgy of cleaning – in those days wealthy families who had more than one house used to retreat from one to another to avoid these dust-laden tornadoes. So dutifully, once a week, I sprinkled my floors with damp tea-leaves or damp grass, and brushed it all furiously with a stiff brush.

Child-care was also a matter of standards in which Aunt Evelyn had definite views. Washing, of course, was all by hand, nappies were boiled and had somehow to be made white; mackintosh pants were taboo. So there was always far too much washing, and since man-made fibres were not invented, nothing drip-dried and everything had to be properly ironed. Feeding on demand would have met with the deepest disapproval, routine was character-building, and unless the noise became unbearable, children were to be left to cry, otherwise you were 'making a rod for your own back'. Pot-training, of course, began at birth – or almost.

Evelyn and her standards were a help to a nervous and inexperienced mother like me, more especially since Andrew at ten days old had developed an acute urinary infection and very nearly died. Mercifully he never failed to suck, and soon became, and continued, flourishing, greedy and fat.

My elder cousin, Elizabeth Fison, went off to the war and joined the WRNS, but her younger sister, our bridesmaid, ten-year-old Gay, was still at home, and needing education. Evelyn organised a small class and found a trained governess; there were Gay, Joanna Bland, Georgie Ross, Hilary Keeble from the neighbouring farm, and three Harter sisters. Thankfully I found Jean, a nice young girl to help with Andrew, lend a hand in the house, and provide an extra ration book, while I retreated happily to help in the schoolroom.

I still felt that I was marking time, while John was moving ahead in so many exciting ways; life seemed to be passing me by, I was no use to the war effort, no use to John, no use to myself. John wrote long and encouraging letters whenever I voiced these complaints, but my feelings remained, and I lived for his leaves. Winter, spring, summer and autumn, I had always yearned to be part of the whole natural year at Stutton, and now I had my wish, though not as I would have wished. But when I could share it with John it was a brief enchantment; the spring was especially lovely when we reverted to our birds'-nesting childhoods, and wandered happily competing as to who could find the most and the rarest nests.

Some time early in 1943, two military gentlemen appeared, and spent a long time in conclave with my Uncle Clavering. After they had gone, Clav came to talk to me and Nancy Bland. The possibility of an invasion was still taken sufficiently seriously to need contingency planning. There might be preliminary parachute landings or commando raids, and, in the event of a real invasion, several miles of coastland would be overrun; Stutton would find itself in occupied territory. A system of gathering and transmitting information about enemy movements, headquarters, numbers etc. was needed – Stutton Hall was thought to be an ideal enemy HQ. The suggestion was that Nancy and I might be trained to become just such information gatherers.

It was made clear to us that, if we were caught, we would have no protection from the Geneva Convention; we would be treated as spies, probably tortured and certainly shot. Since the possibility of invasion did seem rather remote, I began to indulge myself in a pleasant glow of heroism. But, we were told, if we were prepared to volunteer, we must first get permission from our husbands. Permission from our husbands? I was indignant – of course, I would discuss this with John, we kept nothing from each other, we belonged together, but I wasn't his property, it was my life and my death, it was for me to decide. Men didn't ask permission from their wives before they went off to fight. My objections were not taken at all seriously, they were thought to be tiresome and frivolous, and as I was eager to join this 'Mum's Army' I had to submit to extracting a rather reluctant agreement from John. So Nancy and I were enrolled.

In one of the surrounding parklands, a shepherd's hut was stationed beside a wood; inside, beneath a rough wooden seat a wireless transmitter and receiver was installed – Nancy and I had to master one of the Army codes and, at stated times, repair to the hut to transmit and receive imaginary messages. Once or twice we took part in full-scale exercises lasting a whole weekend. I found this playing at soldiers enormous fun – 'Able, Baker, Charlie, Dog' – I can still remember it – I used to walk about the woods and fields, longing for a German parachutist to drop out of the skies, or even a wounded airman would do, might, in fact, be preferable, because, although I liked to fancy myself as a heroine of the Resistance, I knew that if anything real were to happen, I would be very frightened.

Village people and farm labourers were accustomed to seeing Nancy and me around on the estate. During our respective pregnancies we used to go for those healthy walks recommended by little books on how to keep fit before the great event, and in the process we had become firm friends – we were known as 'the Cuckoos', and towards the end as 'the Puffins'. Of course, we didn't always visit the hut together, and were careful, so we thought, to avoid being seen, though Evelyn assured us that everyone in the village knew that something fishy was going on in that hut. My companion spy Nancy was apt to get into trouble with the code, and must have sent off some rather strange messages; we did our decoding together and had a lot of fun, it was difficult to take it seriously. And, of course, in the end nothing ever happened.

In January 1943 I got a telegram from David to say that he was coming on leave. He was not due for immediate leave, so this could mean only one thing: 'embarkation', and so it was. He arrived in excellent form, happy and excited, 'I've learned so much about the battlefield that I really want to get there and see what it's like,' he said.

We had a particularly happy few days; it was traditional winter weather, snow and hard frost, snowmen and snowballs for the children, and ice-skating on the ponds. David and I trudged for miles through the snow, and walked along by the river, watching great flocks of hungry sea-birds. And endlessly we talked: 'Don't just write to me about home and family news,' he said, 'write about all the real things that we talk about, write about what you are reading and thinking, and about John's work'. David had become interested, among many other things, in the paranormal and in spiritualism. 'If I'm killed,' he said in a matter of fact way, 'and if there is any genuine means of communication, you're the one I'll come to.'

We spent an afternoon at Little Hall, playing many of David's favourite records. Our grandmother's memory by this time had nearly failed, though she knew and registered the people like me, whom she saw regularly. She knew David, but once he had gone she never asked about him, and for that I was thankful. So we listened to those old records, and a great wave of nostalgia swept over me. David reproved me, 'It's no good looking back into a golden age, and feeling that everything good lies in the past, it's the future that matters; it's so important to look forward, if you just look back it destroys initiative and hope.' David was full of hope; three years ago he had seemed a bewildered boy, now he was a man. 'I know what you mean,' wrote an Oxford friend, 'he had acquired maturity without losing freshness and frankness, the two qualities which drew everyone to him like a magnet . . . From the first time I met him, I felt that here was someone who was, in himself, altogether admirable and valuable.'

David could only spare a few days at Stutton, he had so much to do, and so many preparations to make, but I went to London for the last day of his leave. We met for lunch at Kettner's restaurant, it was comfortable and relatively empty and we settled down for a good and protracted lunch. During our youthful companionship, it had usually been I who was the leader in thought and discussion, now it was David. He talked of the future, his and mine. His mind was turning, idealistically, towards politics and to the hope of a post-war world, purged of so many of the injustices of the past. Perhaps he thought that in sharing the hardships and dangers of war with so many ordinary Englishmen, he would discover what it was he should be doing for the future in which he so much believed. That he might not return was taken for granted, he seemed to have counted the cost, and found it worthwhile; he was no longer afraid.

We had intended, after lunch, to go to a concert, but the programme of Bach, Brahms and Beethoven, at the Queens Hall, was too popular and we couldn't get seats, so we settled for a more modest, but still enjoyable, performance round the corner. We came out to a cold grey evening, and streets full of people, mostly young, mostly in uniform, a great crowd eddying backwards and forwards.

It was time for me to go and catch my Liverpool Street train back to Stutton, and David had to report to barracks up at Hampstead.

'Well, goodbye Di' – a hesitation. 'It's been lovely.'

'Goodbye Dave, it's been a marvellous day.'

So much more I would have liked to say, so much more I found impossible to say, so much more I would never say. So we turned and went on our separate and opposite ways.

It was some weeks before I heard from David, and then came a letter telling us that he was in North Africa, the 3rd Battalion Welsh Guards had joined Alexander's 1st Army, and together with the 8th Army they were steadily pushing the Germans out of Africa. So I went back to my easy routine, caring for Andrew, working in the house and garden and in the schoolroom where I was busy writing and producing plays for the children. I visited my ageing grandmother daily, and wondered what had happened to the person whom I had known and loved. The loss of mental faculties in old age is bewildering and depressing, but, at least, my grandmother never suffered from the paranoia that so often accompanies senile dementia; she remained sweet and gentle to the last. I felt, somehow, closer to her after her death. I wrote letters, daily to John, frequently to David and to Aunt Tilly, marooned in Kenya.

David's letters were always lively, descriptive, serious and often very amusing, they were enjoyed by everybody. By the beginning of 1944, it

Above John as an RAF chaplain, Yatesbury

Below Fellowship Sunday breakfast

Left Diana, John and Father Paul (*right*) in Leningrad

Below Sergiu Celibidache, John and Wilhelm Furtwängler, during the visit of the Berlin Philharmonic Orchestra, 1948 (*Hulton-Deutsch*)

was clear that his battalion would soon be leaving North Africa for Italy. That year started badly for us, death invaded our little Stutton community. Friends and relatives were killed, two of Aunt Evelyn's young cousins whom we all knew died in the fighting, and Nancy's only brother Dick was killed at Anzio. The Italian campaign which had started so promisingly now seemed bogged down, the weather was terrible and the casualties mounted.

It was the middle of February when Clav came back from his office one evening, and came upstairs while I was putting Andrew to bed. I knew by his face that it was bad news. 'David?' I asked, he nodded. 'Killed?' 'Yes'. David's battalion had gone into action two days after landing in Italy – they played their part in the costly battle for the ruins of Cassino. They were to relieve a company holding the desolate Monte Cerasole to the south-west. They held the summit in the face of continuous and accurate shelling: 'It was so cold that their clothes froze on their bodies, they had no shelter but stone sangars, and the journey down the mountain with the wounded took more than twenty hours'. On the morning of 11 February there was a blizzard, and the Germans attacked; David's company, in the words of their commanding officer, 'fought like fiends'. 'The enemy got on top, and David went to meet them with the Company, drove them back, and himself got killed on the top – of course he was absolutely regardless of any personal danger.'

Those were details that we learned later; for the immediate present, there were just the bare words of the official telegram. John came on leave, but he could only spare forty-eight hours and I was still in a state of numbed unreality. A little later my father came, and we wept together over David's letters, and the letters of condolence that came pouring in. We were a household in mourning.

I wrote many answers to many letters, and, as David's executor, there were things to which I had to attend. I received no communication from the spirit world, though I did have one dream in which David was vividly present, and spoke of his death, which was instantaneous, and not he said in any way terrible or alarming, and I was not to worry about him, he was all right. This was comforting, a part of the process of accepting reality.

I made no parade of grief, that is how the English are trained, and I am very English, but an emotional shock like a sudden bereavement can produce swings of mood over which one has little control. John wrote me many tender and sympathetic letters, and I wrote to him as I felt and sometimes I felt very low. Had we been together, John would have understood these swings of feeling; he needed the personal contact to which he would respond with open and intuitive sympathy. As it was, whenever he thought I was getting better, he would receive another sorrowful letter, and he thought that perhaps he should play the role of a priest as well as a husband. So he wrote me a rather conventionally 'religious' and theologically worded letter, which seemed like a reproof. We must not cling to the dead, love between husband and wife is the highest value for which we must forsake even the love and anchorage of our own family and 'cleave' to each other, and we must think of those who are worse off than ourselves. 'If my words,' he wrote, 'seem to convey any harshness, you must at once assume that to be due to my poor manner of expressing myself and not to my real meaning'. His words did sound harsh, and I was hurt, but I never reproached him, just put the letter aside. David was a part of my life, a part of me that I could never 'forsake'. Love is not rationed, my love for him could in no way diminish my love for John. As for other people, if there is something you can do for them, even some small practical service, that is a real help, but just to contemplate the miseries of others worse off than you merely adds guilt to your own pain.

Once when John and I were together again after the war, quite out of the blue, he said, 'I know I failed you over David'. I would not have put it like that, would only have said that there is no substitute for direct personal experience. You do not understand what it is to bear a child until you have had one, you cannot know – only imagine – what it is to lose a husband, brother, child, until you have suffered such a loss. Now that I have had to tread a much harder path alone I understand a little more. I have noticed that people do often seem to think that, after a certain time, others should 'get over' a loss that they have not themselves experienced. Learning to live, even to live creatively, with pain and loss is another matter, quite different from 'getting over', but it takes a long time.

During the summer of 1944, I spent five weeks in Scotland with Andrew. Ann Tindall, by then Ann Bass, was an Oxford friend, whose parents owned and ran West Downs, a well-known boys' preparatory school in Winchester. For the duration of the war, the school was evacuated to Blair Atholl, and housed in part of Blair Castle. Since it was holiday time, there was plenty of accommodation, as well as domestic help. Ann is a rock of good sense, common and not so common, she is highly efficient with a marvellous sense of humour. Both Ann's brothers had been killed, and her husband Richard was fighting in Burma; their small daughter, Diana, was the same age as

Andrew. Other Oxford friends came to visit, among them Catherine Walker, who says she is not at all efficient, but who overflows with fun and practical kindness, and the results of her cheerful muddle are always impressive. Ann's parents were an exceptional and interesting couple, and the whole atmosphere was relaxed and stimulating. It was all blessedly peaceful.

Nights at Stutton were becoming unpleasantly noisy. Now that the Germans had been driven away from the French coast they were concentrated in Holland and Belgium, much nearer to East Anglia. As well as continued night bombing, unmanned missiles – Hitler's secret weapons – began to arrive. V1s, the 'doodle-bugs', came by day and by night with a steady engine sound and a small light; when the engine and the light cut out explosions followed. Soon after, we had the V2s, which came without warning and without sound, and they were larger and the explosions were more destructive. But in Scotland an aeroplane was a rarity, and was always 'one of ours'.

Blair Castle looks just as a romantic castle should, and is surrounded by mountains, heather- and bracken-covered, while the distant soothing sound of mountain streams seems part of an embracing silence. Occasionally, by courtesy of Mrs Tindall, Ann and I were able to walk for miles over the purple and golden mountain slopes, starting up grouse, mountain hares and ptarmigan already turning white in preparation for the winter snows, breathing air that seemed so much purer and sweeter than any down in the soft and crowded south, and smelling the unforgettable smell of Scotland.

18

Bomber Command HQ

FOR the Fellowship John's departure had been 'like a bereavement'. 'Everyone in the Fellowship loved John, and that love is just as fresh today.' So Joan Edwards remembers. The local Bishop of Sherborne was much distressed, he had seen the work of the Fellowship, and the rising number of candidates for confirmation. But his protests were unavailing.

John's posting remained a mystery. A new chaplain–in–chief had visited Yatesbury and professed enthusiasm for the Fellowship, saying that he wished to see similar initiatives elsewhere. He gave contradictory reasons for the posting, that John was getting stale, and that *The Man Born to be King* was the high point of his work, and it was best to leave then. More probable was a political angle. A mock election had been organised on the camp, and a report of it had appeared in the Communist newspaper, *The Daily Worker*. The election was nothing to do with the Church, John was on leave at the time, and knew nothing about it, but, for the harassed CO, John was a convenient scapegoat.

Whatever the reasons, Bomber Command looked like demotion; instead of having at least three chaplains under him, John would be on his own, and was only the second chaplain ever to work there. There was vague talk about the possibility of his being sent to France in a senior position, but he would have had to commit himself to staying on in the RAF after the end of hostilities in Europe, and that he was not prepared to do.

Bomber Command was a far cry from Yatesbury. John felt lonely, depressed and unwell, and wondered how he was going to tackle his new job. Keeping in touch with the scattered members of the Fellowship was a major task in itself; as chaplains and keen members were posted away, little daughter cells grew up, and eventually there were twelve, six spread over the British Isles, and six abroad, one as far off as Ceylon (Sri Lanka). Rather bravely John wrote to Yatesbury that perhaps it was good for him to have the experience of being a 'posted' member.

The news from Yatesbury was not good. Before he left, John had urged the Fellowship to do everything possible to co-operate with the new padre. But the new padre was not disposed to co-operate with them. Everything now was to be run on service lines, no more Christian names, and proper attention to rank; the democratic atmosphere of the Fellowship was foreign to the service mind. At first Padre Lee tried to stop them meeting together, and there was an attempt to take over the Fellowship room and open it to other activities. Two or three times John returned to Yatesbury in unsuccessful attempts to sort things out. There was a final unhappy confrontation; John spent a night and a day with the Fellowship. He found them at first rather quiet and uncertain, but as he greeted them by name, one by one, the old happy spirit began to revive. John then had a meeting with Lee and got nowhere. Lee said he intended to break up the Fellowship and exclude them from Church life. But John's faith in the Fellowship was justified, they carried on quietly, doing many of the things to which they had been accustomed, unobtrusively helping the Church and the chaplains. Slowly Lee began to relax, until he was finally won over.

Bomber Command was hidden away among the heavily wooded hills around High Wycombe. There was the command side, all secret and technical, and some of it underground, and there was the administrative side that supported the command. Personnel numbered around 1,300; they were mainly technical and administrative, but pilots and aircrew who were 'resting' after their allotted number of sorties were sometimes there as well. From my point of view, Bomber Command was more easily accessible than Yatesbury. Arthur 'Bomber' Harris was a first cousin of my father's, so I was invited to stay at Springfield, his official residence, and to bring Andrew. There were usually interesting people at Springfield, and Arthur, when not too exhausted and weighed down by his responsibilities, was very good company. With his wife Jill, Arthur enjoyed entertaining, and was a humorous, somewhat cynical observer of the human comedy, witty and amusing, and never pompous or self-admiring.

Arthur and John differed in their politics and in their outlook on life, but they had similarities: both held strong views, and were prepared to stand up, speak out and do battle for the things in which they believed. The media labelled them both with public images that were absurdly far from the truth, and which produced regular supplies of 'hate' mail. They developed a sincere mutual respect, and John really liked Arthur.

Early in 1942, Bomber Command HQ had waited with some trepidation for the arrival of Arthur Harris, their new commander-in-chief. He was reputed to be difficult, intolerant and opinionated; he expressed himself in what is euphemistically called 'forthright language' and this did not always make him popular. Perhaps one of the more nervous was the WAAF officer who had served as personal secretary to the outgoing C-in-C. She did not suppose Arthur Harris would want her, and was very doubtful as to whether she would be able to work with such a character. The reality proved different, and she stayed with Arthur until his retirement at the end of the war. She found him kind and considerate, a particularly just man who would listen carefully to all sides of any question, and having made up his mind, would act decisively; she saw nothing of the reputed fierce temper. 'He was,' she said, 'a very compassionate man'. The little that I saw of Arthur confirmed, as she said, that his concern for the welfare of his men, and his distress at casualties went very deep. As for the men who served under him, he gained their respect, affection and often devotion. He was a true leader, 'imaginative, far-sighted, inventive and forceful', and his qualities of leadership were felt throughout Bomber Command.

Arthur was dedicated to Bomber Command. He was, and re-mained, convinced that, given enough men and high-quality machines and equipment, wars could be won by bombing, and many lives could thereby be saved. Any idea that the RAF should be regarded as an appendage of the Army or the Navy was anathema to him, and he much resented the existence of the Fleet Air Arm under naval control.

Arthur did not invent Allied bombing strategy, such decisions were taken by the War Cabinet; the commander-in-chief had to see them carried out effectively. The policy of carpet-bombing of German cities was agreed before Arthur arrived at Bomber Command, and as for perhaps the most controversial action, the bombing of Dresden in 1945, Arthur did as he was instructed to do by the High Command. There is one widely held misconception that should be corrected. It is supposed that when the victory honours were handed out, Arthur Harris and Bomber Command were deliberately omitted. Not so, Arthur was offered the same as the other commanders-in-chief, and pilots and aircrew were awarded the Europe Operational Star. Arthur fought hard for a special campaign medal for Bomber Command, such as had been given to the 8th Army. He was bitter that this was not agreed, since from 1942 onwards, Bomber Command had been constantly in offensive action, and had suffered some 56,000 casualties. He also wanted recognition for the special contribution made by the ground crews. These men maintained and serviced the machines at their dispersal sites in all weathers and all dangers, without their work the nightly offensive could not have been maintained, 8,000 had lost their lives. Arthur considered the Defence Medal an inadequate recognition of such a vital contribution. If his men were not to be properly recognised, Arthur refused any special recognition for himself.

The strategic and moral rights and wrongs of Allied bombing policy have been much debated. Evidence from inside Germany suggests that the bombing offensive may have been more effective than its critics would admit. Nevertheless, towards the end of 1944, public unease was beginning to spread, and this was bravely voiced by the Bishop of Chichester, Dr Bell. John, who had never been, and was not now, a pacifist, shared in this unease. He was particularly distressed by a letter he received from one of the most outstanding members of the Fellowship, who wrote of his part in the bombing of Hamburg:

'It was a nightmare experience looking down on the flaming city beneath. I felt sick as I thought of the women and children down there being mutilated, burned, killed, terror-stricken in that dreadful inferno – and I was partly responsible. Why, Padre John, do the Churches not tell us we are doing an evil job? Why do Chaplains persist in telling us that we are performing a noble task in defence of Christian civilisation? I believe that Hitler must be defeated; I am prepared to do my bit to that end. But don't let anyone tell us that what we are doing is noble. What we are doing is evil, a necessary evil perhaps, but evil all the same.'

John struggled on, trying to work in the pattern of Yatesbury, and by the autumn of 1944 things began to improve. From among the small regular church congregation, a little Fellowship, five men and three women, soon joined by another seven persons, began to flourish. Arthur Harris was co-operative; he agreed easily to John's wish to abolish compulsory church parades, and he was not opposed to the series of talks that John, rather rashly, began to organise. Then, the camp doctor at last accepted that John's constant exhaustion and dizziness might have a physical origin and he was sent to a large RAF hospital near Blackpool, where blocked eustachian tubes and vitamin deficiency were diagnosed and treated. The priest who came to take services in John's absence was 'most impressed by the spirit of the merry fifteen who had breakfast together afterwards' and 'at the sight of a Christian community really in being'. John was discharged from hospital and given three weeks' sick leave, which meant 'home for Christmas'. He had first to return to High Wycombe, so was able to be present at one of his series of talks, that given by Sir Stafford Cripps. As Minister of Aircraft Production, Stafford had been briefed to speak on 'The Christian in Industry', but instead, he had announced his talk would be called 'Is God my Co-Pilot?' An evangelically inclined pilot had recently written a book *God is my Co-Pilot*, and Stafford, taking part in a Brains Trust, had been faced with the question as to whether the team thought it right to associate God with the work of a bomber pilot. Stafford decided to use this occasion to try to answer the question.

His first point was that God is always with us whether we are doing right or wrong, and he concluded that 'in war, as in peace, we each have to frame our judgements upon the basis of what we most truly and honestly believe to be God's will'. Implicit in Stafford's lecture was the question of the supremacy or otherwise of the individual conscience; of the point at which a person, even someone under orders, has to say, 'I must obey God rather than man'. This was dangerous thinking in time of war, and to some of the senior officers, even to raise the question, however obliquely, was tantamount to treason.

After Stafford's talk, John came on leave; he returned to a hornet's nest: 'half a dozen senior officers,' he wrote 'have been working themselves into a fury of opposition to Cripps. And their accounts of what Cripps said are now entirely unlike anything he actually said or could have said.' The result of all this was that Harris had asked his personal assistant Harry Weldon, in peacetime a philosophy don at Oxford, to give a counter-lecture with the title, 'The Ethics of Bombing'. John went, or was summoned, to talk to Arthur. 'Weldon doesn't even believe in God, let alone Christianity,' he protested. However, the lecture went ahead, a lecture John dismissed as more about 'the bombing of ethics' than the 'ethics of bombing'. A local doctor who was friendly with the Harrises and with John lectured him about arguing with senior officers. 'They aren't used to it, and they don't like it.' John, of course, could never see why rank should protect anyone from the cut and thrust of honest debate. So, once again, he was in disgrace.

From the beginning of 1945 John's eyes were more and more fixed on the future. Stafford Cripps was in regular contact with Mervyn Stockwood and with John, and he decided to call together a group of clergy and Christian lay people, to try to work out what part a reformed Church might play in helping to shape and guide the national and international future. John seems to have become some kind of secretary for this group. Then there was the question of the future of the Fellowship. John had once thought that at the end of the war, it should be disbanded. 'I shan't want to do it,' he said, and of course in the end the Fellowship itself had no wish to lie down and die; for many of its members, this had been the experience of their lives, they wanted to carry it forward into civilian life. So John wrote a number of pastoral letters, elaborating his own ideas, and asking for theirs.

What about our personal future? Although John was not particularly anxious to return to Oriel, he made numerous expeditions to Oxford to try to find some possible accommodation; but there was none to be had; all over the country there was a desperate housing shortage, and since I was again pregnant, I was not much practical help. Early in March, John received a summons from Downing Street for an interview with that *éminence grise*, the Prime Minister's Patronage Secretary. For any young priest this means that you have been noticed by those who patrol the corridors of power, you have a foot on the slippery ladder of ecclesiastical preferment, and though John had his share of ambition, he was well aware of its dangers. After an hour's discussion, he was asked to consider a canonry at Worcester Cathedral, or the important industrial parish of Nuneaton – either could lead to higher things. I remember sitting with John in St James's Park, enjoying the ducks and debating our future. We decided on Nuneaton, if offered; although I did not exactly see myself as a vicar's wife, this did seem the place where John would be most likely to be able to put his ideas into practice, so we waited hopefully for a further summons.

There was, of course, enormous relief when Germany finally surrendered on 7 May. Relief – yes – but thanksgiving was harder, and I certainly felt in no mood for celebration, the cost had been so vast: not just my personal cost, the loss of David and of many good friends, but in all those ruined lives and ruined cities, in those great streams of refugees that were to grow and grow. And though we had known something of the Holocaust, we were now faced with it; we saw in live pictures something of the almost unbelievable horrors of the concentration camps as they were 'liberated' by the Allied armies. It was not easy to believe in a God of love and compassion.

John wrote, trying hard not to draw what he called 'false conclusions', afraid that emotional horror would lead to an unreasoning hatred of Germans as Germans, or to a complete loss of faith. No, he said, in a way the dreadful revelations strengthened his own faith, only

Christianity could enable him to face the evils of humanity without despair. And we must not forget the many Germans who had also perished in the camps, and those who had suffered because they had tried to help Jews and other victims – there were many good Germans.

John was now desperate to get out of the RAF. He fretted and fumed and began to feel useless. Everything was being run down, the building used for church services was derequisitioned without consultation, and at weekends most people went away. No further summons arrived from Downing Street, and before long the two possible appointments were filled by others. Perhaps John was already considered too 'dangerous'. 'If God has no *apparently* great work for me to do,' he wrote, 'that doesn't matter fundamentally, it would chiefly be a hurt to my pride, I suppose, yet I'm bound to admit I have a sort of feeling we have some very important part for which we are being prepared. As you say "the fundamental realities are the mysteries of birth and love, the beauty of human relationships, of the lovely world outside, and the sense of the presence of God." '

My side of our war-time correspondence has been lost, but this epistle must have been written following the birth of our baby, always referred to as Elizabeth, but who turned out to be Richard. Unlike Andrew's birth, this was an easy and anxiety-free affair, and in my relief, I was lifted to a real peak-experience; once again I felt that joyous affirmation of life, Traherne was right, Blake was right, Blake was always right, 'Everything that lives is holy'; I felt like singing my own Magnificat.

At the beginning of July came the General Election, and a landslide victory for Labour. John was elated. I, a little to my shame, as I look back, voted Conservative, over-influenced by the family atmosphere of the past three years, and perhaps by patriotic emotion focused upon Churchill. After a week, John got a letter from Stafford: 'Don't fix yourself up too quickly, as soon as I get the chance, I'll have a look around and see if we can't place you somewhere suitable . . .' John wrote to me cautiously, 'Whatever happens, I want to be sure that ambition is not the cause of my next move . . . Yet I think there runs through me a real desire to take the right step now; a conviction (right or wrong, but honest) that God does want us to play a definite part in the higher policy of the Church. This is a new age into which we are plunging. The Church must become related to the new spirit and temper of our age, it must be a strong spiritual arm to minister to the rising Socialist state – to feed it spiritually, and to be God's instrument to declare judgement and mercy upon its sins and errors.'

The new age was ushered in in dramatic and ominous fashion with the ending of the war against Japan. On 6 August, the Feast of the Transfiguration, the first atom bomb was dropped on Hiroshima; three days later, a second exploded over Nagasaki. Shock waves of horror spread around the world; this was more than an extra large, extra powerful bomb; it was something different in kind, a fearful expression of evil. It was too much for John, too much for me, too much for most of us. How could modern war be, any longer, supported by Christians? John telephoned Stafford Cripps. 'What can I do?' said Stafford. 'The Cabinet was not consulted, only Attlee was informed, the decision was taken solely by the Americans.' To John's suggestion that he might resign, Stafford, probably rightly, thought that this would be an empty gesture.

With some difficulty – the lines were almost permanently engaged – John got through to Lambeth Palace. He was answered by a harassed chaplain who said that the archbishop was in hiding at a secret address; in any case, what did he expect the poor man to do? He might summon the bishops, said John, and issue some statement for the guidance of the Church, some protest, some disassociation from this new horror. 'You'd better put your views on paper,' said the weary chaplain; but he did promise that, from among the thousands of letters that were beginning to pour in, he would ensure that John's was, at least, seen by the archbishop.

So John sat down and wrote begging the archbishop to protest officially against the first use of this hideously indiscriminate weapon. How, he asked, could the Western democracies continue to claim that they stood against barbarism? All pretence that we were fighting to preserve a decent way of life had been thrown overboard. His position as a chaplain in an officers' mess was unbearable, enough to make a man physically sick. After some time, the archbishop replied to the effect that now that the war was over, there was no point in protesting, but if in the future any nation were to manufacture and threaten to use these weapons, then would be the time to protest.

After Hiroshima, John described himself as 'a nuclear pacifist'; later, recognising the illogicality of such a position, he became what he called 'a reluctant pacifist'.

So now there was nothing left but to wait for demobilisation and a return to Oxford. I was happy enough with the idea of Oxford, except that it was impossible to find anywhere to live, and we had no transport. At long last, John's papers came through; he was to be released in September. He celebrated the ending of the work of the Church at Bomber Command by organising a huge dance to which all were invited. He introduced the proceedings by emphasising that as this was a Church party, rank was not recognised. So high-ranking officers and other ranks entered into this spirit, and all agreed that it was the best party the unit had experienced. Meanwhile, I had, by chance, noticed an advertisement for a cottage to be let furnished for one year at Brill, a village near Thame, and not too far from Oxford. As there were buses twice a week to Thame and Oxford, we decided to rent Windmill Cottage.

19

Back to 'Civvy Street'

'BRILL on the hill where you'll never be ill'. So ran the saying, and we never were ill, perhaps because those powerful winds that turned the local mill disposed of any evil germs. The top of the hill was a large area of common land, and in the centre, only two or three hundred yards apart, stood the windmill and our small cottage. Round the edges of the hill where the ground sloped downwards were cottages and little houses. Windmill Cottage must originally have been two, built sometime in the eighteenth century to serve the mill. It had been well modernised, it was warm and comfortable, it had a pleasant little garden, and there were splendid views. John and I did almost have to go on hands and knees to get into the room we had selected as our bedroom, and the 'wealth of exposed timbers' would have gone to any estate agent's head. Considering the conditions in which many people had to begin, or resume, their married lives, we were lucky.

Everyone coming out of the Services was entitled to two months demobilisation leave with full pay, but as soon as John knew the date of his release, he announced his intention of returning to Oriel for the Michaelmas term. I was stunned; yet another period of voluntary separation seemed too much. I wrote him a passionate pleading letter, never mind about the double pay, surely we were entitled to just a few months of the married life for which we had so much longed. John, dear John, succumbed to my pleadings, and agreed to remain at Brill, until January 1946. Perhaps I was wrong. John was so eager to become immediately involved in creating the brave new world and the brave new Church, the tasks for which he had been waiting and preparing, and to which he felt he had much to give. Yes, I too shared and believed in his aspirations, but just now, for me, they were secondary, all I wanted was married life with John in a home of our own. After six years of marriage, we now had to discover how to be properly married. Along with thousands of others, we had missed out on the normal period of growing together, becoming sexually adjusted, having babies and children around and, for undomesticated me, getting used to running a household. John never complained, never indicated any resentment, and I never knew whether he felt any.

During our separation, John had suffered a good deal from sexual deprivation, which he wrote about in some of his letters, and I suffered as well, but two pregnancies and births had made it a bit easier for me. Because of John's early conditioning, and subsequent training for the priesthood, anything to do with sex outside marriage was sinful, there was no way that he could relieve, however marginally, his frustrations, and even thoughts were supposedly 'impure'. Perhaps marriage itself was slightly suspect, were not celibacy and virginity supposed to be somehow 'higher' and more dedicated? So John was still somewhat mixed up, and I daresay I was too, and instead of the sexual bonanza to which we had both looked forward, our sex life collapsed completely. Years of enforced celibacy imposed upon normally vigorous young men are not perhaps the best preparation for a happily uninhibited sex life. That we were not alone in our post-war problems was soon evident in the queue of men and women who wanted to come and talk to John about their own difficulties.

Neither of us ever doubted that we truly and deeply loved one another; there were many good things about Brill, and much that we could share. As I was still nursing the baby, Richard, I could not easily leave the cottage for long, but John was not tethered, and was able to get away to Oxford and London for meetings. The Church Reform Group was struggling along; its composition varied as different members brought in others they thought might be 'useful'. The hard core consisted of Stafford Cripps, his wife Isobel, and their daughter Peggy, Mervyn Stockwood, Richard Acland, and Guy Mayfield, another RAF chaplain who had been at Westcott House with John. At first one or two Nonconformists joined, but as soon as the Bishop of Chichester, Dr Bell, agreed to take the Chair, he stipulated that the group must be confined to Anglicans. James Welch from the BBC came occasionally as an observer.

They were a collection of individuals each with his, mostly his, strong views; it proved difficult to reach any consensus. Memorandum after memorandum was produced, criticised, altered, rejected, and most of this work fell upon John. Early on he had written to Stafford pointing out that there were two aims that seemed to be getting muddled: (1) finding a means of relating religion to practical affairs of modern life, in particular factory life, political and economic issues; and (2) reform of the Anglican Church to make it a more effective instrument. John and Bishop Bell wanted to begin with (2), while Stafford favoured (1). The bishop wanted to bring in 'moderate' Churchmen, and at least one good Tory. Richard Acland insisted that a test of membership of the group must be 'to let it be publicly known to regard the private ownership of the great productive resources as evil': this alarmed the moderates, and even a radical like Mervyn. Richard helpfully amended his text to 'That it must be known of each member of the group that he regards the system of Big Business and Monopoly Capitalism . . . as evil'. But even Stafford wanted to change it to something vaguer to do with the 'profit motive'.

John was always impressed by Mervyn's contributions which were radical but practical and down to earth. Mervyn was all for encouraging the clergy to take part in local politics, and stand as councillors; others thought it better to encourage committed Christians to play a more active role. John was impressed too by Stafford's chairmanship and summing up, and later by Dr Bell's – he described both as 'brilliant'.

It was then thought that the group should include more women – Mervyn's reaction to John was 'I suppose we must have a hag or two – I know a couple of dames in Bristol. But perhaps you have a few wenches up your sleeve. Moreover, Isobel may know of a bumpkin on her compost heap. Though in my heart, I agree with St Paul that all women should hold their tongues. John Hayter would be better than a dozen dames.' (I hasten to add that Mervyn has a number of very good female friends including me, and is a staunch supporter of the ordination of women.) Someone suggested they ought to have at least two 'workers', but nobody seemed to know any. Finally a memorandum was hammered out and accepted. It was very long. There was a preamble about the Church of England being out of touch and in need of 'drastic reform'. It went on to call for 'virile Christian cells not only in the Churches, but also in the homes of the people and in factories, public houses, clubs etc.' These were 'to enable the Gospel and the power of the Holy Spirit to permeate all facets of life, social, economic and political, whether local or national'. John's hand is evident here, and there was more about 'the social, economic and political implications of the Gospel', and, 'it is not enough for the Church to proclaim ideals; it must take an active part in political and social affairs'; John's contribution again, with strong support from Mervyn and Stafford. And to allay the fears of the more conservatively minded, 'The Church should not identify itself with any particular political party. But it should openly and in every way possible, condemn any policy of whatever Party, which is against Christian conscience.'

Among suggestions for Church reform were many that have become standard practice: greater lay participation, more democracy, amalgamation of parishes, better training for ordinands, worker-priests, specialist priests etc. As a practical step there was a call for the Church 'to effect reconciliation between us and our late enemies,' and Richard Acland's 'text' was slipped in, but so hedged about with safeguards and reservations, that it was difficult to discover what it really did mean.

The result of the General Election had, of course, made a difference to Stafford's position; as President of the Board of Trade, he was unable to devote much time to the group, though he remained keen and supportive. But there was still, in spite of the memorandum, some disagreement, and Bishop Bell insisted that they must have some idea of a follow-up before taking any public step. James Welch, who had been hanging about on the fringes, launched a whole barrel full of cold water at John. The Group, he said, seemed with one or two exceptions to be 'quite extraordinarily mediocre, and not at all the kind of group which is within miles of initiating any real reform in the Church of England . . .' He thought the idea of an Albert Hall meeting absurd, and bound to fail. As well as James Welch, Stafford began to get cold feet, as did one or two others, and it was finally decided that there was not enough agreement to go forward.

Soon after we had settled at Brill, John arrived back from a few days in Oxford with two large volumes. He was bursting with intellectual and theological excitement. 'You simply must read this, it's brilliant.' 'This' was Reinhold Niebuhr's Gifford lectures *The Nature and Destiny of Man*. I did read it, and noted John's underlinings and approving NBs on nearly every page. Niebuhr had started out as a Christian Socialist and a pragmatic pacifist, though never a Communist, he had been influenced by Marxist thinking. World events had disillusioned him; he was now profoundly critical of Marxism, suspicious of Socialism, and had rejected pacifism, though he recognised the value of the individual pacifist witness. He attacked what he called the 'Utopian illusions and the sentimental aberrations of modern liberal culture'. Drawing perhaps on his Lutheran heritage he elaborated a doctrine of original sin – all men's highest achievements were inevitably tainted by pride and self-interest, and the worst sin was the failure to recognise this fact and to accept that man's finiteness precluded any Utopian perfection. The result was a rather conservative and pragmatic approach to politics, but his conservatism was never an acceptance of the *status quo*; he remained convinced that it was the duty of Christians and of the Church to wrestle with the moral ambiguities of social, political and economic life, and to wrestle in the light of a belief in the primacy of the law of love.

John had moved in the opposite direction, but neither did he believe in Utopias; science and technology were never going to lead humanity to the Promised Land. John could fairly be described as a 'moral idealist' but he could not adopt simple unambiguous convictions that can lead to fanaticism. That, perhaps, is why he was never able to drop the word 'reluctant' from his final espousal of pacifism. Niebuhr's thoughts on the relation between love and justice particularly interested John who had been unhappy with William Temple's statement that in politics, justice must precede love. Niebuhr's formulations were more acceptable.

Apart from Cripps, Acland and Niebuhr, there was another, a more powerful influence in John's life: this was Victor Gollancz. Victor was a fervent 'moral idealist' and a tireless campaigner; not for him the theological paradoxes of Niebuhr, he thoroughly disapproved of him. Victor too had moved, he was still a passionate Socialist, but in the shock of the Nazi-Soviet pact he had abandoned his somewhat fellow-travelling attitude to the Soviet Union exemplified in his leadership of the Left Book Club; the impact of the Holocaust and a severe nervous breakdown had led him into deeper and deeper soul-searchings. While at Oxford, prior to 1914, Victor had fallen in love with the person of Christ, and had made arrangements to be received into the Anglican Church. The war, followed by his marriage, had put an end to that. Now, though he no longer wished to become a member of any Church, he had embraced wholeheartedly the Christian ethic of the New Testament. Victor was an all or nothing man, and the all for him was the Sermon on the Mount, never mind that he didn't and couldn't live up to it himself, that was the standard by which all human behaviour, political as well as personal, was to be judged.

While he was at Bomber Command, John had been able to see quite a lot of Victor whose country home at Brimpton was not far from High Wycombe; I had once met him for lunch in London. Victor's enormous enthusiasms, his loves and his hates – though, of course, nobody ought ever to hate – were infectious. At lunch he was charm itself, and kept my two-year-old son Andrew happy by making absurd monkey-faces at him. No meeting with Victor could be dull, though it was sometimes difficult to keep up with his swings of mood, his elations, his depressions, his joys and his hurts. The subtleties of humour were not for him, but he had an enormous and infectious sense of fun. He could sometimes give his friends a rough time, but it was worth it, every inch of the way.

Victor too wanted a brave new world, and had hopes of the Labour government, though determined to judge their performance by the highest possible standard. I think that Victor at that stage had some lingering Utopian dreams, and he certainly believed that religion and politics were inseparable. Even if John had some sceptical reservations, Victor's vision and absolutist demands fired his own enthusiastic temperament.

So there was John, a race horse pawing and champing to be out of the stable; but he was happy at Christmas, our first family Christmas, so simple, uncommercial, and magical an occasion. We invited Harold and Yvonne Cooper and one of my Oxford friends, and we found a Christmas tree. Three-year-old Andrew, with half-understood explanations about Father Christmas, went to bed as we erected the tree, still a sober green, in our sitting-room. When Andrew came downstairs on Christmas morning there was the tree all light and sparkle and colour, with enticing parcels piled at its foot – I shall never forget his expression of incredulous wonder – it was pure childhood magic. I don't know what we would have done without the German prisoners-of-war, it was impossible to buy anything in the shops, but given wood and tools and bits of material, they managed to produce all kinds of marvels, including a musical merry-go-round for Richard, and a bright red sledge for Andrew. And then, traditionally, heavy snow fell round about, and night frost made it suitably crisp and even – perfect for sledging up and down among the hillocks of the common.

In January John returned to Oriel. I was unhappy to see him go, especially as our sexual problems remained unresolved, but I knew that he had to go. He plunged straight in. He preached a sermon in chapel calling for 'all out Christianity', for the spirit of the early Christians who were ready to turn the world upside down for Christ; he preached a revolution, one of peace, and brotherhood and love, a revolution of and through the Churches, and he invited his hearers to come to his rooms afterwards for coffee. A small group arrived, a little Christian fellowship, and from then on they met regularly once a week in term time. As always, John began gently, asking each one to talk first about his own experiences and ideas. They were a mixed bunch, some who had been too young to fight and were still in their teens, some ex-service men, theological and medical students exempt from military service, and one or two pacifists; later they were joined by Nonconformists and one Roman Catholic; freed from the constraints of Service regulations, John wanted anything he did to be fully ecumenical. So first of all, John listened, before speaking at all about his own experiences. Gradually he led the group, as well as deepening their own spiritual lives, to begin to look outwards to the college, to the university and beyond. He fired them with the belief that not only was there work to be done at the national level, but that, armed with their faith, it was work that they could do.

In the Senior Common Room, John was, said his colleagues, his lively and amusing self, even more argumentative, even more agin authority, but still a man you couldn't help liking. John took over the newly created post of domestic bursar, which meant that he had responsibility for the college staff. When he examined their conditions he found them, in his view, poorly paid, and expected to work far too long hours; so he persuaded the fellows to agree to various changes – he even suggested that, for their own protection, the college servants should join a trades union. Later he introduced a Christmas party for them and their wives and children, and, more revolutionary, a Christmas dinner at which the fellows' wives were invited with their husbands to dine at the High Table, a holy of holies to which they had never before been admitted; Oxford recognised academic women – just – but mere wives had no standing at all.

By the end of his first term at Oriel John was still uncertain about how to proceed; prayer and discussion within his little group seemed to rise to a climax that never quite came, but there was enough enthusiasm and response there to believe that the way forward would somehow be illumined. So John returned to Brill bringing with him another book. This was *Adam and Eve* by John Middleton Murry; it was not at all the kind of book that John would normally have bought. It was a well-written, well-argued attack upon the teaching of the Christian Churches about sex, a passionate rejection of any idea that sex is somehow evil and dirty. The sayings of some of the early Church fathers and supposed saints on this subject are appalling; from the story of Adam and Eve onwards, men, unable to come to terms with their own sexuality, have projected their problems on to women, the seducers, the temptresses, the feared troublemakers who must carry all the blame and be kept in subjection. The result, Middleton Murry declared, was that a young priest, in love with his wife, could be unconsciously ambivalent about the act of sex, not quite sure whether this was truly an act of creative love, or whether it was not, in some way, a concession to the weakness of the flesh. The Roman Catholic Church prohibited any kind of what it termed 'unnatural' birth control, officially it still does, and sex is only permitted in order to beget children. But sex, argued Middleton Murry, is one of the highest expressions of personal love between two human beings, and, as such, is to be mutually enjoyed in its own creative right – a far more Christian attitude and one that accepts the real and equal value of a man and woman. The effect of this upon John was dramatic, a release from lingering inhibitions of which he had barely been conscious, and our sex life flourished again. This time John's return to Oriel did not seem nearly so bleak.

At the beginning of June, another catalyst of a book arrived on the scene. This was Victor Gollancz's *Our Threatened Values*. John was immensely impressed and inspired by it, he gave copies to all his young men, and asked them to read it and think carefully about the challenge that it presented to Christians. That thinking led, in the following term, to momentous results.

When term was over we were able to have our long-postponed honeymoon in the Alps. On Harold and Yvonne's advice we chose St Luc, a tiny Swiss village halfway up a valley that led to the great jagged peaks of the Matterhorn. The journey, in a third-class French railway carriage, was something of a penance; it was crammed with French soldiers, once you had a seat you dared not leave it, even if such a thing had been physically possible, and it took a very long time as the train had to avoid unrepaired bridges and stretches of broken railway track; but we were young, discomfort meant little, excitement was all. And the station at Basle was a revelation; great trolley-loads of almost forgotten good things, unlimited chocolate, bananas, biscuits, cakes and pastries full of sugar and cream – there seemed no end to this cornucopia. At last we arrived, somewhat shaken by a drive up the valley in the local bus, round endless hairpin bends with an unfenced precipice on one side.

We walked through meadows and pine forests, and climbed surrounding mountains – nothing dangerous or precipitous – and the profusion of flowers was lovely beyond all imaginings – nowhere can there be a blue as blue as those rivulets of spring gentians that seem to pour from the melting snow. On our first Sunday, there was a local festival; a son of the village who had gone away to be trained as a priest, returned to celebrate his first Mass in his home church, an occasion for great public rejoicing. The sun shone with special brilliance; long wooden trestles and benches were set up in the main village street, all decorated with wild flowers from the forests and mountains, men and girls wore their best, traditional dress, there was food and wine for the whole village young and old, and for any wandering visitors like ourselves. Eating and singing and drinking, especially drinking, went on the whole afternoon, and, with dancing, into the evening – a golden dream of Arcadia after the darkness of war. And if, after nine months, some new little human creatures appeared in the village how could anyone wonder, or anyone be blamed?

20

A Call to Christian Action

A T the beginning of October, we moved into a small college house in Oxford. John had arranged to go away on a retreat during the period of our move, but I took such a poor view of this that he abandoned it (right or wrong again?). Number 6 Oriel Street was a real town house, tall and narrow, but large enough for us, and only just across the road from the college, so that John could, at least, sleep at home. At one end Oriel Street opens out into a wide area that separates Oriel from Christ Church, and beyond are Christ Church meadows; the other end leads into the High Street opposite St Mary's, the university church, its tall elegant spire beautifully framed in the exit of the narrow street. I was happy; at last our own house, furnished with our own belongings.

John was now absorbed in his work and his plans. *Our Threatened Values* had affected the young men as he hoped; they were all convinced that 'something must be done'. As I reread Victor's book after forty-four years, I am as moved and convinced by his basic appeal as I was so long ago. Of course, much of it is of topical, and therefore historic interest only, some of his political predictions have proved incorrect, and the Socialist dream in which so many believed, and which seemed to promise so much hope, now, in the Nineties, appears in danger of collapse. But the fundamental challenge is as valid now as it was then. For Victor, Liberal Democracy, the flower of European civilisation, is based upon one basic value: 'respect for personality'. This one 'value of values' includes all others, equality before the law, equality of opportunity, freedom of speech and all the hallmarks of a true democracy. It is a recognition of 'the essential spiritual equality of all human beings including ourselves'. 'Love your neighbour as *yourself*'. The real test of such respect must be in the way in which we treat our enemies, those who have failed to respect us. Victor, determined to push any argument to its extreme limit, insists that it is precisely the *worst* evil-doer, the *most* depraved sadist, who is most in need of respect, forgiveness and love. Sadly, he overestimated the ability of governments and people to rise to and sustain the heights of behaviour that he demanded, but he did not overestimate the ardent idealism among the young, nor the abundant springs of compassion and generosity in the public at large.

Victor was not content only to write, he took action. He founded 'Save Europe Now'. This was to press the government to send more food to Germany, even at the cost of a cut in our own rations, and to allow individuals to send their own food parcels. It was to campaign for international action to prevent further expulsions, which were causing untold hardship, sickness and death, and it was to take up the cause of the prisoners-of-war still held in Britain in defiance of the Geneva Convention. By the spring of 1946 'Save Europe Now' had received more than 100,000 offers of support. John was eager to assist Victor in this campaign, and did his best to drum up support in the college and the university; this was a cause that demanded action by Christians, and he was easily able to share his concern with the undergraduates. The Oriel Fellowship continued to meet weekly for prayer and discussion, and since they had taken *Our Threatened Values* to heart, they resolved to organise a public meeting 'A Call to Christian Action in Public Affairs'. John had had some experience of meetings in the RAF, but this was a different, and much more demanding affair, the kind of public platform of which he had, as yet, no experience.

The Oriel men undertook to make contacts throughout the university, and soon there was a group of around 100 undergraduates ready to help, and they began to spread out into the parishes and the town. John made friends with the local Press, and enlisted Dick Milford, vicar of the university church, and the theologian Donald Mackinnon to assist him in preparing a leaflet for the meeting.

There was a theological preamble, an affirmation of God's providence and concern in human history, and a recognition of Christians' total failure to translate their principles into political action.

Those present were to be asked to commit themselves to two resolutions. The first of these was that 'There must be a large increase in the number of committed Christians actively engaged in public life, and Church life must become an example of the application of Christian principles to everyday practical life'. Then followed four suggestions as to how this resolution might be implemented. These included participation in various democratic structures, pressure on the government and the formation of active Christian fellowships within the Churches. The second resolution was more specific: 'In view of the special dangers which arise at this time in connexion with our recently defeated enemies we urge the leaders of the Churches to press the Government for a more Christian policy towards Germany'. This was spelled out in practical terms. Individuals were to consider voluntary service on the Continent, and the Churches were to promote fellowship with German Christians and Churches. The call to Christian Action meant what it said, and was not to be just a general exhortation to virtuous behaviour. In order to emphasise this, and make clear to those who attended the meeting that they were expected to take on an active commitment, copies of the leaflet were distributed by undergraduates throughout the university and the city parishes.

College chaplains and theologians looked somewhat askance at all this activity. Oxford had an eighteenth-century attitude to 'enthusiasm', it was considered vulgar and unintellectual, unsuited to the detached academic ethos of a university. And there was a sizeable majority everywhere that thought Christians should not, under any circumstances, 'interfere in politics'. But the enthusiasm was there, and would not be dampened.

The meeting was fixed for 5 December at eight-fifteen p.m., in the Town Hall. The speakers were lined up: the Bishop of Chichester in the chair, Sir Richard Acland to propose the first resolution; Roger Wilson, ex-secretary of the Friends' Relief Organisation in Europe to follow, Barbara Ward, a distinguished Roman Catholic, and Victor Gollancz to speak to the second resolution. It was to be fully ecumenical and inter-party. In spite of John's well-known Socialist views, he managed to enlist the support of town and university Conservative organisations. All this preparation involved a great deal of time, and John's college commitments began to suffer; his wife began to suffer too. I felt more and more peripheral, I would have liked to have been able to take part in the preliminary discussions, but Oriel was a male enclave; had I been an undergraduate I might perhaps have slipped in to the Fellowship, but as a wife there seemed no way in which I might attend. And John only came back late at night and exhausted. Not surprisingly, he was unable to manage his life and his diary, try as I might to help. One Saturday afternoon, I decided that I must scrub the kitchen floor, and dressed myself in my oldest, dirtiest clothes. But John had invited a venerable professor and his wife to tea, and had forgotten to tell me anything about it; I hope I rose adequately to the occasion. We had other troubles too with social engagements, three times we failed to visit another couple, as John had forgotten the arrangements – that was a particularly embarrassing situation. It became more and more evident that he would have to have a secretary, but secretaries have to live, and must be paid, however minimally. We were lucky to find an enthusiast for John's ideas, but we had somehow to guarantee her a salary, and there was the cost of the printing and publicity as well. John and I decided that we personally had to take the financial risk, and hope that a successful meeting would generate enough money to cover at least some of the expenses.

There were last-minute complications. The Bishop of Chichester insisted that the meeting must begin with prayer, but there would be prominent Roman Catholics on the platform, and they were not permitted to join in prayer with other denominations. As so often, the Quakers came to our rescue, and suggested that there could be no objection to silent prayer. John, not to be defeated, made a special journey to Birmingham to plead with the presiding Roman Catholic archbishop. He returned triumphant: silent prayer could be followed by the Lord's Prayer in which all might join.

By the evening of 5 December, John, always prone to short-term pessimism, especially about the weather, was in despair. It was the end of term, everyone was tired, satiated with meetings and activities, the weather was terrible. It was bitterly cold, a penetrating wind swept round every corner, driving an evil mixture of rain and sleet – whoever would want to turn out on such a night to listen to a bunch of Christians?

By six-thirty p.m., a queue had already begun to form outside the Town Hall, and by eight o'clock it was packed to capacity; hundreds were still waiting in the icy rain. Dick Milford hastily and helpfully offered the large university church just down the road for an overflow meeting; the unfortunate speakers having to shuttle between the two buildings and deliver their speeches twice. The church was soon filled to overflowing, and there were still many who had to be disappointed – at least 3,000 people had turned out, hoping to attend the meeting.

The Bishop of Chichester opened proceedings, and Richard Acland followed with a characteristically rousing speech. We needed, he said 'a religious transformation . . . greater and deeper than that which took place at the beginning of the fifteenth century . . . our responsibility is to deal with the revolutionary age in which we live . . .' His speech was a forceful plea for a responsible, participatory democracy, an appeal to all to share in 'the arduous, exacting, humdrum tasks upon which even relatively good government depends'. He exhorted Christians to abandon their 'almost pathological prejudice against party politics . . . If you keep out of every sphere in which your principles are liable to be compromised, you'll keep out of everything except the grave.' Roger Wilson followed with an appeal for a revival of personal integrity. The most terrible feature of his experience in the work of famine relief in Europe had been to witness the complete collapse of men's confidence in one another.

Victor Gollancz had paid a six-week visit to Germany. He described starvation, the pitiful struggle of life among the ruins, children without shoes, without clothes, babies born into the world with no provision for their most elementary needs, patients in hospitals in agony for lack of drugs, lack of penicillin which was all reserved for the treatment of gonorrhoea, lack of toilet necessities including sanitary towels – Victor was determined to dot every i and cross every t. He ended with a passionate declaration that the world could only be saved by the practice of mercy, reconciliation and love.

Barbara Ward, a brilliant speaker, was able to sustain the high pitch of the meeting. She took up Victor's challenge in regard to British policy towards Germany and other needy countries. 'When the history of our times comes to be written,' she said, 'one of the most remarkable facts that will stand out will be that the man who did most to rouse the conscience of England in regard to its treatment of the Germans should have been, not a Christian, but a Jew.'

The two resolutions were carried unanimously, and as John rose to wind up the meeting, the Reverend Howard Guinness, chaplain to the Oxford pastorate, leaped to his feet and begged everyone who was in a position to do so to send parcels of rationed food to Germany. 'Let's stand up and show we are really in earnest,' he cried. 'I'll be the first.' And some 1,000 people stood up and pledged their intention to make this small act of self-denial.

I hate to think how many meetings I have attended in my life, this was the first, and in many ways and in spirit the most remarkable. The speakers were outstanding, but it was the mood of eager anticipation in that youthful audience that seemed to lift them all to heights of unusual eloquence. And the audience was not one of innocent idealistic young men full of Utopian illusions: many were ex-Service men, and those too young or ineligible to fight would have known loss, fear and disruption of family life. There was no one there who would not, in some degree, have been scarred by six years of war.

John was not alone, that night, in feeling a change in his life. I certainly shared that feeling with him, and there were many who responded in similar fashion. There were young men and women who went on to devote their energies to the deprived and afflicted of the world; men who joined the ordained ministry and carried the experience into their parishes and work overseas, and some became important leaders, Bishop Hugh Montefiore, for instance, and an ex-Service man called Robert Runcie who told me, years later, how impressed and inspired he had been.

21

Post-war Reconciliation

O N 17 December we moved to another college house. Bartlemas is
about a mile up the Cowley Road, opposite what was then the
Regal Cinema, now a bingo hall. A small lane leads off the main road,
and quickly takes you out of the twentieth century. There is an attractive old farmhouse on your left, and on your right a long beech hedge.
Some way further on a little wooden gate opens through the hedge to
Bartlemas.

The moment I saw the house it was love at first sight. It was so
simple and dignified; it was very old, built at the beginning of the
twelfth century with rough, irregular grey stones; a long, low narrow
house with a grey-tiled roof, stone-arched doors at either end, and
plain stone-framed windows. It drew me with an air of romance, as
well as of solid and comforting security; even the stones seemed warm
and alive, nature's material, appearing in all shades of colour, flecked
with gold and green lichen, and shaped and misshaped by centuries of
wind and weather.

There was so much land around; beyond the formal garden with its
lawns and sundial and a few straight flowerbeds, was a large orchard,
and on one side of the house and garden a meadow of rough grass;
stretching away at the back were spacious green swards of the college
playing fields; while tall trees on the boundaries preserved us from
sight or sound of the city. Where orchard and garden met stood a small
chapel, built with the same dignified simplicity and the same rough
grey stones as the house; inside it was unostentatious, light and
beautiful, and here was celebrated the Mass of St Bartholomew, the
patron saint of lepers, hence the name Bartlemas. Chapel and house
had been built around 1125 as a leper hospital, with care for souls as
well as for stricken bodies. And this was not all: on the other side of the
lane was more land, another orchard, and a sizeable vegetable garden,
most welcome in that post-war period of shortages and rationing.

We moved in a snow storm, prelude to a very cold and very long winter, with fuel and food supplies down to a minimum, and constant electricity cuts. Bartlemas had no central heating, but it had thick walls. We just managed to keep the boiler going for hot water, and, with a few flickering gas fires we survived; our happiness kept us warm.

The Hilary term began with an upsurge of Christian and humanitarian activity throughout Oxford, and John was in the thick of it. The undergraduates decided to 'twin' with German universities and started the Oxford/Bonn Committee and the Oxford/Austria Committee; they arranged exchange visits, and an Easter vacation school. Christians worked their way into political clubs, and, inspired by Christian Action, they began to befriend the many homesick German prisoners-of-war in camps around Oxford. There were two specifically Christian Action undertakings; the collection of signatures to a petition for the speedy repatriation of German PoWs, to be presented to the government, and plans for a summer school for teachers from Germany and from our wartime allies. Enthusiasm among the senior members of the university did not quite match that of the undergraduates, but John did succeed in forming from among them 'The Oxford Committee for promoting friendship and understanding with Europe'. John was co-opted, by Victor, on to the Committee of Save Europe Now, which gained much extra support, as did the Oxford Famine Relief Organisation (Oxfam), recently founded by Cecil Jackson-Cole, a remarkable Quaker philanthropist. And of course John did not forget the Fellowship: he wrote them pastoral letters, as well as many personal ones, he arranged one or two small meetings, and undertook to organise a full-scale convention to be held in Oriel over the Easter weekend, when they could discuss their future.

Christian Action needed to be something more than a one-man show, with a small office in Oriel. John got together a committee, with Lord Lindsay of Balliol and the mayor of Oxford as joint presidents, and Lady Pakenham (now Lady Longford), Quintin Hogg (now Lord Hailsham) and Sir David Ross, provost of Oriel, as vice-presidents; they represented the three political parties and three Christian denominations. Later John persuaded Lord Halifax (Conservative), the Earl of Perth (Liberal), and Sir Stafford Cripps (Labour), to become patrons. He found Edward Colegrove, a city councillor as treasurer, for the almost non-existent funds, and set up a finance committee joined, among others, by Jackson-Cole, who gave invaluable advice. Then there was a rather loose committee of advisors, which included much sympathetic help from the Roman Catholic master of Campion Hall, Father Thomas Corbishley SJ.

John did, of course, have numerous college and chapel duties to which
to attend; students to supervise, lectures on the New Testament to
prepare and deliver. Somehow he also managed to put together a
synopsis of lectures on the Acts of the Apostles interpreted in the light of
his experiences at Yatesbury; these he submitted for the prestigious
Bampton lectures, but they were turned down; he had been too long
away from the academic world.

Since Christian Action had spilled out of the colleges into the town,
there were things in which I could share. We lived in a whirlwind of
activity fanned by much innocent hope and faith, and, I believe, some
genuine charity as well – this was to be the pattern of our lives for more
than thirty years. Whoever thought that life married to a clergyman
might be boring? True, I did sometimes feel that I didn't see enough of
John, Christian Action took him too much from home. During term-
time, he usually dined in college, which was pleasant for him, and a help
to family rations. Nanny and I had to make do with dried egg, soup or
the occasional tin of snoek, a particularly unpleasant fish imported in
large quantities from South Africa. I did try whale meat on the family,
but it was so oily it made us feel sick.

We had no car, but John said he was happy to bicycle home to spend
nights with his wife, even though he had to return early to Oriel to take
the daily eight a.m. Communion service. He enjoyed dinner in Hall,
especially when they had interesting visitors and lively discussions; at
other times he would tell me about particularly amusing evenings, and
would recount some of the jokes and anecdotes. The trouble was that I
was never able to find these at all funny; after comparing notes with my
fellow wives, I discovered that they too were equally unamused by
similar accounts of their husbands' 'amusing' evenings.

With spring and early summer, Bartlemas revealed its treasures –
daffodils round the sundial, blossom in the orchards, a wonderfully
scented syringa by the chapel door, and in our rough meadow an
unexpected delight, a wide area of closely growing moon-daisies;
white-petalled and golden-hearted, Bartlemas daisies were, it seemed,
famous, they were so spectacular that local people took walks up the lane
just to gaze at them. Later we had roses, and all along the front of the
house fairy-tale hollyhocks that grew right up to the bedroom
windows. The boys could run around freely and safely, and we found an
excellent school for Andrew, where he seemed entirely happy. Before
long we had hens in the orchard across the lane – no more dried egg – and
fresh vegetables from the garden. We were in paradise.

We were, of course, exceptionally fortunate. But the economic state of the country was getting worse rather than better, rationing of food, clothing and household goods was more stringent even than during the war years. Unreal expectations of the ease and pleasure of victory gave way to grumbling discontent. In order to rally morale, a National Day of Prayer and Dedication was called.

The Archbishop of Canterbury, Geoffrey Fisher, thought that the Church should produce some guidance for the nation, so he wrote to John suggesting that he prepare a pamphlet which, if suitable, would be published anonymously. Fisher had sent a message of support to the Oxford Town Hall meeting, and had, doubtless, received reports about it.

John consulted a number of friends, chief among them, Richard Acland, who came to stay with us. Together, with a few snippets from me, they produced *A Call to National Prayer – a Christian Response*. The pamphlet attempted to address the problem 'How can we achieve justice without sacrificing freedom in a modern technological society?' 'Justice' for John and Richard had to include a reasonably equitable share of the national cake and an acceptance that Britain ought not to pursue its own material interests to the detriment of the poorer nations of the world. 'A society which functions efficiently, which satisfies basic material needs, and by its justice commands the loyalty and willing co-operation of all classes, and which is based upon the widest possible measure of individual freedom and personal responsibility.' That was how John saw it, over-ambitious and idealistic perhaps, but still a noble human aspiration, and certainly a continuing human problem. Geoffrey Fisher seemed reasonably happy and wrote a cautious foreword. The pamphlet received enthusiastic comment in the secular and religious press, but, of course, nobody knew who had actually written it.

John had now to turn his attention to preparations for the teachers' summer school. The party arrived about the middle of July, thirty Germans, five Norwegians, three Dutch, two French, men and women, Catholic and Protestant, all Christians and all English speaking. The two-week programme included lectures by academics, visits to local schools, to Stratford-on-Avon for a performance of *Romeo and Juliet*, and to London to the Houses of Parliament to see parliamentary democracy in action.

For the first few days, the visitors were put up in a hostel so that they could get to know one another; they then separated into ones or twos to stay with families in Oxford; we had two Germans to stay at Bartlemas. Wartime passions still ran high, and this risky undertaking could have been a disaster. Interestingly, the teachers from the Allied countries had all been members of their respective resistance movements, and one of the French girls, a particularly impressive person, had spent eighteen months in Ravensbruck concentration camp.

Everyone was urged to take the opportunity to give voice to resentments and bitterness, to speak of the concentration camps, the Holocaust, the bombing, the destruction of German industry. It was a remarkable experiment in Christian reconciliation, and it was remarkably successful.

At the beginning of September, John was invited by Lord Pakenham, the minister responsible, to visit the British zone of occupied Germany for two weeks. He was shocked by conditions. 'To see Cologne', he wrote, 'is, I think, to assure oneself of the wickedness of our mass raids on other than factory areas'. The plight of the homeless residents was exacerbated by some 100,000 'official' expellees from the East and hundreds of illegal refugees arriving daily. The situation was made worse, and the people more embittered, by the fact that so much undamaged housing was requisitioned for the British Army and the Control Commission. Everyone dreaded the winter and the food shortage.

John's contacts were mainly with the Churches, and those involved in education. In Bonn, the dean of the Faculty of Medicine spoke of anxieties about the health of the students, the rate of malignant TB had doubled since 1945, and starvation was having a mental effect on the young. Everywhere John heard pleas for the return of the PoWs; to suggestions that the men might only add to the food crisis, all said that they wanted their men home and would gladly share their meagre rations. The policy of destroying undamaged factories seemed more and more crazy, not only Germany, but the whole world was desperately short of commodities, and the Germans were being told that they would shortly have to pay for their own imports. There was even a threat to blow up air-raid shelters, now 'homes' for many of the homeless, because such shelters were regarded as affairs of war. At Kiel John was shown the buildings and factories due for demolition, and again he saw the appalling living conditions, some 200,000 refugees in the area – in one case 148 people crowded into one house. At Düsseldorf John was given an introduction to life in the bunkers affecting some 60,000 people. He saw a widow with five children, two out at work bringing in only 25 marks a week each (there were 40 marks to £1), there was 'no gas, no electricity, holes in the walls and roof, hardly a stick of furniture – the woman had no shoes and her youngest child aged 4 no shoes and no clothes, just a pair of breeches and pullover donated, against the rules, by a kind-hearted British major – yet somehow', John said, 'the place was as clean as a new pin'.

His last port of call was Berlin, where he stayed with Robert Birley, the head of the education work of the British Control Commission; that was a happy meeting, and 'Red Robert' was destined to cross our paths in other connections. John had been wondering what, beyond increasing material help to Germany, Christian Action could do to further the work of reconciliation. On a sudden impulse John decided that he would invite the Berlin Philharmonic Orchestra for a tour of Great Britain. Robert Birley arranged for him to meet the secretary of the orchestra, and its regular conductor Sergiu Celibidache. When John put the proposal to them, both men wept. Celibidache said, 'Germany has done evil things to Europe. But our music is at least one small reparation we could make towards the rebuilding of a happier world . . .' The invitation was received with enthusiasm by the whole orchestra; Dr Wilhelm Furtwängler would come to conduct a few concerts, as well as Celibidache, and all would play without fee or salary; profits from the tour would go to relief and reconstruction in Europe.

John returned more determined than ever to continue the work of Christian Action for Germany. Against the background of physical hunger, homelessness and misery, he was aware of a desperate and dangerous spiritual hunger. But work could not continue without money. John's finance committee were appalled by his invitation to the Berlin Philharmonic Orchestra – a wonderful idea, but how could such a risky venture possibly be financed? John was determinedly hopeful. He persuaded the Oxford churches to donate all their collections to a 'Christian Action Sunday', and for the same day he booked the Sheldonian Theatre for a meeting. Quintin Hogg agreed to take the chair, and Victor Gollancz was billed as the main speaker.

Victor made a gargantuan speech on the implications for British policy towards Germany of the Christian imperatives of love, forgiveness and reconciliation. 'To proclaim that the Sermon on the Mount is the word of God, and then to explain it away by all sorts of ingenious devices seems to me, not to put too fine a point on it, rather contemptible humbug,' he thundered. Victor's masterly exegesis was intended to make professing Christians squirm, and it did. As Victor was not a professing Christian, he didn't have to squirm in the same way.

It was unquestionably a magnificent and moving speech, later published as a pamphlet, *On Reconciliation*, and dedicated to John. But as a speech it was far, far too long, people began to slip away, and there was no time for a proper financial appeal. John had, however, prepared and distributed leaflets with a list of practical activities in which anyone could participate, and these got a good response.

Towards the end of February 1948 Lord Pakenham asked John whether he would organise an Albert Hall meeting to rally Christians to a positive conception of Churchill's idea of a Western European Union. John and I supported this movement, and John was well aware of the spiritual vacuum in Europe, and the threat of a Communist takeover. But he was reluctant to undertake such an official government-sponsored meeting, and he did not wish to lead Christian Action into the negative position of a purely anti-Communist crusade. Under pressure from Lord Halifax and Stafford Cripps, he finally agreed, provided the meeting was set in the context of a general call to Christian responsibility and action.

Stafford Cripps was Chancellor of the Exchequer, so he invited John to stay at 11 Downing Street, and put an office and a secretary at his disposal.

There were only four weeks of the Easter vacation in which to fill the Albert Hall; it was hard work and austere living. From six-twenty to seven-thirty a.m. John and Stafford walked round St James's Park, the only time they could talk without interruption. The Crippses were teetotallers and vegetarians, not to John's taste, but he had a high regard and affection for both Stafford and Isobel. Unlike his public image, Stafford was a man of great personal charm, humour and warmth. Isobel was even more warm-hearted, and was apt to rush off enthusiastically after any new cult or guru, anything that would now be labelled 'alternative'.

The Albert Hall was filled, and could have been filled twice over: four thousand applications for tickets had to be refused. Lord Halifax was in the chair, and the platform was heavy with notables, both lay and ecclesiastical. Attlee sent a message, as did Sir Winston Churchill, who said: 'The unification of Europe assuredly offers immense material advantages, and may also be the main road to the peace and future of the world. All those hopes will come to naught unless the structure of the new Europe is built firmly upon more spiritual foundations . . .'

As well as four British speakers, distinguished persons came from Holland, Sweden, Belgium and Italy. Our old friend André Philipe came from France, and Germany was represented by Karl Arnold

(Roman Catholic), Minister President of North Rhine Westphalia, who had been involved in the 1944 plot against Hitler, and Dr Adolf Grimme (Protestant), who had worked in the underground resistance and had served five years in a prison camp. The first appearance of Germans and Frenchmen together on a public platform was a signal of hope.

There were fine speeches, messages of vision and of hope, but all inevitably general, and mostly too long. Stafford spoke last, his concluding words are inscribed beneath his memorial bust in St Paul's Cathedral: 'If man neglects the things of the spirit and puts aside the full armour of God, he will seal the doom of future generations.'

Back in Oxford, a question arose about our, or rather John's, future. The Archbishop of Canterbury asked him to become General Secretary of the British Council of Churches. This, John said, must be considered seriously; I, of course, didn't want to consider it at all.

I think one must admire Geoffrey Fisher for making an offer, which many might have felt to be something of a risk. Fisher was impressed by what he had seen of John's ability, energy and powers of organisation, also by his consistent commitment to an ecumenical movement and to social action; but he must have realised that this was a man of independent character, who would want to go his own way, and who would find it difficult to be bound by authority. For John the offer was something of a turning point. In some ways it looked like a suitable outlet for someone with his convictions, but he had misgivings. How much freedom of action would he have? How far would he be answerable to committees, embroiled in conflicting interests? He went to talk to the archbishop, who was friendly and clearly anxious for John to accept the post. From a personal point of view, it would be a move into the ecclesiastical establishment, and John was still an ecclesiastical insider, he wanted to work through the Church to which he had, or hoped he had, given his life. The outgoing secretary was not encouraging, not much scope for initiative, he said, not much hope of making the organisation alive and effective – perhaps this had to be taken with a pinch of salt, as the man in question was old and tired, but one or two friends, whose opinions John valued, were uncertain. Such a job would certainly mean the end of Christian Action, as an independent movement. There were material considerations: a considerable drop in salary and we would once again be homeless, houses in London were expensive and in extremely short supply, and we were on the way to adding to our family. John put these considerations second; I, rather anxiously, put them first.

We decided to stay in Oxford: Geoffrey Fisher was sympathetic, but genuinely disappointed. I was, of course, enormously relieved, and John was increasingly convinced that he had made the right decision.

22

Bartlemas, Goodbye

I slipped back into the sunlight of Bartlemas, and the contentment of pregnancy. John was busy with college duties, with preparations for the visit of the Berlin Philharmonic Orchestra, and with the fall-out from the Albert Hall meeting. Letters, letters; they poured in, more than two thousand of them from all over England and from abroad; general and vague as the message may have been, it seemed to have touched a need. There was an atmosphere of crisis in the aftermath of war; there were hopes and expectations, but there was fear and uncertainty as well; a real fear that Russia, now in occupation of the whole of Eastern Europe would continue to advance westwards. The hope of the new United Nations, was, to say the least, uncertain and wavering.

Suggestions for action, appeals for help, small groups needing a speaker, too many demands, too many possibilities, these continued to arrive at the Christian Action office, but there was very little money, and only the sketchiest organisation. John was reasonably clear about the way in which he hoped Christian Action might develop. He was determined not to set up yet another top-heavy organisation, he wanted it to remain personal and flexible, with a minimum of administration. He hoped for small 'cells' of Christians over the country, inspired by the idea of Christian Action and tackling local problems, working, as far as possible, through existing organisations. There were a few signs that this might already be happening. A small national executive at the centre would co-ordinate and communicate, produce literature, and from time to time suggest particular objects of Christian concern around which all could unite; reconciliation with Germany and European unity were two such particulars. John was anxious to retain the support of the different denominations and different political affiliations; in the end he was more successful with the denominations than with the politics.

Other things were moving in the great metropolis. In February

Canon Alexander of St Paul's Cathedral had died. He was a sad and lonely old man, his wife had died many years earlier, and he seemed to have no relatives. His chapter colleagues did not love him, they were tired of his autocratic ways, and they concocted a plot to remove him from the influential post of chapter treasurer when the annual review of what are called the greater offices of the cathedral came round. The chapter treasurer held a senior position, and Alexander was the senior canon, so the only hope was to persuade the dean to accept the treasurership. This was unusual, but the dean too found Alexander increasingly difficult, so he agreed, and together they voted the old man out. Alexander was heartbroken, no longer did he have any effective position in the cathedral, he turned his face to the wall, and died soon after. His only friend during those last lonely weeks was the young cathedral registrar, David, now Sir David, Floyd Ewin. He visited the old man daily, and did what he could for him. Just before he died Alexander said to Ewin: 'There is only one man I would like to succeed me in the canonry, and that is John Collins'.

There were other, more influential people, who had the same idea. Stafford was anxious for Christian Action to become a nationwide movement; he had a vision of a Christian Socialist Britain, combining social justice and personal freedom, a positive and Christian alternative to Communism. Christian Action, led by John, might help to pioneer the way, but for that to happen, the movement must have a headquarters in London. So he approached Attlee about the vacant canonry.

As soon as Geoffrey Fisher heard about it, he wrote disapprovingly to Attlee: John would not be an easy member of the chapter, he would concern himself too much with interests outside the cathedral; Dr Wand, Bishop of London, was strongly opposed to such an appointment; nobody consulted the St Paul's chapter, a fact that greatly annoyed the dean. Attlee sent Fisher a spirited reply; in his view John was a man of character, energy and active mind, he was a good scholar, and had shown considerable administrative ability; as an RAF chaplain, he had done remarkable work of which he, Attlee, had had personal experience; John would be a good and lively addition to the chapter. Perhaps to mollify the archbishop, and since this was technically a Crown appointment, Attlee took the unusual step of consulting the Palace. No objection was forthcoming, so on 25 June, he wrote to John saying that he wished to put his name before the Crown for nomination to the vacant canonry at St Paul's.

This offer coincided with the birth of our son Peter; not the best moment for me to face such a prospect. I was appalled by the thought of uprooting our little family from these lovely surroundings, and taking them to that dark dismal house in the heart of the City; I had never, never wanted to live in London, and nothing that John had ever told me about St Paul's had made me want to go there. John was divided; we were so entirely happy at Bartlemas but he was committed to Christian Action, and was finding it increasingly difficult to combine with his college responsibilities; in his heart he was drawn to St Paul's. The pros and cons went to and fro as we talked and talked. Isobel Cripps wrote me a long and sympathetic letter, all about the difficulties of being married to a man with a vision – oh dear, those difficulties seemed to go on and on – but the upshot was that wives had to follow, and, in the end, the rewards were great. The little chapel was our haven of peace and we spent much time in it together and singly; quietly, gently, Bartlemas paraded its summer beauties. We decided that we could not leave, could not deprive our children of their healthy open-air life, of all that Oxford could offer them, including a choice of excellent day schools within easy reach. John wrote a letter to Attlee refusing an offer of the canonry; and we went to bed intending to post the letter in the morning.

But in the morning I knew that that letter could never be posted. I did genuinely believe in everything that John was trying to do; I could not refuse to follow where it led. Although John had not pushed his own wishes, I knew that they were there. I knew too that John no longer belonged, if he ever really had, in the theological ivory tower of Oxford or Cambridge; he had studied and speculated with the best of them; now he had to act. So he wrote another letter to Attlee, saying that he would be prepared to accept the canonry should it be offered him. On 30 July, the appointment was confirmed.

It could have been worse; John would stay at Oriel until Christmas, and take up his new duties on 1 January. Number 2 Amen Court was in a state of complete dilapidation – it had electricity on the ground floor only – and it would take a long time before it could be got ready for a family; meanwhile we could stay at Bartlemas until the end of the summer of 1949.

Arrangements for the tour of the Berlin Philharmonic Orchestra now absorbed John. Mrs Emmie Tillet, of Ibbs and Tillet, took over the organisation and the risks, and a friend of Stafford's offered a bank guarantee of £5,000 for initial expenses. Bureaucratic obstacles and delays were hideous, from the Home Office, the Foreign Office, the Control Commissions, the Russians and the Americans. No sooner were these surmounted, than there was trouble with the musicians' union, who were in dispute with the BBC, and would allow no broadcasting of the concerts, the fees for which were essential. This was settled, all permissions finally given, and the tour was arranged for early November.

Then the worst blow fell, the Russians blockaded Berlin, and it looked as if we might never get the orchestra out. John refused to give up hope. As soon as the Allied airlift got under way, he suggested that the orchestra might be brought out on return journeys; that was ruled out. John turned to private charter companies and found a relatively cheap Dutch firm. This the Russians vetoed. British Air brokers were ready to act, but it took days of negotiations before air and landing space were permitted.

At last all was settled, and the first concert scheduled for 3 November at seven p.m. On 1 November, John was to be formally installed as a canon of St Paul's, how appropriate it would be, he thought, for the tour to open with a concert in St Paul's. The chapter agreed, posters and programmes were printed, and then one of the canons, the archdeacon of London, had a last-minute attack of conscience. It would be immoral, he suggested, to ask people to pay for tickets in the cathedral. He bulldozed his fellow canons, who now said they could only allow the concert if no money passed hands, and they were to be reimbursed for any expenses; an impossible proposition. Mrs Tillet searched rather desperately and was at last able to book the large, gloomy Empress Hall at Earls Court.

Miraculously the orchestra arrived on 28 October. They had no music, the Russians had burned it all, and had also been responsible for the loss of their dress suits. The music, at least, could be borrowed. The first concert was a remarkable occasion, eight thousand people eager to listen to a Bach Suite in G, the 4th Beethoven Piano Concerto, and Brahms's 4th Symphony. For the concerto, John had diffidently approached Dame Myra Hess. As soon as she understood the purpose of the tour she at once agreed to play.

The impact of the evening was overwhelming. 'Dame Myra Hess's playing', said one critic, 'had a touch of the crusader's fire'. Another wrote: 'Scarcely anyone in that vast audience can have remained unmoved at the visible symbol of reconciliation when, after a memorable performance, Dame Myra Hess and Wilhelm Furtwängler stood to receive the applause hand in hand . . . this was not only a notable occasion, but a gesture on behalf of all who preach the Gospel of peace.'

Wherever they went the orchestra were received with friendly enthusiasm and tumultuous applause. Ill luck dogged them at the end, when they were held up in Hamburg in thick fog for an extra six days at extra cost. But in every respect other than financially, the tour did all that was hoped for it, a wonderful spirit was engendered by all those marvellous concerts, and the financial loss was small.

When it came to saying goodbye to Oriel John felt really sad, and Oriel seemed sad to lose him. There were plenty of criticisms that could be levelled against him, but he had a way of disarming his critics. Christopher Seton-Watson remembered him standing in front of the fire in the Senior Common Room and saying, 'I've been a bloody fool haven't I, go on say so, I know I have'. And Seton-Watson remarked on 'the peculiar mixture of astonishment, admiration, exasperation and affection that John was able to inspire', and that was the mixture that he went on inspiring to the end of his life.

For the first part of 1949 John and I led a strange backwards and forwards life. He took up his cathedral duties in January, and rigged up a small study in 2 Amen Court. We bought two beds and put them on the bare boards of what would be our bedroom, and here we camped when John had to be resident at St Paul's. His introduction to the cathedral was not entirely happy. He looked forward to his first chapter meeting, but the subject under discussion which took up most of the time, and was to continue for some eighteen months, revolved round a dispute between the archdeacon and the senior canon as to which of them should take precedence on public occasions, who should walk in the senior position in ecclesiastical processions.

The annual chapter dinner takes place at the end of January, and important City personages are invited as guests; by custom, any newly appointed canon has to speak for the chapter. On this occasion John listened to speech after fulsome speech, an evening of mutual back-scratching and self-congratulation far removed from the reality of chapter and cathedral life. By the time it came for him to speak his frustration boiled over. 'As a dog returns to its vomit so have I returned to St Paul's,' he began. When John's emotions were roused he didn't always choose the most felicitous of expressions. He went on to speak, not very tactfully, of the darker side of cathedral life, he recalled his friend, Dick Sheppard, who had been so unhappy as a canon, who had said, 'those cold, cold stones, they crush to death all that is human in the place' – 'Unless we can bring the cold stones of St Paul's to life, we might as well hand the place over to secular authority as a national monument to a dead past,' John concluded. This was not the kind of speech his audience was expecting, or was accustomed to, and senior guests and ecclesiastics were duly offended. 'His speech suggested that we were a lot of lazy has-beens', said the unfortunate dean. But in spite of ruffled feathers, John's colleagues remained friendly, and their wives wrote me welcoming and helpful letters. 'If you want to be happy at St Paul's,' said Mrs Matthews, 'you must learn to love it'. She did indicate that she had never quite achieved this herself.

John threw himself energetically into cathedral duties. He was installed as chancellor, and as such was responsible for the library. The greater offices were the treasurer, who was responsible for the cathedral 'treasures' and for the floor of the cathedral which included the virgers (that is St Paul's spelling) and the body of voluntary wandsmen who help on Sundays and special occasions. The precentor was responsible for the music and the choir. It was the chapter treasurer, that wielder of power and influence, who was responsible for the cathedral finances.

The library was dusty and forgotten, John wanted to open it up and make it a centre for scholarship. He got the chapter to agree to a paid part-time librarian, and then, by chance, he ran into a man who had a number of important sixteenth-century lay and ecclesiastical manuscripts for sale. The collection included documents concerning the Armada and the Reformation, letters and drafts by Cranmer, and much else. The asking price was £16,000. With chapter backing, John persuaded the merchant bankers Morgan, Grenfell to produce an interest-free loan. He also managed to extract £1,000 from the Pilgrim Trust for the refurbishment of the library. All went well, the library was cleaned up and the manuscripts displayed. There was considerable public interest, and scholars began to arrive. It then transpired, that though authentic and valuable, the documents were much over-priced, and not all had been handed over; there were threats of litigation. In such a climate, it proved impossible to raise money to repay the loan, and the collection reverted to the bank. In his enthusiasm, John had been sadly misled.

In May we had an unexpected bonus. Stafford Cripps had been to Rome and discussed with senior Vatican officials the possibility of Anglican-Roman co-operation in the cause of a United Europe. He now wanted John to follow this up by meeting Dr Gedda, head of

Catholic Action, an organisation with aims similar to those of Christian Action. The visit had to be private and secret, not even Geoffrey Fisher was to be informed.

I couldn't resist the temptation to go as well; for both of us it would be our first visit to Italy. Ignorantly and innocently I had imagined Rome to be built of white marble, instead there was this marvellous honey-coloured city with the whole of European history spread out before us. We arrived to red carpet treatment; as well as meeting Dr Gedda, John had talks with leading moral theologians and other Vatican officials. We were looked after by an Irish monsignor, a lively and amusing character, who took us to the best restaurants, on guided tours of St Peter's, of the Vatican, and of the Catacombs, and who entertained us with accounts of how, during the war, he had helped Allied airmen and soldiers to escape.

I took a day off, and found a local bus to take me to Cassino where David was buried. It was an extraordinary experience. Cassino is – or was – a small town at the foot of the mountain on the summit of which stands the great monastery. I had never seen such a complete and eerie ruin as that haunted place. Just outside on a slope of the mountain was the Allied cemetery, row upon row upon row of graves. I was overwhelmed, not by grief or by any understandable human emotion, there could be none, the dead were completely in possession, life seemed an irrelevance, an impertinence in this huge anonymity of destruction. There was no suggestion of death as a gateway to any fuller life, nor to any possible form of reality. I experienced only nothing or nothingness; it was more than an experience, it was an almost overwhelming compulsion to become part of that total void, a vast longing simply not to be.

Later in the year I went again to Italy with my father and we found Monte Cerasole where David had fought his last battle. This was a completely different experience. We climbed all day in gentle autumn sun, up a long stony track, guided by an Italian who had been a carrier for the military, I suspect for both the Germans and the British. On the rounded summit were grasses and wild flowers, and the uncleared litter of battle, empty sardine and bully beef tins, a few empty water bottles, rotting puttees and socks, as if some careless campers had been holidaying in the sun. The mountainous land all round was marvell-ously wild and beautiful, and far away below were glints and gleams of the river Garigliano as it twisted its way to the sea. Our guide showed us where the two opposing armies had camped, as the struggle for the summit rocked to and fro.

There had been many deaths on that mountain, but the scale was human and personal; I felt sorrow and I felt anger, rage at the endless folly of human beings, of the lunacy that forced men to fight in appalling winter weather for possession of this wild and useless mountain; how could such horrors be repeated again and again and again?

John's discussions in Rome were exciting and fruitful; he and Dr Gedda produced a joint statement, an agreed basis for common action; it went, John said, further than the Malines conversations, which, to date, were as far as any meeting between Rome and Canterbury had got. The document was based on a recognition that both Churches were part of the one Catholic Church, and their common acceptance of the Apostles creed was a sufficient basis for common action. The discussions were adjourned with an agreement to meet again in July. John, always trusting, took with him no copy of the document, and when we returned to Rome there was no red carpet, important persons were unavailable, or out of town, and the document was lost. John had been ill-advised by Stafford; as soon as Geoffrey Fisher had discovered what was going on, he was furious and made representations to the Vatican, that effectively ensured the impossibility of any future discussion or co-operation. This episode was an unfortunate step in a growing rift between John and Fisher, the decline of a relationship that had begun happily and hopefully.

We returned to a last summer at Bartlemas. The sun seemed never to stop shining; it was too hot to be out at midday, but every evening we dined in the garden and drank cool white wine, until the stars came out. Everything seemed to whisper to me, 'Don't leave us, don't leave us, you love us, we love you, don't go away.' John and I paid a last sentimental visit to the Shillingford Bridge hotel, and I wrote John a love-poem; all our hopes and dreams of marriage were being magically fulfilled. 'That's the kind of poetry I like,' John said when I showed it to him. 'Is that what you really think?'

'Of course it is,' I said. And John smiled, he was a great smiler, open, expansive, almost a grin, but this was a little inner, personal smile – a smile for us.

We made the most of the perfect weather, the boys ran around brown and naked, clutching their butterfly nets and chasing the cabbage whites. We salted down runner beans, we bottled pears, stored apples, and even preserved eggs in water-glass, and Nanny made plum jam and delicious elderberry jelly; all those long forgotten houschold skills needed before the days of instant frozen food.

Then, at last, on 1 September, a sad little cavalcade set off for London.

23

No. 2 Amen Court

As soon as we arrived in London the weather broke, dark cloud cover, storm and rain followed for the next few weeks. Our four-year-old Richard, trotting along beside me on the pavement, enquired mournfully, 'Doesn't sun ever come in London Mummy?' London did seem bleak; St Paul's, though considerably damaged, towered above the ruins, devastation stretching away on all sides. But nature had been at work, gaping caverns and broken, jagged walls were colonised, rose-bay willow herb, suitably named the fire-weed, soon covered great areas, new and sometimes rare birds arrived, and found convenient nesting places, and in their busy little to-ings and fro-ings, they deposited seeds of Buddleia, fig, ragwort, wallflowers, and other shrubs and flowers; you could go for a surreal country walk from Amen Court to St Giles Cripplegate.

Amen Court had survived the flames unleashed by German bombers on 31 December 1940, it was still a small green oasis, lit at night by ancient gas lamps. On our arrival, I was told that children were allowed in the Court only between ten and eleven a.m. (Cathedral Matins) and four to five p.m. (Cathedral Evensong). I thought this an outrageous prohibition, I said I would pay no attention to it, and before long other children of canons and minor canons joined the little Collinses at play in Amen Court.

My misgivings about life at St Paul's were not only concerned with our country-bred children. It was the prospect, I wrote to John, 'of being dragged into the lobby of ecclesiastical politics. One must expect – you tell me – to find in ecclesiastical circles the same mixture of envy, malice, self-seeking, bigotry and all uncharitableness as in other walks of life, but what is so nauseating is that in so-called Christian circles it is covered up with a smug, hypocritical show of friendliness . . .'

The process of transformation was still going on inside No. 2; the top floor was for the boys, the first floor for John and me and visitors, and, running the length of the front of the house, was the elegant eighteenth-century drawing room, where poor old Alexander had once kept his coal. On the ground floor, a room, used by previous canons as a study or private chapel, was converted, without, I hope, too much desecration, into a kitchen for me, with the advantage that opposite was John's study, Alexander's capacious one-time dining room; for our eating we had to make use of the sizeable entrance lobby. The basement was the Christian Action office. Slowly I began to appreciate what a beautiful house this was, and how well suited to all that we wanted to do.

Our first secretary left to become a nun, and we were joined by Freda Nuell. As well as being a good shorthand typist and secretary, Freda had qualities that Christian Action needed, a lively mind, a lively sense of humour, and tolerance for all sorts of people, for their follies and misdemeanours – this last particularly in demand at 2 Amen Court.

Conditions in our basement would hardly have passed an official inspection, but here Freda laboured, at first with one junior typist, later with a larger staff. She worked long hours for small financial reward, and held voluntary evening sessions as well. Since John always tried to 'cram a quart into a pint pot', she had to grapple with his diary, as well as putting up with my incursions. Many and varied pastoral problems arrived in the office, and Freda dealt with them with an unsentimental sympathy; she kept the personal heart of Christian Action beating steadily.

On our return from our Roman excursions, John managed to upset his colleagues once more. He was still carried away with enthusiasm following our visits to St Peter's; so he preached a sermon suggesting that St Paul's should invite in living artists, craftsmen and dramatists, the choir should experiment with modern music, the cathedral should not be content to remain just a nineteenth-century museum. The Press picked this up, and there was much indignation. The cathedral organist threatened to resign, and before the next chapter meeting, John received a round robin from his colleagues to the effect that he was the one who ought to resign. With this in his folder, John went to chapter, and when the matter came up for discussion, he, rather melodramatically, tore the letter in pieces – a pity, I would have liked to preserve it. The furore soon died down, and John and the organist became good friends. But it took several years before the cathedral could be persuaded to open its doors to the arts.

In every way, John longed to open St Paul's to the world and its problems, to bring in the world, and take out the Christian message of hope and redemption; but for all his ideas and innovations he had first to persuade his colleagues. On one side of us, in No. 3, lived Canon Demant, a scholar and theologian; there was a kind of critical sharpness about him, the round robin demanding John's resignation had been typed on his typewriter, he did not seem at home at St Paul's, more suited to the Oxford John had left, and there he was soon translated as a professor of divinity. No. 1 housed Marcus and Claire Knight who were friendly and helpful to us both. Marcus was the senior canon, he too was a theologian. He was liberal and progressive, but he was cautious by temperament, and not a man to quarrel with anyone if he could avoid it. John puzzled his colleagues by the fact that, with all his radical views, when it came to the services and the liturgy, he was the most conservative of them all, and they didn't at all understand his affection for Canon Alexander.

Then there was the archdeacon, Oswin Gibbs-Smith, he too was disposed to be friendly, and soon came to drink sherry with John and talk about the chapter. Oswin was a politician, concerned with the diplomacy of chapter and the marshalling of votes. He had ideas – he was a practical and energetic man – but to push his ideas through he had to secure a majority of votes, especially that of the dean who, in the event of a disagreement, had the casting vote. Oswin didn't always succeed with the dean, and was not a favourite with Mrs Matthews; she would make him wait on a wooden bench just inside the deanery remarking that that was where the servants used to sit.

By a mixture of his own powers of persuasion, and the forbearance of his colleagues, John got agreement for a lunchtime series of speakers on world problems, peace, hunger, overpopulation, European unity, world government and others. The talks would be delivered from the large raised pulpit, and that was accepted, it was the best place from which to handle the cathedral's difficult acoustics. But among the speakers, John had invited Lady Megan Lloyd-George – a *woman* in the pulpit, a female presence defiling the purity of that historic male preserve, that could never be allowed! John was taken aback by the reactions of the chapter, but how could he withdraw the invitation, what would the Press have to say? His colleagues did realise that the cathedral might attract some adverse publicity, so they searched for a compromise, and after much debate, they found one. A special podium was to be erected beneath the overhanging pulpit, and Lady Megan might speak from that. My comment: 'Perhaps God won't notice her tucked away underneath'.

John was concerned to promote a coming together of the different Christian denominations, also a concern of Geoffrey Fisher who had preached a sermon suggesting an interchange of pulpits. Once again John persuaded his colleagues to allow him to experiment with the six-thirty voluntary Evensong on Sundays, and during his months in residence, he began to invite distinguished Free Churchmen to preach. This proved very successful, the whole service came to life, and there were much larger congregations than usual; the Free Churches are dedicated to the proclamation of the Word, and the preachers were impressive and sometimes brilliant. But the *Church Times* had been watching developments at St Paul's with increasing disapproval, and soon weighed heavily into the attack, refusing to report anything to do with the cathedral when John was canon-in-residence.

Nothing daunted, John got agreement for a number of leading Christian laymen to preach, the conditions being that they should all be Anglicans, and the series should be politically balanced. That presented no problems, and in January 1950, Sir Stafford Cripps preached the opening sermon. His sermon was widely and not always accurately reported, and trouble erupted. The preachings had been arranged for many months, but just prior to Stafford's appearance, the government called a snap General Election; it was widely and incorrectly assumed that John had invited him in order to make propaganda for the Labour party. Rather against my advice, John had allowed himself to be proposed for membership of the Athenaeum. His nomination attracted wide support, but as soon as reports of Stafford's sermon appeared, his main sponsor withdrew, and John was, in effect, 'blackballed', a distinction that he shared with Stafford.

John still hoped to be able to do much of his work through the cathedral, he had ideas and schemes and suggestions for money-raising, but his colleagues feared that he thought 'too big' while he felt that they thought 'too small'.

There was one piece of work that he had to perform in the course of his duties, that gave him especial pleasure. The east end of the cathedral had been badly bomb-damaged, and, as part of the reconstruction, it was decided to create a memorial chapel for the Americans who had been killed while based in Great Britain. In 1951 General Eisenhower came to hand over the Roll of Honour, and John was in charge of arrangements for the memorial service. This earned him a letter from the dean that he treasured all his life: 'I must tell you how deeply I valued your words on the telephone about the great service, and say that the service itself was perfect. I don't think in all my years here I have ever known one which was so moving and exactly right, or one in which everything went with such complete smoothness and dignity. This is due primarily to you and I shall never forget it.'

Much of John's time and energy was now devoted to Christian Action; he was determined to test his faith in wholehearted engagement in the complex problems of human living, but he still wanted the movement to have a valid theological base. At the beginning of 1949 he published a small book, *A Theology of Christian Action*, based upon three lectures he had given at Lichfield Cathedral. This little book is a distillation of John's thinking and studying, it is 'modernist' but orthodox, and still shows the influence of Loisy and of Niebuhr. Though a little dated, it stands as a clear and effective statement of a theological basis for Christian Action.

Now the basement of 2 Amen Court began humming and re-verberating with the tapping of typewriters, the ringing of door and telephone bells, and the comings and goings of people. John assembled his council, a few faithful friends from Oxford, Father Tom Corbishley, Christopher Seton-Watson and Frank Pakenham, and newcomers from London such as Leslie Paul, a writer and theologian, Howard Marshall, journalist and broadcaster, and Sir George Schuster, an industrialist, and soon we were joined by Dame Florence Hancock and Sydney Bailey, a distinguished Quaker and writer. The movement became a limited company and Stafford Cripps applied his brilliant legal mind to ensuring that it was registered as a charity. We had two treasurers, and proper accounting, and respectability was strengthened by the nomination of representatives of the Archbishop of Canterbury, the Roman Catholic Archbishop of Westminster, and the Moderator of the Free Church Federal Council.

Jackson-Cole urged the fledgling council to run a road safety campaign, 'Don't drink and drive'; from the point of view of extensive publicity, it was very successful, whether it saved any lives is another matter, perhaps things had to get worse before they could get better. Jackson-Cole was now so involved with Oxfam that he asked that his place be taken by a Quaker colleague Raymond Andrews; to Raymond he said 'John needs someone to keep an eye on him so he doesn't do anything reckless'.

Raymond approached Christian Action with detachment and caution. He was enthusiastic about the kind of things that John wanted to do, but he was suspicious of what he called 'clever-and-well-connected people who knew everybody'; he wanted to be surer of John's values and motives before committing himself fully. 'John's charm was one reason why I was quickly won over,' he wrote, 'but not, I think, the main reason. Many will tell of his charm . . . its effect on me . . . was to draw out whatever I was able to contribute, and enable me to see its importance. But it was the man behind the manner who inspired loyalty.'

On the council there was a good deal of discussion and planning, first of all for a weekend conference to be held at Oriel in April 1950, of which I have two vivid memories. The first is not pious; John had placed a 2/6d (12½p) bet on the Spring Double, and the first horse had won. The second was to race on the Saturday of the conference, and I, and once or twice John, kept slipping out to listen to the radio. In a thrilling finish, the second horse won, and John's 2/6d produced £250, which, in those pre-inflation days was wealth. I am afraid we didn't give our ill-gotten gains to the poor, or to Christian Action, we used it to take the family to Italy for a holiday.

My second memory is of a heated row. The object of the conference was to help Christians to face the 'Challenge of the Times', and John had invited Victor Gollancz to be the first and main speaker. There was nothing Victor liked more than challenging Christians on their own ground, pointing out – which is not very difficult – how far we all fall short of behaviour enjoined in the New Testament. As always, he spoke passionately and brilliantly; largely an exposition of Socialism as the only possible political affiliation for Christians, any form of Conservative capitalism was irredeemably wicked. As John was still struggling to maintain some political balance in Christian Action, this went down badly with some of the participants, and led to an increasingly angry exchange between Victor and a distinguished and, as far as John was concerned, sympathetic judge. John managed, though with some difficulty, to persuade the judge not to leave the conference immediately, and Ruth, Victor's wife, restrained him from returning the next day to continue the attack.

Victor and Ruth used to spend the week in London, and now that we were there as well, we saw more of them, and I was able to get to know them as well as John did. John was something of a disciple of Victor's, he supported his humanitarian causes with enthusiasm, and he admired the depths and sincerity of Victor's spiritual insights and struggles. Victor was a man of extremes and contradictions; the gently undulating middle ground where most of us live was not for him, his joys were more intense, his sufferings more acute than those of less sensitive mortals. He had a violent temper, and great gentleness and sweetness, he was a puritan *bon viveur*, an ardent feminist whose all-female household revolved entirely around his own wishes and well-being, self-deluding and self-critical, an overpowering egoist who responded with immediate sympathy to anyone in trouble, mean and generous, a fervent critic of the profit motive, who lived by the profit of his thriving publishing business, though he was always ready to publish worthwhile books that he knew would never make him any money.

One could go on cataloguing Victor's contradictions – they exist in all of us, and few do not compromise with their highest aspirations, but these failings can be reasonably well contained and covered; Victor's were unconcealed, blazoned abroad with such vigour, that he was easily exposed to accusations of humbug and hypocrisy. But he struggled hard with his temper and his ego; there was nothing insincere in his passionate aspiration to personal goodness, the 'hunger and thirst after righteousness' that would not let him be. And he longed to explain to everyone else – particularly to politicians – how to be good, how to usher in the kingdom of love and peace, the kingdom of God on earth – the tradition of the great Hebrew prophets burned fiercely and relentlessly within him.

Ruth may have seemed to many too self-effacing, too subservient to Victor, but she was a strong woman in her own right. She had been a suffragette, and before marriage she had trained as an architect, and as an artist, but could only continue her painting when she and Victor were on holiday together. Ruth firmly repudiated any idea that Victor was difficult to live with, she treated him partly as the Messiah and partly as the son she had never had – the Gollanczes had five daughters. Victor adored Ruth and relied on her completely, he never ceased to proclaim his devotion to her, but that did not prevent him from having an actively roving eye. I often heard him discourse upon the dreadful sin of sexual jealousy, a rather convenient view for anyone with adulterous desires, especially as he was, at least in theory, dutifully supported by Ruth.

Around this time, 1950, Victor published his anthology *A Year of Grace*, for me, his most enduring testament, more effective than any of his own writings. He was reacting, he said, against anti-religious humanism, and anti-humanistic religion, and he put together an arrangement of quotations from an immensely wide field, the result of his omnivorous reading. He drew from many sources, Jewish, Christian, Muslim, Hindu, he quoted poetry, philosophy, theology, mysticism and fiction. Through the words of others, Victor expressed his love and enjoyment of the world, and his own essentially religious humanism. It is a view of life with which John and I had much affinity. Victor dedicated the book to his first grandchild, Timothy, and to our son Peter Victor, whose godfather he was – a consistently generous, helpful and affectionate godfather.

Victor was interested in Christian Action, and full of good advice. Work for peace and reconciliation was for John an essentially Christian concern but, apart from the Quakers and one or two minority pacifist groups, there seemed little effective Christian witness. That was Victor's view, and in the dangerous situation created by Communist China's invasion of Korea, he suggested that he and John should write a joint pamphlet.

Christianity and the War Crisis was a plea to world leaders to put aside national pride, talk to each other as human beings, and use the resources now poured into armaments for a massive international campaign on behalf of the world's poor. The pamphlet had such a success that Victor followed it with an appeal for support that resulted in 8,000 signatures, and a flow of money, so he founded 'The Association for World Peace'. But Victor soon lost interest and abandoned the organisation to a committee chaired by the young Harold Wilson. He, with Richard Acland, changed it into 'War on Want'.

Meanwhile, John, in his search for a specifically Christian witness, proposed that Christian Action should, as a first step, organise a conference for pacifists and non-pacifists in more or less equal numbers. There were a few words of caution from the council. 'Peace', much trumpeted by the Soviets and their followers, was in danger of becoming a dirty word, indicative if not of outright Communism, at least of naïve fellow-travelling. John was never much influenced by words of caution, and he had active support from his Quaker colleagues.

The conference was arranged at Elfinsward for early December. It was interesting and valuable, and did much to promote understanding of different viewpoints. The proverbial aggressiveness of some pacifists was softened, many discovered that they might after all be able to work constructively with those with whom they disagreed. The Quaker contribution was invaluable, the Society of Friends has been pacifist since its beginnings; they have no psychological need for aggression, their views are accepted and respected. No one at that time knew that Attlee had already, and in secret, taken the decision to develop Britain's own atom bombs, and the technical possibilities of a hydrogen bomb were already on the horizon. The Christian Action

Council was pleased with the success of the conference, and considered the possibility of sponsoring jointly with the Quakers a delegation to Russia to talk with Russian churchmen and the Russian Peace Committee; Sydney Bailey had numerous international contacts, and agreed to work out preliminary plans.

John preached rousing sermons on the subject of peace. He believed that Christian Action, because of its unofficial nature, could and should tackle the difficult and controversial areas of national and international life, from which the official Churches shied away. It was not long before reading another book stirred us into action in another controversial issue.

24

Into Africa

THE book that John and I read together soon after it appeared was Alan Paton's *Cry the Beloved Country*. It was sold out almost immediately, and has been continually reprinted; my 1988 copy lists twenty-five impressions; it must have been read by millions. People who knew little or nothing about South Africa were shaken out of ignorance, and some began to care about what was being done to black people in that far-away land. There may have been guilt somewhere, awareness of the history of slavery and segregation in America where the book was widely read, and, in Britain, an uneasy post-Imperial questioning, but the reaction, I think, went deeper, something to do with the desire of human beings to be able to believe in a better image of themselves. Alan Paton does not batter your sensibility with accounts of the injustice and suffering caused by racial discrimination, his exposure is subtle, imaginative, and ironic; it creeps into you like yeast in dough, it grows and it lasts. 'A story of comfort in desolation' is the sub-title, and the desolation is powerfully portrayed, but the desire for reconciliation was a dominating force in Alan's life and work, and there is reconciliation here. *Cry the Beloved Country* is a book that stirs and tears the heart. There, in South Africa, a member of the British Commonwealth, John and I saw injustice writ large.

The problems of race and colour were much in our minds, and at a meeting with the sponsors of the Albert Hall meeting, John proposed that Christian Action should try to work in this area. There was an immediate reaction, one after another of these eminent persons got up to say that this would be fatal to the organisation, it was a most explosive and controversial issue, it should be left well alone. There was a solitary voice from the Editor of the *Church of England Newspaper*, who said that he had understood that the purpose of Christian Action was precisely to try to tackle such difficult issues. Few seemed to agree with him.

Other things were pushing us in the same direction. Soon after we were settled in Amen Court, Victor Gollancz telephoned saying that he wanted us to meet someone who he thought might be helped by Christian Action. Would we come to dinner at the Ivy? We went, and there we met Michael Scott. He made an immediate and sympathetic impression on us both; he had a lean, ascetic appearance, and looked as if he slept in his clothes; he was an unconventional Anglican priest, a kind of holy vagabond, but what drew us to him was his acute perception of injustice, and his personal identification with deprived and suffering human beings. John wanted to help him as much as possible.

Michael had gone to South Africa in 1943 to recover from an attack of TB, but he was soon in trouble with the authorities. He supported Indian passive resistance in Durban, and was arrested – Gandhian non-violent resistance was one of Michael's preoccupations. He lived with Africans in a particularly deprived shanty town, but with the advent of the Nationalist government in 1948, and the beginning of the legal imposition of apartheid, such behaviour was unacceptable, and the authorities soon got rid of him; in 1950 he was declared a prohibited immigrant. But Michael had, meanwhile, been to South-West Africa (Namibia) and had seen the sufferings of the Herero people, and the steady loss of their traditional lands. Since their chief, Hosea Kutako, was not allowed by the authorities to travel abroad, Michael had been deputed, as his representative, to plead the Herero case at the United Nations; this he was on his way to do. The UN was presumed to have taken over the responsibilities of the League of Nations, which, at the end of the First World War, had mandated what was then German South-West Africa, to South Africa. Michael was finding no support for his cause from the British government, nor from any official Church bodies, and John promised that when he returned from New York, Christian Action could at least offer him a public platform, and St Paul's a pulpit.

John was becoming an old hand at organising and publicising successful meetings; on 17 April 1950 the Central Hall, Westminster, was filled to capacity with people wanting to hear Michael Scott, and an overflow meeting had to be hurriedly arranged. Although Michael was not a great orator, he was a powerful personality, and his speech was inspired, prophetic and profoundly Christian. He quoted the South African Minister of Labour: 'The non-Europeans will *never* have the same political rights as Europeans: there will *never* be social equality; the Europeans will *always* be boss in South Africa.' Michael gave illustrations of the iniquities of apartheid, but he was constructive

in his appeal to the British government to develop those areas of Africa
for which it still had responsibility. He pointed out that apartheid was
'obstructing the natural, social and economic development of all races,
the white races included'. There was a problem for Christians, so often
exhorted to be law-abiding citizens, when the law itself becomes an
instrument of injustice and oppression. 'It may be that in South Africa
we Christians will have to face the necessity of challenging the
supremacy of a legal system which knows no moral law.' Christians
might have to accept, he said, the penalty of an unjust law, rather than
acquiesce in it. 'This quite simply was the Gandhian way, and I am not
convinced that it was not the way of Christ, to resist the lawlessness of
the law.' After forty years I can still be moved by Michael's words as I
recapture the spirit of that remarkable meeting.

Christian Action was now fully launched into the field of race
relations; a Race Relations Fund was established and began to be of
assistance to coloured students and immigrants working in London. As
well as preaching peace, John preached anti-apartheid and anti-racist
sermons, and these were no more popular, if anything they produced an
even more extreme reaction; the roots of prejudice reach down into
some very murky depths in the human psyche. Soon there was another
project sponsored jointly by Christian Action and the Race Relations
Committee of the Society of Friends; a lecture tour for Alan Paton,
which was quickly set up for the autumn of 1950. To open the tour, Alan
Paton was to preach in St Paul's.

Our meeting with Alan was one of the many, very many rewards of
John's work, and we became friends 'for life'. Alan was a man who
inspired love and affection in many people. He was a deeply serious,
deeply Christian man, and he was tremendous fun, with a deliciously
ironic sense of humour. After this happy meeting, Alan usually spent a
few days and nights staying with us at Amen Court, whenever he visited
London, and we developed an evening ritual. John and Alan were both
'wine-bibbers', but Alan never wanted to go to bed; he would talk about
religion, literature, politics, race, life, well into the small hours.
Eventually, as John and I flagged we would go to bed, at least, we would
prepare for bed, taking with us another bottle of Alan's favourite red
wine. Alan would also prepare, and would then arrive in our bedroom,
where John and I were comfortably installed in our large double bed,
and the discussion would continue until the bottle of wine was empty;
luckily Alan only had to get next door to the spare bedroom.

Alan preached a beautifully phrased sermon, he called it 'the great
obedience', obedience to God rather than to men. The cathedral was

packed – in those days, National Services apart, it was only John's enterprises that ever filled St Paul's. On this occasion, the chapter had agreed that any money from the collection over and above the average £15 could be given to the Race Relations work of Christian Action. They could hardly have anticipated the resulting £88, which may not today sound very much, but if you add at least one inflationary 'o' you may see what it meant to us then.

Because of Christian Action's race relations work, John became involved in the complex situation caused by the marriage of Ruth and Seretse Khama. John was friendly with Tshekedi Khama, Seretse's uncle who had acted as Regent during Seretse's minority, but he was also sympathetic to Ruth and Seretse. John was particularly angered by the discreditable part played by the Anglican Church. Ruth and Seretse were both sincere and practising Christians, anxious to be married in church. But the British government persuaded Dr Wand, Bishop of London, to forbid the marriage, and the young couple were forced unwillingly and with difficulty into a registry office. This was a shocking example of politics interfering in religion.

'I will never forget', Ruth, now Lady Khama, wrote to me, 'and Seretse did not forget either the immense moral support that John gave us in those bad days . . . he was very influential in restoring my faith in the Church and its priests'.

Unfortunately this affair led to a disagreement with Michael Scott, who supported Tshekedi. John had invited Michael to run the race relations work of Christian Action, but Michael too was an individualist and wanted his own organisation, solely devoted to African affairs; so with support, especially from David Astor, he founded the Africa Bureau. Michael was not an easy man to work with, and he and John had such very different temperaments that co-operation between them could never have lasted for long.

John's activities outside the cathedral, and his sermons from the pulpit did bring trouble upon the long-suffering dean. 'Now and then,' Matthews wrote, 'strangers have commiserated with me on having such a colleague, and I must own that there have been times when I could wish that he had not said provocative things, because so many people think that a dean is a kind of headmaster who can keep his canons on the right lines. How many times I have informed irate correspondents that, even if I wished to censor a canon's sermons, I had no power to do so! I am afraid that sometimes I have said, "If you want to accuse Canon Collins of heresy, you must write to the Bishop of the diocese and state what heresy you accuse him of." I do not suppose the bishop has ever had an accusation.'

Angry letters were one thing, but in the beginning of 1951, John's activities resulted in more substantial trouble for the dean and chapter. A certain General Martel, possessed by anti-Communist fury, decided that the Church of England was harbouring dangerous reds in its bosom. He proposed to purge it by organising pilgrimages to signify Christian abhorrence of tyranny, and to stir up Christian conscience and action against Communism; the first pilgrimage suitably was to Canterbury Cathedral, and was aimed at Hewlett Johnson, the Red Dean, who certainly was a Communist, though of a peculiar kind. Harry Pollitt, one-time secretary of the British Communist party, used to refer to him as 'that bloody red ass of a dean'. The pilgrimage took place, but there was no great following, and the general turned his attention to St Paul's, decidedly in his view in need of purgation. Innocently the dean at first agreed to be present on the day, and to lead the pilgrims in prayer, but the chapter soon realised that this might give credence to the idea that there was a Communist, or Communists, on the chapter; whatever John's colleagues may have thought about his activities, they knew that he was no Communist. So it was agreed that the pilgrims might come and kneel for private prayer, but that was all, they would not in any way be officially welcomed. General Martel then invited the dean to lunch, and the chapter boldly suggested that John should go too, so together they repaired to the Cavalry Club. This must have been a very strange lunch party, it did not appear to have arrived at any degree of mutual understanding.

On the appointed day a small group arrived at the cathedral; they attracted little attention. General Martel then wrote to the Press implicating Westminster Abbey as well in harbouring Communists. This was too much for both St Paul's and the Abbey. They threatened a joint libel action, and the discomfited general had to withdraw.

John had learned the importance of cultivating the Press if he wanted to get his message across to a wider public, and he needed their help to raise money. As Amen Court was on top of Fleet Street, it was not difficult to pursue friendly relations. John believed in trusting professional journalists who had a job to do, and he was rarely let down. He had a group of friends on the *Daily Mirror*, the editor, Sylvester Bolam, the cartoonist, Philip Zec, and their brilliant columnist, William Connor, alias Cassandra. These were men with a social conscience, sympathetic to much of what John was trying to do, and they did their best to slip in items of social concern, among all the 'popular' material.

The editor of the Press Association too was a friend, and when he saw that John was preaching at St Paul's he would ring up and ask if there was anything that needed a wider coverage. John always stressed that he wanted publicity only for his work, he asked expressly for no personal items. But of course, certain papers were editorially hostile, whatever their individual journalists might have felt, and the Press is a double-edged weapon; it must make headlines, take words out of context and attract attention.

There was one controversial sermon that I did not want John to preach, I thought it would be counter-productive. King George VI had undergone an operation for lung cancer, and it was arranged that he should go to convalesce in South Africa. I remember very well one of John's Westcott House pupils coming to us in a state of indignation about this – 'John, it is monstrous to give respectability to such a government, you must protest,' he said. 'You must preach a sermon in St Paul's.' I knew that this priest had just been elected a member of the Church Assembly, and I didn't see why John should always be the fall-guy in controversy. 'Why don't you raise it in the Assembly?' I said. 'Oh, I couldn't do that,' was the reply. 'I am much too new, much better for John to do it.' And, of course, that is what John did. The cathedral was not pleased, the Palace was not pleased, and the archbishop was angry. I suppose I was cowardly.

I was wholeheartedly behind a request that came to us from South Africa. It was from Father Trevor Huddleston of the Community of the Resurrection, who was in charge of a black mission parish in what was then Sophiatown, Johannesburg. The African National Congress led by Chief Albert Luthuli was at that time dedicated to a policy of non-violence. The influence of Gandhi was still strong in South Africa, and not only among the Indian community. Manilal Gandhi, one of the Mahatma's sons, still lived in Natal in an ashram, where Gandhi's ideas and teachings were followed. The Christian influence too was strong, and Luthuli himself was a devout believer.

The ANC together with the Indian National Congress had decided upon a campaign of non-violent resistance to unjust laws. They had written dignified letters to the government asking for talks, expressing their willingness to co-operate in solving some of the problems of the townships, insisting that they were not anti-white. Their appeals were rejected, so they decided that they must act. They listed fifteen new laws and said that their campaign would focus on six of these, including the Separate Representation of Voters Act by which the 'Coloured' community was deprived of the votes to which they had hitherto been entitled, the Group Areas Act, by which Africans were being forced out of areas where many had lived for generations, and the hated Pass Laws. An African had to carry on him seventeen documents, failure to produce one meant immediate arrest, a fine or, more often, imprisonment. These laws were now to be extended to women. The ANC put out an appeal – 'With clear consciences and the knowledge that we are armed with lofty humanitarian principles common to all the great philosophies and religions of the world, we appeal for that moral and practical support which will enable us to enter into the liberty and dignity which is the birthright of all men everywhere.'

This was not an appeal that Christian Action could ignore, and Father Huddleston asked John if we could raise money to assist the families of those who would go voluntarily and peacefully to prison. He had a small committee chaired by Alan Paton, and they would ensure that all monies would be properly distributed. As yet we had not met Trevor Huddleston; this – the 1952 Defiance Campaign – was the beginning of our anti-apartheid work together.

John accepted the challenge immediately, and the Christian Action Council supported him. He preached sermons, wrote letters to the Press, spoke at meetings and drafted appeals. Within a few months £1,450 was collected, and sent to Father Huddleston. Some 7,000 volunteers came forward, and the prisons were filled, ugly reports began to emerge, stories of torture, of electric shocks, much that over the years has become all too painfully familiar. Sentences were harsh, two months' imprisonment with hard labour for walking through a 'Whites Only' entrance, one month's hard labour for sitting on a 'Whites Only' bench, lads under twenty-one were automatically whipped.

Nobody worked harder at publicity than John, but it was tough going, 'Lambeth doesn't help,' he wrote – Lambeth did not hold with law-breaking, however just the cause. 'Can you ask Ambrose Reeves (Bishop of Johannesburg) to write to Cantuar?' he suggested. But Cantuar listened to other voices, Trevor was considered too extreme, and already he and his superiors feared that he might be arrested.

Thousands of Africans and Indians went peaceably to prison and behaved with amazing discipline in spite of provocation. They were joined by a tiny handful of whites. True, the Archbishop of Cape Town had said that there could be circumstances in which Christians might defy unjust laws, and the Bishop of Pretoria said the same, but both stopped short at urging their flocks to join the resistance; had there been greater white support things might have been different. Then the police began to shoot; Swart, so-called Minister of Law and Order, gave instructions that they should take drastic action; 'they have been told to shoot first,' he said. In the Eastern Cape a peaceful prayer meeting was broken up, and as the Africans walked quietly away they were attacked by bullets and bayonets – all the casualties in the hospitals were wounded in the back. The police then got into their trucks and drove up and down the location firing at random into the houses – a man was killed sitting at his kitchen table, as were others at an indoor beer party. Nobody had attacked the police; when an ANC man asked for a megaphone so that he could calm the crowd, he was immediately shot at, and the man standing next to him was killed. Not content, the police went into the hospitals and began arresting the wounded; to have been shot was considered evidence of violence and rioting. Families began concealing their wounds, and dared not even go to doctors' surgeries.

Incidents such as this, attested by lawyers, doctors and eye witnesses, occurred elsewhere, and of course, as was intended, the crowds reacted. They began throwing stones and rioting, and over the country four Europeans were killed, but already the police had killed fifty Africans and wounded hundreds more. The non-violent campaign had to be called off.

The role of the police as agents provocateurs has become increasingly evident over the troubled years of South African history – one after another peaceful demonstration has been violently and indiscriminately attacked; the pattern of police behaviour here recounted has been sickeningly repeated, while brutality and torture in the prisons has become ever more extreme.

With its espousal of the Defiance Campaign, Christian Action began to lose any respectability that it might have had. It had already lost two of its first patrons; Stafford Cripps had died in 1951, and this was a real blow to John personally, and to the movement. In spite of his heavy public responsibilities, and of increasing ill-health, Stafford never lost his concern and support for Christian Action. Our Liberal patron, Lord Perth, sympathetic but remote, had also died, and now Lord Halifax decided that he must resign. He had been viceroy of India during the period of Gandhi's passive resistance campaigns, he could not now be seen to support similar law-breaking in South Africa. Frank Pakenham agreed to replace Stafford, and he has stuck to us nobly in spite of disagreement with some of John's activities. Frank, good Christian man as he is, is not afraid of appearing eccentric in a cause in which he believes. Before long, we also lost the representatives nominated by the heads of the official Churches.

John's efforts to achieve a political and Christian consensus within Christian Action had no personal motivation, he longed only to involve the Christians, especially his fellow Anglicans. As Edward Carpenter, a keen supporter, said, 'The thought of standing over against the Church was far less palatable to John than standing over against the State. He wanted the Church to come in and to approve what Christian Action was doing. Indeed he saw it as a handmaid of the Church.' But it was a vain hope, John's temperament and his particular gifts were against it. Years later, Edward Carpenter, by then dean of Westminster Abbey, wrote: 'A group should not seek any official recognition, unless it is willing to be geared down to the pace of the slowest vessel in the convoy . . . I remember a prominent Bishop, in respect of an equally prominent public issue, counselling the Church to go slow . . . this seemed like urging a tortoise to lose speed.' John was no tortoise.

25

Confrontations, Separation

WHILE the number of individual Christian Action supporters increased steadily, the autonomous 'cells' did not develop. Christian Action never became the national movement for which Stafford Cripps had hoped, but because of John's flair for publicity it remained in the public mind. John described the movement as a 'gadfly' to prick the consciences of Christians, and stir them into action.

The gadfly continued stinging, and sometimes there were unforeseen results. John preached a sermon in St Paul's in which he referred to the then South African Prime Minister, Dr Malan: 'Let us sympathise with Dr Malan in his difficulties, let us be charitable to him, poor, wretched man hag-ridden with fear; we know that only love can cast out fear; but as well expect a man with delirium tremens to discover in his heart the love to destroy his illusion of pink elephants, as to hope that the Nationalists can by a wave of a wand change their whole policy from one founded on fear to one founded on love.' This somewhat confused but colourful metaphor naturally caught the attention of the Press; it penetrated into South Africa and was received with outrage by some of the white population, and it, with other pronouncements, was observed by Geoffrey Fisher, who wrote with displeasure. John replied: 'You criticise, you say, my capacity for wise judgement, for my part, I am equally convinced that your judgement on the South African issue is at fault.' John enclosed a letter from Trevor Huddleston as to how he saw the situation and the need for pressure from outside, and John begged Fisher to consider it carefully. Fisher relied on advice from the Archbishop of Cape Town, who did not approve of Father Huddleston, and his activities. John went to discuss the matter with Fisher. The discussion became more and more heated, and ended with Fisher seizing John by the lapels of his jacket and shaking him violently, and John saying, 'You're trying to be a headmaster, if I would just bend over and take six of the best, you'd be satisfied.' That same evening Fisher wrote a note to John: 'This afternoon's conversation must have left a very nasty taste in your mouth and in mine. At least it is Ash Wednesday. I think we had better forget all about it, and recognise in each other the human liability to unwisdom, and the Christian desire to seek wisdom.'

John responded immediately and apologetically to this magnanimous gesture: 'I am extremely grateful to you for your very generous letter. I am very sorry for my part in making it so acid. The last thing I would wish to do is to cause hurt to the Church; and I am certainly sorry for the offence caused by my comment on Dr Malan.'

Our lives were not all controversy and drama, there were friends old and new, contacts with the Yatesbury Fellowship, and there were holidays. We solved the problem of getting three, and soon four, lively boys into the freedom of the country. Occasionally generous friends lent us their houses, but in August John usually took a 'locum', he attended to the minimal demands of the parish and we lived in the vicarage; for one month we became part of a small rural community. It was a wonderful way of exploring the English countryside.

We experienced Ottery St Mary, the vicarage where Coleridge was born and spent his boyhood; Dartington, and the Hall where we enjoyed the magnificent gardens and the summer music school; a crazy place on the Yorkshire moors, where a half-mad old cleric lived with his mentally retarded daughter, and the Anglicans had all migrated down the road to the Methodist chapel; a locum in Shropshire which must be some of the loveliest country in the world, closely rivalled by Dorset, where a small river ran through the vicarage garden and nourished at least five pairs of kingfishers. These were happy days, and for John a rewarding part of his ministry. The parishes were at first alarmed at the prospect of this firebrand cleric, then relieved to find him human and approachable, and inevitably some came with their personal problems.

My birthday came in the middle of the summer holidays and nearly always we managed to eat lobsters, not yet all exported to France, and still reasonably priced, and of course there would be a bottle of John's best white wine. In 1951 we were in the Isle of Wight, and on my birthday evening we left three boys with our Dutch au pair, and drove to Yarmouth where we dined off local lobster accompanied by draughts of dry white wine. We felt happy and reckless as we returned, we had thought that perhaps we shouldn't have any more children, but 'Why not?' we said. 'Why don't we just take a risk and see what happens?' and what happened nine months later was the birth of Mark Nathaniel.

Mark was my National Health baby, and I could not have had better care or greater happiness; I felt as I had felt after Richard's arrival, the world was a paean of praise and joy. But then the hormones began to work in the opposite direction, and I fell into what I suppose was a post-natal depression, only it wasn't exactly depression, but a horror that I might harm my baby. I would have killed myself first, I was terrified of being left alone. For some time, I struggled on my own, and then I told John, who was sweet and sympathetic, but bewildered. In his distress he talked to Victor. So then I too went to talk to Victor, who was at his very best, loving, gentle and wise. He questioned me closely, and I found I could talk to him easily. 'You aren't in any real danger,' he assured me. 'Offer your suffering to God,' he said. 'I really mean that sincerely.' And that is what I tried to do and slowly the nightmare lifted, and normality and happiness returned; help in time of trouble is something I do not forget. I wasn't a particularly bad case, but, painful and frightening as it was, I do not entirely regret this experience; it has given me a sympathy and an understanding of people who are driven to do terrible things when gripped by irrational compulsions that they can neither understand nor control.

In 1953 St Paul's was only peripherally involved in the Coronation of Elizabeth II, but the choir joined others to sing the service in the Abbey. This gave John an idea. Through his American contacts he found that there might be support for a tour of America by the famous choir of St Paul's Cathedral, as a money-raising venture. St Paul's was chronically short of money, so John put the idea to the chapter, who agreed. The tour was scheduled for October and November 1953, and I managed to make suitable arrangements for the boys, so that I could go with John.

On 24 September our party of fifty-eight boarded the *Queen Elizabeth* at Southampton. There were thirty boys between the ages of eight and thirteen, eighteen professional men, two organists, a minor canon, the headmaster of the choir school Jessop Price and his wife Eileen, and one or two teachers and matrons to look after the boys. The choir was to give concerts, in halls or churches in forty cities.

We went everywhere in Greyhound buses, a fine way of seeing America. It was exhausting, but there was so much of interest and excitement that it is impossible to select. The singing was a revelation. Released from the swirling echo of St Paul's, we heard, as if for the first time, the clarity, richness and balance of the choir. The professional men were all fine singers, and with and above them was the soaring purity of the boys' voices. 'Ours don't grow like that,' said the Americans. 'Is it your climate, or your diet, or are they just made different?' No, not different, only trained in the long and unique tradition of English church music.

We drove north to the lakes and forests of Canada, and down to the deep South of America. John did a certain amount of preaching en route, but was warned that, when in the South, he must on no account preach on the racial issue. That, of course, is exactly what he did, with no apparently alarming results. We were shocked by the poverty of so many of the black people, living in miserable wood and tin shacks on the outskirts of those affluent Southern cities. 'That's how they prefer to live,' our white hosts assured us. 'They're much happier with segregation.'

At New Orleans we contacted some of the leaders of the black community. They assured us that they did *not* wish to live segregated lives; segregation was a perpetuation of slavery, they all had slave ancestry. These were moderate people, hoping and expecting to move slowly towards equality and integration with the whites, the signposts were in the right direction, but they acknowledged that the pace was painfully slow.

John was frequently exhausted, he also carried a burden of responsibility. The tour expenses were heavy, but he dared not present the chapter with a financial loss. He had to persuade all concerned to allow their daily expense allowances to be centrally administered by himself for economy, and his powers of leadership and conciliation were fully stretched. There were a few troubles among the men, grumbles about food, money, accommodation, as well as personal rivalries and bickerings; John never allowed these to fester. The boys showed extraordinary resilience, in spite of late nights and early mornings. They appeared unaffected by the adulation they received, spoke naturally and unselfconsciously on radio and at Press interviews, and people marvelled at their easy good manners. In fact, they thoroughly enjoyed themselves.

In 1953, America was gripped by anti-Communist hysteria whipped up by Senator Joe McCarthy. In Washington we lunched with an Episcopalian minister, who gave us a copy of a book he had written, preparatory to launching a nationwide anti-Communist crusade, aimed primarily at the Churches. His views horrified and alarmed us. He was evidently an able and respected man, but his 'crusade' was to be a full-blown witch hunt, made more ruthless and unscrupulous by the apparent authority of religion. We knew there were valid reasons for mistrusting Russian intentions, but this approach was a fantasy. Communism was the devil incarnate, individual

Communists possessed diabolical cunning, they were infiltrating everywhere, subverting the nation, they must be mercilessly exposed and rooted out, anyone remotely left wing was under suspicion. We saw and heard too much of this, too many people victimised, too many careers smashed, homes broken and friendships destroyed. Such irrational hysteria leads to persecution and war.

We saw the darker side of American life, but we experienced the overwhelming friendliness. Americans and Canadians opened their hearts and their homes to us, no trouble was too much.

When the time came to leave, partings were emotional, the head boy and one or two others were in tears, as was one of the hard-headed businessmen responsible for the tour management. It had been a triumphant success; all expenses had been met, there were bonuses for the men, the staff and the choir school, and a small profit for the cathedral.

The chapter, and especially the dean, were pleased with John, the greater offices were now shuffled around, and John became precentor with responsibility for the choir and the choir school. This made both John and the choir happy. John fixed regular meetings, an improvement in salaries, and more freedom for the men to arrange deputies. I had not altogether learned to love St Paul's, but I had certainly learned to love the choir and its music.

It was good to be home, and have our children around us. For John, of course, there was a huge pile-up of work and correspondence. Many letters arrived at 2 Amen Court, some expressing support, some enquiring, some sending money in response to appeals – these were always very welcome – and a fair proportion that were angry, abusive and obscene. For about six months I personally received a weekly postcard announcing that six 'buck niggers' were about to abduct and rape me. I informed the police who were entirely uninterested; no such excitements occurred, and eventually the cards ceased. Some of the angriest missives came from South Africa.

Among these was one that was different, from a Mr Jack Shave, a wealthy Durban paint manufacturer. He wrote that he and his friends had been much distressed by reports of John's sermons on the subject of apartheid, he felt sure that John could not understand the reality of the situation, and must have no idea of how much the white people had done and were doing for the 'natives'. He would like, therefore, to invite John to stay with him and his family for a month during which he would show him what the situation was really like. He would send John a first-class return air fare, and his only condition was that John must undertake to report honestly and publicly upon everything that he would see. The letter was sincere and generous; it was an offer that could not be refused. John accepted his proposal gladly, but pointed out his belief that apartheid, however humanely implemented, was a denial of the teaching of the New Testament; this was a principle he could not abandon, though he would, of course, undertake to report fully and honestly upon everything that he saw. He said that he would like to spend a further month at his own expense, travelling to other parts of South Africa and meeting other people. Mr Shave seemed happy with these conditions, and the visit was arranged for June and July 1954.

John and I had now been married for close on fifteen years, and we wanted no more separations, we had had quite enough of that during the war. We discussed the possibility of my going too, but, in the end, I knew that I ought not to leave the children again for as long as two months. So on 2 June I saw John off from London airport on, what was then, a long and circuitous journey. I missed him more than I would have believed possible and his letters told me that he felt the same for me. We shared so much, the high moments of love, and of beauty in nature and art, the comfort of complete physical intimacy, our children, what has been called 'the poetry of the trivia of married life', and all its humour too. And there was John's work, nearly all of which took place in the house. I can think of few professions other than that of a priest, in which a wife can, if she so wishes, be so much a part, and an essential part, of her husband's life. And I was very much a part; John liked to discuss Christian Action with me, and – just occasionally – he took my advice. Sermons were often tried out on me, 'trying it out on the cat' he called it. When he had speeches, articles or letters to the Press to prepare I would do a draft, which he would, often to my annoyance, tear to pieces, then, since his criticisms were usually valid, I would try again, and a joint version would finally emerge. We argued quite a lot, we both had strong views, but our disagreements were about means, not about the ends that we shared. John thought I was the argumentative one, I thought it was he – a familiar case of mutual projection. I did not feel that I was submerging my essential self, it all seemed a happy fulfilment.

So now I busied myself with home and children, and with Christian Action in which I began to take an increasingly active part; I wrote to John every day, and lived for his letters which, though also written daily, tended to arrive erratically. Many friends were kind and helpful, and I had two happy weekends with Victor and Ruth Gollancz. The second visit was more than a weekend, since after it Victor planned to take the three of us for a brief holiday in the Cotswolds. One of his American authoresses came for Saturday and Sunday, and we took her into Oxford for the day, a rather sadly nostalgic outing for me. Christ Church Cathedral was magnificent, filled and scented with all white flower arrangements from a recent wedding.

After a discussion about marriage in which Victor maintained that 'men are much more self-sacrificing in marriage than women, and their difficulties and sacrifices and responsibilities aren't understood or appreciated by women', Ruth, who was quite the most self-sacrificing wife I have ever known, was sent on another expedition into Newbury to cash a cheque – as Victor said that she hadn't drawn out nearly enough money for our holiday, it was to be 'a real gala with nice little lunches and dinners and bottles of wine'.

The holiday was all that Victor wanted it to be, and I was wonderfully loved and looked after, he and Ruth could not have been kinder to me. We started off with a slight mishap; Ruth, who always drove, hit, without quite killing, a crow that was feeding in the middle of the road. Victor covered his eyes with his hands, and burst into loud sobs; Ruth stopped the car, got out, and calmly finished off the unfortunate bird – great relief for Victor, and, of course, for the crow, and happiness restored. The Cotswolds in perfect June weather must be as lovely as anywhere in the world, so many villages with roses clambering all over their honey-coloured houses, and flowers gener-ously planted outside as well as inside the garden walls. We were enchanted by it all and Victor's generosity knew no bounds. He paid me many compliments, and sometimes assured me that he was falling in love with me, but I never took any of this very seriously, he said the same to several women, but however much he might sometimes wish to stray, Ruth remained supremely the one woman in his life. I was very fond of Victor, I greatly valued his friendship, but I never found him in the least sexually attractive.

So, for me, the time passed, though all too slowly; for John these were two of the most momentous months of his life; good-hearted and well-meaning Mr Shave had no idea what he was letting loose. Years later, Trevor Huddleston wrote: 'I remember very well the announce-ment of the invitation in the South African Press, and my immediate reaction. It was one of fear and doubt. I was afraid that John might all too easily succumb to the deceptive warmth of hospitality which I knew would be offered him in Natal, that he would see only the surface things in a society well provided with a veneer of western Christian civilisation. I was doubtful whether any English ecclesiastic, however well-disposed, could at all assess the reality of such a complex situation in one short visit, more especially when it would make life so much easier to return to St Paul's Cathedral with some bromide assertions about the need for patience, understanding and the desirability of avoiding rash judgements on situations so much more fraught with the dangers of misrepresentation than elsewhere. I need not have worried! But then in those days I did not know John.'

26

Deeper into Africa

THE South Africa that John entered in 1954 had already had six
years of Afrikaner Nationalist government; 'grand apartheid' was
taking shape, much of it already on the statute books. The vote was to
be removed from the Coloured people of the Cape, and the population
had been registered by race; complete separation could now begin.
Separate amenities, public transport, shops, lavatories, recreation,
were all in force. The Group Areas Act under which millions of
Africans, Indians and Coloureds were to lose their homes was in place.
Mixed marriages were illegal, as was the right to strike. Under new
Pass Laws every male African must carry a reference book containing
eleven documents; failure to produce immediately any one of these
resulted in imprisonment or fine. The Bantu Education Act designed
to 'fit' Africans for permanent servitude was about to become law.

These laws which were supposed to make everybody happy had to
be enforced by others; including the Suppression of Communism Act,
under which anyone whom the minister 'deemed' to be a Communist
was a Communist, never mind if he were a dedicated Christian or had
never had any dealings with the Communist party. Upon anyone who
too actively opposed government policy, could be inflicted the kind of
death in life of a banning order. Dictators and dictatorial regimes who
profess only to have the interests of their people at heart, and who
assure the outside world that those same people are happy and
contented, always find it necessary to enforce all such happiness and
contentment by increasing repression and terror.

John knew all this, but his knowledge was theoretical, now he
would see the human effects of apartheid, he would meet and hear its
supporters and those who were opposed to it. Perhaps symbolically
John was greeted at Johannesburg by Mr Shave's manager, by the
Anglican Bishop Ambrose Reeves, and by two ANC leaders, Walter
Sisulu and Yusuf Cachalia, and, of course, by the Press. Ambrose was
clearly anxious to keep this headstrong priest under control, so he took

charge, the Press were allowed photographs only, and John was swept off to Bishops House for the night. He was exhausted, but rest was not yet, Ambrose kept him up talking until after midnight. The next morning was devoted to organising John's programme, and a very full one it was to be, no opportunities for straying into dangerous or unnecessary paths. But Ambrose was a good man, and soon won John's admiration and affection.

John caught an evening flight to Durban, and arrived at the Shaves' comfortable but unostentatious home at seven p.m. Jack Shave had seven children, three by his first wife who had died young, and four by his second wife Ruby. She created a happy atmosphere throughout the house, and her three stepchildren loved her as their own mother. Jack Shave was a keen, rather simple Methodist, he neither drank nor smoked, but was not a puritan. He was kind and charitable, though apt to express his conventional views rather forcibly. John soon saw how much Jack Shave was liked and respected at his works, and in the community.

John was swept into a round of visits, schools and hospitals for non-whites, many of them excellent, and in the evenings Jack Shave's friends would come to continue the process of impressing upon him 'the reality of the situation'. As Trevor Huddleston had predicted there was courtesy, kindness and generous hospitality, there was more, there was real VIP treatment. The senior administrator of the province in Pietermaritzburg gave a dinner in John's honour, and he took the next day off so that he could show John round personally; he said that he had had instructions from Pretoria to lay on all facilities for Canon Collins. They progressed, John said 'from here to there like a Royal tour'. They visited a wonderfully equipped hospital for Africans and Indians, a native village, a school, a home for indigent old people, a nursery school, then lunch with all the chief officials: 'five courses, wines and cigars', followed by visits to three Indian schools, two municipal African markets; here John was told that he might shake hands with the African manager, though innocently and unofficially he had been shaking hands with Africans all along the route. Then followed a large hostel for African migrant workers, and a model African village. John was impressed by the work, and by the men who showed him round, 'all first-class men with decent outlook and ideals' . . . 'but somehow', he wrote, 'it all spoke to me of tragedy – despite the excellence of the work and of those responsible – they were quite unaware of their air of superiority . . . There is an atmosphere all the time that this is a white man's country into which by some misfortune a vast number of Africans has intruded.' It never seemed to occur to anyone that instead of having things done *for* them, Africans and Indians might prefer to do things for themselves.

John got on well with the Afrikaners he met; in spite of their rigid ideology, they seemed somehow closer to the Africans than many English-speaking whites, and some were liberal and honest.

John had a wide interest in the human scene, and would listen and talk to all manner of people, including classic 'bores', for whom he was something of a magnet. So his officially conducted visit to Zululand and the game parks was enjoyable. He was especially interested in the attitude of the government paid chiefs. They spoke through interpreters and dutifully followed the Nationalist party line, expressing gratitude and contentment. Fed up with this on one occasion, John said suddenly, 'So you wish me to return to England and report to our Queen and Government that you are perfectly happy with things as they are, and wish for no changes?' Caught unawares, the chief replied in perfect English, 'No, no, you mustn't do that, things could be much improved'. So ended that particular interview.

John was getting restive, he wanted to meet Africans and Indians, talk to them alone and see how they lived. Seven African servants moved barefooted around the Shave household, they had been there for many years, and were clearly well-treated and contented. 'They prefer not to wear shoes,' John was told. 'It's what they're used to.' When he questioned one of them, the African replied with a smile, 'Shoes cost a lot of money'. Whenever John did manage to speak to Africans and Indians alone, which he did at every possible opportunity, he got a very different picture from that presented by his white hosts.

Contact with the segregated white Churches was not particularly encouraging. On John's first Sunday a young Anglican priest just out from England told him that he had asked one of his churchwardens for advice about African servants. 'You can't trust any bloody coon,' was the answer. The evening was better, when John attended the Indian Methodist mission where a special interracial and interdenominational service was held, and Father Zulu, an Anglican priest, 'preached a lovely sermon on racial unity'. After the service, John was besieged by a crowd of Indians all clamouring to shake him by the hand.

Later on in his visit, John was invited to speak to a mixed race gathering of Anglican clergy. After his talk, one white priest after another got up to explain how important it was not to be in too much of a hurry, how complex the situation was, he must have seen how much was being done for the Africans, segregation was in everyone's interest, the Africans preferred it, and John mustn't listen to Communists and agitators. The African clergy remained silent. The chairman seemed well satisfied, and looking round confidently he asked whether their African brothers had anything to add. There was a long silence; John felt more and more nervous, then Father Zulu stood up and said, 'Canon Collins has so admirably analysed the situation, and so forcibly expressed the only Christian attitude to this problem both in thought and action that I can only subscribe to every word. Canon Collins has said it all.' There was immediate agreement from all the African priests. Afterwards a number of the white priests confessed that John's speech represented the only right and Christian position; but if they were to preach this from their pulpits, and open their churches to all races, their white congregations would vanish, and with them most of the financial support upon which the churches depended for their existence, and for their missionary activities including their hospitals and schools.

John went to visit Father Zulu, a fine and impressive priest who eventually became an Anglican bishop, but only after he had been three times nominated, and three times rejected. He begged John to continue with everything that he was doing and saying. Though cheerful and dedicated, he did comment on the disparity in church stipends, he, with his large parish and seven children, was paid £20 a year, a newly ordained and unmarried white priest would begin his ministry on £355 a year.

The meeting with Father Zulu was a rewarding personal contact, and there were others. A visit to Gandhi's son, Manilal, who lived at Phoenix, a self-contained little ashram. Here, said John, 'were holiness, wisdom, simplicity, happy family life, joy, peace, love – Manilal is the prophet of the still small voice'. Then there was the meeting with Chief Albert Luthuli recently deposed from his chieftainship by the government. The meeting was arranged with difficulty, there was no public place in Durban where a white and a black man could meet for a private talk. Ruby Shave explained awkwardly that her social life would come to an end if she were to receive an African into her house as a guest, and the same was true of other white families who were approached. Eventually a sympathiser was found, a listed Communist, who had had his passport removed, and who at once offered his office and all facilities. John was enormously impressed by the chief, educated, well-informed, a devout Christian and dedicated to non-violence; he was president of the African National Congress.

'Educated Africans', said Luthuli, 'are not supposed to know what *real* Africans in the reserves think, though oddly the whites are supposed to know. In fact, Africans in the reserves are quite well-informed, nationally and internationally, for instance, they follow with interest what goes on at the UN.' 'He is moderate, anti-violence, wise and courageous. It is quite fantastic that he should be treated as an inferior person,' John wrote of Luthuli.

Among the Indians John found bitterness and frustration. He was entertained to a buffet supper by Dr Naiker, president of the local Indian National Congress, which was working with the ANC. Under the Group Areas Act Dr Naiker, a highly qualified professional man, would lose his comfortable home, as would most of those present, numbers of whom would be relegated to slum conditions or to sharing with other families. Most of the men, and a number of the women, were professionally trained and highly educated; as much as the legislation, they resented the personal insults and affronts to human dignity to which they were constantly subjected.

John's first sight of an African location was Cato Manor, two miles outside Durban, and he was appalled by the slum conditions, 'about 60,000 African men, women and children living in shacks without water, light or sanitation'.

It was time to move on, and John felt really sad, he had grown very fond of the whole Shave family, and they had done their very best to make his visit happy. Ruby Shave had been somewhat unsettled; in the end she admitted to John that she had to agree with all he said, but he represented the ideal and not the practical, and she feared much for the future of her children; with all of which John could not but sympathise. Of Jack Shave, John wrote that he had 'established a friendship based upon an acceptance of the fact that I shall probably disappoint him in what I have to say when I get back. He now asks only that I shall remember their difficulties, and sometimes point out what there is of good being done here, which, of course, I shall be happy to do.'

Back at Bishops House, John was plunged into talk and plans with Ambrose Reeves until two-thirty a.m. His first visitor next day was Father Trevor Huddleston.

'A wonderful person to meet . . . with a heart of gold.' Unlike ninety-nine per cent of white South Africans and a majority of white clergy, Trevor Huddleston, as priest-in-charge of the Community of the Resurrection Mission in Sophiatown, lived among the Africans, he lived with them and he loved them; if any white man in South Africa could truly claim to know the Africans, understand their lives, their feelings, and their aspirations, it was he; but the whole of Sophiatown where he exercised such a marvellous ministry was under threat from the Group Areas Act, and would soon be demolished to make way for Europeans. 'Of course you must carry on as you have been doing,' said Trevor. 'The reason there has been such a furore over your visit is because South Africa *is* sensitive to criticism from outside, however much they may claim that their problems are unique and only they know how to handle them.' He suggested that Christian Action might work on a sport and cultural boycott of South Africa, and whip up opposition to the Bantu Education Act especially among the Churches. He identified this Act as one of the most vicious pieces of legislation, and one that would be most bitterly resented in the years ahead. He spoke of conditions in the townships, and of his special loves, the children. With the help of concerned white people he had been able to start a voluntary feeding scheme for African children. 'If it weren't for the Jewish community here,' he said, 'I don't know what we should do about social welfare among the Africans, seventy-five per cent of our voluntary helpers are Jewish.'

There were meetings at the university, the Institute of Race Relations, with the trades unions, and many others. John was driven to Orlando for lunch at the home of Nelson Mandela. He and Oliver Tambo had together opened the first all-African law firm to operate in Johannesburg; Nelson was the leader of the ANC Youth Movement, and had been volunteer No. 1 in the Defiance Campaign. He lived with his first wife and children in a small three-roomed house for which he paid £1 15s. rent per month; it had bare brick walls, concrete floors and no ceilings. As with all African homes that John visited, it was spotlessly clean, and he was served a very nice lunch. Nelson's wife and children did not eat with the men. After lunch Nelson came with soap and a bowl of water, and conducted John to the outside lavatory, a bucket in a tumbledown shed.

John was much impressed by Nelson Mandela, by his personal dignity, intelligence and balance; he confirmed all John's views and impressions. He referred, as everyone did, to 'the Congress' – this was an alliance of the ANC, the Indian National Congress, the all white Congress of Democrats, and the Coloured People's Organisation. The Congress, Nelson said, was not really Communist, but government policy, and the absurdities of the Suppression of Communism Act were driving it in that direction; it was not the direction in which the present leadership wished it to go, but the Communist party was the only white organisation that accepted non-white members, and worked with them on equal terms, it was completely identified with the struggle against apartheid, and it stood unequivocally for full democracy and universal suffrage. There was little time left, Nelson warned, for there to be a possibility of real co-operation between black and white.

John slipped away to visit Christopher Gell, a young man he had met at Cambridge. A year after his marriage, Christopher had had an attack of polio that left him completely paralysed; he had to live in an iron lung. But from his invalid bed he bombarded the Press with articles, letters and protests. He was exceptionally well informed. 'For all that most white South Africans know about Africans they might as well be living in Timbuctoo,' he said. John found his visit wonderfully stimulating and informative, and he marvelled at the courage of Christopher and his wife Nora who did everything for him. It was agreed that John would send copies of his sermons or articles on South Africa, so that any misrepresentation could be corrected, and Christopher would write regularly with information. This invaluable correspondence continued until Christopher's death in 1958.

John went on to visit the Reverend Arthur Blaxall's home for blind Africans. He wrote of a deaf, blind and dumb African whose face lit up with joy when he touched Blaxall's beard; Blaxall then 'spoke' to him through vibrations in the hand. It had taken years of patient training for Blaxall and his wife to learn and teach this method of communication.

Back in Johannesburg the hectic round of meetings began again, but in spite of his unalleviated tiredness, John was settling happily into the Reeves family with their four children. Life was far from easy, Ambrose was under constant pressure, frequent anonymous telephone calls threatened the lives of himself and his family, shots were fired into the house, and the police did nothing. 'The cruelty and beastliness of this place is beyond belief,' Ambrose said.

Oliver Tambo came to Bishops House and took John to his office for a meeting with a few members of the ANC executive which included the general-secretary, Walter Sisulu. John thought they were slightly 'cagey', but as Oliver drove John back he opened out. He was a keen Anglican, and had had thoughts of becoming ordained. He was beginning to despair of the timidity of the Church: fine statements but so little action. Father Huddleston and Bishop Reeves were the ones who gave him and others a small ray of hope. Oliver was certainly no Communist, but he said, 'If you are drowning and someone throws you a rope, you don't stop to ask about his political beliefs'. If only more Churchmen would come out openly in support of the Congress, it might halt the way in which many politically minded Africans and Indians were being driven despite themselves towards the Communist party. Earlier in the day John had heard the same thing from a meeting with the Indian National Congress. John felt very drawn to Oliver, a man with intelligence and dedication, without self-seeking and with an exceptionally warm and attractive personality: a truly Christian spirit. Soon both he and Nelson Mandela, along with Chief Luthuli, were banned under the terms of the Suppression of Communism Act.

Dinner with Sir Ernest and Lady Oppenheimer of Anglo-American was a rather different experience. John had already met Harry Oppenheimer who had said, quite pleasantly, that John's 'interference' was helping Malan, and making the task of the Parliamentary opposition, the United party, much more difficult. But he added that, of course, John must speak according to his conscience. Ambrose and Margaret Reeves accompanied John to the dinner, a magnificent affair. 'Talk of marble halls,' John wrote, 'and rooms large enough to fit in two or three houses . . . they have 60 servants . . . and yet there was a feeling of unhappiness despite all the diamonds, pearls, good food and drink and beautiful dresses – also much bosom only just concealed'. 'How could people like this know or imagine the life of Africans in the locations?'

John was next invited to Pretoria for discussions with the principal government officials at the Ministry of Native Affairs. It was a very high-powered and intellectual discussion, and John had to be alert and on guard. They evaded anything to do with principle, and did not answer John's questions about repression. 'They showed', he said, 'a combination of obstinacy and brilliance . . . a ruthless team with most of the cards in their hands'. 'The opposition should realise what they are up against, the English-speaking whites especially tended to underestimate these astute politicians.'

For lunch John was driven nine miles out of Pretoria to the African location to meet a Mr Tema, an African minister of the Dutch Reformed Church. John was curious to discover what could be the feelings of an African in this reactionary and apartheid supporting Church. After lunch, Mr Tema asked him into his study. 'Now that we are quite alone,' he began, 'I want to tell you that what you say and what you do have made you one of the great spiritual leaders of my

people.' 'I nearly jumped through the ceiling,' John said, 'then Tema
let himself go . . . he remains in his Mother Church, but the African
ministers and members are out to redeem it. He does not, of course,
preach segregation, and he is a member of the ANC – 'the only
"political instrument" worth supporting'.

John was returned to Johannesburg in the Pretoria mayoral car 'with
flag flying'. By way of contrast he went to spend the evening at the
home of advocate Bram Fischer who had invited in some of his friends.
Bram was a genuine as well as a 'listed' Communist, as were most of
those present. 'And yet,' said John, 'I felt more in common with this
group than with say the clergy group in Durban'. Over the years John
and I have known a number of South African Communists, most of
whom seem more concerned with the abolition of apartheid than with
Communist theory or economics. Many of them are fine people of
rock-like integrity, who have made great personal sacrifices in the
cause of African freedom. Bram Fischer came from an old and
respected Afrikaner family, but he identified himself wholeheartedly
and selflessly with the non-white people of South Africa. John thought
him charming.

For his last weekend in Johannesburg, John was invited to Ros-
ettenville to stay in the Priory House of the Community of the
Resurrection. Trevor Huddleston was away, so John was looked after
by a former Westcott House pupil, Martin Jarrett-Kerr, who had been
suspicious of what he saw as a worldly right-wing priest, 'John I', at
Westcott, and who now met this notorious radical, 'John II'. Martin
took him off on a visit to Orlando, of which John wrote:

> It was the worst thing of my whole tour . . . municipal shelters put up
> seven years ago as temporary housing for thousands and thousands of
> Africans – a pit open-air lavatory for hundreds of houses, quite exposed
> and opening into a ditch in which the children paddle and bathe . . . one
> tap for about every hundred families – in some parts even less. No roads,
> just rough tracks in the veld; mostly tumbledown shacks; only home-
> made braziers with which to warm themselves – nothing but insult to
> human dignity.

On Sunday evening there was a meeting in the Priory of about forty
African clergy attended by Ambrose. He had told John that he thought
he was unwise to speak openly in favour of the Congress in the way
that Trevor Huddleston did. 'I don't think you'd find any of my clergy
are members,' he said. At the meeting there were many frank speeches

expressing opposition to apartheid. John decided to take a risk; he asked if any of those present were members of the ANC. There was a long silence, then at the back one man stood up and produced his card, 'I wouldn't have any congregation to preach to if I didn't support the Congress,' he said, and one after another got up waving their cards of membership. 'Well I'm damned,' said the bishop.

Contacts in Cape Town were mainly political, left wing and Communist; some good people, some whose party line clichés maddened John – such as the man who spoke admiringly of the dean of Canterbury and asked John's opinion. John's reply that he thought the dean a vain and rather stupid man whose views had little to commend them was greeted with a pained silence. A meeting with the Liberal party produced a good, if somewhat academic discussion, but John felt that they were, perhaps inevitably, so concerned with trying to win white votes, that they inspired little confidence among the non-whites.

Tea with the Anglican dean was not 'political', a group of worthy people discussing the evil moral consequences of the system of migratory labour, the breakdown of family life, rising illegitimacy and spreading venereal disease. White South Africans have a schizophrenic attitude to sex, the men are obsessed by an idea that the one thing African males want is to rape white women, a crime that is punishable by death, though rape of black women by white men, a far more common occurrence, is relatively mildly punished. They accuse the African of every kind of sexual immorality, but think nothing of separating vigorous young men from their wives and families for years at a time.

Cape Town gave John a first-hand experience of the Coloured community, those sad often frustrated human beings trapped in a no-man's-land between black and white. He heard stories such as that of a family in which two little girls were not allowed to see or speak to their brother, because he had 'passed for white' and could, therefore, go to a better school, and even of twins who had to be separated because one arrived noticeably black, and the other apparently white. The police would conduct snooping raids in the Coloured areas, to see if white men were sleeping with Coloured women. They thought nothing of breaking into the women's homes at night, stripping them naked, and roughly searching the house. An academic friend told John that eighteenth-century church registers showed one in ten marriages registered as between black and white.

John saw terrible living conditions for the Coloureds on the Cape

Flats, 'undrained and considered unfit for Europeans, scenes of desolation and misery. For three months of the year some of the houses more or less under water and all surrounded by wet mud'. But the most moving experience of John's brief Cape Town days was an evening meeting in the African location of Lange.

He was asked by the African welfare officer to attend a private meeting; so that a representative group of Africans might welcome and thank him, and tell him frankly what they felt about the present situation. 'They wanted me alone,' John wrote, 'with no other white people, "as we can only trust a very few" . . . very trusting, very flattering, and very saddening . . . There were about 30 people present, and a series of speeches which for thoughtfulness, balance and presentation were excellent; but what frustration, what a growing resentment, what a depth of bitterness welled up into their words.' It was made clear that they were all solidly behind the work of the Congress. The evening ended with African songs, 'so full of sorrow, of yearning and of courage . . . the only dud speech', John noted, 'came from the parson (a Presbyterian)'. After this meeting John said, 'It is the African women who will save South Africa,' and he mentioned especially the names of Lilian Ngoyi and Annie Selinga, leaders of the ANC Women's Committee.

Back in Johannesburg, John got a warm welcome at Bishops House, especially from Margaret Reeves, who said how much they had missed him. On his last Sunday, he celebrated Communion at an Indian Christian church, and in the afternoon addressed a large meeting of the Congress, organised by Walter Sisulu, who took the chair. John's speech was carefully worded, and, he thought, moderate and non-controversial. He did say something of all he had seen, and described South Africa as 'a pleasant mad-house'. He stressed the importance of personal integrity in all who would lead their fellow men, and expressed his concern that the Congress should remain true to the principle of non-violent resistance and struggle. The Press was in attendance, and crowded round John, taking photographs of him with Walter Sisulu and other leaders.

Monday morning Press reports expressed anger and outrage, not so much about what John had said, but at the fact that he had dared to identify himself with the struggle of the Congress, and had spoken to an audience of non-whites brought together by non-white political organisations; the whole affair was written up as a Communist plot.

The next day was homeward bound – a twenty-four-hour flight to London, in which John happily had the companionship of Ambrose Reeves.

I was at Heathrow to meet them.

27

Consequences

JOHN had been met at Heathrow by the Press, and his comments were widely disseminated. 'The Canon Collins Controversy' was in full swing in South Africa; it now erupted in England. Trevor Huddleston brought his strong guns to bear on the London *Times*: 'Canon Collins has exaggerated nothing; his statements have been entirely accurate, and anyone who knows what the African people presently suffer could add to them very considerably. The extreme sensitiveness of White South Africa to criticisms of any kind is an indication of its sense of guilt . . . South Africa today is a very sick country.'

John was pleased by a thoughtful article from an ANC member that concluded: 'We on the African side hear and recognise in Canon Collins' pronouncements the voice of the Christian conscience raised from across the seas in protest against betrayals of values considered sacred and precious in the Christian tradition.'

While the whites were calling John a traitor to his profession, a politician and a Communist, it was the Africans who recognised that he spoke and acted simply as a Christian priest.

Number 2 Amen Court had been relatively peaceful in John's absence, now it became a hubbub of activity. John had to give interviews, write articles, compose carefully worded letters to the Press, and respond to numerous invitations to speak up and down the country.

His immediate concern was somehow to counter the Bantu Education Act. The purpose of this iniquitous piece of legislation was openly proclaimed by the South African government: 'The native will be taught from childhood that equality with the Europeans is not for him.' 'There is no place for the Bantu in the European community above the level of certain forms of labour.' 'Education should stand with both feet in the Reserves, and have its roots in the spirit and being of Bantu society.'

In pursuance of this cynical programme, all primary education was to be in the vernacular; few were able to afford secondary education, as Africans had to pay for uniforms, and books (free for white children), and even then instruction was to be primarily in Afrikaans. Parents and children were to clean and maintain classrooms, and since Africans were not to be allowed to undertake skilled work, manual subjects would be substituted for academic and technical ones. This was all in line with the attempt to build up a phoney 'Bantu culture'.

It was the Christian Churches which had pioneered African education, and since this saved money for the central government, it made them substantial grants. These were now to be withdrawn as Christian education 'created wrong expectations on the part of the native'. There were threats to expropriate Church schools that would not toe the line.

John sought an interview with his old friend and enemy Geoffrey Fisher; he hoped to persuade the archbishop to sponsor a scheme to raise £100,000 to enable the Church in South Africa to save at least some of its secondary schools and training colleges. The archbishop was not unsympathetic, but said, as usual, that he must consult the Archbishop of Cape Town. A few days later he wrote to John to say that he was handing the scheme over to the British Council of Churches, and he proposed to send two ecclesiastics to South Africa to report on the situation.

Messrs Greaves and Fenton Morley returned after two weeks, announcing that reports (John's and Trevor Huddleston's!) were much exaggerated, things were not so bad, the South African Church was doing all that could be done; outside criticism and interference were not helpful. As far as the official Church was concerned, opposition to the Bantu Education Act died a natural death, except for Ambrose Reeves who proposed to close all the schools in his diocese rather than 'co-operate in any way in furthering an education policy which violates the principles from which all true education ought to spring'. 'Church schools', the bishop said, 'must not be used to indoctrinate children with a racial ideology that is clean contrary to the Gospel'.

With all the activity John was getting more and more tired, sometimes he looked grey with exhaustion. There was not much I could do since I was only recovering rather slowly from a viral pneumonia contracted during our summer 'locum'. I felt anxious and generally frustrated. I had begun to want to play a more responsible and personal part in Christian Action: behind the scenes I did quite a lot, I spoke at small gatherings, and during our last year at Oxford I had written a brief book on the origin, aims and progress of the movement; this Victor had obligingly published, an act of friendship, since it didn't make him any money. During John's absence in South Africa, our vice-chairman, Canon Edward Carpenter, was in charge, but many day-to-day decisions were made by Freda and myself. On John's return, I suggested that I might be co-opted on to the council as a full member. I was a little surprised when he did not immediately jump at my suggestion, he said he must consult his colleagues.

The colleagues seemed happy to welcome me. At the first meeting that I attended, I disagreed with John on some not very important point; quite sharply he shut me up. I was surprised and hurt, I thought I had made a valid point. With hindsight, I should perhaps have been more sensitive and tactful. Though John had shed much of his conventional and old-fashioned upbringing, he had not, I realised, altogether shed his attitude to marriage. Had I wanted to follow an independent career, he would not have objected, although he might not have liked it; he genuinely thought of our marriage as a partnership, but there seemed to be a senior and a junior partner. I remembered a good-humoured argument we had had with two married Christian friends, the men both supporting the Pauline view, that the man is 'the head of the woman'. If there was disagreement about some important decision, they said, then someone would have to make the final decision, and that someone had to be the man. That was not my idea, it sounded logical, but was unrealistic. If you had such a disagreement, you had to live with it, and work it out together, you might arrive at a compromise, or one, *not necessarily* the woman, might eventually accept the other's viewpoint. However, at the time, this all seemed rather academic, John and I were so completely happy and at one.

What with separation and illness, we needed time alone together, so we set off for a comfortable hotel in Torquay. The Sunday morning after our arrival, I, still convalescent, had a luxurious breakfast in bed, and John got up to go to Communion; but he never got there. The church was on top of a hill, and he got so breathless that he was unable to climb up. I had been nagging, yes nagging, him to see a heart specialist, but he had done nothing. 'Come on,' I said. 'We're going straight back to London, and you're going to see a doctor.' For once, John submitted, he felt and looked really ill.

Dr Bedford was a distinguished cardiologist who practised privately and at the Middlesex Hospital. He examined John. 'There's nothing wrong with your heart,' he said, 'but your lungs are in a shocking condition. You must go and see my colleague at the Middlesex, Dr

Scadding.' This good doctor immediately ordered John into hospital, and he was given an amenity bed, just off Dr Bedford's ward. They drained a lot of nasty fluid off his lungs, and then set to work to try and discover the cause of the trouble. Although the lungs were cleared, John did not recover, he was still very ill. Preliminary tests were inconclusive; I realised that there could be unpleasant possibilities.

Friends were marvellous and helpful; none more so than Victor. He visited John every evening on his way back from his office, and kept up a regular supply of books, something that John much appreciated. Later Ruth told me that Victor, who was a friend of Dr Bedford's, thought John was going to die, and was in a state of near panic on his behalf. Later, one afternoon, I was alone with John, and Dr Bedford in his long white coat arrived with his retinue of registrars, assistant registrars and students, there must have been about six of them in white jackets of varying lengths. Dr Bedford, who was known in the hospital as 'God', demanded absolute silence when he was examining his patients; this time it was not an examination but a verdict; there was a deathly hush, and he looked grave. 'You needn't go,' he said to me, and I felt that he must be about to pronounce the death sentence. But what they had finally discovered was that John's was a case of pulmonary tuberculosis – an unforeseen and unwelcome consequence of his South African visit. John must stay in hospital for at least two to three months, and be treated with the new drugs that were just coming into use.

Since I and the children were contacts, we all had to visit Dr Scadding to be screened and – in the case of the children – inoculated. After he had listened carefully to my chest, Dr Scadding said, 'Has anyone ever told you that there might be something wrong with your heart?' 'Certainly not,' I replied rather indignantly, after all, I had played every kind of game, had even been a Lacrosse Blue at Oxford, and had borne five children. 'Well,' he said. 'I would like you to go and see my colleague Dr Bedford.' So to Dr Bedford I went, and he confirmed that I had a congenital hole in my heart. 'There's nothing we can do about it,' he said. 'Try not to walk up too many hills or stairs, no more mountains please, and come and see me once a year.'

Whatever troubles I might experience were in the future; it was John's recovery that mattered. I now had plenty of responsibility, rather more than I had bargained for. Christian Action was fine, with Freda and her helpers in the basement, Edward Carpenter as chairman, and a lively and active council; I was glad that I too could play a part in shaping policy. But I had another, more immediate, responsibility, something of an anxiety: this was Mr Sparrow. Although we were all supposed to be never having had it so good, beggars still frequented Amen Court.

I am not sure how Mr Sparrow came to us, but John took a fancy to him. He came from prison, where, on and off, he seemed to have spent a lot of his life. He had hardly any possessions, and his only shelter was a bed for the night in a Rowton House – those hostels for the real down and outs. But Mr Sparrow said he wanted to make good, and to use his skill as a watch and clock mender; he still had a few tools. John tried him out on one or two watches, and found that he did indeed know his trade. There was a small back room in the basement as yet unused, so John had it fixed up as a workshop, got a few more tools for Mr Sparrow, and persuaded our friends to send us their clocks and watches for repair.

For a time all went well, Mr Sparrow had a key to the back door, and came in and out regularly. There was something endearing about him; he showed us crumpled and grubby photographs of his children, thin, large-eyed pathetic little miniature Mr Sparrows. Later, I learned that bigamy was only one in the long catalogue of his crimes, that included nearly everything short of rape and murder. But Mr Sparrow's feeling for children was real, he was kind and goodnatured to our boys, and took a particular fancy to Richard; he produced a broken-down old watch (could it have been stolen?) and spent a long time repairing it. He was offended when I offered to pay for his time and labour. 'It's a present for Richard,' he said with dignity.

But now things were not going so well, he came in late, sometimes not at all, there were bits of watches and clocks strewn all over his work table, nothing got finished, his hands shook suspiciously, and I feared he was drinking. One day he arrived, coughing badly and obviously ill. With the help of our local doctor, I managed to get him a bed in a hospital, and went to fetch him and his pathetic little bundle of belongings from the grim Rowton House where he bedded down. 'It isn't the same,' he said. 'What's gone wrong, it doesn't feel the same.' I am afraid he sensed my suspicion and lack of trust; he had been upset when John was taken away; while John was around he had felt at home in our basement, and though he had every opportunity for exercising his other trade of stealing, he took nothing. He never came out of hospital; I visited him occasionally until he died; yes, I did everything that could have been expected of me, but, humanly speaking, I knew that I had somehow failed Mr Sparrow.

This was a strange period in our lives. John never said he was unhappy in hospital, he was a good patient, he made no complaints, obeyed instructions and was popular with the doctors and nurses. He would have liked an occasional drink, so we asked Dr Bedford. 'I don't think a glass of sherry a day would hurt you,' he said; so I brought along a case of John's favourite brand. The next morning he was woken up as usual between five-thirty and six a.m. by a young nurse; she handed him his pills and a glass of brown liquid – 'Whatever's this?' he said. 'Your sherry,' she replied, 'You're to have one glass a day.' Once that little matter was clarified we had some convivial evenings with ourselves, and with visiting friends.

Christmas without John seemed a bleak prospect. As with most families, we had evolved our own ritual, and since children are deeply conservative this had to be properly observed. Foraging expeditions into Suffolk produced a Christmas tree, holly, fruit, vegetables, and often a brace of pheasants and a couple of cockerels. We prided ourselves on our tree, the tallest in the Court, displayed in a window of John's study for all the world to admire. There was some family disagreement over the decoration, as we were evenly divided between Classics and Romantics. The first, John, Andrew and Peter wanted everything restrained and symmetrical, the Romantics, Richard, Mark and I preferred our magic tree to be smothered in a glorious, glittering abundance of tinsel, coloured baubles and coloured lights; the Romantics, with their vulgar taste, usually won. There were fine and joyful services in the cathedral, plenty of carols, and singing of a heart-catching beauty. At home all was thoroughly traditional with stockings and a huge Christmas dinner, usually on Boxing Day as I couldn't manage religion and cooking at the same time.

One Christmas Eve stands out, as late in the evening John and I were in the basement rather despairingly faced by two cockerels in need of plucking and cleaning. As we scraped and fumbled inexpertly there was a ring at the back door – a Christmas Eve beggar. John brought him down, and I groaned inwardly. He was a strange rather wild-looking person; he saw our cockerels, and smiled happily. 'I used to work on a chicken farm,' he said. 'I'll do them for you.' And in next to no time they were perfectly plucked and cleaned. We offered him food and drink, we would have offered him a bed, but he refused everything, even money. He talked to John for a while, and said he had just come out of hospital – a psychiatric hospital we understood – he assured us that he was all right and had somewhere to go to, and off he went, quite cheerfully into the night. We never saw him again.

Towards the end of January, John was pronounced sufficiently recovered to leave hospital, but not to return to Amen Court, and not to consider starting work again until September. Dr Bedford was able to arrange for him to go to Osborne House, one large wing of which was given over to a convalescent home for officers and ex-officers. So, on a bitterly cold morning I took John by train to the Isle of Wight. The building looked formidable, but inside it was warm and comfortable, and the rooms large and well furnished. It was run on strictly Service lines. The superintendent, an ex-military gentleman, came to inspect John. 'Report for PT at nine a.m. tomorrow,' he informed him. I protested in the strongest terms; John had been confined to bed for nearly three months, and such a regime would have killed him, so the sentence was reduced to the occupational therapy class, where ageing colonels, admirals, and air-commodores made bedroom slippers and rugs for wives and daughters.

After a month at Osborne House, John was much better, but not yet ready for life at Amen Court. Hilary Flegg, a South African friend, wrote from Majorca and asked us to join her, but we had financial problems. A day or two later, John opened a letter and out fell a cheque for £250. This was from John Oram, whom John had befriended on a Suffolk locum, and to whom he had passed on a Stock Exchange tip that had been given him. Oram had made a handsome profit, and this cheque came as a thanks to John, with the proviso that it was to be used by him personally, and not given to any of his good causes. We had a month's perfect holiday in Majorca, an as yet undiscovered little paradise.

I persuaded the chapter to allow us to let No. 2 until September, and we rented part of an old house in Devon that we had seen advertised. The house was attractive, and the countryside beautiful, but Slapton Sands was not a success; the weather remained bad, Mark was constantly ill with tonsillitis, Peter was bored and tiresome, and we all found the climate enervating. Then Richard developed mysterious trouble with his knees, and ended up in Great Ormond Street Hospital; there was a national rail strike, and that made it difficult for me to visit him. It was a horrid feeling having no home base, and I wished we had not let 2 Amen Court.

This low ebb of Collins family fortunes was much lightened by our eldest son Andrew gaining a scholarship to Eton. We had had a serious debate over the education of our children, we wanted to help them to grow up feeling neither superior nor inferior to any other human being or group. We wondered whether we should send them to State schools, but their friends and relations would be at private schools, and that might produce just the kind of chip on shoulder that we wanted to avoid. We consulted my old boyfriend Ronald Lunt, now headmaster of a State grammar school. He was in favour of private education. 'If you have any money to spend,' he said, 'use it on a good prep school, and then let them find their own way'. So that was what we did, and in due course, all Andrew's brothers also found their own way to Eton. We were lucky in having clever children, they were happy at Eton, and the older boys were fortunate enough to have the enlightened and liberal Robert Birley as their headmaster. We hoped that the less desirable aspects of such a privileged education would be counteracted by the influence of their home.

I didn't know what we should do when we had to leave Slapton on 25 June, but Victor and Ruth generously came to our rescue, and offered us their country home until September. They were only there at weekends, and the rest of the time we had the run of this pleasant house full of books and with a large and lovely garden. The boys all loved it, and without such true friends we might have had a rather miserable summer.

John, as ordered, did not work, but we both had time to think and talk and be with each other, and with our children. South Africa had affected John deeply; apart from the injustice, the human cost of apartheid, and the corruption of human relationships that the system imposed, it raised in extreme and dramatic form the whole issue of religion and politics. If you were an African, there was literally no area of your personal life that was not covered by some piece of discriminatory and political legislation. Even the whites, for whom it all seemed materially comfortable and convenient, were hemmed in, and subject to unpleasant penalties if they refused to toe the apartheid line. To say that religion must have nothing to do with politics was to say that it must have nothing at all to do with people's lives. 'How can you love your neighbour, if you are never allowed to meet him?' asked Trevor Huddleston. And how could a government calling itself Christian ensure that an empty ambulance would leave a badly injured African child lying in the street, because, by political decree, this 'whites only' ambulance was not permitted to take a black child to hospital?

John was deeply disappointed by the failure of the official South African Church to make an effective stand against apartheid. Synods passed resolutions, individual bishops spoke out, but there was no effective action; the existence and maintenance of the institution was always, in the long run, more important than the sufferings of individual human beings. Consciences might be eased by charitable activities, and schemes for alleviating human distress, but nothing was to be done to attack the root of that distress, because that would be 'political'.

Coming home, though the situation was nothing like so extreme, many people, especially those of a conservative persuasion, and many ecclesiastics still pronounced comfortably that religion must have nothing to do with politics. Apart from the tradition of the Hebrew prophets and the theology of the Incarnation, this attitude seemed an absurdity, when bishops were politically appointed, and sat in the House of Lords as part of the legislature of the land. What were they doing there if not to fulfil some political role? Geoffrey Fisher was capable of, and on occasion did, stand up to the State, but he was at heart an organisation man, concerned inevitably with preserving the institution; he did not care for those who rocked the boat. Increasingly John found that much as he longed for his fellow Christians to be with him, more often than not it was the agnostics, the atheists, the rational humanists and the Communists who rallied to the causes that he embraced.

So John and I talked and discussed the future work of Christian Action. I was with him all the way in his South African work, but I remember saying to him that I felt that Christian Action would lose credibility if it did not face the challenge of modern war, and especially of nuclear testing and the threat of nuclear war. He accepted and agreed, and I knew that from now on we would be a working and an equal partnership.

Although John had been saddened by official Church attitudes, he still had the support of many Christian friends, and he was a loyal and in many ways a traditional Churchman. He had never thought of himself as, or wanted to be, an outsider, so much of his religious and spiritual life depended upon the forms of worship that he practised and performed as a priest. His religion was deeply personal, but, in the end, he would always support the individual rather than the institution.

Under John's influence I too had become a keen and conscientious Churchwoman; for many years, I found this helpful and sustaining, and I wanted to be entirely with John. At one stage I went regularly to confession, but this did not last long, as I found it unhelpful. Perhaps it was life at St Paul's, perhaps it was the Church's attitude to John, but I was beginning to wobble. I had always been more interested in the mystical side of religion, and had read many of the Christian mystical writers; I reached out to the writers and poets of other religions. John was inclined to be uneasy about this, afraid I was 'going a-whoring after strange gods'; he was not without appreciation of mysticism, but it was not for him, his temperament and his heart were more concerned with the immediate and everyday affairs of human beings. We were complementary but not contradictory.

One weekend Victor announced that we were to have a visit from Arthur Koestler. Ever since he had been in a Spanish prison under sentence of death, daily expecting to be led out to execution, Koestler had been a powerful opponent of the death penalty; now he believed that the time was ripe to launch a campaign for its abolition. As Victor had proved himself the most effective campaigner of his generation, he was the man to run it. Victor was all enthusiasm, he was passionately opposed to the death penalty, and for John it was equally abhorrent on Christian grounds; the first speech that I had ever made in my life was at a school debating society when I proposed the motion that the death penalty should be abolished.

So we all sat in the sunshine in the garden at Brimpton planning this new campaign. Koestler was writing a book on the subject, *Reflections on Hanging*. He said that he would leave his regular publisher so that Victor could publish the book with his usual speed and efficiency. John, through Christian Action, would take on the Churches.

We were ready again for life and action at 2 Amen Court.

28

South Africa Defence and Aid: How It All Began

IT was such a relief to return to our own home, that I almost began to love 2 Amen Court; but after the easy tranquillity of Brimpton the impact of our London life arrived like a whirlwind. It had been full and active; in the next few years it became hyperactive; I had complained that it was like living on a railway station; it soon became a railway station at permanent rush-hour; but these were exciting, exhilarating and rewarding years.

The empty red leather surface of John's large Victorian desk was soon – in one of his much-used phrases – 'snowed under': there was so much to read, to catch up on and to answer. There was a lengthy report from the delegation that had at last got itself to Moscow in May. One of the group, Sir John Lawrence, was a fluent Russian speaker, and already knew the Soviet Union. He noted small improvements and considerably greater openness in discussion with foreigners. One hopeful Christian Action stalwart remarked that the Peace Movement, enthusiastically embraced by the Orthodox Church and the Baptists, was the only place where there was any contact between theology and worship and the outside world of politics. Could the Russian Churches perhaps develop some social ethic via the Peace Movement? However cynical the political leaders may have been in their promotion of this movement, there was no question about the widespread horror of war, and of alarm at the possibility of a rearmed Germany; after their atrocious suffering, the Russian people longed ardently for peace.

There was an account of a meeting for Ambrose Reeves. This was intended to raise money for a joint effort by Christian Action and the Africa Bureau to counter the Bantu Education Act. But we found too many differences of approach, so Christian Action had organised a full and successful meeting, and had handed over the collection, around £1,500, to the Bureau to run their own fund.

John, like his desk, was quickly 'snowed under': Christian Action, capital punishment, chapter deliberations and sermons for the next month in residence. I had hoped that we might now institute a new regime whereby sermons could be started at least by Friday morning, and not hastily finished around two a.m. on Sunday. But my efforts at persuasion failed; 'I'm just clearing the decks,' John would say, and when I persisted he would add, smiling, 'You're an old bully': I might just as well have kept quiet.

John preached some powerful sermons on capital punishment, nuclear tests and weapons, and on all manifestations of racism. He continued to raise money for Christian Action's African work, responded to appeals from Trevor Huddleston and Ambrose Reeves, and began to do the work of Defence and Aid in the Central African Federation. Once more John got into trouble with the Archbishop of Canterbury by objecting publicly to the archbishop's statement that 'Men are not equal in the sight of God, but are equal in the love of God', and to his comment on affairs in Southern Rhodesia to the effect that 'the solution of the problem merely lies in doing simple acts of kindness and courtesy to one another'. Fisher objected in his turn to John's sermons, and they had a prolonged, semantic, theological correspondence that got nowhere. Fisher finally wrote in exasperation:

> Your method seems to aim at fostering distrust between the races; in so doing you are, in my judgement, betraying the Gospel. I was doing precisely the opposite. If you do not like my method you need not go out of your way to abuse and misrepresent it. I dislike your method, but I have never attacked it or you in public.

Perhaps Geoffrey Fisher had a point, though John would have argued that the views of an archbishop were likely to be influential, and if they were, as John believed, based on dangerous misunderstandings, somebody had to challenge them publicly. It was a sad ending to a relationship that had begun well, and in later years John did, I think, regret it.

John's return to the anti-apartheid scene produced a predictable new crop of hate mail and of worse. As well as in South Africa, there was unrest in the three provinces of the Central African Federation, and one morning our daily help arrived on the doorstep in tears.

'Whatever is the matter, Mrs Welch?' I asked.

'They want to hang Canon Collins,' she sobbed. 'It says so outside'. And sure enough, our old enemies the League of Empire Loyalists had been at work in the night, and had painted slogans in large white lettering along the respectable wall of 2 Amen Court: 'HANG CANON COLLINS – BANDA'S REBEL HEADQUARTERS'. They had used indelible paint, so there the slogans had to remain, somewhat to the embarrassment of our ecclesiastical neighbours. Later we had bricks through a downstairs window, car tyres slashed, and threatening telephone calls. 'I wonder,' wrote Trevor Huddleston, 'whether at any time in its history that quiet and lovely Wren house had dreamed of being such a revolutionary place!'

Christian Action worked hard at the Anti-Capital Punishment Campaign, publishing leaflets, circularising the clergy, arranging seminars and organising petitions. This last got John into trouble, this time with the Archbishop of York.

Meanwhile, under Victor's enthusiastic and energetic chairmanship, the Campaign was making progress. He had assembled a powerful all-party committee and an impressive list of sponsors. There had been considerable public disquiet over recent executions, notably that of Derek Bentley, a mentally retarded and illiterate youth who was hanged for the murder of a policeman, not committed by himself, but by his companion Christopher Craig, who was too young to be executed; and more recently by the hanging of Ruth Ellis, mother of two young children who, when drunk, had shot her lover, after he had beaten her up so badly that she had had a miscarriage. The time, as Arthur Koestler had sensed, was ripe.

The Campaign was to be officially launched at the Central Hall, on 10 November, with a galaxy of star speakers who were only to be allowed a few minutes each, except for Victor and Gerald Gardiner. Victor asked me to take the chair at an overflow meeting just across the road at Church House, so there could be an easy shuttle-service of speakers. I was somewhat nervous at such a prospect. The main meeting and the overflow were sell-outs, and some 400 people had to be turned away. I didn't have much to do except introduce and thank the distinguished speakers. The only one that I afterwards remembered at all clearly was J.B. Priestley: he made a brilliant speech but seemed thoroughly out of humour, as if he disliked the whole business, and whereas the other speakers had made polite gestures towards the chair, Priestley ignored me; he was not, I decided, a nice man.

John was a keen member of the Campaign committee, but he found himself in an uneasy position in the growing rift between Victor and Arthur Koestler. John's and my opposition to the death penalty arose from principle and Christian conviction, but we were not always happy with Victor's extreme expression of his absolutist position. But of his brilliant campaigning there was no question, and on 6 February 1956, on a free vote in the House of Commons, capital punishment was rejected by 283 to 262 votes. Unfortunately that was not the end of the story; all the Conservative government did was to allow time for a private member's abolitionist Bill moved by Sydney Silverman. This passed in the Commons, but was thrown out by the Lords. Instead of allowing the Silverman Bill to return to the Commons to become law, the government brought in its own 'Homicide Bill' abolishing hanging for various categories of murder, and retaining it for others. This, as the judges and law lords had warned, proved unworkable, and abolition was only finally achieved under the 1964 Labour government, when Gerald Gardiner was Lord Chancellor.

In 1956, the year of Suez and of the Hungarian uprising, one of the two events that were to shape John's and my lives in the years to come took place in South Africa. On 5 December, in the early hours of the morning, a favourite time for the security police to pounce, 156 men and women of all races were arrested and charged with high treason – the penalty for which was death. Without waiting for committees or agreements – he got those later – John sent £100 to Ambrose Reeves. He asked him to brief the best available counsel for the defence of the accused, and guaranteed that Christian Action would raise a fund to pay legal fees, look after the accused, help rehabilitate them if and when they were released, and meanwhile care for their families and dependants. Ambrose responded immediately; he set up a corresponding Treason Trial Fund to raise money from within South Africa, and got together a committee to administer the funds.

The accused were a remarkable collection of people from all over South Africa, from the most distinguished to the relatively modest. There were some whom John had met and admired, Chief Luthuli, Nelson Mandela, Oliver Tambo, Walter Sisulu, Dr Naiker, Lilian Ngoyi – many more, in later years, became our friends and colleagues. There were a number of prominent Christians, and a number of Europeans, including a Methodist minister. There were three other clergy, eight lawyers, seven doctors, one member of parliament, and the most distinguished African professor, Dr Z.K. Matthews, with his son Jo. All these diverse people were united only in their opposition to apartheid, and in the fact that they had, in 1955, attended the great Congress of the People which had adopted the Freedom Charter.

It was largely on the basis of this mildly social-democratic document

that the State hoped to base its charge of high treason. The Charter
advocated universal suffrage, nationalisation of the mines and a few
other major industries, maternity benefits, holidays with pay, a
National Health Service, free and equal education, freedom of speech,
equal rights for all. It could have been based on the Beveridge Report,
or have served as a rather old-fashioned Labour party manifesto.
Nowhere in the document was there any suggestion that these
desirable objects were to be achieved by anything other than non-
violent means. The Freedom Charter is uncompromisingly non-racial
and is prefaced by the statement: 'South Africa belongs to all who live
in it'. Throughout all the years of oppression, the ANC has never
deviated from this non-racial policy.

John was determined to ensure maximum publicity for the Treason
Trial, partly to help with fund-raising, and partly to ensure that the
South African government would know that the eyes of the world
were upon it. He approached Gerald Gardiner to ask if he would attend
the preliminary hearings as an observer. After consultations with
Justice and with the Bar Council, it was agreed that Gerald would go
representing both Christian Action and the Bar Council.

On Gerald's return early in 1957, Christian Action put on a Central
Hall meeting for him, and afterwards published his speech as a
pamphlet. This was a masterpiece of clarity and legal discretion. He
drew attention to the manner in which the Nationalist government had
openly packed the judiciary by appointing 'judges who shared its
views'. But, said Gerald, we might still hope that at least some of the
appointees would put law before politics, and over the years, some of
them have. He noted that the South African definition of treason was
very much wider than the British, and he examined the Suppression of
Communism Act, under which some of the accused were also
charged. According to this remarkable law, 'If you were a Communist
forty years ago and had left the Party you are still a Communist today.
And whether you are or have ever been a Communist, you are a
Communist if the Governor-General says you are.'

The preliminary hearings were likely to last at least three months, as
a minimum of 10,000 documents had to be examined. The reason for
this extraordinary state of affairs was 'that any document that is found
on the premises of any organisation of which you are alleged to have
been at any time a member or active supporter, can be used against
you. That is to say that if you were a member of an organisation 10
years ago and resigned from it, any document found on the premises of
such an organisation can still be used as evidence against you.'

The first few days of the hearings were something of a farce, though Gerald reported that the magistrate in charge was fair and impartial. He noted that the prosecuting 'Counsel' were not in fact 'Counsel' and not even members of the Bar: they were civil servants. At first there were no loudspeakers, so nobody could hear what was said; this went on for four days of appearances and adjournments. Meanwhile, the accused had been put into a large cage of tubular scaffolding and wire-netting, upon which some wits had hung notices saying 'Do not Feed'.

Outside the Court there were crowds, and Gerald happened to witness a disturbance during which the police lost their heads and started shooting; Gerald protested publicly about the behaviour of the police, and this prompted a letter to the London *Times* from the minister concerned disputing Gerald's version of events, and insisting that the police had only fired blanks. Gerald replied: 'By the time the Bishop of Johannesburg had picked up two bullets in the street which he showed me, and a member of the Bar had picked up a bullet which he showed me, and I had seen an obvious bullet-hole in a plate glass window behind the crowd, I was beginning to think that this statement was erroneous.' The crowd, he added, was good-humoured and non-violent, and the police action was quite unnecessary. Serious bloodshed was averted by the Bishop of Johannesburg who threw himself between the police and the crowd. 'I do not regard it as accidental,' Gerald concluded, 'that this is the first time in the history of the Church of England that it has openly assisted in the organisation of a Fund to defend men and women charged with High Treason in a foreign land (which is a remarkable thing if you come to think of it), and that it is the first time in the history of the Bar Council that they have been represented at a foreign trial . . . The Church and the Bar have always been the last bulwarks for civil liberty . . . These are matters from which no-one who is interested in civil liberties can afford to disassociate himself.'

John's fund-raising energies now met their greatest challenge. He employed every means: public meetings, circularisations, advertisements, letters to the Press, concerts, entertainments, exhibitions. Opening letters at breakfast time became more and more exciting, the family had bets on the amounts, our mathematical son, Peter, totted up the daily score, and luckily this rose steadily enough to meet the requests that arrived regularly from Ambrose Reeves.

29

The Campaign for Nuclear Disarmament

For some time, the Christian Action Council had been debating its attitude to nuclear weapons and nuclear tests; there was a division over whether or not we should try to launch a fullscale anti-nuclear campaign. Edward Carpenter was keen to do this, and so was I. John was heavily involved in race relations, but was ready to throw his weight behind any such initiative. There was public disquiet, as yet rather uninformed, over the possible health hazards of nuclear tests. The Conservative government's white paper of 1955 contained a proposal for Britain to manufacture its own hydrogen bomb; and if you manufacture, you must, of course, test. In the spring of 1957, the first H-bomb tests took place in the Pacific on Christmas Island.

I was restive at the failure of the Christian Action Council to act; of all the issues in which we were involved, it was nuclear weapons about which I felt most deeply. It was not just a fear of the appalling consequences of a nuclear exchange that drove me, with so many others, it was the knowledge that the tests were already threatening the health and the lives of children everywhere. Early in 1957, a small committee was formed in Hampstead calling itself the National Committee for the Abolition of Nuclear Weapons Tests (NCANWT). Lord Russell was its president, and a Quaker, Arthur Goss, the chairman. Dr Sheila Jones, a physicist and social scientist, was one of the driving forces, and now that capital punishment was in abeyance, Peggy Duff had been taken on as secretary. John thought the committee too much of a halfway house, a full-scale anti-nuclear campaign was needed, but I felt that it was, at least, a beginning, and I attended the committee meetings. This small group with its slender resources did a tremendous work of publicity and propaganda, it was a springboard for the greater campaign that followed.

The first action, organised by the committee, in which I took part was a march culminating in a meeting in Trafalgar Square; I was asked to chair this and to be one of the main speakers. This was much more daunting than the capital punishment meeting; a 'chair' on the plinth beneath Nelson's column sounded bleak, and as for speaking, it would be impossible to read from a script, it might rain and blow my paper away; but I could not refuse. I learned my speech by heart, and walked up and down our drawing room rehearsing it. This caused great merriment among my young male chauvinists, imitating Mummy making a speech became a regular family joke. I don't remember any mimicry of Daddy speaking or preaching, though there was plenty of Daddy belching – adolescent masculine fun. It was just as well that I did do all that rehearsing: we slogged through rain and wind, and when we reached the Square the rain bucketed down with even greater violence drenching us all – but, in spite of the weather, we had a good turn out.

There were various burgeoning anti-nuclear groups and activities, among scientists, among the Quakers, and in the Direct Action Committee, but what finally drew all the efforts and anxieties together was, once again, the power of the word. On 2 November 1957, the *New Statesman* published a long article by J.B. Priestley, 'Britain and the Nuclear Bomb'. Priestley, always readable, wrote at his most serious, one after another memorable phrase came tumbling out, and his humour enhanced rather than concealed his powerful moral concern. Every argument was dealt with; the article was not pacifist but was a powerful plea for Britain to renounce any reliance upon nuclear weapons.

John and I were not alone in being impressed and excited by this vigorous article, the *Statesman* experienced an avalanche of letters in support of Priestley, and a second article produced a further avalanche. The editor, Kingsley Martin, sent all these to the Hampstead Committee. They were already debating the possibility of becoming an all-out campaign against the Bomb, and had begun to circularise their list of eminent sponsors to invite their views. Arthur Goss was convinced that such a vital campaign should be led by important national figures, and here was the opportunity to bring this about; Arthur wanted nothing for himself, only an effective campaign to abolish nuclear weapons.

Meanwhile, as a result of the response to Priestley's articles a small group met at Kingsley's flat in the Adelphi; it included J.B. Priestley and his wife Jacquetta Hawkes, Commander Sir Stephen King-Hall, who was interested in working out effective strategies of non-violent resistance to aggression, and George Kennan, who had just delivered the Reith Lectures, 'Russia, the Atom and the West', in which he had questioned the whole nuclear strategy. All were agreed on the need for a national campaign. Kingsley Martin believed that the Hampstead Committee would be ready to sink their own identity in a larger movement, and would bring with them that seasoned and effective campaigner Peggy Duff. Canon Collins of St Paul's was suggested as a possible chairman.

Peggy Duff was deputed to take John along to be introduced to Priestley. This was to be an exploratory meeting, the Priestleys had some reservations about this ecclesiastic: they recognised his effectiveness as a campaigner and fund-raiser, but were not attracted by his public image, which was as misleading as public images always are. We too had some prejudice about the Priestleys, also unfounded and unjust. John, of course, hoped and perhaps assumed that he and Christian Action might be part of any national campaign, but he had no idea of becoming its chairman. 'What was Priestley like?' I asked, and was surprised and pleased to find John so enthusiastic. 'It was the most successful introduction I ever made,' said Peggy Duff.

Shortly after, the Priestleys invited us to dinner in their Albany flat, John had a prior engagement that he could not alter, so I went, a little nervously, on my own. The only other person there was Laurens van der Post's wife, Ingaret, whom I already knew. Jacquetta came to greet me, and I was momentarily intimidated, such a beautiful and elegant woman in her long evening clothes, with an alarming air of distinction and formality – I was wearing something short and ordinary. But even then, I think I sensed there was a great deal behind that appearance that I could not have immediately articulated, but later found to be true: a vulnerability, perhaps a shyness, an imaginative inner life, even a wildness, and a determined honesty, all of which contributes to the fascination of Jacquetta's personality. And Jack, to whom I had taken such a dislike on that Church House occasion, was smiling and welcoming, turning into an entirely delightful host and companion, announcing in his richly seductive voice how happy he was to be spending an evening with three women, he much preferred their company to that of men, they were so much more interesting. By the end of the evening, I knew that Jack and Jacquetta were our friends for life.

Further discussions with the Hampstead Committee resulted in a decision to call together a meeting of the committee's sponsors, and any other interested people. So on 16 January 1958, some fifty people assembled in John's study in 2 Amen Court. They decided to launch the

Campaign for Nuclear Disarmament (CND), and they asked John to become its chairman.

CND and South Africa were not our exclusive commitments over the next six years. Christian Action had other things to do, and so had we, but these two issues certainly dominated our lives. To write of them together, as we lived them day by day, with so much activity, so many different meetings taking place in our house, would throw any would-be reader into confusion. This cannot be the place for a history of CND, so mine must be a selective personal account of how the movement affected John and me.

The first executive committee, appointed from among those who assembled at 2 Amen Court, consisted of Lord Russell (president), J.B. Priestley (vice-president), Canon John Collins (chairman), Ritchie Calder (vice-chairman), James Cameron, Howard Davies from the United Nations Association; Michael Foot, Kingsley Martin, Arthur Goss and Sheila Jones from the Hampstead Committee, and Professor Joseph Rotblat, a distinguished nuclear physicist, who had abandoned anything that might be used for nuclear weaponry, in order to devote himself to medical research. We soon lost Howard Davies and Sheila Jones, but were joined by Lord Wilmot, Sir Richard Acland, Frank Beswick MP, Jacquetta Hawkes, Benn Levy, the playwright, Lord Simon of Wythenshaw and A.J.P. Taylor. The list of sponsors was eminent and respectable: it included three bishops, Gerald Gardiner Q.C., the Very Reverend Sir George Macleod, and many well-known names from the worlds of the arts and entertainment.

Our aims were simple: to persuade Britain to abandon unilaterally all reliance on nuclear weapons; to work for disarmament negotiations; to ban nuclear tests, missile bases, overflights of aeroplanes carrying nuclear weapons, and the export of nuclear weapons and facilities to other countries.

There has always been an attempt, quite unreal, to make some kind of hard and fast division between 'unilateralists' and 'multilateralists', as if the former were somehow, by definition, opposed to multilateral negotiations. The reply of the Campaign was simple: 'unilateralists are multilateralists who mean it'.

CND had a name, an executive, a policy, and Peggy Duff. Peggy's apparently inexhaustible energy, her resilience and her organising skills were phenomenal, all the more so because she gave no appearance of efficiency, in fact seemed thoroughly slapdash, but the results were remarkable, her determination and powers of improvisation somehow ensured that it was nearly always 'all right on the day'. She had good judgement, managed to get on with a vast diversity of human beings, she swore, she drank, not excessively, she smoked – excessively, she was fun. Peggy loved the Campaign and the campaigners, especially the marchers, I don't think she loved the executive, and was somewhat ambivalent about the chairman, but she initially supported executive decisions, even if her sympathies some-times lay elsewhere; she was a political animal, she wanted to get rid of nuclear weapons, and, at least at first, she saw that this was most likely to be achieved politically.

Owing to the wise and unselfseeking leadership of Arthur Goss, the Hampstead Committee handed over its bank balance, its office, and a booking of the Central Hall for 17 February.

This meeting was the public launching of CND. The hall was sold out, as were five overflow meetings, the speeches were brilliant, some of the best public speakers in England spoke on our platforms, and the spirit of the meeting reminded John of the Christian Action launching in Oxford. The Press ignored the occasion.

The Campaign began publishing documents and pamphlets designed to put our case to the public. For pacifists and nuclear pacifists alike the moral case was overwhelming. We should never use these wholly indiscriminate and horrific weapons whose radioactive poisons threatened not just our supposed enemies, but ourselves, neutral nations around the world, and generations yet to be born. There was a further rational and strategic case put with wit and brilliance by A.J.P. Taylor in one of the first Campaign documents, *The Great Deterrent Myth*.

Duncan Sandys' defence white paper of 1957 must be reckoned one of the most extraordinary ever advanced by any government. No provision could or would be made for the defence of the civilian population, and in the event of an overwhelming Russian conventional attack Britain would be prepared to use her nuclear bombs first. It was a plan for national suicide rather than national defence.

Meanwhile the small activist group of pacifists called Direct Action were planning a protest march at Easter from London to the nuclear weapons research centre at Aldermaston. This was to be a peaceful demonstration, although the Committee was also planning acts of Gandhian-style civil disobedience. The executive was somewhat wary of mass demonstrations, and they were wary of Direct Action. They wanted an informed and intellectual campaign to persuade the British public, and through them their political representatives. John's instinct was surer, he believed that a mass campaign was needed as well to impress vote-hungry politicians. CND was not a single issue campaign like capital punishment, it had deep roots in the national psyche, and affected the whole of national life. He persuaded his colleagues to give their support and blessing to a march to Aldermaston, but not, at that stage, to identify the main campaign with it, nor with Direct Action.

On the morning of Good Friday, 1958, John and I were in Trafalgar Square, at the rally to speed the marchers on their fifty-two-mile, four-day slog to Aldermaston. There must have been at least 4,000 people, and there was the same atmosphere of dedication and moral purpose that had informed the Central Hall meeting. There, hoisted up, was the great black banner that we came to know so well, with 'March from London to Aldermaston' painted on it in white lettering, and there were dozens of little lollipops all bearing the CND symbol, white on a black background. The drooping white lines represent both the semaphore for ND and a despairing gesture – 'the death of man'; the enclosing circle is both the world and the unborn child, now threatened by radiation.

John addressed the gathering, and slowly the march moved off, for John and me the urge to go with them was almost overpowering. But we were conditioned to believe that on Good Friday we had to be in church, so, as the square cleared, we walked across to St Martin's-in-the-Fields where Father Huddleston was conducting a three hours service. No priest could have been better fitted for such an occasion; but in spite of his deeply devotional and relevant addresses, our hearts remained with the march.

On Sunday evening John went to Reading where the weary marchers were to spend the night before their final stretch to Aldermaston. The local constituency Labour party had laid on a meeting in the Town Hall, at which John spoke. The 300 or so marchers, all who were left of the thousands who had set off on Good Friday, loyally turned up with some of the local supporters. John felt enormous sympathy and identification with the marchers, but was disturbed by some of the speakers. Michael Scott attacked all politicians and political parties, and urged the campaigners not to waste time on them, but to make it impossible for any government committed to nuclear defence to govern. This declaration of anarchism upset the Labour party organisers, and worried John.

The next day we both joined the final rally on the Falcon Field at Aldermaston, and we then drove Michael back to London. We discussed the possibility of an anti-nuclear movement within the Churches, and John suggested to Michael that he might lead such a movement from within the Campaign, but, after thought, Michael refused. It would never have worked: Michael was a loner, he became more and more committed to non-violent civil disobedience, almost as an end in itself.

All over the country CND groups sprang up like mushrooms; there was an extraordinary upsurge of conviction and moral revulsion, and money flowed in, almost unsolicited, to the Campaign office – as a gesture of good-will we gave £300 to Direct Action for the expenses of their march. After the local and regional groups came the specialist groups: the Women's group and the Christian group, in both of which I was active, the Scientists group, the Architects group, the Press and Publicity group, the Labour Advisory group, the Universities CND – Youth CND and others followed. Somehow or other all these different and differing groups, as well as thousands of individuals, had to be held together in an effective and realistic mass movement – a huge challenge, and a headache for the chairman.

The Women's Committee, one of the earliest specialist groups, was the brainchild of Jacquetta Priestley. Membership fluctuated, those I recall clearly are Dr Antoinette Pirie, Reader in Ophthalmology at Oxford University, Marghanita Laski, Margaret Lane (Lady Huntingdon), Storm Jameson, Dr Janet Aitken, and Mrs Kitty Wintringham. We were not active feminists but we did cherish an idea, enthusiastically supported by Jack Priestley, that the world had for too long been dominated by masculine values of competition, logic, the pursuit of power, fantasies of honour and glory, and the macho image that must never be allowed to lose face. This must now be balanced by feminine values of co-operation, intuition, preservation, rather than destruction, and care for the future of the race. We were not alone in our ideas, women's anti-nuclear groups proliferated, and soon there were voices from overseas, from America, 'Women Strike for Peace' ('strike' interpreted in both its meanings) and in Canada 'Voice of Women' led by a redoubtable lady called Helen Tucker.

Far from the hurly-burly of 2 Amen Court the Women's Committee met in the elegant calm and seclusion of the Priestleys' Albany flat. We planned a women-only meeting, all males excluded, even male journalists – perhaps we feared they might be tempted to mock us. Peggy booked us the Church Hall, Westminster, for 29 June, and we mustered as many distinguished and well-known women as we could for a supporting platform – yes, for good tactical reasons we were unashamedly élitist. This was another remarkable meeting, imagina-tively planned by Jacquetta. The speeches were short, everyone kept strictly to their allocated times. We had collected official 'quotes' from Britain and the USA, and these were read alternately by two actresses. They were effectively horrifying. The meeting concluded with an eye-witness account of the survivors of Hiroshima and Nagasaki, and a reading of extracts of letters from a young Japanese woman whose husband had died after appalling suffering. We had a number of excellent women journalists to cover the meeting, but the men got their own back on us, and the general Press made no mention of the occasion.

The Women's group produced a pamphlet *Tomorrow's Children*, full of scientific information about the long-term effects of radioactive poisons. Much of the information we got from Toni Pirie, for whom I developed affection and an enormous respect for her personal and scientific integrity. She would let nothing pass if she were not absolutely certain of its scientific accuracy. While government scientific advisors were busily working out what might be 'safe' or 'permitted' levels of radiation, I remember Toni's repeated assertion, now, at long last, accepted by the scientific community, 'There is *no* safe level of radiation'.

It was hardly surprising that the public understood little about the long-term and irreversible genetic effects of nuclear tests: two of the most dangerous and long-lasting substances, Caesium 137, and Strontium 90, did not exist in the world until nuclear explosions put them there. They were now accumulating in our food and in our bodies, and were particularly dangerous to growing children. Meanwhile, the Prime Minister, Harold Macmillan, announced blandly, 'There is no evidence that anyone has been harmed by nuclear tests'. Now after thirty years, we learn from released government papers, that officials were doing their best to suppress public knowledge about the effects of radiation, lest a public outcry might put a stop to the British H-bomb tests. Families of British servicemen, who were exposed to the Christmas Island H-bomb tests of 1958, are in process of suing the government. A proportion of these men have died from leukaemia and multiple myeloma, two forms of cancer clearly associated with exposure to radiation.

There were CND activities all over the country. It has been said that during the first year of the Campaign there were some 290 meetings under its auspices. There were marches, pickets, leafletings, demonstrations at rocket bases organised by Direct Action, lobbying of MPs, a stream of letters in the local and national press; there was hardly a day when there was not some activity in any place anywhere in the British Isles. I am amazed at how hard we all worked, and that was especially true of the local groups, most of whose members had full-time jobs, but who were prepared to give up leisure, holidays, sleep for a cause in which they believed. After thirty years it requires some imaginative effort to recapture our feelings, but fear of the outbreak of nuclear war was very real.

The first Aldermaston march was something of a publicity break-through, the Campaign could no longer be ignored by a mainly hostile Press. The line now was to write us all off as a bunch of emotional hysterics, manipulated in some sinister fashion by the Communist party. The fact was that the Communist party was originally opposed to CND, and while some eager and genuinely idealistic Communists joined in as individuals, it was not until 1960 that the party line changed, and the British Peace Committee decided that it, and its members, might be permitted to take part. There were never any Communists on the National Executive, and the Communists, unlike Direct Action, never tried to 'capture' the Campaign, they were hard-working, reliable, and did not support law-breaking.

By now, CND had been observed from overseas, there were anti-nuclear movements in Sweden, Switzerland, Holland and a larger movement in West Germany. After a weekend meeting in London, The European Federation against Nuclear Weapons was formed with a troika of presidents, Dr Heinz Kloppenburg, a Churchman from West Germany, Dr Heinrich Buchbinder, a Swiss writer, and John. There was a grand finale to this weekend. The sympathetic Mayor and City Council of Frankfurt invited the CND executive and foreign delegates to fly over, all expenses paid, for a final consultation in this anti-nuclear city. John was in residence at the cathedral, and was unable to leave, but he preached a rousing anti-nuclear sermon at Matins, which was attended, in comradely fashion, by a number of our atheist and agnostic colleagues, en route for Germany.

As Easter approached, the Campaign, with the amicable agreement of the Direct Action Committee, took over the organisation of the Aldermaston march. Jacquetta Hawkes suggested that we should reverse the direction, and march from Aldermaston to the seat of political power in London. This effectively would make CND's political point, and would have the added advantage that the march would attract larger numbers as it approached the capital. So, on Good Friday morning, John and I and Jacquetta set off in a hired car for Aldermaston.

It was raining when we got to the Falcon Field, and the whole place seemed a chaotic mass of extraordinary looking people floundering about in the mud; a vast tangle of mackintoshes, placards, lollipops, vehicles with loudspeakers desperately imploring people to assemble in groups, put their bags on the baggage lorries, go there, come here. Groups of students had slept out all night in order to be in time for the march, Elsan lavatories had been put up, and the splendid, solid Co-op van that always drove in front of the march, was serving cups of tea and coffee.

Soon friendly and familiar faces began to emerge from the crowd, and those who were able struggled to the centre of the field where John and Michael Scott conducted a brief Good Friday service. Richard Acland, an Anglican lay reader, spoke a few words, and as we sang our last hymn 'O God of Earth and Altar', the rain stopped, and the sun came out.

Somehow or other everything fell into place, baggage loaded, groups organised, holding up their identification banners and slogans: 'Reading CND', 'Oxford CND', 'Friends Peace Committee', 'Kent CND', 'What is morally wrong cannot be politically right', 'Force may subdue but love conquers', 'Join up, do your bit', and as the march progressed contingents from overseas appeared. The Co-op van rumbled off and the executive lined up. John always wore his cassock on the march, partly to emphasise the Christian presence, and partly so as to be easily identified by the police or the Press or in any emergency. Then came the original great black banner with only two little words crossed out and altered – March ~~to~~ from Aldermaston ~~from~~ to London, and tied on top a bunch of daffodils – new life – new hope.

We set off almost at the stated time of one p.m., and marched in silence past the grim-looking Atomic Weapons Establishment. And then the gaiety and excitement bubbled up, the bands played and people sang, the marshals and outriders motorcycled vigorously up and down counting the numbers. We stopped for tea on a village green – the Co-op van there before us – and refreshed, we marched on into Reading in a gold and green spring evening. I found a long-tailed tit's little lichen-covered nest in the hedge as we passed by; everything had a lyrical quality about it; we laughed, talked, sang, made new friends, shared food and drink – we seemed part of a new spring, a real rebirth.

Those who slept at Reading had a rough time, bare boards, few blankets, no hot meals, and little sleep, but they were all back in place next morning ready to set off for Slough. This was the longest and hardest day, blisters appeared, first-aid cars were more and more frequented, and there were occasional calls for doctors. It was already dark when we reached the outskirts of Slough.

John and Peggy always made special efforts to be on friendly terms with the police, and so far all had gone well. At Slough we had a new lot, and we were joined by a stranger with a curious shut-in face, who insisted on walking alongside the executive: we concluded that he must be from MI5, CID, or some such sinister body. Instead of marching us straight into the town the police diverted us into the back streets, and there was chaos for everyone trying to find baggage and accommodation in the dark; it was really tough after such a hard day's march.

The next morning numbers and spirits were undiminished. I walked out of Slough with a local man who had been responsible for getting a hall where fifty or sixty students had slept on the floor. To his amazement, these young people had got up early, washed up every utensil they had used, and swept and hoovered the hall, leaving it cleaner than when they went in. We were scrupulous about litter, there was never any left behind after our picnics.

Easter Sunday morning John always spent in St Paul's. I got up for the early Communion service, and then joined Jacquetta on the march. That Sunday we got the wind and the rain; it took several people to hold up the heavy banners. There comes a stage when you are wet right through, and as your feet become waterlogged and numbed, the soreness and blisters seem miraculously relieved. We had no idea what we would find in London, but we came in like a victorious homecoming army. All along the way the pavements were crowded with sympathisers cheering and clapping, we could hardly believe it. When we got to Whitehall the crowds were denser than ever; we marched up in silence, only the drums beating out the morse signal for ND, and an almost endless march trudging along behind us – 30,000, 40,000, 50,000. We couldn't help feeling rather noble and triumphant, perhaps the blood of all my military ancestors leapt up in exhilaration in this so different kind of parade.

There was a final brief rally in a packed Trafalgar Square, with encouraging speeches from the plinth and, of course, from our star outdoor speaker, Michael Foot. At the end a lone voice called out, 'Three cheers for Canon Collins' – a spirit of harmony that was too good to last.

Afterwards I made a point of corresponding with a large number of people who had taken part in the march. I got letters from Christians, atheists, Communists, from a woman of seventy-one and a man of seventy-six, who had marched the whole fifty-two miles, from mothers of families, from children, from a blind man, from a paralysed spastic boy who had been brought up from Colchester by his local group and pushed in his wheelchair from Victoria to Trafalgar Square. Many were people who would probably have agreed about nothing else but the banning of the bomb. All wrote of the wonderful spirit of friendliness and co-operation, and all seemed to feel that the march was one of the great and most hopeful experiences of their lives.

30

Visiting Russia

WHILE I was happily working with the Women's Committee, John was struggling with the whole campaign. Shortly after the Central Hall meeting, a co-ordinating committee was set up to bring together so many diverse groups. I have admired John's skill as a chairman over many years, he managed to get through the business expeditiously, and still allow everyone to have his or her say. I never remember him shutting anyone up in a way likely to leave hurt or resentment. But chairing meetings of the Council of Christian Action or Defence and Aid, relatively small groups of likeminded people, was a very different matter from CND councils and committees. The original executive was soon enlarged to include representatives from the regions and the specialist groups, and that made it much more unwieldy. When the campaign decided that it must have a democratic constitution with an elected executive and chairman, annual general meetings became an all-day ordeal.

The inspiration behind both Christian Action and Defence and Aid was Christian: John's personal faith developed out of his RAF experience and he put his personal stamp on both movements. CND was secular, the moral impetus out of which it sprang was as much humanist and rational as Christian, perhaps rather more so. I would guess that professing Christians were always a minority within the campaign. Christians tended to be obsessed by the anti-Christ nature of Russian Communism. So John had to be a different kind of chairman, he could not impress his personal vision upon this diverse crowd, only try to hold them all together and help to steer them towards the goal that all desired. This was not only endlessly time-consuming, it also demanded endless patience.

Apart from meetings and tactical disagreements, there were plenty of happenings. One particularly interesting one for John and me came in the form of an invitation from the Metropolitan Archbishop of Moscow, to spend three weeks in Russia as guests of the Orthodox

Church. Stalin was dead, and Khrushchev had initiated a small thaw, people were beginning to travel to Russia. Christian Action's earlier delegation had slipped through a minute chink in the Iron Curtain, and CND, for a variety of complex reasons, was of interest to the Communist Party. We realised that our visit must have been officially sanctioned, and we knew also that it would be misinterpreted – more material for the Communist smear. Only the clever Quakers seemed to be able to avoid this particular innuendo in their peacemaking efforts, the rest of us were automatically suspect. Co-existence, however, was now Russia's officially proclaimed policy, and we believed in bridge-building, we would take advantage of this opportunity, and be prepared to put our heads in the bear's mouth.

At the beginning of July we boarded an Aeroflot jet, en route for Moscow, where we were met with a dazzling display of friendliness and hospitality. There was champagne, vodka, wine, brandy, mountains of caviar at every meal, including breakfast. We were housed in a private suite in the best hotel, very comfortable, except that the plumbing didn't work very well, and we were quite unable to do justice to the enormous meals that were continually offered to us. The Russian Church seemed remarkably well-heeled, or was it only the good boys who got such treatment?

Our impressions were crowded and contradictory, and that is how they remained. I kept a diary, and one day I find myself in love with Russia and the Russians, on others so oppressed by the dreary, claustrophobic society that I can hardly wait to get away. Apart from its dark, cruel side, State Communism seemed interminably grey and boring.

We had endless talk about peace and how to achieve it. All professed themselves convinced that America was planning an aggressive war against Russia; they were just as certain about this as our own planners were that, but for 'the Bomb', Russia would launch an immediate attack upon Europe. Most of the time we felt that discussion was getting nowhere.

We had much more sophisticated talk with Russians who had been allowed to travel abroad. There was a delightful evening with Sergei Obratsov and his wife; he was director of the famous Moscow Puppet Theatre. Their flat was large by Russian standards, and was crammed with every kind of exotic object, as well as five cats, a canary, a poodle, and masses of tropical fish. Talk flowed, wine and vodka flowed, good fellowship enveloped us, we ate and drank from nine-thirty until midnight – everything delicious. We drank toast after toast, to peace, to each other, to the arts, to the eternal friendship of Britain and Russia. Obratsov was a great man for peace. He told us about a broadcast that he had made, 'What ordinary people can do for peace'; we must fight against talk about '*the* Germans', '*the* Russians', '*the* Americans', there were no good or bad nations, 'just individual human beings, good and bad, the same everywhere with the same desires and aspirations, the same wish to live in peace'. He proposed a toast to 'the one human individual', which, of course, we all drank with enthusiasm. We parted with mutual embraces, in fact our entire visit was punctuated by kisses, John kissing and being kissed by men, and me by women, I don't remember any transsexual kissing, that would not have been approved.

An afternoon out in the country *dacha* of the writer Ilya Ehrenburg was less convivial, but very interesting. With his long experience of the West, living for many years in France, he was an important figure, and seemed to have the ear of Khrushchev. 'He looks,' I wrote, 'like a man who has seen everything and experienced everything, and remains detached and rather cynical'. He was cautiously optimistic about the possibilities of genuine co-existence; largely through his efforts the government had established an arrangement for the exchange of teachers with France, he hoped they would soon do the same with England. He understood very well that CND would be finished once it could be convincingly labelled 'Communist', but he urged some co-ordination with the suspect World Peace Committee all the same.

I went for a walk in the woods with Mrs Ehrenburg; we talked about books. She knew Pasternak well and had read the banned *Dr Zhivago*. She said it was absurd for the government to have treated it as a political book, Pasternak was a completely non-political person, he never even read the newspapers.

John and I were much moved by the Orthodox liturgy; in spite of its length and complexity, it seemed to have a real simplicity, and the chanting, in those deep bass voices, was hypnotically beautiful. Our first attendance was in a packed Moscow Cathedral, where we were honoured guests. John was taken off with the priests into the holy of holies behind the altar, where no mere woman may penetrate, but I was well looked after with a natural friendliness and curiosity. At the end an old lady embraced me, and sent messages of love 'to all the believers in England'; others kissed my hand and gave John and me little bunches of roses.

There were stretches of boredom and frustration, there were good experiences and some good discussions, but when we tried to raise the ugly aspects of the regime, all shied away, or said that that was all in the past. Priests would not talk politics, except for the ever-present topic of 'peace', that apart, they told us that 'religion should have nothing to do with politics' it was 'not the business of the church to interfere in politics', words that to us had a very familiar ring.

Things were better outside Moscow, and Kiev was particularly relaxed and agreeable, if rather too hot. I much enjoyed a day spent in the Young Pioneer's camp out in the pine forests. The amount that was done for the children everywhere did seem impressive. This lot were extremely friendly and eager to practise their English, they seemed to have been very well taught. I was amused by their code of conduct, eleven rules which echoed almost word for word those of our own Boy Scouts and Girl Guides, minus, of course, any reference to God. Nobody was very pleased when I commented upon the similarity, the Russian revolution not only had to be the best, it had to be unique.

Leningrad, that beautiful city, was a delight, as were its artistic and architectural treasures. There I made a real friend, Helen Petrova, Professor of English language and literature at the university.

We heard terrible stories about the siege and the war. My friend Helen had lost her husband, her little boy of four had died of starvation, as had both her parents-in-law. Father Mikhail, a sweet gentle old priest, who looked after us, had lost his three children. In that terrible time, he said, he had had to bury more than 1,000 people. Elsewhere we were told that the whole generation of the 35-45s was missing from the population. It was inconceivable that these people could ever want another war. We saw hardly any sign of militarism, no uniformed soldiers, and we were told that university students were exempt from military service. Khrushchev's Peace campaign, whatever its motivation, had struck deep chords in the hearts of the people, the glorification of peace seemed excessive even for John and me, but we hoped and believed that it meant something more than a cynical political ploy.

About this time I began to edit a quarterly journal for Christian Action (it still survives in the far more professional and competent hands of Canon Eric James). Freda had produced, sporadically, an informative newsletter, but by now, there was so much going on in the basement of 2 Amen Court, that she had very little time left over, and this was something that I could do and enjoy. I wrote a short article on our impressions of Russia and the Russian Church. Some of our more Conservative supporters thought it much too sympathetic, they didn't hold with 'supping with the devil', and the writer Leslie Paul, himself an ex-Communist, resigned on the grounds that we had been 'taken in' by the subservient and time-serving Russian Church.

Forty-two years of atheist indoctrination had failed to eradicate the Orthodox Church. Certainly it existed and functioned by permission of the all-powerful state, but it did function, and not only old ladies went to church. One weekday evening we visited a church in Leningrad that was filled with the young and the middle-aged on their way home from work – our interpreter was amazed.

Perhaps Father Paul who accompanied us everywhere was really a KGB plant, but we could not be mistaken in the warmth, the friendship and the generosity that we met. Communism had not produced a nation of brainwashed robots, the human spirit was alive, and there were good reasons for hope.

John still hoped to be able to raise support for CND from the Churches. There were many who joined as individuals, and vicars who brought contingents on the Aldermaston marches, and to other demonstrations; but the hierarchy, with few exceptions, remained in support of government policy. Geoffrey Fisher, in one of his off-the-cuff remarks had observed that 'it might be within the Providence of God for the human race to destroy itself with nuclear weapons', whatever that fatalistic statement might mean. But John had given up attacking Geoffrey Fisher, he merely referred anonymously to the words of 'an archbishop'. He did protest rather more fiercely and demonstratively against Robert Stopford, when he was appointed Bishop of London, on the retirement of William Wand. According to some archaic law, the dean and chapter of St Paul's were required to endorse the appointment of the incoming bishop by a unanimous vote. The sting in the tail of this apparent exercise in democracy was that anyone who failed to vote for the Crown's nominee was to be carried off to the Tower of London, and would be unlikely to retain his head upon his shoulders. John was normally something of a traditionalist, but he thought this piece of history too absurd, so when the chapter met in solemn conclave to 'elect' the already appointed bishop, John broke tradition and voted against him. He gave two reasons to the Press, the first that he thought the whole business of the election was a mockery, and the second that Stopford had stated publicly that it would be better for Britain to be completely destroyed by nuclear bombs than to have to submit to a Communist occupation.

Of course, there were other voices within the Church, more from the Free Churches and the Roman Catholics than from the Anglicans, though there were increasing numbers who, while not going the whole way with CND, were dubious and uneasy about the moral implications of nuclear weapons.

Christian Action and the Friends' Peace Committee got together to organise an Albert Hall meeting, 'Modern War Challenges Christians'. We aimed to present the Christian case for nuclear disarmament in the widest possible terms, intellectual, moral and aesthetic; we intended to appeal, not to the fear of death, but to the instinct for life. Speakers were both pacifist and non-pacifist, Anglican, Free Church, Quakers and Roman Catholic, and our Judeo-Christian friend, Victor Gollancz. The meeting was packed and hugely successful, but as usual, the Press took no notice.

Out of this Albert Hall meeting came Christian CND, an all denominations group run by Christian Action and the Friends' Peace Committee. We published pamphlets, held special services, organised pilgrimages, arranged deputations, held conferences and discussion groups. All these small, and not so small, efforts added up. The British Council of Churches, whom we lobbied, produced somewhat timid documents for discussion, the World Council of Churches meeting in December 1961 in Delhi, went further, and committed themselves to the statement: 'The use of indiscriminate weapons must now be condemned by the Churches as an affront to the Creator and a denial of the very purposes of creation . . . Christians must also maintain that the use of nuclear weapons or other forms of major violence against centres of population is in no circumstances reconcilable with the demands of the Christian Gospel.'

The Anglican hierarchy continued indifferent to this statement. John, in spite of all his rebellions and disappointments, remained a loyal Churchman to the end of his life. I became increasingly disenchanted with orthodox, and especially with institutional Christianity.

One aspect of our campaign that was especially exciting was the wide and generous support that we had from writers, poets, painters, sculptors, musicians and those involved in the performing arts. CND was creative, imaginative and inventive, it appealed to the mind, the imagination and the moral sense of the people.

The Direct Action Committee was certainly imaginative and inventive, and their illegal activities got far more publicity than the more traditional methods of the mainstream campaign. The Committee staged a number of symbolic demonstrations at East Anglian rocket bases, where participants would attempt to block the entrances to these bases by sitting or lying down on the road. They would then allow themselves to be picked up by the police and bundled into police vans, and, when charged with obstructing the highway, they would elect to go to prison rather than to pay fines. These demonstrations were non-violent, self-disciplined and impressive, and, of course, they attracted media attention.

Many campaigners saw no reason why they should not practise civil disobedience and play a role, even an official role, in CND. But by and large they understood and accepted CND's legal and democratic position. The practitioners of non-violence regularly tried to persuade the whole campaign to their methods at every AGM, there were resolutions to that effect, but these were always rejected. Keen Labour party members, and the Labour Advisory Group, thought civil disobedience politically damaging. They were even more alarmed when Direct Action tried to convert campaigners to a policy of Voters' Veto; everyone was to make clear that they would not vote for any candidate not pledged to work for British unilateral renunciation of the Bomb. Direct Action deeply distrusted politicians, and their compromises and duplicities, they wanted their own activities and their movement to remain pure and unsullied. The chairman of CND, poor chap, sat there to be shot at from both sides, though, it must be confessed, with rather more venom by some of the pureminded practitioners of non-violence, than by the despised and compromising politicians.

John was in a difficult position. He had a genuine sympathy and respect for the practitioners of non-violent civil disobedience. He had supported such movements in South Africa and in the Southern States of America, he was an admirer of Gandhi and of Martin Luther King. But in Great Britain there were no unjust laws nor customs oppressing nuclear disarmers, we could write, speak and demonstrate freely with the active assistance of the police. But the campaign leaders were under pressure to state publicly where they stood, and a policy had to be formulated.

A compromise was worked out. CND aimed to persuade the British public by legal and constitutional methods, but it worked alongside other organisations with similar aims but different methods. Individual campaigners were free to practise civil disobedience and to take part in Direct Action demonstrations as long as it was clear that they were not in any way committing CND itself to any illegality. John went further than this, acting upon a suggestion of Peggy Duff's, that CND should lay on a supporting march at one of the Direct Action rocket base demonstrations. This proved successful, and impressively dignified.

In order to express further solidarity of aim, Jacquetta and I went, on behalf of the Women's group, to visit two of the women demonstrators imprisoned in Holloway jail. We took with us whatever small gifts were allowed by prison regulations, and within the limitations of what might or might not be mentioned, we had a good visit. We got the feeling that they were happy to see us, and we thought them an impressive couple. Both came from comfortable middle-class families, and could well have afforded to pay any fine imposed, but they had chosen prison. After their release, they wrote an excellent book exposing some of the more horrible and stupid aspects of prison life.

The 1960 Aldermaston March was bigger than ever. That year we had our four sons marching with us, and Andrew, in his last year at Eton, organised a school contingent with its own banner and slogan, 'Eton College detests the tests'. As a result of letters from irate parents he got into some trouble over this, and was hauled up before the headmaster, a not unsympathetic Robert Birley. But he had managed to persuade a sympathetic house master to allow the exhausted marchers to sleep on his floor – subversion was slowly gaining ground.

Subversion was also gaining ground in the trades unions. The Fire Brigades' Union, under John Horner, led the way when it adopted unilateralism. It was soon followed by the influential Transport and General Workers' Union, with its huge block vote, and an Aldermaston marcher, Frank Cousins, at its head. Other unions followed, and all seemed set fair for a CND triumph at the Labour party conference in Scarborough at the beginning of October. The politically minded supporters of CND wanted less and less to do with civil disobedience.

Compromises seldom satisfy everyone for long, and campaigners were in a hurry. The first rumblings of trouble came, perhaps surprisingly, from Lord Russell, at one of the regular meetings that John held with the great man whenever he came to London. In spite of Russell's antipathy to the Christian Church, John thought they had established an amicable and constructive relationship. But by the late summer the atmosphere seemed to have changed, Russell was a sponsor of Christian Action's Defence and Aid Fund for Southern Africa, and he began to question John suspiciously about the administration of the Fund's finances. John could think of no source for these suspicions other than Michael Scott and the Africa Bureau. Michael was already accusing John of discrimination and misuse in the distribution of the very considerable sums of money that Christian Action had succeeded in raising.

Russell spoke of the need for CND to support Direct Action, as a means of publicity and of gaining quicker results. He pressed for the introduction of Campaign membership and a democratic constitution with an elected executive and chairman. John promised to put these proposals to the executive, though privately he thought the administration entailed would hold up the real business of campaigning. The executive rejected membership, but agreed on democratisation, and Peggy Duff produced a more or less workable constitution. As for Direct Action, John contented himself with saying that he thought the Campaign should abide by the decision agreed and formulated by the executive. He invited Russell to speak at a rally in Trafalgar Square a few days before the all-important Labour party conference at the beginning of October. This was to be the grand finale of a CND march from Edinburgh to London, right down the centre of England. It was intended to impress the Labour delegates assembling at Scarborough.

Other meetings between John and Russell followed, uneasy but at least superficially friendly, and Russell continued to press his views on direct action. Just before the Trafalgar Square rally, Russell wrote to John saying that at the rally he intended to speak in favour of civil disobedience. John was alarmed, and begged him not to do this on the eve of the Labour party conference. Frank Cousins was called upon for his advice, and he too begged Russell not to speak openly for illegality. Russell agreed to postpone any statement, and John expressed his gratitude.

A week later John was rung up by Victor Gollancz to say that he had received a letter signed by Lord Russell and Michael Scott, inviting him to join a Committee of 100 people to organise and take part in a campaign of mass civil disobedience; what was all this about? John was astounded, in all his meetings with Russell there had been no hint of any such project. He telephoned members of the executive who had also heard nothing. John telephoned Russell, who appeared embarrassed, but said that the letters were only meant to discover how much support there might be for this new effort, and nothing would be made public until after the Labour party conference.

Worse was to come. Through a careless mistake of identity, a copy of the Russell–Scott letter landed on the desk of John Connell, a right-wing journalist strongly opposed to CND and the story was prominently featured in the *Evening Standard*. Number 2 Amen Court was immediately under siege by the media.

John contented himself with restating the position of the Campaign in regard to civil disobedience. He telephoned Russell who was distressed by the premature disclosure of his plans. He said that he had acted as an individual, as was allowed by the agreed compromise policy, and that this did not commit the Campaign; a somewhat disingenuous argument since Russell as president was in a different position from the rank and file members.

Russell offered to resign, but at a hurriedly summoned and therefore small executive meeting, John persuaded them not to accept the resignation.

The hostile press, were, of course, delighted at the appearance of a split in the Campaign, and various inaccurate reports appeared. Russell and Michael Scott, not content to let matters rest, sent a joint statement to the Press containing further inaccuracies, and false accusations against John. He was already at Scarborough for the crucial Labour party conference, but returned rather wearily to London and again telephoned Russell. He begged that there should be no more statements to the Press, and that they should meet and resolve their differences for the sake of the Campaign. At first Russell refused, but later agreed on condition that they each brought a witness and the discussion would be tape-recorded. This seemed farcical to John, but anything for the sake of peace, so he asked the peace-loving, but shrewd, Arthur Goss to come with him.

They met from Monday to Friday in Russell's house, in company with the tape-recorder. John and Arthur were innocents, and it never occurred to them to insist upon having their own recording. Every time they seemed to be getting near an agreement, Russell would go upstairs to confer, and would return having changed his mind.

There was a brief moment of harmony when the tape-recorder was switched off, and they listened to the news report from Scarborough. The Labour party conference had voted for a policy of unilateral nuclear disarmament for Great Britain. But harmony soon faded, and what was finally produced was a 'Statement of Amity' to the effect that the president and chairman intended to continue 'working together for nuclear disarmament', and a statement would be issued after a meeting of the full campaign executive. John and I were due, almost immediately, to go on holiday, Russell too was going away. They agreed the Statement of Amity was to be published and circulated, and there would be no more statements until after the next executive meeting. John and Russell shook hands and parted.

John and I crossed the Channel, and drove south to the Dordogne heading for Les Eyzies. It was such a relief to be away that bad weather didn't matter. We had warmth, comfort and high quality French cooking. And we were lucky enough to be almost the last tourists to be allowed into the famous Lascaux caves, before they were closed in order to preserve the paintings. How far away and foolish seemed our petty squabbles, and how incredible that governments were preparing to destroy the civilisations towards which humanity had struggled over so many thousands of years.

We returned home a few days earlier than expected. On top of the usual pile of documents on John's desk was a copy of a seven-page document from Michael Scott which he had circulated to the executive, the regions and the groups of CND. These reiterated complaints against John already disproved, concluding with the assertion that he had failed to publicise the Statement of Amity. This was soon disposed of by the office worker who had delivered it to the Exchange Telegraph. It was Russell and Scott who had chosen to ignore the Statement of Amity.

As well as Scott's memorandum, there was a formal letter from Lord Russell which read: 'I hereby tender my resignation as President of the Campaign for Nuclear Disarmament. My reason for doing so is that I find it impossible to work with the present National Chairman of the Campaign. Nonetheless, I profoundly believe that the Campaign is doing good and most important work and I shall continue to do my best to support it.'

The full executive duly met on 5 November. All relevant documents were examined, and the twenty-eight-strong executive passed a resolution expressing unreserved confidence in the chairman. Russell was persuaded, very unwillingly, to withdraw a vitriolic attack upon John that he had sent to *The Observer* for publication. Russell's resignation was accepted with regret, and great appreciation of his past services to the Campaign was recorded.

The next AGM in March 1961 was run on the new democratic constitution; John was re-elected as chairman unanimously. The conference also passed a resolution to the effect that 'CND, Direct Action and the Committee of 100 are three techniques in a united attack on preparations for nuclear war.' And they asked John to invite Russell to resume the presidency. This John duly did, and Russell duly, but quite reasonably, refused. The Campaign always wanted to have it both ways: they wanted both legitimate action and civil disobedience, both John and Russell.

CND caused John and me a number of personal problems; it seemed to arouse even greater hostility than the racial issue. It was considered unpatriotic, even traitorous, as well, of course, as being Communist or favouring the Communists. I had some bad times with senior members of my family. But on the whole, families will go on loving however much they may disapprove, and, as far as mine were concerned, there were no final breaks. In fact, a family myth grew up that John wasn't really half a bad fellow, it was I who was the extremist and who spurred him on in all his subversive activities.

A more difficult and sadder problem arose with Victor Gollancz. During the weeks when CND was being formed, Victor was away in America buying books, and by the time he returned, the executive was in place and the campaign was under way. John proposed that Victor should be co-opted on to the executive, but this was met by opposition from all. John did his best to persuade them, but to no avail. Victor, they said, could not be in any campaign without trying to dominate it; he would be incapable of holding together a movement of such diversity as CND. Victor didn't help himself by vociferously criticising the campaign because it was not one hundred per cent pacifist, but he was deeply wounded by his rejection. He persuaded himself that John, out of jealousy, had deliberately chosen to launch CND when he, Victor, was out of the country, and had then been responsible for not inviting him to join.

Victor clung to his conviction of John's jealousy. In his bitterness, he turned on me, suggesting that it was partly my fault, I wanted John to stand on his own feet, and not play second fiddle to Victor; it had never occurred to me that John wasn't standing on his own feet. The friendship was sorely tried and was never quite the same again, at least between Victor and John. In the end, Victor half-accepted that perhaps John was not wholly to blame, his real affection and generosity reasserted themselves and we saw each other nearly as often as before. Victor swallowed his pride, became a sponsor of CND, sat on its platforms, and spoke at its meetings, putting the moral case against nuclear weapons with his usual fire and fervour.

John might have been happy to resign from the uncomfortable chair of CND, but he was never a man to retreat under fire. He owed loyalty to all who had supported him, and he believed deeply in the cause, so he stayed to struggle. Gaitskell too meant to struggle, he announced that he would 'fight, fight and fight again' to get the vote for unilateralism reversed. The Campaign for Democratic Socialism was well organised and effective, it worked hard within the Labour party and there the influence of CND began to decline. But in the country at large, CND appeared to be forging ahead.

The Committee of 100 put on a star-studded demonstration, many famous names of stage and screen took part. They sat outside the

Ministry of Defence, and the police rather sensibly took no action, so the demonstration eventually broke up; but it got a good share of the media. The next time the police were not so accommodating and arrested over 800. The majority paid fines of £1 and went home.

By now a new and enigmatic figure had attached himself to the Russell entourage: this was a young American student called Ralph Schoenman. It was rumoured that the Committee of 100 was his idea, also that he was an agent provocateur, or an agent of the CIA. Nobody ever knew, but he appeared to gain a powerful influence over Lord Russell. Schoenman announced the aim of the Committee as 'We want to put the Government in the position of either gaoling thousands of people or abdicating'.

That year we decided to change the Aldermaston ritual, and split the march into two, one huge march made it difficult for the marchers – those in front had to crawl along – very exhausting – while those at the back had to run to keep up. So one march went as usual from Aldermaston, and another from the American base near Wethersfield in Essex; that was the one I decided to join. We hoped to be able to synchronise a meeting at the bottom of Whitehall, and march together up to Trafalgar Square.

The Wethersfield march was enlivened by Randolph Churchill, who parked his car in front, and stood on the verges shouting abuse at us as we passed by. When the weather permitted, he positioned himself in a deck chair beside a record-player blaring out patriotic songs intended to drown the peace-orientated singing of the marchers; peace, to some, is a dreadfully subversive subject. I suppose Randolph enjoyed himself, the march certainly enjoyed him. But I remember another figure, a woman who stood in the rain to watch us, and who clapped and called out, 'Well done – carry on'; I stopped to speak to her and thank her for her support, and she wept as she said, 'My husband is dying from leukaemia, please go on protesting'.

The weather was terrible that year, but wind and rain never deterred the marchers, young and old and middle-aged, long hair, and short back and sides, the banners, the bands, the guitars and the funny hats. 'The real lost souls don't wear their hair long and play guitars,' wrote J.B. Priestley. 'They have crew cuts, trained minds, sign on for research in biological warfare, and do not give their parents a moment's worry.'

'This is where the Churches ought to be,' said our friend Canon Edward Carpenter, as we marched together. 'Out on the streets with all these young people.' But the Churches were deaf to the call from

Aldermaston. I had had a letter from the chairman of the Bradford Christian CND group, who wrote of shock and disillusion. 'We thought we were merely up against apathy but it is, in many cases, antagonism that we have to meet.'

By some miracle of timing – Peggy Duff was a genius at organisation – the heads of the two marches did meet exactly as planned at the bottom of Whitehall; that was a wonderful and emotional moment. The street had been closed to traffic, so ten abreast we marched, or rather some of us, including me, hobbled up to Trafalgar Square. My blisters turned septic, and my unsympathetic doctor said it served me right.

We had had an agreement with Direct Action that there would be no civil disobedience on the march which had its own special ethos. But this year a new, less happy spirit entered. Ralph Schoenman, and one or two others, had spent the four days moving among the marchers, and trying to persuade as many as possible to join him in a sit-down in front of the American Embassy. Some two or three hundred followed him, and there were scuffles with the police and arrests. The next morning the daily papers were full of this small piece of illegality, and had nothing to say about the march itself.

John was beginning to think in wider terms of an international disarmament movement. Khrushchev had suspended Russia's nuclear testing, and the British and Americans had refrained from further tests. Khrushchev had also called for universal and complete disarmament. Nobody took this very seriously, the Russians were given to Messianic visions, though these were not always completely insincere. John paid several continental visits this year to try and galvanise the European Federation, and we received another invitation to visit Russia, this time as guests of the Peace Committee.

There were plenty of people who advised us not to go, we would be 'playing the Communist game' yet again. Opposition often goaded John to do what he intended to do, so we went, and took with us our eldest son who had managed a respectable Russian 'O' level.

On our first visit, we had met and disliked the chairman of the Russian Peace Committee. We didn't expect much from this second visit, but we felt that we ought to try. But being the guests of the Peace Committee was not nearly so much fun as being guests of the Church. Khrushchev had just initiated an anti-drunkenness campaign, so no party member was ever allowed to be seen drinking in public, and alcohol was in relatively short supply; caviar seemed to have disappeared altogether.

We detected a faint thaw in our conversations with the committee, they promised to make our proposals public through their magazine. When we stressed the need for both sides to desist from hostile propaganda, they replied that the Russian government *never* indulged in such discreditable tactics. We had to protest vigorously against this travesty of fact.

Despite our disagreements, all remained friendly, and they sent us for a little holiday to one of their 'sanatoriums' on the Black Sea at Yalta. This was a beautiful place, with exotic flowers and shrubs, and peacocks in the gardens. There were graded walks through the grounds, suitable for differing degrees of fitness, as this was supposed to be a kind of health clinic, and was full of bustling women in white trying to look like nurses. However, when I began to suffer from bad sunburn, and asked for something to relieve it, there was a lengthy wait until they came up with a raw cucumber. Swimming was strictly regimented, and the sexes were segregated. I was happy with the women who were fat, friendly and jolly, and we were all able, quite unselfconsciously, to swim naked. When we were asked what we wanted to see, I said that I wanted to visit Chekhov's house. 'Yes, yes, of course,' they said, but we had to go through a tedious ritual of factories, sanatoriums, and Young Pioneer camps, and by the time we got to Chekhov's house it was closed. Perhaps his humorous, perceptive and sympathetic view of the human tragi-comedy was not considered properly revolutionary.

Our visit was not without results. A huge world Peace Conference in Moscow was being planned for 1962, and they were anxious for our support, and for the participation of CND. They assured us that we would be able to speak quite freely, even to criticise Russian policies, and speeches would be published in their Press. John, too, had been cherishing the project of a cultural and political Peace Conference, attended by Western peace movements and by Communists and fellow-travellers who would not be in a majority and would not be able to dominate the Conference. The Peace Committee appeared interested and moderately sympathetic.

On our return, John talked to the British Peace Committee, now enthusiastically behind CND. They were rather tiresome on the march, always trying to get their banners into full view of the television cameras, who were only too eager to photograph them. But John's most important and helpful contact was with Professor J.D. Bernal, a well-known Communist; he understood John's idea and promised to support it; they planned for September.

Under Khrushchev the Cold War swung, somewhat unpredictably, from thaw to freeze, and on 31 August he resumed Russian nuclear testing. CND immediately put on a 'March of Shame' to the Russian Embassy, where John delivered a strongly worded letter of protest. A few days later CND had to march to the American Embassy, as America resumed testing. In spite of this set-back, plans for John's conference went ahead. The American anti-nuclear campaign SANE, so-called because it described itself as a Campaign for a Sane Nuclear Policy, was alarmed at the idea of facing the Communists, and even some of the CND executive were uncertain. After a long debate, the executive did vote by seven to five to support the conference, but John was anxious to avoid any further splits in the Campaign, and invitations were issued in the names of the European Federation and of Christian Action, which met the expenses.

After a struggle, John had got agreement that invitations should be issued on a basis of not less than six Westerners to every five Communists, and that anyone from the West thought by Western delegates to be a fellow-traveller would count as a Communist. Sixty people finally assembled at the Russell Hotel, the Americans put aside their fears and it was a truly international gathering including representatives from one or two non-aligned countries such as India. The two Russian delegates were Ilya Ehrenburg and another writer, a playwright, Korneichuk, who was a member of the Supreme Soviet.

I don't quite know in what capacity I was allowed to attend this conference, but I sat through the four days. I have to say that John chaired it brilliantly, and spent many hours of the nights persuading and soothing those inclined to be intransigent. It was a practical conference, and agreement was reached over the problems of a divided and rearmed Germany, and on more general problems of disarmament. They then turned to the thorny issue of nuclear tests. It had been agreed that no statement would be given to the Press anywhere unless it had the unanimous agreement of the conference. Any individual could veto the statement as a whole or in part; and there were to be no minority reports. In view of the Russian resumption of testing it seemed very unlikely that the Russians would be able to agree to the condemnation that the rest of the conference clearly wanted, they had to sit and listen to some very strong statements.

'It was at this stage,' John wrote, 'that the Indian delegate, Jayar Prakash Narayan, passed me a little note which read: "the man of God never despairs".' John took fresh heart, and the recollection of this incident was to help him through many other difficult and discouraging occasions.

After lengthy discussions, and another midnight session, an

agreement was hammered out. It read: 'We deplore the resumption of nuclear testing, and, reaffirming our attitude, we oppose war, nuclear weapons and all nuclear testing of any kind . . . both as intensifying preparations for nuclear war and as a danger to the health of present and future. We call on the Governments now carrying out or planning nuclear tests to halt them immediately, not to resume such testing and to come to an agreement on a permanent and controlled test ban, separately or as part of general disarmament.'

It was signed by all, and after Ehrenburg had appended his signature he turned to John and said, 'We have taken a step for peace here, but it may mean war for Korneichuk and myself when we get back to Russia.' However, they both survived.

On 17 September we were involved in a different affair. The Committee of 100 had announced plans for a great 'sit-down' in Trafalgar Square. But the police and the government were getting tired of the Committee of 100, thirty-six of the more prominent members were summoned to Bow Street, and when they refused to be bound over to keep the peace for a year, they were sentenced to two months' imprisonment. With almost unbelievable folly Lord and Lady Russell were included among the thirty-six; gallantly they refused to be bound over, and were imprisoned along with the others. Russell was eighty-nine, and his sentence was reduced on medical grounds to one week, but he had already and inevitably become a national and international martyr and hero.

On 17 September the police put a Public Order Act ban on a large area around Trafalgar Square – it stretched as far east as Temple Bar. In a tense and excited atmosphere the CND executive met in Amen Court, and decided that they must express solidarity with the demonstrators, and opposition to the actions of government and police. They would march to Temple Bar, and then try as private citizens, with no intention of causing a breach of the peace, to make their way to Trafalgar Square. Peggy Duff had cunningly got the whole of the London Region out, and they were waiting and ready. So John led a march of several hundred down Fleet Street until they were met by a cordon of police, who, after some persuasion on John's part, gave permission for each one to continue as an individual.

The Square was packed. There were literally thousands of people; numbers were sitting, and on the periphery greater numbers were walking round and round as the police would not allow them to stand still. John found the officer in charge, he explained his position and that of CND and he asked if he could go about and see if possible that his own

Above CND: Jacquetta Hawkes, Ritchie Calder, Tony Greenwood, John, Frank Cousins, Emrys Hughes MP, on the march in 1962 (*Hulton-Deutsch*)
Below Marchers arrive at Trafalgar Square, 1960 (*Reuters*)

Left Oliver Tambo speaking at a Christian Action meeting. Frank Longford (Lord Pakenham) is in the chair (*S&G*)

Right John, Father Huddleston and American jazzplayer Lionel Hampton at a concert for Defence and Aid (*Alan Vines*)

people didn't get swept off into civil disobedience or get themselves arrested without cause. The officer easily gave permission, John was well known to the police.

Walking round and round got rather exhausting, and as John and I had already arranged to have dinner with the Priestleys in the Albany, we took time off. After dinner we both returned, John moved about, but I felt I must join the circular treadmill. It was damp and dark by now, and tempers were beginning to fray, there was an atmosphere quite different from any other CND demonstration, a feeling of suppressed violence, a crowd that was growing angry and rather ugly. I didn't like it. Nor did I like the attitude of the police. I stopped for a brief moment, and a hefty policeman stamped deliberately, and heavily on my foot. Arrests were beginning, the Black Marias were filling up, and suddenly I saw John being driven away in one of them. He was taken off with a number of the sitters, and dumped in a Bow Street police cell; he was extremely, but, of course, non-violently, angry.

I didn't quite know what to do, so I decided to return to the warmth and friendship of the Albany, and a stiff drink, and there we all waited. Eventually John turned up looking somewhat dishevelled; he had been told that he would have later to appear at Bow Street charged under the Public Order Act with a breach of the peace. 'But I was only trying to *keep* the peace,' he protested.

Rather late we returned home, there were only about 500 people left determined to keep a vigil until the following morning when Lord Russell was due to be released. It was then we heard that the police got really rough, arresting people and beating them up. Adam Roberts, whom we knew, and knew to be an entirely truthful young man, was kicked almost unconscious by the police; a doctor examined him in the morning and confirmed his injuries. It was a nasty business.

Ironically, one of the real CND martyrs was Victor Gollancz. He and Ruth had come, with no intention of sitting down, to observe the demonstration. They were proceeding peaceably up Whitehall, when Victor slipped and fell and, being a heavy man, he broke his hip, and had to be rushed off to hospital. As soon as visitors were allowed I went to see him, and was greeted with, 'Now I know what the Crucifixion was really like'. Poor Victor, he did have a very low pain threshold, and I am sure suffered a great deal, but he was soon quite enjoying his martyrdom. Ruth kept him well supplied with special food, he was able to have his favourite secretaries in and direct his affairs, and he was soon arranging bridge fours in his room.

When John finally appeared before the magistrate at Bow Street, I was in Court with our barrister son, Andrew. It was a strange experience – a pathetic procession of drunks, prostitutes and petty pilferers followed one another and then suddenly there was John, in his clerical dress, looking extremely out of place. The policeman who had arrested him, Sergeant Uzzell, gave evidence. 'What did he say when you arrested him?' asked the magistrate. 'He said, you're a bloody fool,' the sergeant replied. I had never, in all our married life, heard John use the word 'bloody'. I let out a whistle of disbelief, and got disapproving looks all round, especially from the magistrate and other court officials; Andrew was rather embarrassed. John was defended by a sympathetic solicitor, and it didn't take long for the case to be dismissed.

Meanwhile, the Labour party conference had reversed the 1960 Scarborough decision, and had voted *against* a policy of unilateral nuclear disarmament for Britain.

31

Infighting in CND

N INETEEN sixty-two was a year for peace conferences, in two of
which John and I were personally, though separately, involved.
The most dramatic of these gatherings was the huge 'World Congress
for Disarmament and Peace' in Moscow, in July.

As well as taking part, John had agreed to be one of the sponsors of
this event, as had Barbara Wootton and Lord Russell. All three were
members of the Labour party, and the Labour executive, fearful of
accusations of fellow-travelling, promptly decided to expel them. This
made the party look foolish, and the British Press had a lot of fun over
it. Somehow or other, after a time, the expulsions quietly lapsed.

In Moscow some 2,800 people representing 121 countries assembled. The largest group was American, 190 of them, and the
British mustered 142. As well as John, the CND contingent was led by
Sydney Silverman and Kingsley Martin. Our old friends the Committee of 100 were there, and Arthur Goss went as an observer for
Christian Action. Of course, there was a large Communist majority,
but non-Communist representation was substantial and vocal.

The heads of the eighteen nations engaged in disarmament negotiations at Geneva were invited to put their views. Macmillan replied
only that the British position was well known, Kennedy did not reply
at all. Statements were read from the other heads of state, and
Khrushchev spoke for two and a half hours. There were many
representatives of 'liberation movements' from Africa and the East,
vociferously demanding that the Congress pay attention to their
anti-imperialist calls for freedom and revolution, but, as Arthur Goss
commented, 'the real breakthrough in Moscow was that the Congress
was dominated not by the expected speeches laying all the world's
troubles on the Western imperialists and warmongers, but by a call for
disarmament and peaceful co-existence. The Soviet speakers left no
doubt that their longing for disarmament is as strong and sincere as
ours.' But, throughout, there was the same blind spot that one always

found in talks with the Russians, their unwavering conviction that 'the nuclear weapons of the West are aggressive and menacing, and theirs are protective, only forced upon them by the build-up of Western nuclear power'.

The Russians had to listen to some strong criticism of their policies from John and from the rest of the British contingent, as well as from the Americans, but they kept to their promise that all speeches and statements would be fully reported in the Congress documents, and in the Soviet Press. CND literature was allowed to be distributed inside the Congress only, but the Committee of 100 took their banner and their leaflets out into Red Square. These were gently confiscated by the police, but the Committee members were able to talk freely and put their views to the numerous Russian onlookers.

The high spot of the occasion for John was an hour's private interview with Khrushchev. 'My impression of him,' he wrote, 'was of a brilliant peasant, human, full of wit and humour, but withal a politician to the fingertips, and one who would make no concessions to ideals or emotions where what he regarded as interests of State were at stake.'

To John's surprise, Khrushchev said that he was sorry when Dulles died, they had understood each other. 'It's like this,' he explained, bringing his large rough hands slowly together, 'as we got closer and closer to the flash point, we both knew that at the critical moment' – and here, just as his fingers were about to touch, he quietly slipped one hand above the other, and concluded with a grin – 'we should avoid an ultimate clash.' He was uncertain, he said, about the brash young Kennedy, and wondered whether he had enough political clout to carry out the promises he had made at their Vienna meeting. When John asked that Russia should give a lead by declaring that she would not carry out any more nuclear tests, whatever the Americans might do, Khrushchev revealed how well informed he was about affairs inside Britain, by enquiring slyly whether the Anglican Church as a whole would support a similar request to the British and American governments.

Meanwhile, a very different kind of conference was being prepared – on the initiative of the Canadian 'Voice of Women'. Fifty-one women assembled in Canada in September, among them, Jacquetta and I as delegates from CND. There was an impressive group from the American 'Women Strike for Peace', led by Dagmar Wilson, slight, dark and attractive, one of those small, wiry people charged with nervous energy; I felt an immediate rapport with her. These were brave women too, the atmosphere in America was very different from the more tolerant British climate. When they returned, they were hauled up before the Committee on un-American activities; to venture to talk with Communists was decidedly un-American.

The women from Eastern Europe and the Soviet Union were also impressive. There were four Russians led by Olga Tchekchetkina, who had an important job on *Pravda*. Olga was clearly a party member, and all had been carefully selected for their intelligence, expertise and clear dedication. Olga spoke excellent English, and it was impossible not to like her for her liveliness, friendliness and quick, if slippery intelligence, she was charming and persuasive.

Our Conference was intended to produce concrete and sensible ideas for the implementation of International Co-operation Year which the UN had hopefully designated for 1965, and it did produce a number of good proposals, mostly concerned with education. Jacquetta and I joined the cumbrously worded 'Getting people to press Governments to take steps in 1963 to show sincerity in disarmament'. Jacquetta chaired the group, and I was the rapporteur. We produced a lengthy report, full of what we considered excellent ideas and suggestions for the gentlemen conferring at Geneva, but I fear they took little notice of our admirable proposals.

Our CND women's group continued its peaceable activities. We arranged another women's meeting, rather more lighthearted than the first, as it was largely a send-up of Civil Defence. Once more we collected quotes, many from America which was suffering an attack of nuclear war nerves. Private enterprise was quick to capitalise: 'Sensational offer – shelter as little as $650 – no cash down – seven years to pay.' This came with 'Completely odorless chemical toilets – the "Bomb" pot $49.50.' The British were more sober: 'Shelter Boycott. Britain will be told to stay calm over fall-out. Shelters would use up steel and other materials needed for more realistic purposes.'

A Civil Defence officer was quoted as saying that if people panicked, he would bring out a brass band to calm them. Americans, on the other hand, were debating as to whether it might be legitimate to shoot neighbours panicking to get into an overcrowded shelter. The answer appeared to be 'yes'.

This was a year for lobbying, and the women got in first. We gathered in Geneva with representatives from Britain, America, Scandinavia, Germany, France, Canada, Switzerland, and Austria; there must have been at least 100 of us in various groups. We went the rounds of these world-weary men, endlessly and it seemed fruitlessly, discussing disarmament, but it was only with the two giants, America and Russia, that our conversations became charged with emotion – theirs, not ours. All we talked with agreed that the root of the inability to make progress was a human and psychological problem. But as soon as we suggested any practical step to the Russians or the Americans, each side began a wearisome repetition of accusation and counter-accusation. We ended with a silent march through Geneva to the Palais des Nations where the statesmen were gathered. The officials were a little alarmed and suggested showing us round the buildings. But we said that all we wanted was a silent vigil, we would wait until the government representatives came out. Eventually they appeared. Mr Dean, the American, and Mr Zorin, the Russian, sat stiffly side by side looking rather embarrassed, the others stood. Our petition was read out by a Norwegian, and presented with admirable simplicity by Dagmar Wilson. We sat in silence.

We found that the non-aligned and non-nuclear delegations welcomed expressions of intelligent and humane public opinion. Many realised that the gap between the aspirations and moral intuitions of ordinary people, and the policies being pursued by their governments was becoming so wide as to be almost ludicrous.

With all its work, all its lobbying and deputations, CND had never managed to reach the British Prime Minister, so the women thought they would try. Back in 1958 a group of us had lobbied the women MPs from all parties. At that time we were led by Dame Alix Meynell, who had recently retired after a distinguished career in the Civil Service.

So when we approached Harold Macmillan, we again asked Dame Alix to lead us and to make the approach. We assembled an impressive list of distinguished women. Each one of us made a short prepared speech from a different point of view. A good discussion followed. Macmillan obviously took us seriously, and it was clear too that he was very concerned to achieve a Test Ban Treaty, and perhaps we helped to move him a little further in that direction. He assured us that he, personally, had on several occasions persuaded President Eisenhower not to test. It was also clear that he and presumably his advisors were beginning to recognise the dangers in over-reliance on nuclear weapons and the policy of nuclear first strike. It was also clear that our, by then very semi-independent, nuclear force was to be retained in order to give us 'influence' as Macmillan had said earlier: 'It puts us where we ought to be, at the top table'.

Macmillan did half admit that the Pentagon would not be too upset if Britain were to abandon her nuclear capability. All in all, we felt that the deputation had been well worth while; it was all very polite, we got quite a lot of TV coverage, and Dame Alix was interviewed. We heard afterwards that Macmillan had been much impressed.

We followed this effort up with similar deputations to Mr Gaitskell and Mr Grimond. Gaitskell's position was that moral actions must be judged by their consequences, but as Alix Meynell pointed out, we cannot in fact foresee the consequences. He was inclined to be optimistic about the possibility of achieving agreements on disarmament. 'We *can* have freedom and peace,' he said. Jo Grimond, on the other hand, gave it as his personal view 'that the odds are that most of the world will blow itself up in the not too distant future . . . it is very optimistic to suppose that the male animal will give up fighting.'

In October 1962 the Cuban missile crisis blew up. The Americans launched and botched the Bay of Pigs invasion, and Khrushchev installed missiles in Cuba. The American Navy blockaded Cuba, and Kennedy demanded the removal of the Soviet missiles. Russian warships were already en route for Cuba carrying more missiles and other horrors, the American warships were in place ready to meet the Russians, and the air waves buzzed with threats and counter-threats. To a majority of people in Britain it seemed as if nuclear war was only hours away.

There were impromptu CND peace demonstrations; it must be admitted that the rank and file were, unreasonably, more anti-American than anti-Russian. The ninety-year-old Lord Russell roused himself from a bed of sickness and sent off frantic telegrams. One to Kennedy read: 'Your action desperate – threat to human survival – no conceivable justification – civilised man condemns it – we will not have mass murder – ultimatum means war – end this madness.' Another, much more politely worded, was despatched to Khrushchev: 'May I humbly appeal for your further help in lowering the temperature despite the worsening situation – your continued forbearance is our great hope – with my high regards and sincere thanks.'

On behalf of CND John sent a message to the UN Secretary General, U Thant. This was a period of confusion and real fear, and CND's instinctive urge to demonstrate hardly knew what or who should be its target. A few people uprooted themselves and their families, and fled as far away as possible from the centres of population. For thirteen days the crisis continued as the opposing warships drew closer and closer to each other. Then, at the last moment, 'the flash point' so graphically illustrated by Khrushchev, the nuclear giants drew back from the brink. Khrushchev removed his missiles, in return, presumably for an assurance that the Americans would not physically invade Cuba. The Americans quietly and almost unnoticed took some of their missiles out of the European bases that ringed the Soviet Union.

CND tried to point out and to emphasise that, as the arms race accelerated, this kind of crisis was likely to recur, and the outcome might well be a nuclear, instead of a verbal exchange; that was what all those predisposed to support CND chose to believe. Those who had swallowed the conception of nuclear deterrence preferred to believe that the affair proved that the deterrent did work, that at the last minute and in spite of threats to the contrary, no one would really dare to press the fatal button. One thing, however, was quite evident, and that was that, at the moment of crisis, Britain with her very junior deterrent, had no place at 'the top table'!

CND was changing. The original limited objective, that Britain should unilaterally abandon her nuclear capability, had seemed realistic and politically attainable. Of course, we would have preferred America and Russia to abandon their bombs, but it seemed wildly unrealistic to start campaigning against them; we should begin at home. Now, campaigners were beginning to stray from this original straight and narrow path. Many wanted immediate withdrawal from NATO, 'positive neutralism', international non-alignment, general disarmament, and some wanted to include social and human rights issues. The young especially wanted a new heaven and a new earth. There were disagreements about techniques of campaigning, legality or illegality. There were many, including the secretariat who thought CND should act as an 'umbrella' beneath whose capacious spread differing approaches and groups might happily work together.

Many of the first executive had departed for different reasons, the only originals left were Ritchie Calder, Jacquetta Priestley, Toni Pirie and Arthur Goss.

The American Committee wanted a new international and non-aligned peace movement. It was not to be anti-Communist, but would not include any recognisably Communist groups. Both CND and the European Federation were interested, and a conference was planned at Somerville College, Oxford for January 1963.

John meanwhile wanted a follow-up of his successful 1961 London conference, and this would necessarily include Communists. Representatives of the Communist-dominated World Peace Council were due to gather in London in January to discuss this, and John persuaded the European presidents to invite the Communists to Oxford as observers. Peggy Duff warned him that there would be opposition, and she and the CND secretariat were against it.

When John had an idea that he believed in, he could be like a dog with a bone; he went ahead with the invitations. One observer might have been accepted, but the number had swollen to ten. The Chinese had been asked to send one, but they despatched five. John was supported by Jacquetta and Toni Pirie; I feared that he was mistaken and said so to him, but not publicly. CND refused to have the Communists at Oxford, John was acutely embarrassed, the Conference was split, and the whole affair was a disaster. Toni Pirie, one of the most dedicated, hard-working and valuable members of the executive, said, 'It broke my heart'. The outcome of the conference was the formation of the International Confederation for Disarmament and Peace (ICDP) with a Quaker, Kenneth Lee, as chairman. Peggy Duff accepted the position of treasurer, which John thought, correctly, would create a conflict of loyalties.

To add to our general unhappiness, it was bitterly cold, and the central heating in Somerville broke down; only the whisky bottles kept us all going. John wanted to resign at once, but it would have been a further mistake to act hurriedly while in a state of frustration and exhaustion. In addition, we were both due to go to America for a month's joint speaking tour under the auspices of SANE: publicity about the resignation of the chairman of CND would not help our tour.

The month of our American tour was one of the most physically exhausting I have ever experienced; when the Americans hire you, they exact their pound of flesh. But perhaps, in some ways, it was good that we could leave the troubles of the Campaign behind us, and return to the pure milk of the CND gospel – the moral and rational case for nuclear disarmament and peace. Sometimes we spoke together, sometimes we separated, we went east, west, south and north into Canada. We met some fine people, the same kind of people who supported CND, and we returned curiously better.

It was too much to hope that there wouldn't be any trouble on this year's Easter March. At first all went well, and numbers were as great as ever. At Windsor, a contingent switched off and marched up to the castle along a route lined with black and white CND pennants. There our youngest son, Mark, delivered a letter on the subject of nuclear disarmament addressed to the Queen. He was delighted with himself, especially as the TV cameras caught him, and he was seen by some of his school friends.

Meanwhile a group calling themselves 'Spies for Peace' had, rather cleverly, got hold of a secret report plastered with D notices, about the results of Fallex 62, a NATO exercise. A limited nuclear attack on Britain had been simulated, and there was information about underground Regional Seats of Government (RSGs) in which selected people were to be more or less safely housed in the event of such an attack. 'Spies for Peace' discovered the locations of these RSGs, one of which was only a mile off the route of the march. They distributed leaflets and a map urging marchers to peel off and demonstrate at this RSG. A few thousand went off, the majority stayed with the march.

The executive and the marshals also had trouble with a group calling itself 'The March must decide'; they wanted a resounding civil disobedience demonstration as the finale. Fortunately that was not what the majority of the marchers wanted, and since some clever-dick had got ahead of CND by booking Trafalgar Square, we had a rally and a peaceful picnic in spring sunshine in Hyde Park. Of course, being out in the open park made us more vulnerable to the public, and one ill-wisher crept up behind John and emptied a bag of flour over his head. We had a difficult and lengthy job trying to get it all out of his thick, wavy hair.

Inevitably, CND was identified by the media with 'Spies for Peace', and with the disturbances and arrests. John appeared on *Panorama* and disassociated the main campaign from both, but all that that achieved was to infuriate many of the marchers, who thought civil defence was an absurd joke anyway, and that 'Spies for Peace' were fun. It also exacerbated the rift between John and Peggy. 'How could the leadership have been so stupid?' she said. She too thought 'Spies for Peace' were fun, as well as original and inventive, well, they were certainly that, and, as usual, it was they who had made the headlines.

The image of CND was further damaged by demonstrations against the King and Queen of Greece, who came on a State visit in July. There were valid reasons for CND concern, since a prominent Greek peace campaigner, Grigoris Lambrakis, had been murdered by the Greek police. Lambrakis had founded a peace movement with affiliations to CND – they carried the CND symbol on their public protests – he had brought a Greek contingent to the Easter march, and had attended the Oxford conference.

John and the executive hoped to siphon off some of our campaigners' anger and distress by a protest march two days before the arrival of the royal visitors. The march ended with John placing flowers in the shape of the CND symbol against the railings of

Buckingham Palace. But this did not satisfy the militants: there were confrontations with the police, further demonstrations against the State visit, and a number of arrests. All of which was grist to a hostile Press and a cause of confusion to the public.

Happier events were pending internationally; it began to look as if there might be a real breakthrough in the Test Ban negotiations, Harold Macmillan was off to Moscow. Alix Meynell sent him polite good wishes from the women's deputation.

Macmillan returned in triumph with a copy of the signed Test Ban Treaty – one small step forward on the road to sanity. I truly believe that one ingredient in this achievement was the effect of all the educative work done by CND, though Macmillan tried to claim that somehow or other it had been achieved because Britain had so disinterestedly gone ahead and developed her own bomb.

Delighted as we all were with the Test Ban, we felt that it had, in one way, come too late. Nuclear weapons were spreading. De Gaulle, in pursuit, so he said, of 'La Gloire' had already authorised tests in the Sahara, and France would soon have her nuclear weaponry. China was well on the way to producing her bomb; this frightened India into working on hers, and that, in turn, set Pakistan on the fateful road – an unwelcome 'domino effect'. Meanwhile, Israel under permanent threat from her Arab neighbours was quietly developing her own nuclear capability.

John was still in two minds about resignation. We were both completely committed to the cause of nuclear disarmament with all its trouble, its pressures, its up and downs, CND was one of the most worthwhile movements of our times. 'I would rather have been married to the Chairman of CND than to an Archbishop of Canterbury,' I told John. And now, as I look back, I am more than thankful that, whatever happens to the human race, we were among those who stood up and said 'No!' to the evil of nuclear weapons and nuclear war.

There were still many, probably a majority, of CND campaigners who supported John, the executive and their policies, but they were not the noisy ones. John had friends among the radicals as well, he had a weakness for rogues and for eccentric characters.

The campaign continued publishing useful pamphlets and reports, though this side of the work was obscured by the demonstrations, and the more serious publications didn't sell nearly as well as *Sanity* which reported all the Committee of 100's activities, and attacked the Establishment. Around this period, Stuart Hall produced *Steps towards*

Peace, a carefully thought out and moderate document, not particularly well received by the rebellious rank and file.

Eventually John decided that he would make one more effort to hold the Campaign together, and would stand for re-election as chairman at the autumn Annual General Conference.

For the first time, John had an opposer for the chairmanship. He delivered a carefully worded speech, spelling out the policy on which he offered himself for re-election, which was also the policy of the executive. The campaign had voted for a democratic constitution, and they should accept the decisions of a democratically elected executive. John was re-elected as chairman by a two-thirds' majority.

Many were still not prepared to accept majority decisions, and that included Peggy Duff and other members of the secretariat. John felt his position becoming increasingly impossible. There was no 1964 Easter march, instead there were demonstrations in London, accompanied by the usual disturbances. On 12 April John resigned. We both felt it like a personal bereavement, many good friends had already left, but we left many behind.

A dwindling and impoverished campaign was gallantly and effectively chaired by Mrs Olive Gibbs, an Oxford housewife, local councillor and member of the Labour party. Peggy Duff left in 1969 to work full-time for the ICDP, and CND remained a small organisation rather than a Campaign. In the late Seventies and early Eighties it enjoyed a revival under Monsignor Bruce Kent.

When John wrote *Faith under Fire*, he ended his first chapter on CND with the words: 'I had been driven to pursue my ministry as an outsider.' John was often accused of being yet another politician manqué. But the difference between a movement like CND and a political party is the difference between influence and power. Politicians and political parties need power to put their policies into action, some want personal power, all want power for their party. John never wanted that kind of power for himself nor for the movement; he would use reason and moral persuasion to influence and to change the minds of people, and the policies of political parties.

John saw his involvement in CND as an extension of his ministry as a Christian priest. We supported and worked for the campaign because we believed it to be right. But we were not there in order to convert people to Christianity, nor to try, in some kind of back-handed way, to draw them into the Church. That, it seemed to us, would be an affront to human integrity, and our atheist and agnostic friends were people of the highest personal integrity.

So John wore his cassock and his dog–collar, conducted the Good Friday service on the Falcon Field at Aldermaston, preached anti-nuclear sermons, and spoke on Christian platforms. He did not try to thrust his beliefs at his non-Christian colleagues and campaigners. John's chairmanship was criticised both for being too tolerant and for being too autocratic and headmasterly; in the later years of CND it seemed that he couldn't be right.

Mervyn Jones, one of the most perceptive commentators on CND, wrote: 'John was modest, rational and persuasive; he listened to what others said, and took advice; he laboured to achieve compromises, he retreated from positions that proved to be unpopular. Probably no one else could have held CND together as long as he did. But it was precisely his good qualities that aroused antagonism. He had skills that gave an impression of the smoothly professional . . . He liked to arrange matters peaceably and avoid clashes.' Mervyn noted John's conviviality, his liking for 'small talk, jokes, informal social gatherings, wine and cigars . . . to the suspicious and puritanical elements in the movement (and there were plenty of them) it appeared he was what they most distrusted – a politician. His flexibility was interpreted as insincerity; his readiness to compromise was taken to imply that he would abandon any principle to keep the show on the road and to preserve his own position.'

When all is said and done, it was a remarkable campaign, and our joint involvement was one of the most important and formative experiences of our life together. John wrote: 'From it I have learnt a great deal. I have learnt what it is to try to preside over an amorphous body that is constantly in danger of fissiparation and disintegration, where the preservation of unity is a prime consideration, and where overt leadership is, as likely as not, to cause resentment and division. I have learnt the hard way some of the dangers and difficulties of endeavouring to take the Christian Gospel into the heart of politics . . . I have learnt that a priest can as well exercise his priesthood outside the Churches as inside them . . . My whole experience of people has been enlarged, enlivened and enriched. My thoughts, my feelings, my faith have all been given new dimensions, new depths, new horizons.'

32

Extending the Scope of Christian Action

In between the dramas and disagreements, the high peaks and the depressions of CND and Defence and Aid, the work of Christian Action went steadily on. Freda organised more weekend conferences, always cheerful and stimulating events, and as the organisation became better known, more people turned to it for help.

A young priest who had inherited a considerable amount of money appeared; he wished to use this to endow three scholarships for Africans from South Africa to study for graduate and post-graduate courses in England. Would Christian Action arrange for selection of suitable candidates, and administer the fund? So 1958 saw the arrival of Nathaniel Masemola complete with wife and family. Nathaniel was to study law in London. Christian Action found him a flat, and produced from among the members a wonderful assortment of furnishings, linen, four beds and bedding, chairs, a wardrobe and a chest of drawers. Another scholar, mercifully a bachelor, came to study at London University, and a third arrived from Fort Hare to read chemistry at Cambridge.

Then there was World Refugee Year, and Christian Action helped to pick up some of the forgotten ones from the Algerian War, mostly women and children fleeing across the borders to escape the bombs and firing squads of the French. There were some 180,000, penniless and exhausted, who had been omitted, by some oversight, from the funds raised for this special year.

Another project was brought to us by Muriel Gofton, who had been working in Europe among the thousands of dismally named 'displaced persons'. In a TB sanatorium near Hanover, she found a Pole who had been brought to Germany for forced labour, with his small daughter, now another patient. Quite seriously he said, 'Why don't you drown us? We cannot go home – we cannot emigrate – we cannot work – nobody wants us, wouldn't it be cheaper to shoot us or drown us?'

These terrible words inspired Muriel Gofton: she set about finding these victims homes and work.

No country wanted TB patients; refusal and frustration dogged her efforts. Christian Action helped her through the labyrinth of British bureaucracy, and ten families were finally allowed to settle in Scotland. We helped her buy a house in Lanarkshire and then build bungalows for the families. 'Cala Sona', Gaelic for 'Happy Haven', grew steadily, and was an outstanding success.

We could have done more for Refugee Year. John was offered a benefit concert in the cathedral. The Philharmonia Orchestra, conducted by Giulini, would play Beethoven's Ninth Symphony. But the cathedral doors remained obstinately closed.

A few years earlier John had managed to slip in Paul Robeson, by getting him to sing Negro spirituals at Evensong. Robeson was delighted and asked if he might read his father's favourite passage from the Book of Micah, 'they shall beat their swords into ploughshares . . .' The cathedral was packed, and the substantial collection did come to Defence and Aid. I suspect that the chapter did not realise that Paul Robeson was a Communist.

But inevitably most of Christian Action's work was concerned with Southern Africa. Part of the basement in Amen Court was already occupied by a young South African, Patrick van Rensburg, who was organising the Boycott Campaign. At first, this was a modest affair of oranges and sherry, but the idea grew, and in 1960 the campaign was transferred to an outside office, and was merged with the new Anti-Apartheid Movement, which, one way and another, was helped off the ground by Christian Action.

Good secretaries have to act as guard dogs for the protection of their overworked bosses, but Freda felt there was something impressive about a quiet young Indian from South Africa who arrived in 1958. He was highly intelligent and well informed, and seemed so seriously and sympathetically interested in the work of Christian Action. Freda let him through. John too was captured and charmed by Abdul Minty. 'I would like to join Christian Action,' Abdul said, 'but I don't know if I can. You see I am a Muslim.' This was not quite what John had expected, for a moment he had to think. Then he asked a question, 'Do you respect the life and teaching of Jesus of Nazareth?' 'Of course,' Abdul replied. 'Muslims regard Jesus as a great prophet.' 'Then you are more than welcome,' John replied. Abdul has spent a lifetime of quiet, dedicated and highly effective anti-apartheid work; he was a close associate of Bishop Ambrose Reeves, as he now is of Archbishop

Trevor Huddleston. Since he went to live in Norway with Kari
Storhaug they have together made a big contribution to the work of
Defence and Aid.

In South Africa the Treason Trial proper had just begun. Two years of
preliminary enquiries had resulted in sixty-five suspects being released. Christian Action had just managed to keep pace with the
requests for legal costs which arrived regularly from Ambrose Reeves.
Then came a further request. Ambrose wrote that whatever the trial's
outcome, there were likely to be many more trials of a political nature.
The South African government was determined to crush any opposition to its apartheid policies. Could the Christian Action Fund extend
its terms of reference to cover new crises and new trials? John seldom
looked before he leapt, but I doubt if either of us quite realised that this
meant a continuing commitment until whenever apartheid would have
finally disappeared. For John it was to be a lifetime's commitment.

F. H. Lawton QC, a friend of Christian Action, went on our behalf
to observe the opening of the Treason Trial. On his return, he helped
John to draw up the new terms of reference for what became 'The
British Defence and Aid Fund for Southern Africa'. The Fund set out
to: 'provide means of assisting and defending those in Southern Africa
who are the victims of unjust legislation or oppressive and arbitrary
procedures; support, sustain and comfort their families; rehabilitate
the accused if and whenever possible; and keep the conscience of the
world alive to the issues at stake'. The term 'Southern Africa' was used
to enable the Fund to operate in South-West Africa and in the Central
African Federation; particularly in Southern Rhodesia which remained
a repressive white regime long after Zambia and Malawi had become
independent. Later a further clause was added: 'assist in the development of a non-racial society based on a democratic way of life'.

Fresh appeals from South Africa were not long in coming. There
was a particularly horrible case in the Lady Selborne township,
reported to us by Hannah Stanton. African women had gathered in a
church hall after a peaceful protest over the threat to extend the Pass
Laws to women. Suddenly the police burst into the hall, drove the
women out, and, as they tried to escape, they were assaulted and
beaten up. There were head wounds, concussions, broken legs and
broken arms: seventy-one women required immediate medical treatment. One policeman was heard to observe with satisfaction, 'I shan't
forget this day, we gave those Bantu girls a jolly good hiding'. When
Hannah Stanton went to protest to the superintendent, asking if he

realised that his men had treated the women worse than they would treat animals, he replied that he did not regard Bantu women as women. British Defence and Aid sent £3,000 to finance a case for damages against the Minister of Justice.

Another appeal came from Sekekuneland, where during disturbances four people were shot dead by the police, and an unpopular and corrupt government-appointed chief was murdered. Defence and Aid paid legal fees for the seventy people who were arrested and charged with public violence and murder. Fourteen were condemned to death for the murder. Without proper defence, said Ambrose Reeves, many more might have faced execution. But John had hopes of somehow saving the fourteen from death, and when C.R. Swart, the governor general of South Africa, was in London, John discovered that he and his aides were housed in the Dorchester Hotel. He marched off, and managed somehow to get into the suite where the South African delegation was staying, and confronted Swart with a letter appealing to him to exercise his prerogative of mercy. Something either in what John had to say or in the contents of the letter must have moved Swart. A year later, John heard from an African friend who wrote, 'I see in today's paper that the death penalty on the 14 Sekekuneland men has been commuted to life imprisonment . . . I choose to think and I believe that your dramatic encounter with C.R. Swart in the Dorchester had some effect after all.'

Much more money now had to be raised. The British public was becoming better informed about the situation in Southern Africa. This was due in large measure to the book *Naught for your Comfort* that Trevor Huddleston had written after his recall from South Africa in 1956. He wrote out of a passionate love for the African people to whom he had ministered during his years in Sophiatown, and a passionate, though restrained anger at the injustice and deprivation inflicted upon them. This book was nearly as widely read as *Cry the Beloved Country*, and certainly as influential.

The amount of money that John managed to raise singlehanded was remarkable. By 1959 it was around £177,000 (multiply by at least ten for a present-day comparison) and the cost of raising it was less than ten per cent. We were wonderfully supported by creative artists of all varieties. Our records tell of benefit concerts and recitals, and benefit theatrical performances. John got black jazz artists over from America to give midnight concerts in the Festival Hall, and he planned an international exhibition and sale of contemporary art.

None of the work of Christian Action would have been possible without the support and generosity of so many people, not famous, not rich, just people with decent human instincts, compassion, hatred of injustice, and a willingness to help those in trouble.

The pressure on our basement was, by this time, becoming almost overwhelming: six typewriters, three telephone lines, and a dictaphone in constant use. Freda also made extensive use of the willing voluntary helpers who surrounded us. 'Working parties' met regularly in the evenings as well as in the daytime. It was one of these voluntary workers who came to stay. George Hamilton was a keen Methodist, who had just retired from Hambros bank. He was especially interested in Christian Action's race relations work, and he came to offer his services. He became honorary treasurer both of Christian Action and of the Defence and Aid Fund, and stayed with us for ten years, steadily refusing anything in the way of remuneration. George was soon joined by Maud Henry who came from Jamaica with her family to live in England. She shared George's unselfish commitment to our work, and they made a particularly happy and effective partnership.

In between two highly successful public meetings in 1958, John and I spent a wonderful week on Iona, staying with George and Lorna Macleod. This island has its own special magic with its mists and sunshine and cloud, its softly shifting lights, and rainbow fragments appearing and disappearing. Iona is a place where you cannot help but feel that you tread on holy ground. George's Iona Community had a great deal in common with Christian Action; the same emphasis on political and social involvement, the same commitment to peace and peace-making. The community was rebuilding the ancient and beautiful Abbey, and this was nearly completed. So now this was a place to which the members could return and share their work and experience, a place that gave them a cohesive sense of community. It was something John would have liked for Christian Action; he still hankered after the spirit of the Yatesbury Fellowship, but that could not be reproduced, least of all in the heart of the City of London. We had to do the work that we had to do, in the circumstances in which we found ourselves.

33

Turmoil in Southern Africa

EVERYONE knows about the shootings at Sharpeville on 21 March 1960. The police opened fire upon an unarmed crowd demonstrating peaceably against the Pass Laws; sixty-nine people were killed, and 186 wounded, they were shot in the back as they fled. There were similar disturbances in Cape Town, where Philip Kgosana of the newly formed Pan African Congress (PAC) led a march on the city. There were shootings by the police at Langa and Nyanga.

The shootings at Sharpeville shocked the world. John immediately pledged the British Defence and Aid Fund to provide for the families of those killed and wounded, to pay medical and funeral expenses, to finance a legal enquiry into the shootings, and to fund claims for compensation against the police. The commission of enquiry found that the shootings were unjustified, but the government immediately rushed through a Bill granting indemnity to the police for their actions.

John was not cautious about financial commitments, but, in fact, money poured in to the British Fund, already known for its support of the Treason Trial. Our postman was unable to get the letters through the letter box; they piled up on our breakfast table. Contributions came from Canada, Denmark, New Zealand, Australia, British Guiana, Tunisia and Nigeria; £1,000 each was donated by the governments of Sierra Leone, Jamaica, Ghana and Liberia. There was an overwhelmingly generous response from within Great Britain. One of the most significant contributions came from Sweden.

There were many fresh visitors to 2 Amen Court that year, among them a young Swedish writer, Per Wastberg. Per and his wife Annalena had spent eight months' study in Rhodesia and South Africa, and on his return to Sweden, Per wrote a series of articles powerfully critical of apartheid. Public opinion was aroused as well by the broadcasts and writings of the Reverend Gunnar Helander, who had returned to Sweden after many years as a missionary in South Africa.

Together Per and Gunnar set up a Swedish Fund for the victims of apartheid and popular anti-apartheid pressure became so powerful that the Swedish government responded and inaugurated a special commission of support for the liberation movements of South Africa. Per came to the basement offices of Defence and Aid, but he soon found his way up to the study and to John and a glass of sherry. It would be hard to exaggerate the significance of this meeting for Defence and Aid. Not only did money raised from the Swedish public now come directly to BDAF, but the Swedish government led the way in contributing to the Fund, and became over the years its major supporter.

After the Sharpeville incident, the South African government panicked. Within a week, it declared a State of Emergency; the ANC, the PAC, the Congress of Democrats, and the Communist party were banned. The security forces then proceeded to arrest and imprison men and women of all races who might, in any way, be supposed to be against the government's apartheid policies. Nearly 2,000 people were detained, and some 1,800 Africans were rounded up on the pretext that they were 'idlers'. There was no consideration for family commitments: both parents would be taken away with no time or opportunity to make provision for small children, breadwinners were hauled off, leaving their dependants destitute. There was widespread poverty and distress among many families of detainees.

South Africa was in a state of shock, and that included the white community. The Bishop of Johannesburg set up an Emergency Fund to collect food, money and clothing for the families of the Sharpeville victims and the detainees; similar funds sprang up in Pretoria, Durban, Port Elizabeth, East London and Pietermaritzburg. Cape Town raised a fund for the victims of Langa and Nyanga. There was an immediate and generous response from the whole community. Existing organisations gave money and assistance – the Black Sash, the Red Cross, the Society of Friends, and the Christian Council of South Africa. African self-help organisations took children into nursery schools and crèches free of charge; a number of municipalities, including Johannesburg, remitted current and arrears of rent; doctors and lawyers gave their services free or for only minimal charges. All through South Africa, there was 'an even larger group of whites fighting for the rights of Africans (and others) than ever before'. But the government remained frightened, obdurate, and without pity.

The South African Funds that had sprung up around the country to bring assistance to the victims of Sharpeville and Langa, now began to organise themselves. Since they relied so heavily upon the Christian

Action Defence and Aid Fund, they decided to call themselves Defence and Aid, and to adopt similar terms of reference. They had a board of trustees, which included our old friend Alan Paton and the new and sympathetic Archbishop of Cape Town, Joost de Blank. Their headquarters were in Johannesburg, and to their continuing appeals Christian Action responded as best it could. The majority of white South Africans were, however, almost unaware of the misery of the detainees' families, although so many were involved.

Bad as things were, they were to become much worse. From now on, the story is one of increasingly savage repression, and of more and more draconian legislation. Banning orders, that peculiarly South African kind of death-in-life punishment, were scattered throughout the community, landing upon anyone the government feared might cause trouble. White people who tried to help those of other races were likely, sooner or later, to receive one of these orders, sometimes with the addition of 'house arrest'; there was no appeal. It was impossible to meet all of the legal and welfare needs, though the South African Committees made valiant fund-raising efforts, and Christian Action exerted itself to its full capacity.

There was an additional problem of refugees. In the uncertain and dangerous atmosphere of the State of Emergency, many people left South Africa – for London or Europe; others, especially Africans without passports, fled to the British Protectorates of Swaziland, Basutoland and Bechuanaland, and there they were stuck, without money, and with the South African government threatening their extradition back to Pretoria. They could not travel through the Central African Federation, as the white government there would give them no guarantee of immunity from arrest and extradition, it was not even safe to put down in transit on any Federation airport. The British Fund managed to get money out to help them over their immediate difficulties, but somehow they had to be enabled to travel on to safety.

By good fortune, Dr Nkrumah was in London, and asked to see John to discuss the refugee problem. Ghana, he said, would do what it could to help, and he suggested supplying planes for an airlift, provided BDAF would pay for the refugees' keep and any further travel expenses. There were still complications, as no large aeroplane could put down on the inadequate landing facilities in the Protectorates; small aircraft would have to be chartered to fly as far as the Congo, from where it would be possible to proceed safely to Ghana.

Other refugees found their way to Dar-es-Salaam, but they too had financial problems. Before the great exodus, the ANC executive, with considerable foresight, had decided that someone must be sent over-seas to lead an external mission to rouse world opinion, and persuade the nations and the UN to act against apartheid. They chose Oliver Tambo, who was soon joined by Robert Resha, another executive member and ex-Treason Trialist. Oliver had reached Dar-es-Salaam from where he wrote to John describing the plight of the refugees; BDAF sent money and arranged to bring Oliver to London; then, through the Ghana airlift, his wife and children were brought out to safety. While some of the exiles stayed in Africa, many came to London, and had to be helped to settle in this new country. At the invitation of Dr Nkrumah, John flew out to Ghana to welcome the safe arrival of the first plane-load of refu-gees. The British Defence and Aid Fund spent some £10,000 on the whole refugee enterprise.

Oliver Tambo is one of the gentlest and sweetest-natured characters I have ever been lucky enough to know. But beneath that gentleness and moderation is a selfless dedication, founded upon a deep Christian faith and belief in the future of his country and his people. It is Oliver who has held the ANC to its non-racial policies. It is Oliver, too, who insisted, with John, that help from Defence and Aid must be given without discrimination to all who suffered through active opposition to the policies of apartheid. Robert Resha was a very different character, lively, ebullient and full of humour. For some time he represented the ANC in London, and would come and give John an acute and amusing analysis of the political situation in and outside South Africa; Robbie was always worth listening to with his sharp insight into personalities and affairs.

Now our offices overflowed, and parts of the Defence and Aid work found temporary homes in spare rooms in minor canons' houses on the other side of Amen Court. Some South African exiles came to work for us and we were joined by John Morrison from the Iona Community who took over our publications and Christmas cards; Dame Laura Knight and John Piper each gave us designs, and John Morrison also helped with general money-raising.

Back in South Africa, Ambrose Reeves was under pressure from his diocesan clergy to leave the country, they feared both for his personal safety and for the possibility of his arrest. This was a cruelly difficult period for Ambrose and his family. The previous year they had been on holiday on the coast when their younger boy Nicholas, swimming in a rough sea, got into difficulties; his elder brother John immediately went to his rescue, got Nicholas to safety but was himself swept out to sea and drowned. I don't think that John's parents ever got over his death; we don't 'get over' such losses, we only learn, as we must, to live with them as a part of ourselves. John Reeves was a truly golden young man, a history scholar at Cambridge, and destined, to his parents' delight, for ordination. Ambrose had recently been ill and in hospital, and the family were subjected to continual abuse and death threats: shots fired through their windows made the threats real. Margaret Reeves had had enough of white savagery. In this atmosphere of anxiety and pressure, Ambrose decided to leave; fearful that he might still be detained at the airport, he fled to Swaziland. He came on to London, and arrived to stay at 2 Amen Court. He announced that he wanted to tell the world what had really happened at Sharpeville. But the world already knew, and was not deceived by any protestations from the South African government. Soon afterwards, Ambrose was joined by his family, who stayed with us for two months. I don't quite know how we all fitted in. Margaret Ann, the elder Reeves daughter, was engaged to be married, and she soon took herself off, leaving us with Ambrose and Margaret, Kay and Nikki. Our three elder boys were away at school, only Mark was at home; it was a tight squeeze, but a happy one.

From Ambrose's personal point of view, the decision to leave South Africa was a sad mistake. An uncharitable world viewed him as a shepherd who had deserted his flock, and when, some months later, he decided to return to his diocese he was immediately deported. Ambrose was a brave, good and gifted man; the English church treated him shabbily, it never offered him a proper job.* Ambrose was not someone to be left to rot; he devoted himself for the rest of his life to continuing the fight against apartheid, and he was for many years chairman of the Anti-Apartheid Movement. Prophets don't work for rewards, and don't expect any this side of the grave.

Many horrifying stories of personal suffering came to us from South Africa, and I reported numbers of them in the *Christian Action Journal*. As always the Indians and Africans came off worst. An Indian detainee wrote: 'The moment we enter prison we cease to be human – we are spoken to like cattle – fed like cattle – sleep almost like cattle and carry on our toilet activities like cattle . . . The whites are separated in jail,

---

* In 1961, the Archbishop of Canterbury, Michael Ramsay, did recommend Reeves for the vacant Bishopric of Blackburn. The Prime Minister, Harold Macmillan, refused to appoint him, saying that it would exacerbate already strained relations with white South Africa. The negative effect upon black opinion was not considered. Politics took precedence over religion.

with better conditions of course. The white murderer . . . is treated better than the black philosopher.'

Trouble was widespread throughout Southern Africa. In South-West Africa at Windhoek, a demonstration of Africans protesting against a relocation order was fired on by the police, and a number were arrested and charged with public violence. BDAF paid for their legal defence, and all were acquitted.

In the Central African Federation, Southern Rhodesia was in turmoil. Terence Ranger, a history lecturer at Salisbury University, together with his wife Shelagh, had got together a Legal Aid and Welfare Committee, and when it could, BDAF sent them money. In July 1960, hundreds of Africans were arrested after disturbances in Bulawayo; 515 were brought to trial, and only 128 were convicted. BDAF was able to supply £1,500 for this crucial case.

But Terence Ranger was still writing desperately to John that the test period in their work for the detainees came with a long tedious drag after all the hearings were over, and the great majority released, and after the issue had almost ceased to be a live one. The British Fund had become their only source of money from England and was crucial. In many ways the situation in Southern Rhodesia was as dangerous as that in South Africa. British moral responsibility was greater even for Southern Rhodesia than for South Africa. As well as the abhorrence shown for what the Afrikaner Nationalists were doing, there should also be more abhorrence shown for what our fellow Britons were capable of doing.

It was much harder to raise money for the Federation than for South Africa, and even there it needed some dramatic and widely reported incident to rouse the general public. Thankfully, there was a core of loyal supporters who contributed steadily to the Fund, after the dramas of life and death, and throughout 'the long tedious drag' when human need remained as acute and painful as ever. BDAF's audited accounts for the year ending June 1960 show that while £8,000 was sent to Southern Rhodesia, £74,000 went to the South African Defence and Aid Committee, and £65,000 to the Treason Trial Fund. Money raised for one purpose cannot legitimately be transferred to another, but the British Fund did manage to see that Southern Rhodesia was not left without help when help was crucial, and the selfless work done by Terence and Shelagh Ranger until their deportation in 1963 is beyond praise.

We were aware of, and were trying to deal with a great deal of human suffering, and many of the cases that came to us were heartbreaking. But neither life nor work could always be grim. We were especially involved, with the help of John Morrison who was an artistic chap, in trying to collect pictures for the benefit Art Sale. My husband had suggested that, unless they wished otherwise, artists should be offered a percentage of the sale money for their works. Pictures were not only their living, they were their capital: you didn't go around asking barristers to give you a portion of their fees, stockbrokers to give you some of their deals, so why should artists be expected just to donate their works? This seemed a good idea, and many artists were interested, and most were very generous. For several months we had a beautiful little bronze seated figure by Henry Moore in our drawing room. I really longed to be able to keep it but knew we couldn't find the money it was likely to fetch.

We still needed more exhibits, and more big names, and I think it was John Morrison who introduced us to Jan le Witt, an émigré Polish artist. 'We must go to Paris,' said Jan, 'and approach the artists personally'. He seemed to know everybody, and to know where they were to be found, so off we went, John and me and Jan.

It wasn't quite so easy to find and approach the artists. The best way, Jan assured us, was to try and get to them through their mistresses, or, rather more rarely, through their wives. Once or twice we tried this only to discover that the mistress in question had recently been discarded, and was certainly not going to help us find the new one. But we did visit a number of galleries and were given several promises. I remember especially lunching in a café with Giacometti, and spending an afternoon in his studio surrounded by those strange, yet strangely powerful, elongated figures. Giacometti was enthusiastic about the cause of Defence and Aid, and was ready and eager to give us – yes give – a major work. But, alas, we ran into difficulties with the gallery to which he was contracted. 'These galleries think they own their artists body and soul,' said Jan gloomily. Later in the year John and I stayed with friends in the South of France, and spent a whole day trying to reach Picasso. He appeared to be living on top of a mountain, and was so securely guarded that nobody could find him, friends and mistresses were of no avail, and we finally had to give up. But our efforts did yield results, and the following year we had a successful and profitable exhibition and sale at Christie's.

34

The Rift: John Collins and Michael Scott

THE early Sixties were full of trouble for John. While he was struggling with CND and the Committee of 100, he was under attack in regard to Defence and Aid. There had been rumblings of this, but after the inflow of money following the Sharpeville incident, Michael Scott and the Africa Bureau began to complain about John's use of funds, suggesting that there was some misuse; they demanded a form of power-sharing. They had, they said, encouraged their supporters to contribute to Defence and Aid; they should therefore have some control over how the money – not just theirs, but all the money – was spent. Many people and organisations had contributed often considerably more substantially to the Fund, no one else demanded such control. The Africa Bureau was not a great money-raising organisation: they concentrated upon producing and circulating much valuable information, and upon public and political pressure.

John had enlisted a number of well-known, influential, and interested persons as sponsors for the Fund, many of whom were ready to sign letters, appeals and advertisements. He was in process of asking a number of these to act as Trustees, and to form an Advisory Grants Committee. He told Michael about this, giving him the names of those concerned. Michael said nothing to John, but proceeded to circularise the selected sponsors with his view of affairs, including his various complaints. John was angry. He had previously suggested that the Africa Bureau should nominate some of its own people to serve on such a committee; this they had refused. Michael now began his accusations about discrimination against the PAC. In a confused situation such as that following upon the Sharpeville shootings, and when there can never be enough money to go round, some, perhaps many, are apt to feel that others may have done better than they have. Michael listened to one particular PAC character, M., who was a bit of a rogue, and who came with numerous false accusations. As John himself was only too liable to be taken in by rogues, we should not perhaps blame Michael too much for this. Whenever any such case came to John's notice he immediately investigated it, and found these allegations of discrimination to be without foundation.

Michael then demanded that the financial affairs of Christian Action in its handling of Defence and Aid be investigated by independent assessors. John replied that Christian Action was a registered charity, its accounts were audited annually, and had to be presented to the Charity Commissioners; anyone was welcome to come and inspect the accounts. It is, of course, fairly easy to 'cook' accounts, but John was responsible to the Christian Action Council, and in George Hamilton and Freda Nuell he had two models of strict financial probity. In fact, the allocation of money was almost entirely in the hands of the Defence and Aid Committees inside South Africa. They, too, had non-discrimination written into their constitution, and were scrupulous in observing this.

There were influential people who supported the Africa Bureau, and who were in a position to damage the credibility of Defence and Aid. There were others who were, quite reasonably, anxious that the various anti-apartheid movements should present a common front to the public. The Africa Bureau was asking for a board of management or council to control the money, and on which they would have equality of representation with Defence and Aid.

The accusations about misuse of money were always vague and generalised, no specific instances were ever produced. And it should be noted that no great scandals or calamities have befallen either John or Defence and Aid in its thirty-five years of successful operation.

Another suggestion was that the Fund should sever its connection with Christian Action – the word Christian might be counter-productive. This produced immediate protest from inside and outside South Africa, from Oliver Tambo, Chief Luthuli, Jusuf Dadoo (not a Christian), the Archbishop of Cape Town and Alan Paton: all expressed the wish that 'in any reorganisation of the Fund, the connection with Christian Action should be retained and there should be no suggestion that there is any break with the Fund as it already exists'.

John was much more inclined to be accommodating to the Africa Bureau than I was. The Christian Action Council had no wish for change, they had seen the work for which they too were responsible, and had seen it effectively and scrupulously carried out. I was indignant about the whole affair. At one stage in these troublesome and time-consuming negotiations, John was ill, so I had to represent him in a meeting with the Africa Bureau. I was tough when someone protested that, under a proposed arrangement, the Bureau members would not have their 'proper rights'. I replied sharply that they had no rights, it was Christian Action that was prepared to offer them some; the point was taken.

John did make one bad mistake around this period. His ANC friends were anxious for a political fund that would be able to produce money for projects outside the terms of reference of Defence and Aid. John had talked to Michael about this, who had replied that he had been thinking along similar lines. Then, under pressure from the Africans, John went ahead without further consultation and launched a political Fund. This provoked a furious response from the Africa Bureau, and an unpleasant public attack upon John in *The Observer*.

John got on well with Lord Hemingford, the Bureau's Chairman, and had friendly and constructive discussions with him. John pleaded for a year's trial of his original sponsors' proposal with Africa Bureau representation, and offered that, since the Bureau had special interest in the Central African Federation, all money raised for that should be handed over to their control for distribution. But this was again rejected.

In spite of hostility and unpleasantness, and against the wishes of the Christian Action Council, a formulation for a joint board of management with which the Africa Bureau agreed was at last arrived at. Frank Longford was to take the chair, and with the help of our friend Ronald Simms who was head of public relations for the Conservative party, Oliver Poole was persuaded to act as treasurer. The board lasted for less than a year. John continued his money-raising efforts, but no extra funds came in as he had been assured that they would. John was somehow expected to produce all the cash and then hand it over. He was frustrated too, as he could not now respond immediately to the urgent appeals that kept coming from South Africa. It was Frank Longford who saw what was happening, and decided to disband the board. 'It wasn't John who was the difficult one,' he said.

Uncharacteristically, John was so dispirited by this whole wounding business, that he contemplated winding up Defence and Aid altogether, he had plenty of other things to do. This prospect produced horrified reactions from South Africa, from Rhodesia, and from the exiled South Africans; Chief Luthuli wrote begging John to continue. And so John decided that we must soldier on. But spread of rumours about supposed mismanagement of the money, coupled with suggestions of Communist influence, did have their effect. The TUC withdrew its support, and the Labour party blew cold. However, solid support always came from where it mattered most, from South Africa and the South Africans. So with the kitty nearly emptied, and the need to raise at least another £200,000 as soon as possible, John returned to the task.

Michael continued his sporadic attacks on Defence and Aid. When governments, through the UN, had begun to make contributions to the Fund, Michael went so far as to visit New York to make fresh demands for its financial affairs to be 'independently investigated'. He was a very strange character, and I cannot profess to understand him, nor why he turned so bitterly against John. Michael provoked extreme reactions, of approval and of disapproval, and I suppose that the same could be said about John. I have known people sympathetic to the cause of African freedom, who thought Michael a dangerous troublemaker, and a somewhat inhuman and insensitive character. He was accused of being ruthless in his exploitation of people, never for personal ends, only for the causes to which he was dedicated. 'Michael doesn't have warm red blood in his veins,' said Alan Paton. I have known others who have worked with Michael, who regard him with love and admiration, and speak of his pastoral feeling as well as his dedication. And, at first, John and I were disposed to be counted among the friends and admirers. Colin Legum suggested that Michael was somewhat paranoid, and that this grew worse as he got older, and was accompanied by an intense suspiciousness, a characteristic feature of paranoia. Certainly Michael was obsessive on the question of money, and John was not the only person, nor was Defence and Aid the only organisation, that suffered unjustly from his attacks.

Many people thought of Michael as a saint. He fitted the popular stereotype: he was celibate, appeared to have no home, was careless of personal safety and personal comfort, and was ready to dash off to any place in the world that he thought might be in need of non-violent protest and civil disobedience. There was no doubting, and I certainly do not doubt, the sincerity of his dedication to the causes in which he believed. Freda Levson, who knew him well, said, 'Michael wasn't a saint, but he was a prophet.' And with that I would concur; Michael was a courageous pioneer in the causes of anti-apartheid, anti-racialism and peace.

Although people have used the word 'saint' to me in connection with John – one friend described him as a 'devilish saint' – I would prefer the word 'prophet'. All the same, with his warm overflowing humanity, his ready sympathy with all manner of men and women, John did seem to me (hardly an unbiased witness) to be a man who was good through and through. 'What do you feel like when people call you a saint and say how good you are?' I once asked him. He gave me a funny little smile and said, 'I know different'.

John was a lover of life in all its forms, pleasurably married, comfortably housed, a cheerful connoisseur of good wines. Superficially he could have been seen as just a worldly priest, in contrast to Michael's eccentric other-worldliness. In fact, I think, there are good and not so good ways of being either worldly or unworldly, both have their temptations. John and Michael, in their different ways, confronted worldly power, and when they thought their causes required it, they both made use of the power and influence that were available. Perhaps neither was totally immune to the temptations of such power.

John did try to extend olive branches to Michael, and my last memory is of an occasion when John had invited him to preach in St Paul's. Michael appeared genuinely moved by this, and as he sat with us both in John's study I felt an echo and a faint stirring of the friendship that might have been.

35

Trials and Tribulations

THERE were causes for rejoicing in the Sixties. John was still desperately raising money for the Treason Trial that dragged on and on, but by 1960, only some thirty persons remained on trial. Mary Benson reported to Christian Action that, in spite of the appalling frustrations, uncertainties and discomforts of their lives, the morale of the accused was high. 'How do you do it?' she asked one of the Africans. 'It's physical culture,' he replied. 'I get up in the morning. I do my exercises. I put on my clothes, then I put on my smile, and I come to the Court.' Legal defence had amounted to no more than £400 per head, and this was a great tribute to the generosity of the South African lawyers. During the first years of the trial, there had been 400 dependants involved, but the accused had refused to accept more than £11 a month for their families, although the breadline in the cities was estimated as around £25 per month.

The South African government made frantic efforts to secure convictions. It passed two pieces of retrospective legislation, one to enable the police to produce unproven documents as *prima facie* evidence, a second to make legal the setting up by the Minister of Justice of a special court to try the case, consisting of three judges selected by himself. The accused were being tried on the basis of their support for the Freedom Charter: all had been present when it was adopted at the great Congress of the People in 1955.

The proceedings remained farcical throughout, and on 5 March 1961, Bram Fischer, one of the team of defending counsel, wrote to John, 'The Crown argument has lasted three months, and has exposed the fantastic unreality of the case. It tried to prove (1) Congress policy was one of violent overthrow, and (2) This conspiracy one joined by becoming a member of Congress'. But, Bram continued, the evidence of non-violence was so overwhelming, that the Prosecution resorted to the suggestion that the supposed conspirators *intended* 'to provoke police violence, which would raise "political consciousness", and would lead eventually to such retaliation by the masses as to sweep the State away'. There was never any difficulty, Bram observed, about proving police violence, it went on all the time. But he continued: 'dozens of reliable rank and file members from all over the country showed that they had never heard of any policy of violence. The plot, therefore, has shrunk and become "semi-secret", and now the Crown is at a loss when trying to determine who is and who is not in the plot. This has led to their dropping one conspirator after another, and has led to so absurd an argument that Professor Matthews, a vice-president, who has been in the ANC and its activities for twenty years, knew enough of the plot to be a conspirator, but not enough to be able to testify to what in fact ANC policy was. Can you beat it? I can't believe even Rumpf can now convict.'

And he couldn't. A few weeks later, all were acquitted unconditionally. This was a moment when we felt that if Christian Action had done or did nothing else, it would have justified its existence 156 times over, in contributing to the rescue of all those men and women. There was plenty more to come, but nothing perhaps as dramatic and uplifting as the triumph of the Treason Trial.

There were changes at St Paul's in 1961. The archdeacon of London was promoted to become dean of Winchester, and that left John in the position of the longest serving and therefore the senior canon. It also left vacant the position of chapter treasurer, which would, by custom, be filled by the senior canon. John would have liked to be chapter treasurer; he had ideas and schemes for raising money for the cathedral – he was good at finance. I sometimes remarked that if he would devote his considerable talents to following the Stock Exchange and the Turf, we might be rich. But John's colleagues were nervous of him, and machinations went on behind the scenes.

Appointments to the greater offices of the cathedral were made at the annual chapter meeting held this year at the end of November. The dean announced that he had given much 'anxious thought' to the question of the chapter treasurership, and had decided to nominate Canon Hood for election. This was endorsed by a formal vote with one dissentient - Canon Collins. John explained that he had no personal objection to Canon Hood, but he did wish to protest at the method by which his nomination had been obtained.

This episode resembled a repeat performance of the way in which poor old Canon Alexander had been ousted from the position of chapter treasurer. John's colleagues might have been forgiven for

Above left Paul Robeson at St Paul's (*Reuters*)
Above right Coretta, widow of Martin Luther King, at St Paul's (*AP*)
Below John, Michael Ramsey, retired Archbishop of Canterbury, and Mervyn Stockwood, Bishop of Southwark, at Amen Court after the wedding of Prince Charles and Lady Diana

Above The family at home at Amen Court: Peter, Mark, Diana, John, Andrew and Richard
Below Adelaide Tambo, John and Diana at John's seventieth birthday celebrations

thinking that he was involved in so many outside activities, that he might not have sufficient time to devote to cathedral affairs. John had thought about this and had already decided how he could arrange his affairs. It would have been rather more decent and more friendly to have discussed the matter with him first. The chapter might also have feared that with John's appointment, money from the City might diminish: businessmen did not appreciate being told, from the pulpit of St Paul's, that they ought not to invest in South Africa. But there were men in the City prepared to put the interests of the cathedral above any feelings they might have about particular deans or canons. And John had friends in the City.

John did, it is true, manage from time to time to embarrass his colleagues, as with one December sermon. During this month there were Christmas trees at the west end of the cathedral. Visitors and others were invited to place, around these, gifts for some of the really poor London parishes, toys, clothes, household necessities etc. John was disgusted by the way some people used this as an opportunity to discard broken, used, and sometimes dirty objects. He alerted the Press, and preached about the true meaning of Christmas giving. But the next day, his colleagues were not pleased to see newspaper photographs of John in the cathedral displaying a pair of soiled and dilapidated lady's corsets.

There was another occasion for which I have to blame myself. John was due to speak at the annual St Paul's day dinner. He disliked after-dinner speaking, and asked me if I could think of a suitable story. It had to be something easily memorable and brief, John was not a good raconteur, and frequently forgot the punch line. So, rather reluctantly, I dredged around in my mind, and came up with one I had heard from my father. This was standard material about a couple of Irishmen, lifelong friends and drinking companions. As one lay dying, he told the other that in his cupboard was a very special bottle of whisky that he was keeping for some very special occasion when they could polish it off together. His last request to his friend was that he would pour this over his grave in celebration of their long and happy alcoholic friendship. 'Of course I'll be glad to do that for you,' was the reply, 'but you sure wouldn't object if I passed it through my kidneys first'.

The dinner was an all-male affair, no sex mentioned, but I thought that this story might just do, and John seemed quite pleased with it. It went down very well at the bottom end of the table among the choirmen, wandsmen and others who worked in the cathedral, and the less important guests; there were guffaws of laughter, even some of those higher up began to laugh until they saw the archbishop's face, and a frosty silence descended.

Christian Action continued with its activities public and less public. I ran a part of the *Journal* called 'Freda Nuell's Logbook'. I described a few of the pastoral problems that Freda patiently dealt with. Sometimes practical help would come from the London network of Christian Action supporters, at others Freda, with John's help, would battle with immigration officials, local councils, Social Security bureaucrats and other such bodies. It was all unspectacular, individual and parochial, but it was an essential part of Christian Action.

The early Fifties and Sixties were periods of more or less full employment, but there were always the dirty and boring jobs that nobody wanted to do. It was a Conservative government that began recruiting among the unemployed in the West Indies, and there was a big response, so big that the government hurriedly passed the Immigration Act, and racial prejudice began to be openly and sometimes violently expressed in Britain.

Christian Action planned a public meeting, 'Colour prejudice must go'. The young Martin Luther King was to speak from the US, Robert Resha from South Africa, and Stuart Hall from the West Indies. For an important meeting, we would pay to have posters displayed on the Underground, but this time, to our amazement, these were refused. The title, we were told, was 'too political'; somewhat ironical, as so many West Indians found employment with London Transport. No amount of argument could persuade the management to accept the posters. Perhaps it was thought they might spread dangerous ideas.

Nevertheless, we had a remarkable meeting. Martin Luther King, raised in the tradition of Southern Baptist preaching, was a master of dramatic timing, contrast and pace, his words were powerful and poetic, fuelled by a visionary fervour that was irresistible. Robert Resha too had a vision of a non-racial society, and his speech sparkled with wit and with a delightful earthy humour. Stuart Hall, a young bright academic, referred to the two previous speakers as 'the voices of the future'. In the light of history, he brought us back to the present day. 'The same ships which took Africans to the US, took Africans to the West Indies which is my home. There was, in those days, a triangular trade. They sent out from this country beads and presents for the natives, they took from Africa human lives, and they brought back from the West Indies and from the Southern States of the US cotton and sugar . . . 300 years of economic and social neglect in my country has at last washed up on yours . . . if on the basis of legislation only thinly disguised as racial, you close your doors to people who have suffered at the back end of your empire for 300 years, you will have turned your backs on all those voices of the future which you have listened to so comfortably tonight.'

Nineteen sixty-one ended with another cause for rejoicing: the award of the Nobel Peace Prize to Chief Albert Luthuli. He was invited to Oslo to receive the prize in person on 10 December, and he wrote to John to ask if he would accompany him for this occasion. John was, of course, delighted, and as he met the chief at London airport, Luthuli said: 'It is wonderful to place my feet on free soil. I am so happy to be here.' The South African government had removed Luthuli's passport, but they gave him a brief dispensation to travel to Oslo. A large audience assembled for the award ceremony, the men all wearing their sober dark suits. So they were startled when Luthuli appeared, resplendent in the regalia of an African chief, with a fine leopard-skin headdress. Some of the South Africans were alarmed, quite the wrong image they feared, but Luthuli carried it off magnificently, and spoke of his people's yearning for freedom and for peace, and of the problems in trying to reconcile the two. There were those, especially among the exiles, who tried to persuade Luthuli not to return to South Africa, where he would undoubtedly be penalised and silenced; he could be an invaluable ambassador to the international community. Luthuli was firm, he had given his word, he would return to live and die among his people.

The South African government played down any significance that the Peace Prize might have, and on the chief's return they imposed upon him an immediate banning order. For the rest of his life, he was confined to his tribal area, and nothing that he wrote or said was allowed to be quoted.

While the world was honouring Luthuli for his leadership of the ANC and his commitment to non-violent resistance, his followers back in South Africa were making different plans. Following the shock of Sharpeville, the ANC executive met and, after prolonged discussion, decided that nothing was to be gained by peaceful protest; all that happened was that unarmed protesters were shot down and killed. The time had come to 'counter violence with violence'. Led by Nelson Mandela, they founded Umkonto we Sizwe (Spear of the Nation). Their object was to keep strictly to sabotage, the destruction of buildings and installations; as far as possible, they would avoid human casualties. The PAC was not dedicated to non-violence, and they now founded Poqo, which aimed to go beyond sabotage, and if necessary to fight to free South Africa by 1963.

Walter Sisulu wrote to John to ask whether the British Defence and Aid Fund would continue its political defence for those charged with acts of violence. Robert Resha was sent to Amen Court to explain the change in policy. Although the intention of Umkonto we Sizwe was to avoid casualties, they recognised that people might be killed accidentally in the course of sabotage operations; men could then face capital charges. The South African committees were already under hostile government pressure; they decided that they could not pay defence for sabotage cases.

This was a difficult decision for John, and for the Christian Action Council. All recognised that it was the unprovoked violence of the State and its trigger-happy police that had driven the ANC to this change of policy. But John was a pacifist however reluctant, as were several of his council. Yet he believed, and had said publicly, that it was not the business of outsiders or sympathisers to tell the Africans how they should conduct their liberation struggles. The blood-stained history of Europe and of the Christian Churches hardly entitled them to criticise others who took up arms in an evidently just cause.

John reached the decision with the help of his council. Sabotage cases could not be allowed to go undefended; whatever a man had done, he was entitled to as fair a trial as the laws of the country would allow – this was crucial to the democratic rule of law. And the families and dependants of those on trial or in prison must be supported. As well as continuing to respond to appeals from the internal committees, the British Fund would now have, in cases of sabotage, to deal directly with South African law firms.

Nelson Mandela slipped out of South Africa to undergo guerrilla training, and to organise supplies of arms. Just before he returned, he came to lunch with us in Amen Court. I remember well how impressed I was by the quiet yet powerful dignity of this young man, and his twenty-seven years in prison have only enhanced that dignity. All those years ago he showed qualities of courage, and of leadership that could develop into statesmanship.

Cases arising out of the State of Emergency came pouring in from South Africa, and the Sabotage Bill of 1962 led to more. At first cases were almost entirely ANC. The PAC took a hard line, it would not recognise the legitimacy of the white courts, and would accept neither bail nor defence. By 1962 the organisation abandoned its hard line, and, with one exception, all cases on the books of Defence and Aid for that year were PAC cases.

Newsletters from South Africa continued to detail distressing cases of human suffering, which convey the reality of the situation better than statistics of the many trials. Even if men had been acquitted in court, or had been released after serving a sentence, persecution was not ended. They would have lost their jobs, and would find it almost impossible to find other work; if they did succeed it was more than likely that the Special Branch would visit their employer, and they would be dismissed. Without work, a man was liable to be 'endorsed out', that is, sent back to one of the 'homelands' where he had been born. For men and their families it was a story of endless hardship and frustration.

During 1962, the South African committees and Defence and Aid in London just managed to keep pace with the appeals that reached them, and the internal committees wrote that, in the trials for which defence was available, there were considerably more acquittals than convictions.

It was not always easy to get news in time for trials held in magistrates' courts in remote areas, nor was it easy to trace and to keep track of all those in need. Ideally a number of field and welfare workers should have been employed, but, of course, there was never enough money for such a scheme. The committees often functioned with little more than a secretary, and a good deal of voluntary help. Under the circumstances, it was wonderful that they achieved so much.

Between September 1962 and March 1963 Defence and Aid South Africa reported that it had never had so many cases to deal with, but that no one who appealed for help went unaided.

The signs for 1963 were ominous. As resistance grew, so did repression. The General Law Amendment Act was now on the statute book, and this contained the sinister 'ninety-days provision'. The police were empowered to hold suspects in solitary confinement without access to family or lawyers for ninety days, and if necessary for a further ninety days. Later the provision was extended to periods of 180 days, and some people simply disappeared into the prisons.

During 1963, some 3,355 persons were detained. People were picked up indiscriminately, many innocents including children were arrested. If a son for whom the police were searching was not at home, they arrested the father, and vice-versa, friends or neighbours who might happen to be visiting were taken off, many youths and boys were thrown into prison, and remand followed remand.

Nelson Mandela had returned to South Africa unobtrusively, but the police caught up with him, he was tried for leaving the country illegally, and sentenced to five years on Robben Island. Walter Sisulu kept the flag flying for Umkonto we Sizwe, and carefully controlled sabotage operations were carried out; nobody was killed. But it could not last. On 11 July 1963 the police swooped upon the ANC base at Rivonia, and arrested Walter Sisulu, Govan Mbeki and others, including four whites, two of whom escaped and fled the country, leaving Lionel Bernstein and Dennis Goldberg under arrest.

The Rivonia trial opened at the end of October, with a Defence team led by Bram Fischer. Mandela was brought from Robben Island to be tried along with his colleagues on the fresh charge of sabotage. Walter Sisulu and his co-accused were held in solitary confinement for eighty-eight days while the Prosecution prepared its case. Sisulu gave evidence that he was pressurised, under threat of death, to testify against his associates. He, of course, refused. The Sabotage Act carried the death penalty; so, once again, men were on trial for their lives. The trial was sufficiently notorious and well publicised for money to come in from abroad and from Britain; this would all be earmarked for Rivonia. But there were hundreds of smaller trials of people unknown to the public. The South African Committees wrote that there were now more convictions than acquittals. Sadly, almost desperately, they said that, for lack of sufficient funds, they were for the first time having to turn away people who appealed to them for help.

Money-raising was John's first and most pressing priority, but we did begin to wonder for how long we would be able to keep pace with the ever-increasing demands, and John had to do it all himself. As well as all the well-tried methods, John embarked upon one unusual enterprise. A young Coloured artist, Ronald Harrison, painted a picture of the Crucifixion. It hung quietly as an altar piece in a church in the Coloured Area of Cape Town. But it was noticed and reported to those in authority, and there was an immediate furore in the South African Press. The picture was banned and declared 'indecent'; there were demands for its confiscation, even its destruction. It was a somewhat crude and entirely conventional representation, except that both the Virgin and the figure nailed to the cross were black. The features of the crucified young man were said to resemble those of Chief Albert Luthuli, though Luthuli was an old man, and Ronald Harrison had never seen him. The Christ figure was painted with obvious feeling and sincerity. There were two other figures, white Roman soldiers, one piercing the side of Christ with a spear bore the features of Dr Verwoerd, the Prime Minister, the other looked like Mr Vorster, the Minister of Justice. White South Africans, especially Afrikaners, were outraged. Never mind the fact that Jesus of Nazareth, far from being the white Aryan figure depicted in European art, would have been a dark-skinned, Semitic Hebrew, to the racially conscious whites, the picture appeared almost blasphemous.

As soon as John read the story he acted on impulse. He got in touch with friends in Cape Town and with the artist and arranged for the picture to be surreptitiously shipped to Britain; it could be used to raise money. It attracted a lot of Press interest, was shown on the BBC and on ITV, and exhibited in the crypt of St Paul's. It was then bought by the newspaper, the *Sunday Citizen*, and taken on tour round the country to raise money for Defence and Aid. It did very well, and we were able to send a substantial contribution to Ronald Harrison, who was living with his family in conditions of great poverty. He hoped to be able to train as a professional artist.

There was a further and sinister development in Southern Rhodesia in 1963, in the form of Bills to amend the Law and Order (Maintenance) Act by imposing mandatory death sentences in certain cases of arson and injury to persons or property, or attempts to commit those crimes. A Christian action group (independent of ours), wrote from Salisbury asking for help in financing protests against the 'Hanging Bill'. 'This means', they wrote 'that instead of a fair punishment being assessed by an experienced judge with full knowledge of the facts . . . the judge's proper function will be usurped by the Executive, which will be able to fix the sentence in advance'. We sent £200, and although the Bill was passed, we were glad the protest had been made.

It was an appeal published in the *Observer* for Defence and Aid money for Rhodesia that got John into serious trouble. This was an advertisement signed by a selection of John's eminent sponsors. In this advertisement John told the story of a restrictee, George Nyandoro, a sick man in need of a serious operation. It was a complicated story, and of course, John ought to have checked the details, but he was much pressed, and he took it all from George. The High Commissioner for Rhodesia wrote to all the signatories asking them to withdraw their signatures, as the story was one-sided and inaccurate. John was alarmed, and wrote at once to the faithful Terence Ranger, who replied answering all the points; the High Commissioner's letter was, he said, 'most misleading'.

But the damage was done; although George's story was essentially true, there were minor inaccuracies. John drafted a letter to the High

Commissioner for the signatories to sign; it apologised for inaccuracies, but stood by the essence of the story. Victor Gollancz was one of the signatories, he was way up on the moral high ground. He drafted his own much more abject apology, and persuaded several of the sponsors to sign his version. He had seen the High Commissioner, he told us, who seemed a decent and honest man, he had spoken to an eminent Rhodesian surgeon who had told him that George was a complete scoundrel, the worst possible case that John could have chosen.

Victor felt he must resign altogether from his sponsorship of Defence and Aid, and he carried Lady Violet Bonham-Carter with him. She described John, rather inaccurately, as a 'holy crook'. Victor was not going to slip quietly away; he intended to leave in a fanfare of righteousness that might be extremely damaging to John and to the Fund. I decided that the only hope was a personal plea. I put John's side of the story, and begged Victor to consider the damage to the work of Defence and Aid. For some time I got nowhere, but eventually he began to listen, and finally agreed to take no further action; neither of us could bear any idea of breaking such a true and long-established friendship. In the end John only lost two of his sponsors. But it was a serious mistake, and one that was never repeated.

Repression in Rhodesia increased in severity, and from our point of view, the worst piece of news was that Terence Ranger was first banned, and the following year deported with his wife. They had both done such admirable work, and had kept us constantly and reliably informed about the situation. Fortunately the committee they had founded could still function, and we were still able to transmit funds through it.

John never worked harder than during these years; he worked hard in the cathedral as well. St Paul's was negotiating for a new choir school. The City Corporation would buy the old Victorian school in Carter Lane, and a new one would be built on a bombed site belonging to the corporation on the south-east of the cathedral. The outgoing chapter treasurer had been in charge, but this was now to be the work of the precentor. John found a thoroughly unsatisfactory agreement, and with much help from the chapter clerk, his friend David Floyd Ewin, he spent the next three years working on new negotiations. John was interested in the planning and building of the new school, and he managed to negotiate a new financial agreement on terms much more favourable to the cathedral.

Throughout these action-packed years, John found the Christian Action Council a welcome respite from the dramas and power struggles of CND and the African work. True, he was inclined to rush into action, and then report to the council what he had undertaken in their name. He called it 'putting on a white sheet', and though I remember a number of 'white sheets', there were few objections.

The council was not a rubber stamp. Members had their own ideas and were ready to oppose John. He genuinely welcomed constructive criticism, and that was what he got. When there was a division of opinion, John would say that we must extend the right hand of fellowship to those who wanted to go in a different direction. The Reverend Harold Goodwin, an old-fashioned right-wing liberal, did observe that he wished it didn't always seem to be the left hand that was extended. Council membership fluctuated from time to time, but many stayed with us, Raymond Andrews and Michael Graham-Jones, a member of the Oriel Fellowship, from Oxford days, and John Prevett, who, in spite of the hostility of his local vicar, had been a keen supporter since his school days. Serious disagreements were few, John found the council an unfailing source of encouragement and strength, and always acknowledged that he could not have done his work without them.

36

Private and Personal

SOMEHOW John and I managed to have a life of our own, personal to us. Although I did sometimes say that what I would really like would be a period of dull domesticity, I would very soon have got bored. I believed in what John was trying to do as sincerely as he did, and the fact that I was able to make my own contribution to it enriched our marriage, and added immeasurably to the interest and excitement of my life. Of course, the pressure on me was much less, as I did not have the final responsibility; my pressures, mild as they were, came from home and family. But we both needed some respite and retreat from it all, and we were fortunate in having so much to help us on our way.

When I tell my daughters-in-law that I don't remember the boys being much trouble, they laugh at me disbelievingly, I must be idealising the past, suffering from old age nostalgia, like imagining that childhood summers were always fine and sunny. True we did have one wayward though charming son, but the really serious troubles are those that come later in adult life.

As well as the summer locums, we began, now and then, to take the boys abroad. CND friends, Ira and Edita Morris, owned an enchanting small château in France, at Rozay-en-Brie. As they were always away in August, they lent it to us. The garden was a wilderness, the house out of another century, only mildly modernised; it was like something in a fairy tale that might suddenly dissolve altogether; we loved it.

Sometimes we drove on to Italy to visit the parents of our friend Jennifer Graham-Jones. Joan and Andrew Tomlinson were an interesting and unusual couple. In the Thirties they had founded and run a successful progressive school, Beltane. When this folded up some years after the war, they emigrated to Italy where they taught English language and literature. They both, perhaps particularly Joan, had a wonderfully sympathetic understanding of young people and their

problems. They had settled at Sestri-Levante on the north Italian coast.
Monte Bello is a small mountain at the end of a little peninsula; houses
are built on the slopes that face the mainland, and at the top,
constructed on different levels, is their house, Villa Pace. On the right
side it looks down on Porto Bello, with its gaily coloured fishing boats
beached along the sands, and its circle of modest houses plastered and
painted in all the sun-colours of Italy. On the left is the wide sweep of
the Sestri-Levante bay, and behind are the mountains. Here Jennifer
and her parents organised what was originally meant to be an August
summer school, but which turned into a holiday for friends and their
families. It was excellent for our boys, plenty of young of their own
ages, sea and sun, swimming and boating, expeditions along the coast
and up into the mountains, fun in the evenings. And there were always
groups of adults sitting around involved in some fascinating and
stimulating discussion. John and I loved Villa Pace too, but we also
liked to go there out of season, and stay quietly with Andrew and Joan.
They were very good company, and when they were not teaching, we
would sit in the shaded and sweet-scented garden that Andrew had
created on the top level of the villa, and talk around our many mutual
interests.

There were good friends from CND, such as Marghanita Laski and
her publisher husband, John Howard, who invited us to their French
homes. Agnostics abound, but true atheists are rare, they take religion
seriously – and Marghanita was a true atheist. She particularly enjoyed
theological debate, for which she was well equipped. She also enjoyed
Anglican services in St Paul's, though sometimes a little shocked by
lapses of taste or deviations from orthodoxy. Perhaps Marghanita had
never really escaped from her orthodox Jewish upbringing, she just
reversed it into a religion of atheism; she was a very moral and upright
person, and she and John were the kindest of friends.

It was Jack and Jacquetta Priestley who became and remained our
specially dear friends. We spent weekends with them, at first in the Isle
of Wight, and then at Kissing Tree House, near Stratford-on-Avon.
Later we all four went on holiday together.

I see Jack and Jacquetta in a classical light – Jacquetta with a touch of
the goddess, a mixture of Athena and Aphrodite. She is a fascinating as
well as a beautiful woman; beautiful women are not always
fascinating. Jacquetta, with her 'Mona Lisa' smile, hides a secret, and
people love secrets, they feel challenged to try to discover them. You
don't get away with sloppy thinking or sloppy use of language with
Jacquetta; if you ask her a question she will pause, determined to

answer clearly and honestly; she is a very honest person. This may sound forbidding, and some can be intimidated by the air of formality with which she surrounds herself, but the reality is different. 'Ice without and fire within,' said Jack, and within is emotion, passion and vulnerability. With all her intellectual and scholarly gifts, Jacquetta is modest and self-deprecating, she judges herself rigorously. People who know Jacquetta well find it easy to love her.

Jack was a ministry of all the talents, in music, painting and writing, a wonderfully many-sided and many-gifted man, his interests were as wide and all-embracing as his reading; to anything that engaged his attention he brought his entirely individual, intuitive and brilliant perceptions – you never got to the end of Jack. He was a Pan figure, with the earthiness of a satyr, and the creative power of the god who brings magic from the pan pipes. He once told me that his favourite chapter in *The Wind in the Willows* was 'The Piper at the Gates of Dawn'. That was my favourite too. I have met people who didn't know Jack, who thought him difficult, aggressive, rude; quite the opposite, he was easy-going, affectionate, sympathetic, generous and kind. There was always laughter and fun with Jack, and he too was reliably honest – if he said he was pleased to see you, sorry to see you go, if he paid you any kind of compliment, you knew that he meant exactly what he said.

Jack and Jacquetta were a perfectly balanced and complementary couple. If you are happily married, one of life's best extra gifts is friendship with another happily married pair, for each of whom you feel an equal affection, and who are equally interesting and under-standing. John and I have been wonderfully fortunate in our friends.

Nineteen sixty-three put a temporary stop to my interesting and exciting life. When I paid my annual visit to Dr Bedford, he shook his head, my heart was becoming enlarged. True I was getting breathless. I no longer climbed up to the top of the house, and hills were a problem.

'There's a new operation which seems to be getting results,' said Dr Bedford. 'I'm not going to advise you to have it, operations aren't a tonic, there's always a risk. All I can do is put the pros and cons either way, and then you'll have to make up your own mind.' I liked and trusted Dr Bedford, I knew he would tell me the truth. 'There's no hurry,' he said kindly. 'Suppose you go away and think about it.' So I went away and thought. It was obvious that the one person to whom I would automatically have turned, was the one person who could not advise me. If things went wrong, John would inevitably, however unjustifiably, suffer an unbearable sense of guilt. In fact, there was really no one I could ask, the decision had to be mine alone.

I stopped thinking, and got on with our busy life. I have found that when faced by a difficult decision the best thing is not to go on chewing over and worrying at it, but to absorb yourself in something else. Then slowly, unconsciously, what you have to do will emerge. After some months, I knew that I must choose the hope of a fuller life, rather than the probability of a long, slow, or perhaps not so slow, decline.

The operation was arranged for the beginning of May. I was worried about John, who was not good at looking after himself. The boys were away at school or university, and after the dailies had left, and the office workers had gone home, he would be on his own. I entrusted him to the partial care of Ninka, an old friend from Oxford. Her first husband was one of John's Oriel colleagues. Ninka was now living in Brighton with her second husband, but she had a part-time job with Defence and Aid helping to fund-raise, so she was accustomed to spend two or three nights a week at Amen Court. Ninka was a good friend, lively, amusing and warm-hearted, supported good causes, was kind to old people and helped disabled friends, as well as conducting a series of amorous adventures.

I went into the Middlesex Hospital for the operation. It was a long and tedious day before I was finally taken down to the operating theatre; it was meant to be much earlier. Poor John didn't know what was happening, and had to wait for news until after nine p.m. My father and stepmother went round to share his anxious vigil. I was very touched by my father who had given up drinking and smoking as a gesture of solidarity with me. However much we fought, I always knew that he loved me as I did him. Ninka was a family friend; all the same he and Madeline were a little surprised to find her settled cosily at home with John, and even more surprised to find that she was staying the night.

I shall not forget my first moment of consciousness, I was alive – alive – alive. Life seems unbelievably wonderful and precious if you feel in any danger of losing it. Friends, those mainstays of our life, rallied round. I did know that many people were praying for me, and thinking of me – and I prayed too. Throughout I felt borne up on a great wave of confidence with only the smallest niggle of doubt and fear.

After a few days when I felt a bit stronger, I was able to sit up and look in a mirror; I got a nasty shock. I had pictured myself sitting up in a flower-filled room, wearing some deliciously seductive négligé, all ready to receive admirers. In preparation, I had had a fresh permanent wave, and a special hair set. But before the surgeons were ready to carve me up, it had, apparently, been necessary to reduce my body temperature to its lowest point; I had been laid in a bath of ice-cold water, and nobody had thought to put on a bath cap. The gaunt face that greeted me in the mirror was surrounded by a most unattractive frizz of hair. I looked a perfect fright, and began to cry.

After that little set-back, I started to enjoy myself. John arrived with an extravagantly beautiful nightdress from Fortnum & Mason, one that I had toyed with, and rejected as being far too expensive. Flowers poured in, from all the CND groups, the Christian Action and Defence and Aid supporters, and from our friends. My room overflowed, I felt like the most popular girl in the school.

Dr Bedford arranged for me to go to Athlone House, a convalescent home next door to Kenwood, where John and I sometimes walked on the rare occasions when I was able to tear him away from the tangle of papers on his desk. Now that I could walk a little, I was able to enjoy the extensive grounds and garden of Athlone House.

Those early weeks were full of wonder, a kind of rebirth. As I had had virtually no post-operative pain, I had needed no powerful drugs that might have produced hallucinations or an artificial sense of well-being. Life itself was enough, colours were more vivid, scents more intoxicating, bird-song more enchanting, people were infinitely kind and lovable; my body was very feeble, but I myself had never felt more wonderfully alive.

Nowadays this operation is routine, absurd to make such a to-do about it. But then I was told that it would be at least a year before I would be able to do very much, and so it was. Amen Court was altogether too active; I stayed away with friends and relatives, and then tried to make do at home with cook-housekeepers. The first one was sex-obsessed and dotty. She began to drop dark hints about dreadful goings-on in the basement, sometimes to the considerable embarrassment of visitors. One morning, Freda appeared in floods of tears saying that she must leave at once, the housekeeper had accused her of having an affair with John. Needless to say, it was the housekeeper who left abruptly. Then we had a sweet and capable girl from South Africa.

Aunt Tilly wrote from Kenya saying why not come for a month to the farm. She sent me a first-class air ticket, so, in the middle of February, I flew away. This time John would not be alone, Andrew was now living at home reading for the Bar, and our nice Felicity from

South Africa would run the house and look after them. All this period was much, much worse for John. Like many people who give out a great deal to others, he was apt to keep his own feelings inside himself. If things were bad, he said, to talk made them worse. I am the opposite, I want to get things out of myself, and then I feel better. We never quite resolved this difference between us, but I think that those who keep their feelings inside tend to suffer more.

Kenya restored me to strength, and it was an interesting time to be there, a few months after independence. There were serious problems of unemployment and an escalating birth rate, and my Uncle Hugh found the results of Africanisation frustrating. But there was a general feeling of hope and optimism.

Joseph Murumbi, an old friend whom we had known in his student days, was now the Foreign Minister. He rang and said he would like to take me to meet Jomo Kenyatta. We all three had lunch in the Parliament buildings. I was impressed by the old man, a real father-figure. He had been detained for ten years by the British, and, in an amused way, he introduced me to some of his fellow detainees; they all seemed to think it a big joke. For the first two years, Jomo said, he had been allowed no books, and for another only religious books. I expressed suitable commiseration. 'No, no,' he said. 'It was a good opportunity to study the scriptures of the great world religions.' 'Which impressed you most?' I asked. 'The New Testament and the *Bhagavad Gita*,' he replied. 'They've made a great difference to my life.'

A number of MPs came up and were introduced to me; they looked absurdly young, one or two said they had been on Aldermaston marches. They all knew about John, so I gained some reflected glory. In the middle of lunch another young African appeared and spoke to Jomo, who was evidently pleased. 'That's the chairman of KADU, the Opposition party,' he said. 'He's a very nice fellow'. How British that sounded, but then, before the war, Jomo had studied at the London School of Economics.

Back on the farm, life was peaceful and sybaritic. The climate was perfect, it was springtime, everything was at its freshest and best. I wrote to John daily; I was in a beautiful place surrounded by kindness, but I was dreadfully homesick, I longed for John and our life together, I longed for our children and our friends; I had been too much away.

37

Martin Luther King in St Paul's

Appeals – appeals – appeals! They came flooding in from South Africa, and from Rhodesia. No wonder John looked tired when he met me at the airport – no wife to nag and bully him to eat properly, and get to bed in reasonable time. But in spite of these, usually futile, efforts of mine, John always said that he couldn't bear the house when I was away. I felt guilty at leaving him, it is always worse for the one who is left behind, and I felt the same when he was away.

A council member, Betty McCulloch, had taken over the editorship of the *Journal* while I was out of action, but now I was happy to take it back, it would be a good opportunity to catch up. The news from Southern Africa was uniformly bad. The main Defence and Aid Committee in Johannesburg reported in June 1964 that in the previous six months, they had spent *twice* the amount that they had spent in the *two preceding years taken together*. The government was determined to try to destroy completely all resistance to apartheid. The ninety-days clause was a gift to the security forces, and reports of torture throughout the prisons began to reach us. Almost every major trial in the last six months had brought to light the use of physical and mental torture to induce confessions.

Africans were picked up, sometimes indiscriminately, kept in solitary confinement, and tortured until they broke down and were forced, often on pain of death, to give evidence in Court for the police. Some of them were illiterate, and had to learn their evidence by heart. One journalist reported that 'it was like hearing parrots come to Court'.

In August 1964 Looksmart Solmandle Ngudle was found hanged in his cell. The police said it was suicide, but at the inquest funded by Defence and Aid, witnesses gave evidence of the infliction of frightful tortures. This was only the first of a succession of such cases; the most notorious being that of Steve Biko.

From Rhodesia too came stories of increased repression. Two men had been saved from the gallows by the intervention of Defence and Aid. But we failed to save the life of Richard Mapolisa. He had accompanied a friend who had thrown a home-made bomb through a house window in the European quarter; it caused minimal damage. Only Richard was caught and charged. He faced the mandatory death sentence, since the law did not distinguish between principal and accessory. After Richard was condemned to death, Defence and Aid financed an appeal to the Privy Council in London. The appeal was dismissed.

John knew that it would soon be impossible for his relatively small organisation to meet the demands made upon it, but help was at hand. In 1963 a new visitor arrived at 2 Amen Court. This was E.S. Reddy, a UN civil servant, and head of their newly formed Centre against Apartheid. Reddy's skilful, patient lobbying, his practical initiatives, and his concern for individuals were to bring help and comfort to thousands both inside and outside South Africa. Reddy understood the UN, his diplomatic skills enabled him to steer a course between the conflicting interests of groups and people all clamouring for money and attention. He dedicated himself to the elimination of apartheid, and the value of his work cannot be over-estimated.

In December 1963 Reddy engineered a resolution of the General Assembly appealing to governments to contribute to organisations assisting the victims of apartheid. And in the summer of 1964, the special UN sub-committee on apartheid visited London; John appeared before it, and described the work of Defence and Aid. The committee was able to see the accounts, and investigate the way in which money was handled.

John realised that it would be easier for governments and international agencies to contribute to an organisation that was itself international. Groups collecting money for the British Defence and Aid Fund already existed in Sweden, Norway, Ireland, Holland, Switzerland and Australia. So, early in 1964 representatives from some of these groups got together in London, and formed themselves into the International Defence and Aid Fund for Southern Africa (IDAFSA). John was elected president, and was supported by an elected presidential committee, consisting of the Reverend Gunnar Helander from Sweden, Kadar Asmal, originally from South Africa, then lecturer in international law at Trinity College, Dublin, for Ireland, and Gilbert Rist, an academic from Switzerland. BDAF, the parent body, now became one of the affiliated committees, but the administration of the Fund remained with it and with Christian

Action. This had considerable advantages in keeping down the cost of administration.

In October 1964, IDAFSA was designated as one of the organisations to receive money from governments for its work against apartheid. Our first contribution, requested by Reddy, was of £1,875 from the Indian government; this was followed in 1965 by Iraq £997, the Philippines £445, Sweden £35,805, the USSR £3,572, and £10,000 from the government of the Netherlands. Soon both Norway and Denmark were contributing regularly.

Towards the end of 1965, a resolution, moved by Nigeria and seconded by Sweden, was passed in the UN General Assembly, authorising the setting-up of a UN Trust Fund for aid to the victims of apartheid. The object was to enable governments who did not wish or were not able to contribute to non-governmental organisations to make their contribution. At the request of the African States, the Swedish ambassador to the UN became chairman, and over the years the UN Trust Fund has been second only to Sweden in its support for IDAFSA.

It was an enormous relief to have the main burden of fund-raising eased, though BDAF still had to continue its money-raising efforts, as did the other affiliated committees. It was now possible for John to have some much-needed administrative help, and this came from among the South African exiles in London. Rica and Jack Hodgson, members of the banned South African Communist party, had arrived in London in 1963 after a hair-raising escape. Rica had fund-raised successfully for Defence and Aid, and now came to ask if John would employ her in spite of her Communism. John was not going to begin discrimination in the office, and Rica never let her beliefs affect any of the valuable work that she did for Defence and Aid.

Soon Defence and Aid left our basement and Amen Court altogether, and established itself in nearby offices, but with the enormous expansion of its work, John needed more assistance. He learned to trust Rica's judgement, so he asked her advice. Rica knew that the senior position in IDAFSA must not go to a Communist. She suggested another South African, Phyllis Altman, who arrived in London in 1964. Phyllis and Rica made an excellent team, Rica, warm, extrovert and outgoing, Phyllis more complex, introverted and talented. As well as their efficiency, loyalty and dedication, they both had a nose for the spies and informers who were constantly trying to infiltrate the Fund. They were a good corrective to John's tendency to trust everybody.

Christian Action was also expanding. With a new archbishop, Michael Ramsey, it had become more respectable. Perhaps that was only because John had been around for some time, and the Church had got used to him. So now we got back our official representatives, and were rejoined by our old friend, Father Tom Corbishley. The Archbishop of Canterbury's representative was a newcomer, Uvedale Lambert. He told us later that he had been nervous of accepting this assignment, afraid that he was being asked to join some dangerous radicals and left-wing extremists. Instead he found a group of reasonable and moderate Christians. It was Uvedale who suggested that Christian Action might try to do something about the serious increase in homelessness in our major cities. The council immediately welcomed this, and launched a national appeal, 'Homeless in Britain'.

Meanwhile, as John had a contract for a book, a semi-autobiographical account of his ministry and his work, he could not devote himself full-time to any of his projects. The council decided that more help was needed for Christian Action as well as for Defence and Aid. So the post of 'executive director' was advertised, and Ian Henderson was selected.

'Homeless in Britain' did well, we published articles, one whole issue of the *Journal* was devoted to the subject, John preached about it in St Paul's. At that period it was estimated that Britain lacked around one million houses, the worst areas being Greater London, Birmingham and Clydeside. In London alone the LCC had between 5,000–7,500 homeless on its books. At first we supported individual efforts. Bruce Kenrick set up the Notting Hill Housing Trust, and two weeks after it was formed, it bought its first large house with a grant of £1,000 from Christian Action. We helped the Simon Community to get off the ground, and supported Abbeyfields. By April 1965 we had launched the first Christian Action Housing Association. This project developed well, and at one time there were some nineteen Christian Action Housing Associations all over the country. Only a drop in the ocean of misery and squalor, but one that affected a great many human beings and their families. Later, led by Ian Henderson, we turned our attention to the real misfits who slept rough and wandered the London streets.

In South Africa, the Rivonia trial drew to its end. Mandela's long address to the Court has become a classic statement for all who struggle for freedom and human rights. His concluding words are well known, but will bear repeating: 'During my lifetime I have dedicated myself to this struggle of the African people. I have fought against white domination, and I have fought against black domination. I have cherished the ideal of a democratic and free society in which all persons live together in harmony, and with equal opportunities. It is an ideal which I hope to live for and to achieve. But if needs be, it is an ideal for which I am prepared to die.'

On 11 June 1964 Judge de Wet pronounced the verdict of guilty for all except Rusty Bernstein who was acquitted. The following day sentence was given – life imprisonment. The men were taken to the maximum security prison of Robben Island, placed in the lowest prison category, and set to hard labour, breaking stones in all weathers. BDAF paid all the Defence's costs, £19,500, in this momentous trial.

A happier event was the award of the Nobel Peace Prize to Martin Luther King. He wrote to John asking whether Christian Action would lay on another meeting for him on his way to Oslo, and John arranged as well for Martin to preach in St Paul's on the Sunday. People who attended that service still speak of it with awe. 'He gives the impression,' I wrote, 'of a deeply solitary person, a man who has wrestled with God . . . he came to London from a sick-bed, and was clearly exhausted. But the feeling of his inner strength remains with one; he moves through the crowds, through both execration and acclamation, his eyes fixed on a distant goal . . .'

Martin Luther King's preaching was, if anything, more powerful even than his public speaking. The sermon was a plea for wholeness of living, an insistence upon the interrelatedness of peoples, nations and problems, a thoroughly Christian Action assertion that 'you cannot separate economic, social, political and racial problems, you cannot separate religion and politics'. He reiterated his belief in non-violence, calling himself a 'pragmatic pacifist', and he spoke of the three myths surrounding the subject of racial integration. The first was the old chestnut of the natural 'inferiority' of coloured people. The result of slavery followed by segregation is that coloured people are poor, are ill-educated, are sometimes physically unfit, sometimes fall into crime, and often believe they are inferior, but these results of segregation and oppression are then used as reasons for its continuance. He spoke of the myth of time, which is simply an excuse for doing nothing, in the irresponsible belief that time will somehow solve all problems. But time, he said, is neutral; it can be used constructively or destructively, and it is often used more effectively by the bad people than by the good people. And he spoke of the myth that nothing can be solved by legislation: all that is necessary is to change the heart. It is true, he said, that hearts need to change but something can be achieved while they are changing. 'Morality cannot be legislated, but behaviour can be regulated. The law cannot make a man love me, but it can stop him lynching me, and that is quite important to me.'

38

After Twenty-Five Years

J OHN never found it easy to settle down to writing, one reason why articles and sermons got left to the last minute. He tried Amen Court, but I soon realised that we would have to go away. Aunt Tilly had a house at Botesdale, on the Norfolk–Suffolk border. She had now returned to Kenya, so she offered to lend us Crown Hill House, and here we spent October, 1964. We worked in the mornings, and walked in the afternoons. Beyond the village was a large area of field and marshland, home of wild birds and wild flowers, and producing an unfailing supply of fresh mushrooms, which we cooked in every conceivable manner.

On 21 October we would have been married for twenty-five years. We decided to give a small buffet supper in celebration. It was a weekday, so our sons were working, John's family were too far away, but friends and relatives could come from Stutton, including our bridesmaid Gay and her husband, Peter Strutt. Yvonne Cooper had died in 1956 after a severe stroke, and Harold had returned to his native Suffolk. He was near enough to come and spend the night with us.

Some of the lovely antique furniture that my grandparents had collected for Stutton Hall now graced Crown Hill House. I filled the rooms with rose pink spindle-berries, a touch of poignancy about those, and they gained added beauty from the turquoise of Tilly's velvet curtains; furniture glowed from centuries of polishing, and old copper gleamed in the lamplight. I thought the setting was perfect. Our supper was prepared by a local lady, and Harold proposed a toast to John and me, Harold knew and recognised happy marriage. It was such a simple, and such a happy occasion.

Though far away in our rural retreat, John and I could not shut ourselves off from the cruel realities of Southern Africa. The one-time Rhodesian Prime Minister, Garfield Todd, wrote in the *Journal*: 'The account against us in human suffering and injustice is already greater than we can meet . . . the future of four million Africans cannot be left in the hands of 200,000 whites . . . Privilege has warped our judgement to the extent that our actions have led to the suppression of freedom, the bypassing of the courts of justice, and the maintenance of a system which gives privilege to a small racial group and limits opportunity for the mass of the people.'

The news from South Africa was worse, the account in human suffering and injustice far, far higher. There were the first three executions under the Sabotage Act. Three more men were then charged with the same murder, they too went to the gallows – six lives for one.

With so many organisations banned and forced underground, the Liberal party chaired by Alan Paton was now the only legitimate multi-racial opposition. The party had once been cautious, now it was open to all races, and stood for universal suffrage and a unitary state. Nearly all who worked for Defence and Aid were Liberals. They were under increasing pressure, as one member after another was banned. A group of young Liberals, increasingly frustrated by the ineffectiveness of political action, and anxious to identify themselves with the risks and sufferings of their fellow Africans, secretly formed the African Resistance Movement (ARM) and planned their own acts of sabotage. They were betrayed by a fellow-conspirator, and many were given long prison sentences.

The number of trials was alarming. Port Elizabeth alone reported 180 cases pending. Defence and Aid still managed to obtain acquittals, but often only after prolonged efforts and appeals, and those who were finally released would have spent many months in prison. In the Cape Town 'Goodwood' case, it took a twenty-one-month legal fight by Defence and Aid to secure the release of thirty-nine of the forty-four accused.

Reports of torture in the prisons poured out, and Defence and Aid made repeated applications to the courts for injunctions to stop the tortures and the assaults. Ivan Schermbrucker managed to smuggle a note out to his wife, stating that he had been made to stand on one spot for twenty-eight hours, and had been brought to the point of suicide. His application to the court failed. The judge ruled that the courts could no longer protect those citizens held in terms of the ninety-day law. Meanwhile, government ministers continued to repeat that torture was forbidden and was therefore never practised.

Back in Amen Court, we had a visit from Bram Fischer. He was in London to complete a case before the Privy Council; he was also out on bail, having been arrested and charged under the Suppression of

Communism Act. He returned to South Africa, repaid his bail money
and disappeared underground, saying he could no longer serve justice.
Bram could have had a life of privilege, wealth and honour; he chose to
throw in his lot with the poor and the dispossessed.

We had visits from Oliver Tambo. The ANC headquarters were
now in Lusaka, but Oliver had to spend a great deal of time touring the
capitals of the world, lobbying governments and appearing at the
United Nations. All the time, Oliver seemed to grow in stature and in
political wisdom; it was hard to believe that he came from illiterate
parents in a deprived rural area of South Africa. Over the years, Oliver
managed to hold the ANC together, and to build it up into a body that
won world respect – except regrettably from the British government.

In June 1965, John was invited by Mr Reddy to New York to address
the UN Special Committee on Apartheid, on the subject of Defence
and Aid. In the course of his speech he said: 'Because of the tyrannical
legislation of the present South African government, no political
organisation which seeks to change South Africa's racial policies can
function properly in the open, the black political organisations are
banned. Those who wish to continue the struggle have to go
underground.' 'Do you really want to say that, John?' Reddy had
asked. But John did want to say it.

As Reddy had feared, the speech caused a furore inside South Africa.
Of course, it was misreported and misrepresented; what could
'underground resistance' mean other than violent revolution? –
although it is clear from the context what John had meant. Our
constant assertions that we were promoting neither violence nor
Communism were never reported. The South African government
stepped up its Communist-violence smear campaign, and the Defence
and Aid Committees feared that the speech sounded their death knell.

In August, we were staying in France, when John got a bitter and
angry letter from Alan Paton, accusing him of failing to support the
Liberal party, and of giving everything to organisations far to the left.
The accusations were false, especially as Defence and Aid never gave
money directly to political organisations, though John did help
individual representatives. But Alan was at the mercy of hostile
propaganda, and it was some time since we had seen him, as the South
African government had removed his passport. John and I were much
distressed, we both loved Alan, but we were nervous of writing to him
on this subject. In fact most of our communications with the Defence
and Aid Committees were already conducted through accommodation addresses. Someone thoroughly familiar with our work would

have to go to South Africa, but who? It could certainly not be John, he would be turned back at the airport, nor could it be anyone employed in the office, most of them were prohibited immigrants anyway.

It soon became clear, at least to me, that I was the one who must volunteer. I had cousins who had emigrated, and were living in Johannesburg, I could go to them for a 'holiday' visit. Collins was a sufficiently common name for me to be able to slip in on my own passport. Rather reluctantly, John agreed. We told Phyllis and Rica from whom I needed addresses and advice. I went to see Joost de Blank, who had had to retire from being Archbishop of Cape Town following a stroke, and who was now a canon of Westminster Abbey. Joost was a great supporter of Defence and Aid. He too gave me useful addresses, and said I could use his name. Under pledge of strict secrecy, I told my father, who didn't at all approve of his daughter's latest escapade. As Andrew was living at home, he too had to know, but that was all.

I departed, a little nervously it must be confessed, in early October, 1965.

39

Brief Encounter and a Long Farewell

THE entire Dorling family met me at the Johannesburg airport. I am afraid they thought I had come for love of them, and it was true that I was particularly fond of these cousins, father, mother and four boys. I had told none of my contacts that I was coming, and I knew that telephones were tapped and must on no account be used, so I just had to appear on their doorsteps.

My first call was on the attorney Ruth Hayman who handled a great deal of our Defence and Aid work, and who was also a member of the Liberal party, and a friend of Alan Paton. After the first shock she was helpful and sympathetic. Although South Africa is such a large country, at least as far as the anti-apartheid whites were concerned, it was a village, everyone knew everyone. So I was very soon in touch with the people I needed to see.

I suppose I must have been as well briefed as anyone who visits South Africa for the first time; all the same it was a shock, the reality was somehow so much worse. I was particularly anxious not to draw attention to myself, nor to let people know to whom I was married. The result was that I became a split personality. In the daytime I met the Defence and Aid Committees, members of the Black Sash, lawyers who worked for us, I went into the townships and met the wives of political prisoners – I remember especially the strong, brave personality of Albertina Sisulu. In the evenings and at weekends, I mixed with the white business community, and with good decent white people who were not politically involved. Many times I had to bite my tongue, especially as everyone wanted to talk about 'the native problem'. I was treated with generous hospitality and kindness, but on the rare occasions when I dared to raise my voice in mild protest, I was told that, of course, I couldn't be expected to understand the 'natives'.

A few days after my arrival, a case was reported in the newspapers of three white youths who got drunk one evening, and thought they would amuse themselves by 'hunting kaffirs'. On the outskirts of the township they came across an African walking out with the girl he intended to marry. They beat the man up so badly that he had to be hospitalised, then each in turn raped the girl. There was no question about their guilt. They were brought before a magistrate who gave them a lecture on the evils of drink, advised them to join a sports club, and sentenced them to six lashes each. No one I was with or met commented on this case, or seemed to think there was anything strange about it. If a black man rapes a white woman, an extremely rare occurrence, the penalty is death.

I had a useful ten days in Johannesburg, and then I got a message from Ruth Hayman, that a member of the Liberal party had to drive to Durban, and would take me to see Alan Paton. I had no idea what kind of a welcome I would get from Alan. I also knew that his wife, Dorrie, whom I had never met, was dying slowly from emphysema. It was still unseasonably cold when we arrived in Kloof, and Alan met us huddled up in his overcoat, their home was not equipped for such weather. Alan was too surprised to do anything other than welcome us in. Quite soon Dorrie took me aside and said, 'I'm so glad you've come, Alan has been so upset over all this'. So then I thought things would be all right. I took to Dorrie at once, such a strong, straightforward and humorous person.

When my driver friend had to leave, Alan said, 'You can stay here, Diana, we'll talk tomorrow'. I had to tussle with Alan, he could be an obstinate old cuss, once he got something fixed in his mind he didn't easily let go. I think we did arrive at an understanding, I managed to convince him that we were not arming the ANC, nor supporting the South African Communist party. But what mattered to me most was that the personal relationship, the true friendship was restored. Dorrie was a consistent help and support.

Alan was under enormous pressure at that time. Dorrie was clearly very ill, and they both knew that her sickness was terminal. Alan was watched, threatened and hounded by the security forces; they had recently smashed up his car for him. He had been deeply upset by the activities of the ARM, he was passionately opposed to violence, and here were young men of his own party, without the knowledge of their chairman, taking to sabotage. Apart from anything else, he felt, with reason, that this would signal the end of the Liberal party.

Yet with all the turmoil around, all the distress, and the suffering that Alan felt with real personal pain, the atmosphere in this house was one of a deep and loving peace. Alan must have been a rich man, but he and Dorrie lived simply, with one African servant who had been with them for years, and extra help for the garden and sometimes in the house. Before each meal, we held hands while Alan said grace, a real grace, not just a gabbled formality.

I had a problem. For obvious reasons, I could not write openly to John as he had written to me in 1954. We had agreed a code between us, in case of emergencies, and we wrote to accommodation addresses. But there was the problem of all the addresses and the useful information that I was collecting: I could not possibly carry it all in my head. Alan suggested that I should send it through the post, no one really knew how much this was censored, and in any case they couldn't possibly open everything. I took his advice, and he drove me to the nearest letter box. Those letters never arrived, and I suspect that the police were watching, and simply extracted them from the box. It was from then on, I believe, that the police began to follow my movements.

Meanwhile, Alan drove me around the beautiful countryside. He gave lifts to Africans, especially to heavily laden women, something few white people ever dared to do. He introduced me to his friends, fellow members of the Liberal party, and the Defence and Aid Committees, Africans and Indians as well as whites, he took me to see Dr Naiker who had entertained John, eleven years ago. I remember this period as a little oasis of calm and happiness in my somewhat traumatic travels.

Next on my itinerary was Port Elizabeth in the Eastern Cape, but as I knew no one there with whom I could stay, Alan arranged a hotel for me. Port Elizabeth frightened and shattered me. I got a taxi from the airport, and was surprised to find that the African driver spoke to me quite openly about the horrors of the situation; Africans seem to know instinctively who is or is not a friend, or had the bush telegraph been at work? But once in the hotel, I got one or two nasty and threatening telephone calls.

The next day I went to see Denis Scarr, chairman of the local Defence and Aid Committee, and then I was on the network. I was taken under the wing of Peggy Levey, who did a great deal of welfare work in the townships. She would have become my dear friend, had not distance and politics separated us for ever. Peggy took me to the Defence and Aid welfare office, and an African worker volunteered to take me into the African township. Many whites had kept assuring me that Africans had no sense of gratitude, never thanked you for anything, didn't have a word for thanks in their language. I was introduced first as Mrs Collins, a visitor from London; they were all polite and not unfriendly, Africans have good manners. Then 'This is the wife of Canon Collins, a friend of Bishop Reeves and Father Huddleston', and I was immediately embraced, overwhelmed with gratitude.

I had come from the spacious homes of the whites, with their gardens and their swimming pools, now I was taken to the homes of the poor, nothing more than corrugated iron shacks, with no facilities of any kind. I had never seen such poverty and deprivation, conditions in which we would not keep our farm animals, and that in what must be one of the richest countries in the world. But I was welcomed warmly into these dwellings, which were miracles of cleanliness, and every effort had been made to create the atmosphere of a home, the walls were decorated, usually plastered, with pictures cut out of old newspapers and magazines.

As we walked through the township my guide pointed to one rather better-dressed African man. 'That's a police informer,' she said. 'Whenever you see a man as well-dressed as that in the townships, in the daytime, you know that he's an informer. You get so you can't trust your own reflection in the mirror.'

I saw the standard poverty, but the plight of the families of political prisoners and detainees was incomparably worse. 'We would need £230,000 a year to keep all these families on the poverty datum line, £24 a month,' said Denis Scarr. 'All we can manage is £2 5s. a month.' How could these people possibly exist, I wondered. The Fund supplied the poorest families with between ten and fifteen pounds of fortified food a month, and helped some families with rent. The previous winter 300 children had been given one vest and one pair of pants and 100 women got a dress or a cardigan; a local timber firm had donated some firewood.

'We should need at least another £7,500 in order to keep the children at school,' said Denis. He added that with all the bannings and threats it was becoming more and more difficult to get people to work for Defence and Aid.

This was all on the welfare side, even more money was needed for legal defence. The Eastern Cape was being subjected to a terrible onslaught. This was the birthplace of the ANC, and was still a centre of fierce resistance. Port Elizabeth had been an area of exceptionally good mission schools and colleges; there were African families there with three generations of higher education behind them, professional men, university lecturers and intellectuals. Once upon a time qualified Africans voted on the common electoral roll. All this was anathema to

Nationalist ideology. It had to be rooted out by any and every means, and the means were savage and pitiless.

I talked with the lawyers who handled our cases, I spent time in the D and A welfare office, I talked to ex-prisoners and detainees. One cultivated and sensitive young African, a university graduate, told me that although he had been hit and assaulted in prison, the worst thing for him were the regular searches, when, whatever the weather, the prisoners had to stand in a row naked. 'They did horrible things to us,' he said, 'humiliating things that I could not tell to any woman, not even to my mother.'

I could fill a whole book with heart-rending accounts of the sufferings of these people, things that I saw or stories that I heard. I could analyse the injustice, the absurdity and the cruelty of the façade of legality used by the State, but these belong in a history of Defence and Aid. That will be a story of the depths of human brutality and corruption, and also of the heights of human nobility, courage and selflessness.

I had a terrible nightmare while I was in Port Elizabeth. I dreamed that I was in a lunatic asylum, everyone about me was crazy, and the few who were on the borderline were slipping into this hideous morass of lunacy, soon I was the only one left, and I could feel myself being sucked down and down; it was unutterably horrible.

I flew on to Cape Town, and here I stayed with friends of the Patons, Bill and Margaret Hoffenburg. Bill was a Liberal party member, chairman both of the Cape Town and of the National Defence and Aid Committee. He was also one of the most distinguished doctors in the country. Every day and night we looked across at Robben Island where so many of the cream of African leadership were breaking stones by day, and sleeping exhausted on stone floors by night.

I spent a day in an advice office run by the Black Sash, who somehow managed to avoid being banned, in spite of their uncompromising opposition to apartheid. Here I saw numbers of wretched Africans enmeshed in the complex bureaucracy of the Pass Laws; they were struggling like flies in a spider's web, terrified of losing their jobs, of being 'endorsed out' to the barren so-called homelands.

I went to see Albie Sachs, just out of prison, and immediately banned, who told me something of his experiences. I talked with an African member of the Liberal party. 'If we really started something here,' he said, 'do you think the outside world would come and help us?' What could I say? I knew very well that the outside world, fearful for its investments, would continue to pass by on the other side.

Using Joost de Blank's name, I saw the Archbishop of Cape Town. He was polite but distinctly cool, he clearly thought I was a troublemaker. Then I went to tea with an African Methodist minister and his wife. I asked if they had a family. Yes, there were two daughters, but they lived with their grandmother in one of the rural areas. I asked why they did not have them living with them, and the minister pointed sadly out of the window; across the road was one of the hostels for male migrant workers. The Christian whites, particularly the Afrikaners, make a great to-do about the value and sanctity of family life; then make it impossible for the majority of Africans to lead anything like a normal married existence.

Joost had given me the name of a friend, a great supporter of the Church and of many good causes. She invited me to lunch, she was generous and hospitable, a really good woman. 'I was very fond of Joost,' she said, 'but when he first came here he didn't understand the situation at all. His enthronement sermon was most unwise.'

'What did he preach about?' I asked.

'Oh,' she said, 'he preached about brotherly love. That sort of thing doesn't go down at all well here.' She had no idea that she had said anything extraordinary.

Back at the Hoffenburgs we were all woken early one morning by a ferocious hammering on the front door. The Security Police had arrived to remove Bill's passport. I remember the bewilderment of their two little boys, the elder, seven-year-old Derek, saying 'But are they right or are they wrong?' Later, when the police had gone, we sat down to breakfast, all rather grim and silent. I could see Derek struggling not to cry. 'Those are bloody shit men,' he said suddenly and loudly. There was a slightly shocked silence, I was after all, the wife of a canon of St Paul's. 'You're quite right Derek,' I said quickly, 'Those *are* bloody shit men.' Everyone smiled, and the tension was released.

One of my perhaps surprising contacts in Johannesburg was with Robert Birley, who was on a two-year visiting lectureship at Witwatersrand University. He was an unusual example of a gamekeeper turned poacher. 'I don't suppose an ex-headmaster of Eton has ever broken the law as often as I have,' he said with an endearingly boyish delight. He and his wife, Eleanor, were committed to the opposition against apartheid, and did a great deal to help those being persecuted. Robert's joy was arranging scholarships for Africans, and equipping libraries and schools in the townships; Robert had an unwavering and hopeful belief in human possibilities, mark of a true educator and a true liberal.

Mary Benson had deliberately returned to live in Johannesburg, partly, she said, to demonstrate that there were Christians as committed to the struggle as Communists and humanists. It was Mary who organised a meeting with Helen Joseph, just banned yet again. I was to wait at a certain street corner, and watch for a car with a certain number plate. This I duly did, and was picked up by Helen; for over an hour we drove round and round Johannesburg talking non-stop. Helen is an icon of courage, but every time the Special Branch visited her, she told me, she had to hold her hand over her throat because when she was frightened a tiny throbbing pulse would show itself. 'I'm not going to let them see I'm afraid,' she said. 'I can never get used to them,' another woman had said. 'Every time they come to search and raid us I feel sick and weak at the knees.' To end our fascinating meeting Helen took me to see Helen Suzman, a risk, because if caught, she would have been breaking her banning orders, and that would most likely have meant a spell in prison. 'You two obviously know each other well,' said Helen Suzman, and it did indeed feel like that, although this was the first, and sadly, the only time that we have met.

I decided to try and visit the Bishop of Johannesburg; I wanted to see the house where John had stayed with the Reeveses. The bishop received me kindly, he was friendly, a well-meaning but an uncertain and a worried man. 'They are threatening to forbid mixed worship altogether,' he said. 'If that really happens, then will be the time to protest.' It seemed to me that the time to protest had been long, long ago. What a contrast was my visit to the Christian Institute, where I spent an invigorating hour with that splendid renegade Dutch Reformed Church pastor, Beyers Naude. Beyers' Christian faith has led him, not to a repudiation of his Church, but to a total rejection of its attitudes to and its endorsement of apartheid. He is a staunch and fearless campaigner against apartheid and all its evils, and he is respected and loved by men and women of all races. Even his opponents have to accord him a grudging admiration.

Meanwhile, the resourceful Mary Benson was trying to arrange for me a meeting with Bram Fischer, who had eluded capture by the police for several months.

It was not long before I became aware that I was being openly followed. Everywhere I went, there were the same two men. If I was in a restaurant, they were seated at the next table; in any public place, there they were; their car was parked for long periods outside the Dorlings' house. They were like two cats playing with, and subtly softening up, a rather helpless mouse.

After about ten days of this form of intimidation, the cats pounced, arriving as was their custom around five-thirty a.m. I decided that I, a respectable married woman, was not going to appear in my nightdress and dressing-gown before these two young whipper-snappers. I collected my papers together, all my precious notes and addresses, they might have incriminated too many people. I thrust them into the hands of the African servant saying, 'Please burn all these.' He understood the situation only too well. I very much hoped the police were not going to interrogate me, I didn't relish that prospect one little bit. I had a bath, got dressed, and had some coffee by way of Dutch courage, and appeared. They were perfectly polite, they handed me a document to the effect that I was to leave the country on a certain date by a certain flight, or else . . . I was not to return. So I was now a prohibited immigrant, I felt a little proud, almost as if I had earned my spurs.

I shan't forget the day of my departure, 11 November. I had lunch with Joel Mervis, editor of the Johannesburg *Sunday Times*, when the news came through that Bram Fischer had been arrested, and that Ian Smith had declared UDI.

I had intended to go on to Rhodesia to see how Defence and Aid was faring, but this didn't seem quite the right moment for such a visit. My African friends were jubilant over the announcement of UDI. 'Now,' they said, 'Britain will have to act, it could be the beginning of the end'. But Britain had no intention of acting, indeed Harold Wilson had precipitated the declaration, by declaring in advance that whatever the Rhodesians did, Britain would take no military action. The Archbishop of Canterbury, Michael Ramsey, on the other hand, had stated, I thought bravely, that should the government think it right to take military action, it would be right for Christians to support it. I was afraid that John might attack the archbishop, I nearly sent him a telegram, and I wish I had, because he did issue a statement repudiating Ramsey's position; it was one of our more serious disagreements.

Later that evening, unhappy and disorientated, I flew away. It felt like deserting the battlefield at the height of the engagement. I wanted to stay and fight.

40

Defence and Aid Banned

I wrote about South Africa, and all over the country I spoke about South Africa. On 13 December 1965, at a public meeting in Church House, I said: 'I have evidence that the Special Branch is trying hard to frame Defence and Aid. It is busy trying to make out a case . . . that Defence and Aid is financing some kind of Communist plot. If you read your news carefully in the coming months you'll see.'

The London South African Embassy, too, was trying hard to fix labels of Communism and violence both on the Fund, and John. If you repeat a lie often enough, many people are going to believe it, especially if it suits them to do so.

By January 1966, Bram Fischer was on trial. During the preparatory examination, the Prosecution asserted that 'money for subversion entered South Africa from the London-based Defence and Aid Fund'. The only evidence produced was a letter written by John to Walter Sisulu in 1963, which the judge at the Rivonia trial had ruled as inadmissible. A wretched African state witness, who had spent more than 180 days in solitary confinement, and had been routinely tortured by the police, was brought in, to declare that Defence and Aid money had been used by Bram to promote an underground Communist plot. At the trial, the Prosecution dared not produce this witness for cross-examination. Bram stated in Court: 'My trial, which ought to deal only with my political activities, has been used as a platform to smear innocent persons who have in no way been associated with me in my political activities, and whose only sin is their unpopularity with the present Government . . . To my knowledge, no one has ever sought to use Defence and Aid for political purposes.'

We continued to try to do what we could for Port Elizabeth. The South African Committees now found it impossible to raise money from within the country, and were dependent mainly upon us. The Eastern Cape trials were legion. A man or woman would be sentenced for belonging to the ANC: on completion of their prison sentence, they would be re-arrested, and charged with collecting money for the ANC and sentenced to a further term of imprisonment. Next time round, it would be distributing ANC literature, or having an ANC meeting in their house – trials and imprisonments went on and on.

Then, at the beginning of March 1966, came the long-expected news: the Defence and Aid Fund was banned, under the terms of the Suppression of Communism Act. It would now become a criminal offence for anyone in South Africa to receive funds from IDAF for the legal defence and welfare of political prisoners and their dependants.

What was going to happen now? Did that mean the end of IDAF? John was asked. But John had no intention of letting go. Schemes for continuing the work were not long in coming. It was Neville Rubin, an exiled South African lawyer, who suggested that the legal side could be arranged through the legal profession itself. Birkbeck Montagu's, a legal firm just down the road, was accustomed to assisting IDAF. Two of their lawyers, Martin Beyer and Bill Frankel, came for secret meetings with Neville Rubin, John and Phyllis. They decided first to set up three trusts: (1) The Freedom from Fear International Charitable Foundation; (2) The Freedom from Hunger International Charitable Foundation; and (3) The Freedom from Hardship International Trust. John approached a number of prominent and respected persons who sometimes contributed to IDAF, to ask them to act as Trustees. They were prepared, if necessary, to state that money came from them.

As soon as IDAF knew of a pending political trial, we would contact Birkbeck Montagu's. They in turn would contact an uninvolved legal firm, explaining that owing to their South African interests, it would be difficult for them to act, but asking the firm to accept their client or clients for them. This firm would then brief and pay the South African lawyers, and would be reimbursed by Birkbeck Montagu's. It sounds involved, but in fact was simple, and proved to be safe. John never contacted Birkbeck Montagu's direct. David – now Sir David – Floyd Ewin, the cathedral registrar, was a good friend, and John asked him if he would act as the contact with Birkbeck Montagu's. David was fond of John and agreed out of friendship; he hoped to remain anonymous.

Meetings took place, sometimes in the Chapter House, a popular rendezvous as John usually produced glasses of sherry. More often they would meet in the cathedral. John would conduct them into the Canon's Closet up above in the choir stalls, and away from tourists, or if Billy Frankel and Phyllis were meeting on their own, they would sit together in one of the pews, and transact their business in whispers. For a long time, even I did not know the details of these arrangements; all I heard was mysterious talk of Mr X and Mr Y.

Sympathetic South African lawyers no longer dared to reduce their fees for fear of prosecution; this our major donors understood. They were invited to send trusted representatives to inspect our audited accounts, and Phyllis made use of diplomatic bags to send them regular and detailed reports of our work.

A simple arrangement for the welfare work was suggested by Phyllis. As an ex-member of SACTU she was already sending money from individuals in England to families of banned and imprisoned trades unionists. Why could this not be continued on a wider scale? The first correspondents all came from within Britain: they were given the names and addresses of South African families in need, and were sent monthly sums of money for transmission to each family. Special grants were available for medical expenses, funerals and visits to relatives in prison. Families with school-age children got extra money for education, and there were grants for people on their release from prison. Correspondents were told to be careful not to write nor to encourage the recipients to write of political matters. After a few years, Rica took over the Welfare (Clause II) work, and the scheme was expanded internationally. Eventually we had correspondents in Ireland, Holland, Norway, Sweden, Denmark and Canada.

In each country there was a co-ordinator, the only person who knew the source of the money; neither the correspondents nor the recipients were aware of the IDAF link. We were careful to account for all monies disbursed, recipients always had to acknowledge the grants they received. Their letters were sent to the co-ordinator, who in turn sent them, not directly to IDAF, but to an accommodation address from which they could be collected. We have thousands and thousands of these letters; they are moving human documents.

Until 1981, a Swiss committee ran an adoption scheme. Defence and Aid gave them the names and family circumstances of 100 families; the Swiss then recruited 100 'godparents', and raised their own funds.

At first we had some difficulty in finding and locating political trials. Phyllis took all the South African newspapers, and would spend a whole day going through them. The ANC and PAC London representatives brought us information, as well as names and addresses of families in need. Quite soon the South African lawyers knew that they would get funding for political trials, the bush telegraph began to operate, and all seemed to be going miraculously smoothly.

In August John went off to a UN Seminar on Apartheid in Brasilia. He was in defiant and fighting mood, determined to tell the world that the humanitarian work of Defence and Aid continued and would continue 'through channels that are legal not only outside, but also inside South Africa'. He referred to his contentious UN speech, apologising for any embarrassment he might have caused to friends and fellow-workers. He acknowledged that the wording might have been more discreet, but firmly reasserted the points he was trying to make.

41

Death of a Chief

JOHN'S book *Faith under Fire* was published in 1966. There were many reviews, some laudatory, some hostile, many mixed. Joost de Blank wrote of 'the largely unfavourable and unsympathetic appreciation which much of our society has of Canon Collins'. Of the book he said, 'We are confronted by his brashness, his naïveté, his impatience . . . his dislike of authority, and his predilection to speak to rather than from the Church. Many of his sincerest friends would maintain that this is his greatest weakness.' There were a number of clergy who objected to John's strictures upon the Church. He was called exhibitionist, arrogant, egocentric, patronising, muddle-headed.

Philip Toynbee wrote a long and thoughtful article: 'This book does a great deal to vindicate those who have known Canon Collins well, and who have always insisted that his public image does him a great deal less than justice. He emerges as . . . often over-hasty in his words and actions, sometimes too vociferous in self-justification, but more puppyish than conceited, more amiably enthusiastic than self-righteously opinionated. He emerges most pleasantly as a gay (original meaning please) and high-spirited man.'

I need hardly say that in the public image I scarcely recognise the man I married.

These were years of change in the pattern of our lives; the boys were growing up, and beginning to make their own arrangements. Andrew had been called to the Bar in 1965, but continued to live at home, he was always easy and companionable. Richard had done a year's VSO in Pakistan before going to Magdalen, Oxford to read history. In the middle of his course, he announced, to the consternation of his parents, that he wished to become a ballet-dancer. In the foolish way of women – what professions could be more insecure? – I had hoped that one of our children might follow an artistic career, a writer, a musician, an actor – never in my wildest dreams did I consider a ballet-dancer. However, Richard was persuaded to finish his degree course, and was then, to our surprise, taken on for training by the Royal Ballet School; they said he had talent. He was now trying to persuade the Russians to accept him for further training in Moscow or Leningrad. Peter was at Trinity College, Cambridge, chasing quarks and other strange particles, and Mark was in his last years at Eton. The time of locums was coming to an end. We began to think of buying ourselves a cottage in the country.

On 7 October 1966, Victor Gollancz had a severe stroke, and was paralysed down his right side. Like many hypochondriacs, when smitten by a real as opposed to an imaginary illness, he faced it with fortitude. When he came out of hospital he began to practise writing with his left hand, and started to record a rather sad little daily diary. Ruth never left him; when I said something in admiration of all she did, she was surprised. 'But any wife would do the same,' she said. Ruth was not just 'any wife', she was a remarkable wife.

It was unbearably sad to see this man of fire and energy laid so low. 'You will come and see me,' he said. 'You won't desert me?' I promised. We didn't desert Victor, as one or two entries in his diary record: 'Tonight Diana comes to dine with us. That is always for us the chief event of the week. I have grown to love Diana more than any human being except Ruth. She's like an utterly steadfast rock.' His last diary entry on 2 February 1967 reads: 'I only hope I shall feel better soon, and be able to enjoy an hour or two with Diana and John. I just could not bear an evening with them to be a flop. I would sooner put them off.' The evening wasn't a flop. Victor was in a gentle mood, asking Ruth to forgive him for some display of temper. 'Ruth always forgives,' we said. 'And Victor forgives,' said John. That evidently pleased him.

The next morning he had a second stroke, from which he never recovered consciousness, and from which he soon died. Dear loving, passionate, contradictory Victor: we would always miss him.

At the beginning of May 1967, Dr Matthews announced his retirement; he was eighty-six, and had been at St Paul's for thirty-three years. I don't think Walter Matthews could have had an enemy in the world, he inspired affection and respect in the City, in St Paul's and in the Church. Everyone was sad to say goodbye to him. I am tempted to quote something Walter Matthews wrote about John and me; it is flattering, but I hope at least partly true: 'A fact about Collins which I always bear in mind is that he has renounced personal ambition. Both he and Diana are exceptionally able persons, and neither of them is devoid of the natural ambition which goes with ability; but they have never considered self-interest when it was at variance with their ideals.'

Soon after the announcement of Matthews' resignation, the warden of the minor canons came to see me. 'I have been making soundings around the cathedral,' he said, 'and there is only one man that everyone wants to be the next dean and that is Canon Collins. Do you think he would accept it, if it were offered him?' I knew quite well that the deanery of St Paul's was the only post in the Church that John would have really loved. He had a vision of a great cathedral as an ecumenical centre of spiritual, cultural and intellectual life. He longed to be able to try to realise this. I said that I felt sure John would say 'yes', but that I would talk to him. John not only said 'yes', but said that he would arrange his outside work so that he would have time to devote to St Paul's.

So the cathedral planned a campaign, with the exception of the canons, who were hostile. I didn't have anything to do with it, just suggested that all those who really wanted John should write to the Prime Minister, Harold Wilson. There was considerable outside pressure for John, articles in the papers, and letters to Downing Street. 'He won't get it,' Mervyn Stockwood said to me. 'He's got too many enemies.' The ways of ecclesiastical appointments are very strange. It is the views of the influential and Establishment worthies that matter, not those of the men who do the work, and know the cathedral.

It was the most junior member of the chapter, the archdeacon, Martin Sullivan, who was appointed. I don't forget the expression on John's face as he read the letter informing him of the appointment; it was concern for St Paul's, as well as the pain of a personal rejection. In the cathedral, the news was received with shock, disbelief and incomprehension: 'How could it possibly have happened?' 'I don't believe it!' 'They can't do this to Canon Collins!' But they could and they did.

It was not that Martin was unpopular, just that he was not of the calibre expected for a dean of St Paul's. Martin was a decent chap, pleasant, friendly, and popular in the City. I have no wish to question his faith nor his sincerity. There were situations in which he might have had much to give; by all accounts, he had been a good army chaplain, and a good parish priest. But St Paul's was not such a situation.

Tactfully Martin decided to go away until the time of his installation as dean. This meant that John, like his predecessor Canon Alexander, had the bitter-sweet experience of acting as dean for several months, until the day when he, as senior canon, had to install Martin Sullivan.

Some years later Jack Priestley wrote: 'There are times when I wonder if the Church really understands John Collins very much better than the news editor of the *Daily Splash*, who sees him as a possible story now and then. I have never discussed this subject with my friend – we have much else to talk about – but if the Church does not understand him, then I must add that I don't understand the Church. It is rather like a man who, with a certain course to run, leaves a race horse in its stable and uses circus ponies.'

'Who remembers who was Dean of St Paul's when Sydney Smith was a Canon?' wrote one of our friends.

John took this disappointment much better than I did. I had been in two minds about it: I was happy as I was, I had no wish to go and live in the large gloomy deanery across Ludgate Hill, nor did I relish the kind of official life I might be called upon to lead, City dinners and all that. John was not embittered, nor did he waver in his devotion to St Paul's, nor in his loyalty to the Church, he never made things difficult for Martin. I, on the other hand, felt increasingly disenchanted with the whole ecclesiastical set-up; it often seemed so far removed from the faith that many of us cherish in our hearts.

The fact that John had, for several years, been nominated for the Nobel Peace Prize, and never got it, was not really a disappointment. The money would have been nice, and would have secured the future of Christian Action and Defence and Aid, but too much money is not necessarily good for voluntary organisations: better to have to work at it, and involve many more people, as well as governments. Anyway, I felt that the nomination was rather like being recommended for the Victoria Cross, an honour in itself.

Christian Action's 'Homeless in Britain' campaign was going well. More and more we were concentrating on what Ian Henderson called a 'Mission to the Misfits'. We had houses for accommodation and rehabilitation of alcoholics and crude spirit addicts, and homes for unmarried and deserted mothers. Colchester Christian Action was attempting to meet the needs of the old, the handicapped and the discharged prisoner, while a Christian Action group in Hackney had a home for patients from the local psychiatric hospital who had been 'discharged into the community'. It was a hopeful and exciting scene, and of course involved extra money-raising efforts.

Then there was the experimental shelter for vagrant women in Lambeth, opened on 21 June by the Archbishop of Canterbury, Michael Ramsey. Our professional advisor Leslie Tuft had written us an article about these women, he had found twenty-three of them between twelve and two a.m. in intensely cold January weather wandering about Waterloo Station. 'Five had been discharged from prison, seven had received psychiatric treatment. Most appeared disturbed. The behaviour of at least a dozen was bizarre and overtly psychotic . . . They were not sleeping rough by accident . . . If they tried to sleep on benches or in waiting rooms, the police would move them on as not being bona fide travellers. What was needed', he wrote, was 'casual accommodation for casual people'. This is what the Christian Action Shelter aimed to provide. The shelter would refuse no one, and would be non-coercive, except in cases of violence. It would provide short-stay accommodation and basic food which the inmates would prepare for themselves, it could also be a day refuge. As it developed successfully this experiment attracted much interest from social workers, and other concerned bodies.

John continued to preach the kind of sermons that upset people. On Christian grounds, he spoke against the use by the Americans of fragmentation bombs and the chemical weapon Napalm in Vietnam. He read out an account of the horrifying physical effects of these weapons. Several people walked out. They had come to St Paul's, so they said, for peace and quiet, not to have to listen to a 'political' sermon. When Bishop Crowther was expelled from South Africa, John criticised the South African and the British Churches for failing to protest. A correspondence in the *Church Times* followed, justifying the attitude of the Anglican Church, and attacking John.

In a long letter to John, Oliver Tambo, himself a sincere Christian, gave a rather different view: 'the best that can be said for Christianity is that over the years – no, over the decades and even centuries – it has gone to sleep, for if it is not, if it is wide awake, then it is for me difficult to escape the feeling that Christianity is fully implicated in the perpetration of so much of the evil that bedevils the world of our day . . . If the Church was not busy sleeping, it would be up and fighting evil all the time at all places, and would, if needs be, follow the Master to the Cross . . . Instead, those who seek to lead the Church into action and resistance against policies and practices that can only be described as a monstrous sin are ostracised, victimised and treated with official displeasure by the authorities of the Church and the Chief Priests of the Christian Faith . . .'

A great Christian and a great South African died in 1967. Chief Luthuli was mysteriously run over by a train. John arranged a memorial service for him in the crypt of St Paul's. He conducted many of such services for African, Indian and white opponents of apartheid who died or were murdered. Alan Paton had described the chief as 'the shadow of a great rock in a weary land'. Now he was among those who spoke at Luthuli's funeral: 'They took away his chieftainship, but he never ceased to be Chief. They took away his temporal power, but he never ceased to have his spiritual power. They took away his freedom, but he never ceased to be free. He was indeed more free than those who bound him. . .

'There are some people who will think that the story of his life was a failure. . . The real story of his life is the story of his fortitude. If you win in life, you are a successful man. If you lose, you are an unsuccessful man. But if you go on whether you win or lose, then you have something more than success or failure. You keep your own soul. In one way Luthuli lost the world, but he kept his own soul.'

42

A Russian Plot

JOHN was now invited to a number of international conferences, of dubious value apart from the all-important one of meeting and talking with different people. Whenever possible, I went with him. So it was that in the spring of 1968 we found ourselves in Prague attending the Third Conference of the All-Christian Peace Assembly. This was convened under the chairmanship of Joseph Hromadka, a professor of theology, and was initiated and financed by the Russian Church, which presumably meant with at least the backing of the Russian State. At first the whole affair was boycotted by the West, but gradually attitudes softened, the Russian Church joined the World Council of Churches, and the British Council of Churches decided it was worthwhile to go to Prague. John always believed in trying to talk with your opponents.

Of course, the real reward, the real excitement was Prague itself, that beautiful but decaying city, now suddenly, in this famous spring, filled with such an infectious sense of hope and of new life – the birth of 'Socialism with a human face'. Students can be tiresomely rebellious, but they can fan the winds of much-needed change, so that they become an irresistible hurricane. The Prague students came to speak to the conference, and very impressive they were. We travelled everywhere by public transport, people spoke to us, wanted to shake us by the hand, there was laughter, there were tears of joy. It was impossible not to share in this new hope, not to see the light in people's faces, to experience their sudden openness and friendliness, and to feel their sense of release.

Our personal feelings of elation were overshadowed by an announcement in the middle of the conference of the assassination of Martin Luther King, a beacon of hope in another part of the world, for so many of his oppressed countrymen. Back in England, John decided this was the right moment to launch a Martin Luther King Memorial Fund, to try to meet the increase of racist behaviour and discrimination in Britain, and to give assistance in matters like work and housing to coloured immigrants.

This initiative started well, and a considerable amount of money was raised, but I was nervous, not about the cause, nor the need for it – Enoch Powell had already made his 'Tiber running with blood' speech – but because I felt that both John and Christian Action were in danger of becoming over-extended. We supported various small efforts in the field of race relations: one was the building of a Martin Luther King adventure playground in Islington, something requested by Trevor Huddleston who had returned from Masasi, Tanzania, and was now Bishop of Stepney. We made future plans, which included a visit by Coretta King.

Coretta arrived in London on the evening of 14 March 1969 with her two elder children, and other relatives and friends. We were alarmed at all the extra people, until we learned that they were the ones who had supported Coretta through the whole of the last terrible year. Two friends had given up their jobs – and it was not easy for black women to find good jobs – but they had dropped everything, and come to look after Coretta's home for her, while she tried to cope with the multitude of demands made upon her – she had had more than 100 requests for speeches, and was under contract to write a book.

I think we had planned too exhausting a schedule for this exhausted woman, but everybody wanted to see her. She was besieged by the Press who all wanted to know her reaction to the death sentence passed on Earl Ray, her husband's assassin. All she would say was that capital punishment was contrary to everything in which she and her husband and family believed, but that she was sure that there were more fingers on that trigger, and that the whole conspiracy to kill her husband ought to be brought to light.

The most impressive event of the visit was Coretta's sermon in St Paul's. The cathedral was nearly as full as it had been for her husband, and she rose magnificently to the occasion. This young and beautiful woman who had been so suddenly and tragically widowed stood high up in that great pulpit, an emblem of courage, dignity and serenity. When she spoke, her voice was both beautiful and powerful, her sermon radiated love, forgiveness and non-violence. 'Many despair,' she said, 'over the evil, violence and unrest in the world today. Beyond all the turbulence I see signs of a new social order, a new dawn, a new day. I believe this because I believe there is a divine plan, and that love is the unifying element in the universe . . . Christ has promised to make all things new. Now is the time to open all things to God – now is

the time to challenge all race privileges, and to embrace the spirit of
love to bring in a new day of humanity.'

There were other conferences for John; in June we went together to
Stockholm for a meeting of the UN Special Committee on Apartheid.
Over the next years we paid many visits to Sweden. They were a
pleasure for us, as well as being valuable for Defence and Aid. We
stayed with Per and Annalena Wastberg, often in their country home
about twenty minutes' drive out of Stockholm. This was an old
wooden farmhouse, surrounded by unspoiled country and forest. The
long, low house was painted the traditional earthy red; inside were the
original wooden floors, and in every room wood-burning stoves with
their simple and beautiful old tiles. Per and Annalena had even
managed to find and clean some of the original wallpapers – lightly
sprigged with small field flowers, and looking as fresh and bright as
ever. The furniture was all of wood, and all of the period. John and I
loved Stora Saby.

Although we still received and collected a great deal of information
from South Africa, it was not so easy as before the banning. John had,
for some time, felt the need for a research and information department
of IDAF, but there had never been enough money. Then, in 1969,
Alex and Gurli Hepple arrived, forced out of South Africa by repeated
bannings. They were both academics, and Alex came to John with a
proposal that exactly fitted with what John wanted – to produce
information that would be scrupulously accurate, and without any
political or polemical bias. For some time, the Hepples' little department operated on a shoe-string from their home, until John was at last
able to persuade the sympathetic Swedes that this really was an
essential contribution to the struggle for freedom in Southern Africa.
They then agreed that a portion of their grant might be earmarked for
information. From such modest beginnings grew both the publications and the research and information departments of IDAF. These
have produced material that has been used and trusted by the UN, and
by governments and organisations around the world.

John had built up a number of channels of family welfare assistance,
that were able to supplement Phyllis and Rica's growing list of
correspondents. By devious routes, money went to Alan Paton, and to
Archbishop Hurley, the Roman Catholic Primate in Durban. In 1966,
the PAC London representative, Barney Desai, had asked John if he
would come to the Hotel President to meet a friend. There was
something mysterious about this, someone whom Barney clearly did

not wish to bring to Amen Court. At the hotel, John was introduced to Imam Abdullah Haroun from Cape Town. He was aware of the sufferings of the families of political prisoners in his area and wanted to be able to assist. With Barney's help another channel for the transmission of assistance was worked out. After a time Barney, who was a lawyer, came with a letter saying that his 'client' needed more money, as he wished to establish a new 'depot' in Port Elizabeth.

This was too good to last, and in 1969 Barney brought John another letter from the Imam, who wrote: 'The Special Branch have been hounding me continually because of the role I play in aiding the poor Africans who suffer horribly under the discriminatory laws of our so-called Christian Government . . .' The Imam was arrested and imprisoned. He managed to smuggle out a letter written on a scrap of lavatory paper in which he said, 'If you hear that I have died in prison by accident, you will know that it will not have been an accident' – a sure indication that he was being tortured. It was not long before the Security Police announced that the Imam had died from a heart attack, later amended to 'a fall' down a stone staircase.

In the crypt of St Paul's, John held a joint Anglican-Muslim service. There were readings from the works of Rabindranath Tagore, Khalil Gibran (*The Prophet*) and the Quaker, Jeremy Naylor. John and two Imams officiated. It was one of the most moving of the many memorial services that John held in St Paul's.

For a great deal of the educational assistance, we worked through Robert Birley, and his South African contacts. Eminently respectable people, this end, were recruited; they included Dame Lucy Sutherland, principal of my old college, Lady Margaret Hall, and my tutor Miss Lea.

In Rhodesia, Phyllis Altman was building up an impressive scheme of education by correspondence for men in detention. It began with letters from twenty-two students who wished to continue their studies, and soon there was a flood of requests. Wisely, Phyllis got advice from the ZAPU and ZANU representatives who knew most of the detainees. They also knew that a number of them had been school teachers, and these were asked to 'vet' the new applicants, and to advise as to whether they were reasonably equipped to pursue their chosen courses. It was as a part of this scheme that Robert Mugabe obtained his impressive string of degrees.

Our son Richard had at last departed for Russia. After many months of 'Niet! Niet!' the Embassy telephoned and announced that he could go to Moscow – tomorrow if he wished – to join the Bolshoi. It wasn't quite tomorrow, but with the help of Robert Birley, Sir Gilbert Inglefield, Dame Ruth Railton and others he was given a Churchill scholarship. John's left-wing contacts and the Old School tie worked well together.

The dark cloud, that August, was the announcement that Russian tanks were in Prague. The blaze of hope that we had seen in the spring with so much excitement was brutally extinguished – replaced by a small but tragic blaze when the student Jan Palach burned himself to death in protest. Only after twenty years could hope soar again, phoenix-like from the ashes.

Along with so many, John, in his personal capacity, and on behalf of Christian Action, protested to the Russian Embassy. In spite of this the Russians seemed to remain friendly. They looked after Richard well, housed him in the famous Moscow conservatoire, and the best Bolshoi teachers gave time to him. After we returned to London, John got a mysterious telephone call from the Russian Embassy, asking him to meet one of their staff at a certain restaurant. John never thought about any kind of risk, so off he went. The Russians had a proposition. They were prepared to supply money and submarines in an attempt to rescue political prisoners from Robben Island. From John they wanted advice, contact with prisoners, and if possible a detailed map of the island and of the prison buildings. John was too intrigued to reject this proposal outright, and further meetings were arranged. At one of these, his new friend arrived with presents of vodka and caviar. John was sufficiently alert to say that, sad as he was to refuse, he really could not accept such a generous offer – his friend appeared genuinely upset. They were, he said, a real token of friendship, but John stuck to his refusal.

I was never at all enthusiastic about this hare-brained scheme. I thought success was highly improbable, and I felt sure that John's meetings were being monitored by MI5, and information no doubt being relayed to their opposite numbers in Pretoria. We knew that our telephones were tapped. At first we thought it was South African agents who had somehow managed to fix the 'bugs', but one day Gerald Gardiner, by then Lord Chancellor in the Labour government, happened to be in the study when John received a call; as he put the receiver down, Gerald said, 'By the way, John, I hope you don't trust that machine.' So it was our own people – a fact that made and makes me very indignant.

Much to my relief, the scheme eventually foundered when John realised that the Russians were only interested in getting out their own people, members of the Communist party. At first, not even Nelson Mandela was to be included, he wasn't a Communist. This kind of selectivity was something that John could not accept, and he withdrew.

There were new faces on the Council of Christian Action. We were joined by Canon Eric James, a long-time supporter, who now began to play a more active role from within, and by a close friend, Nadir Dinshaw. Nadir comes from a wealthy Parsi family living in what is now Pakistan. The Parsis are Zoroastrians, a religion founded some six centuries before Christ, and once dominant over the Middle East, until it was driven out and replaced by militant Islam. The Parsis are inaccurately described as dualists, but are much more like the Quakers, children of the Inner Light, small in number, but great in spirit. Their religion is personal and tolerant, with a particularly strong emphasis upon practical works of mercy and compassion. Nadir was educated, and now lives, in England; at some stage he became a Christian, and brings to his faith a welcome understanding of the spiritual value of Eastern religions.

Another Council newcomer was Colin Hodgetts, a young priest who had first appeared at a Christian Action conference. He was a talented, imaginative and visionary young man. He had been a teacher, and had written and produced plays for a youth theatre during his first curacy in Hackney. He was enthusiastic about Christian Action. Colin was a child of the Sixties, with their qualities and their defects. This was a period of loosening up, questioning of authority, a turning inwards, the era of Flower Power, the counter-culture, the search for alternative ways of community living, and the development of the permissive society. Even the Anglican Church went through a period of loosening, with the publication of *Honest to God* in 1963. John didn't think much of it, due no doubt to his academic training; he said it contained nothing new. The new element, of course, was that it was written by a bishop in an accessible style. But for me the book brought a sense of release. I had for long felt that the clergy allowed themselves to appear to subscribe to much that they could not – literally – believe, and much that I certainly couldn't believe; though I never wanted to be driven to say that I was not a Christian.

Colin was swept away by the new thinking, with the emphasis upon personal freedom to choose and to experiment. When I asked him to write for the *Journal* on how he saw the future for a movement like

Christian Action, he called his article 'The Love Generation'. At the end of 1969 Ian Henderson resigned from the position of executive director of Christian Action, and the Council appointed Colin Hodgetts as Ian's successor.

43

A Legacy of the Sixties

ON 21 October 1969, we had been married for thirty years: that was the day on which Mill House, Mount Bures, on the Essex-Suffolk border became our country home, an embryo home as yet. It needed much work, and we didn't finally move in until the summer of 1971. As we had searched for the last eighteen months I had noticed an ambivalence in John, whenever we saw anything at all possible, he discovered some insuperable objection to it. I guessed that he feared a hidden plot to lure him away from London and the work to which he was so much committed. There were plenty of objections to Mill House – a surveyor's report that said 'Don't touch it', relatives who thought we were dotty – but I was getting desperate. John saw this and withdrew his objections, and became as enthusiastic about it as I was.

Mill House stands on the highest part of a plateau between two rivers, the Stour to the east, and the Colne further away to the west; it looks down over the Stour Valley. There is a smaller valley to the north-west where a lively little tributary runs down into the Stour. We soon understood why they built a windmill here: unrelenting gales from the south-west, and piercing winds that seem to blow without interruption from the North Pole or from Siberia. But the view over the Stour valley is inexhaustibly beautiful. The wide sky, beloved of landscape painters, is continually changing; it pours its lights and shadows over the undulating slopes on the further side. Here where fields fold over one another, the seasons bring their own colours, bare trees standing singly and in small woods, ploughed land and the green promise of winter wheat break into spring with its symphony of green, the fields fade into the paler greens and gentle yellows of early summer, then the trees begin to darken and the fields to ripen into the rich golden bronze of the harvest, and still to come is the autumn colouring of the trees, and later still perhaps, the sparkling beauty of snow and hoar frost.

The windmill was demolished long ago, but two little workmen's cottages remained, and were turned into one house by successive owners. Somehow I knew when I first entered it, that this was a house that had been loved, and in which people had been happy. There were nearly two acres of unkempt garden and orchard attached, and we began to tackle these even before the house was ready. 'Plant as if you are going to live for ever, and live as if you are going to die tomorrow'; that is true country wisdom. We didn't, need I say, do so well with the second part, but we did plant many fine trees that we were unlikely to see in their full glory. Shall I ever see the tulip tree in flower? This is rose country, so we filled the place with sweet-scented old-fashioned roses, and, inspired by Vita Sackville-West, sent them climbing up available old trees. We had to have spindle-berries, so we dug up a number of bushes from the sand cliffs along the Stutton river, and they have all flourished. 'I don't aim at tidiness,' I said. 'I want a romantic tangle.' No problems about the tangle, the romance often seemed more inside me than outside in the garden, but now and then, when the weather and the seasons have been kindly, the dreams have come true.

In 1973, our son Peter, armed with his PhD, went to continue chasing weird particles at the Weizmann Institute just outside Tel Aviv. An old friend, George Appleton, who had, all too briefly, been a canon of St Paul's, was now the Anglican archbishop in Jerusalem; it seemed the perfect time to visit Israel.

The Weizmann Institute was immensely impressive, Peter said that the quality of research was higher even than at Cambridge. It was beautifully laid out, shaded by trees and full of flowers and vegetables. The personality and the idealism of Dr Weizmann, the first President of Israel, had stamped itself upon the whole place. He had bought it as a desert, and much research had gone into making this and other deserts blossom. We were received as honoured guests.

Staying with George and Madge Appleton was the best possible introduction to Jerusalem, to its history and to its present problems. George is a good and holy man, he was trusted by Jews and Arabs, and by Christians and Muslims. He had started a number of small but hopeful peace initiatives. We became well aware of the vulnerability of the Israelis, and the ever-present pain of the Holocaust, as well as of the suffering, dispossession and bitterness of the Arabs. The Israelis we met said that the occupied territories were negotiable, some said they didn't want to hang on to them, all said they could never give up Jerusalem. Attitudes have tragically hardened.

John and I loved the peace of Galilee where we drove in a hired car. We stayed in the local YMCA, just outside Tiberias. We had a large room with a balcony overlooking a small bay. Here we sat and watched innumerable birds, and at evening little fishing boats came, and the men cast out their nets as they have done from time immemorial. In the morning they were still there, often looking as if they 'had toiled all night and taken nothing.'

We explored the countryside in all its fresh spring beauty, walked by the lake in the evenings, and had our most memorable of many picnics on the top of Mount Tabor, the Mount of the Transfiguration, where we found a field literally carpeted with golden asphodels – were they 'the lilies of the field'? But even here, on the Golan Heights, in the kibbutz near the frontiers, there were too many reminders of war.

If you go to Israel as a believer, your faith may well be strengthened and invigorated, if you go with doubt and disbelief, these may well be reinforced. It is easier to feel close to the New Testament in Galilee, but that is sentimental, Jerusalem is an essential part of the story.

At the end of 1972 John had resigned as chairman of Christian Action; he remained as president, and I continued to play an active part on the council. Our long-term friend and supporter John Drewett took over as chairman, but died from a sudden heart attack within two months, and Michael Graham-Jones stepped temporarily into the breach. From 1976–1988 Stephen O'Brien nobly held the chair.

Christian Action continued working for Africa and for the homeless, but our new director, Colin, had been to India and had absorbed the ideas of Gandhi. He longed to create a Christian community, non-violent and non-coercive, that could experiment in alternative styles of living. So in 1972, he persuaded the council to borrow money to buy Eastbourne House with its adjoining vicarage in Bethnal Green. Eastbourne House was a large run-down building which had once been a community centre. John was indulgent towards Colin and his ideas, and many of us were sympathetic. E.S. Schumacher, ('Small is Beautiful') had become a member of the council, and we had participated actively in the Gandhi Centenary Year. But was it wise to tie Christian Action down to bricks and mortar, would it not lose its freedom and flexibility?

Colin moved into the vicarage, and opened it to people who were homeless and penniless, and had other problems. He gathered a young group to work on the building, and they did do a fine work of restoration. The Christian Action offices would eventually move in, and financially underpin the unstructured community. Colin and his friends identified society as coercive and basically violent, they rejected politics which gave people neither power nor responsibility. Colin wanted 'a creative alternative at the grass roots community action level for those who forswear actual rule'. From Eastbourne House, they might provide free 'alternative' schooling, a holistic health centre, 'barefoot' lawyers and other experiments.

Soon there was trouble, the vicarage became overcrowded and attracted the displeasure of the local council, and the local people looked on suspiciously. They heard rumours of young men and girls sleeping in open dormitories, possibly smoking cannabis, and with their sturdy working-class morality, they were not much interested in alternative lifestyles.

Finally the council felt unable to confirm Colin's appointment as director. Christian Action offices did move in, and we began to run more conventional projects for the community. In the end Eastbourne House and the vicarage were sold to Globe Town Community, a local group, who have made it once more a flourishing community centre.

It is easy to dismiss the Love Generation and the 'alternatives' of the Sixties as absurdly idealistic and impractical. The truth is that life without rules is a prescription for the Kingdom of Heaven: it requires a degree of inner strength and self-discipline that is seldom if ever achieved, even after years of training.

I do not think Christian Action was wrong to give Colin his head, nor do I want to dismiss the ideas and aspirations of this period. We would do well to look at where our worship of Mammon and its allied technology has led us; we see an increasingly violent world, the pollution and rape of natural resources, factory farming, and economies buttressed by a lethal international arms trade. Perhaps those rebellious young were not altogether mistaken.

44

India, Africa, and Home

JOHN and I were invited by the Gandhi Peace Foundation to attend a Peace Seminar on 'The relevance of Gandhi for the present day'. This was in January 1970, in Delhi, and following it we were to be taken on a tour of the ashrams. We arrived in New Delhi on the morning of the Republic Day celebrations. Mark, who was having a year off before going to Oxford to read medicine, met us at the airport, long-haired, dreadfully thin, and wearing the approved Gandhi-style white kurta and pyjama clothing made from hand-spun khadi cloth. We found Delhi full of young Europeans trying to look like Indians, and young Indians trying to look like Europeans – is that called cross-cultural fertilisation? We were pleasantly housed by the Gandhi Peace Foundation, and Mark stayed in what I suppose was the Indian equivalent of a youth hostel.

Our first evening in Delhi was a delight, huge crowds everywhere, noise, light and above all, colour. Scooters, rickshaws, unbelievably ancient taxis held together by string, sacred cows wandering about, and monkeys chattering in the trees. The noble official buildings of New Delhi – the shortlived British Imperial dream – were picked out by numerous small bright lights, making a dazzling succession of sparkling silhouettes, and everywhere among the grass, the trees, and the squares, fountains ran merrily with coloured waters. It was a brilliant clear evening, and suddenly, to my great delight, a huge flock of emerald green parakeets came shrieking out of the glowing apricot sky. One of my father's bedtime stories, my favourite story, had been about finding and collecting, under difficulty and danger, a green parakeet's feather.

We were tired, and stood on a street corner trying vainly to pick up a taxi. All were full and raced past with horns blaring. To drive is to hoot in India, but nobody takes the slightest notice of the ensuing row. A taxi, already occupied by an Indian gentleman, drew up. 'Please let me help you,' he said courteously. 'Where do you wish to go? It is no trouble to me, I am delighted to take you anywhere.' We got in gratefully and answered his polite enquiries as to who we were and what we were doing. He was charming and enthusiastic.

Driving in India is alarming; we were negotiating a particularly busy roundabout when our host suddenly shouted, urging our bewildered driver to go in a different direction. 'There, there,' he cried. 'A wonderful Swami in that taxi. A genuine holy man, you would be so interested to meet him. We must catch him.' Our driver waltzed round a lurching bus festooned with humans, between three scooter rickshaws buzzing along like angry bees. He managed to avoid a couple of sacred cows, but the Swami had vanished into the traffic. 'He really *understands* meditation,' said our friend regretfully, as we abandoned the pursuit.

Unlike John, who had to attend dutifully, I sat rather lightly to the conference. 'An awful lot of hot air,' John said. But as always, he was able to make valuable personal contacts. We met our old friend Jayar Prakash Narayan, and had a meal with one of Manilal Gandhi's sons whom John had met in South Africa. And John made a new friend, who later came to stay with us in London, and with whom we kept in touch until his death. Gora was born a high caste Brahmin, but he had concluded that it was religion that was responsible for the cruelty and injustice of the caste system. So he had set up an atheist ashram, and had his large family of boys and girls married off to surrounding Untouchables. His children could not be given traditional Indian names, since these were all of gods and goddesses, so they were called by some event in the year of their birth, Salt Tax, Round Table Conference, War etc. Mark went to stay in the ashram and found everyone apparently living happily, and merrily propagating atheism.

John and I joined the queue of people who every morning were accustomed to present their problems to the Prime Minister. Indira Gandhi was a strange woman, immensely powerful in personality as in fact, but she had a pronounced nervous tic that suggested hidden tension and strain. We talked mainly about IDAF—India had always been a loyal supporter of the whole anti-apartheid movement.

We managed to take time off with Mark to explore old Delhi, and to give him some substantial meals; in the spartan life of the ashrams he had clearly not had enough to eat. One day we all went by train to Agra to visit that architectural marvel, the Taj Mahal. There are some places, some buildings, whose beauty and impact cannot be ruined by tourism or vulgarisation; the Taj Mahal is one.

How can I select out of the multitude of our impressions? At Ahmadabad we stayed in a well-run and reasonably comfortable ashram. There had been bad Hindu-Muslim riots here, and the Gandhians were doing their best to succour the bereaved and the wounded and to effect some kind of reconciliation. Here we visited a beautiful old palace overlooking the river. Rabindranath Tagore used to stay there: he would walk up and down the terrace composing some of the poetry in which I had delighted from my early youth. Calcutta, by contrast, seemed like hell on earth – Indians will live and survive in conditions that would make most people give up altogether.

We spent a night or two in the ashram of Gandhi's most famous follower Vinoba Bhave. He was the man who had started the Bhoodan movement, walking all over India, and persuading wealthy landowners to give away land to the poverty-stricken peasants.

Varanasi – formerly Benares – is the holiest city in India. It is full of temples, and it is full of lepers. As soon as anyone shows signs of leprosy, he or she is immediately turned out by family and friends, and can only live the life of a beggar – Varanasi is full of beggars. Sometimes lepers lie around in the streets, literally rotting away: stinking carcasses, the remnants of whose diseased flesh is slowly devoured by thousands of maggots.

We visited a leper colony, run by an elderly doctor, a former president of the Indian Medical Association. Devout Hindus at a certain age decide to leave public life, and devote themselves to prayer and meditation, or to some form of active service. This doctor ran single-handed a colony of seventy-five lepers; he had founded and maintained it out of his life savings. He would take his Land-Rover into the city and collect the worst of the abandoned cases of the streets. These he would treat with drugs and operations, and would attempt to heal their psychological wounds, and to rehabilitate them. He was their physician, psychiatrist and spiritual guide. As they recovered they began to work, digging, planting, spinning, carpentering, so that they could return to their homes to lead self-respecting and self-supporting lives. His own life was simple and austere, he was one of the most remarkable and dedicated people we had ever met.

Life in the ashrams was certainly spartan, high thinking and plain living. No alcohol, of course, we ate mainly dhal (lentil soup), yogurt, fresh fruit and vegetables; we frequently slept on boards. It wasn't much to John's taste, but he accepted it all gallantly; he was one of the most uncomplaining of men. I thrived on it, I have seldom felt so fit, and suffered from none of those internal upsets that usually seem to afflict travellers in India.

One of the most primitive, but most delightful ashrams was just outside a tiny village in Gujarat. It was composed of simple but well-designed mud and dung huts, shaded by mango trees that were just coming into flower, and set among wheat and cotton fields, plantations of bananas and still more mangoes. The village was entertaining 27,000 school children for a special Gandhi celebration, 3,000 of them were billeted in our ashram. There was no running water, no electricity, but everything, including the latrines, was kept spotlessly clean. A simple homemade extraction plant had been set up behind the latrines; this drew off the methane gas contained in human excrement, and converted it into use for cooking and lighting; what was left behind went to fertilise the fields. No gas, so no flies – all a splendid example of Gandhian self-help. This neat arrangement posed a little problem for us, since paper (the Indians use water) snagged up the works, fortunately John had a box of matches, and that solved our difficulty.

In a field nearby was a mobile kitchen staffed by volunteers. Here they fed between 5,000 and 7,000 people twice daily, and very good food it was. We ate with our hands, using large vine leaves for plates; these were then fed to the sacred cows – so no tiresome washing-up.

Nearby too was a mobile eye hospital. Ten top surgeons gave two weeks of their time to go out into remote country districts; there they set up a primitive hospital. Latrines were dug, water and electricity laid on, word spread round, and sufferers arrived. As many as 300 operations were performed in a day, cataract, trachoma, and other ailments. Sight was restored to thousands who would otherwise have remained blind, and the success rate was as high as that in more conventional hospitals.

A rather more extreme example of self-help was proffered to us by two elderly gentlemen who arrived early one morning saying that they had discovered the secret of long life and perfect health, and they wished to communicate it to the esteemed visitors. The panacea for all ills was simple. First thing every morning you must drink a large tumblerful of your own urine.

We left from Bombay, which seemed nearly as full as Calcutta of homeless families living on the streets. But here we were met by Nadir, who generously put us up in the best hotel, and I have to confess that this return to the fleshpots was very welcome. It was a pleasure too to meet some of Nadir's family. If I loved Indians for nothing else, I would have loved them for the way that they opened their hearts and their homes, not only to us, but also to Mark in his wanderings. However poor the area or the family, Mark was always generously welcomed and given food and shelter.

We loved and we hated India; we were alternately enchanted and exasperated, inspired, appalled, fascinated, repelled, hopeful, despairing; every set of opposites you can think of: the exquisite beauty of the Taj Mahal and the vast human dustbin of Calcutta. India is deeply materialist and deeply spiritual. Wherever there is an Indian, there is a shop, somebody selling something, even if it is only a few rusty nails. There are all the touts and the sharks and the beggars, and there is the special horror of mutilated child beggars. But there are the selfless saints as well. Some of our most indelible memories were of the prayer meetings; sitting cross-legged on the ground under the stars, and listening to the prayers, Hindu, Buddhist, Christian and Muslim all mixed up together, for India is like a great sponge absorbing everything into itself. The chanting is ancient and strange, it is haunting, sad, tender, beyond the reach of words; it is something we could never forget.

'This is a nation,' said the Pope, 'that has pursued God relentlessly down the ages'. The pursuit goes on.

From India we flew to Africa, John wanted to see how money given by IDAF to South African refugees was being spent. I stayed with Tilly and Hugh in Kiambu and John went to Tanzania, then together we went to Zambia.

Lusaka is a rather dreary place, more like an extended suburb than a city. We lunched at State House, with Kenneth Kaunda and his wife, and were much impressed by the simplicity of their life. Kenneth said grace before lunch, and apologised for using his own language. 'I can't talk to God in English,' he explained. There were plenty of noises off from some of the children who appeared later. This is a musical family, and each one of the six – or is it seven – children plays some kind of a musical instrument, African and/or European. Kenneth spoke, as did Julius Nyerere, of his commitment to the cause of the liberation of Southern Africa, and of his determination to try and assist the refugees. But both countries, in the early stages of development, have their own economic and social problems. Both Nyerere and Kaunda wanted to work for a peaceful and harmonious African continent. It was after this visit that Kenneth Kaunda announced the award to John of the Zambian Order of Freedom, their highest honour for foreigners.

We had also been invited to a UN conference in Addis Ababa, on the twin topics of African economic development and the means of liberating Southern Africa. Like all conferences, there was a great deal of talk, and some questioning as to whether accelerated industrialisation really was the best route for independent Africa. Robert Resha, one of the participants, arranged for John to have an audience with Haile Selassie. So John was escorted past the famous lions and into the audience chamber. Here, on his throne, sat the Emperor, surrounded by subservient courtiers. He seemed a lonely and anachronistic figure; Julius Nyerere and Kenneth Kaunda were living in a different world. Addis Ababa was useful; it was the headquarters of the Organisation of African Unity, and there were a number of UN officials there, including our good friend Mr Reddy.

John was well satisfied with the visit. As well as talks with Nyerere and Kaunda, he talked with UN and Church officials concerned with refugees, and with numerous members of the liberation movements. He inspected their accounts carefully, and was able to state categorically that he was 'wholly satisfied that the money that we have provided has been used for such purposes as are consistent with our terms of reference'.

Back in England, we found the news from Southern Africa as bad as ever. When Ian Smith declared UDI, he made a contemptuous remark about the lack of ability of the African citizens of the country. Just to make sure, he detained a large number of the more able in prison camps. They and their families needed continuing assistance.

It was not just evidence of Africans' ability that offended Ian Smith and his all-white government, it was also evidence that black and white could live and work harmoniously and responsibly together. Such evidence was provided in Cold Comfort Farm, pioneered by Guy and Molly Clutton-Brock. The farm was a co-operative of about forty people, most of them Africans. They worked eighty-eight acres of land about six miles outside Salisbury. Molly Clutton-Brock ran a clinic on the farm, and at a time when Rhodesian farming seemed to be in decline, Cold Comfort Farm was flourishing. But not for long. The area was first designated 'for European occupation only'. Then, at the end of 1970, the Farm's treasurer Didymus Mutasa, a remarkable man, a Christian and pre-eminently a 'man of peace', was handed a detention order; he was considered to be 'a danger to public safety'. Soon two high-up members of the Special Branch arrived to hand Guy Clutton-Brock a notice depriving him of his Rhodesian citizenship, and within a short time he was forcibly deported. Guy was a dedicated believer in Gandhian non-violence. He too was considered 'a danger to public safety'.

Ian Smith maintained that the Africans were happy under the rule of the white man; those who were not were just agitators and Communists. So in 1972, the British government sent an enquiry headed by

Lord Pearce, to try to discover the true African opinion, and to find out what kind of a future they wanted for themselves. African leaders asked Defence and Aid if they could provide independent lawyers to assist them in presenting their evidence. We hired an experienced solicitor and a distinguished QC, Sir Dingle Foot. But the Smith government refused to accept Dingle Foot, so, instead we sent a young man who had been practising successfully for seven years, our eldest son, Andrew. He, of course, cost the Fund much less than Dingle Foot would have done.

Andrew stayed in Rhodesia for a month. He did a very good job, and the Africans trusted him. Their evidence was overwhelmingly opposed to Ian Smith's all-white government, and clear in their wish for independence and self-government. Later we sent Andrew again to Rhodesia, with his wife, also a barrister, to do some more work for IDAF. But by that time the authorities had realised who he was, and politely asked both of them to leave and not return. Ian Smith ignored the evidence presented to the Pearce Commission, and the country was exposed to eight more years of bloody war and destruction.

From South Africa came the familiar stories of brutality and torture. Winnie Mandela and twenty-one others had been arrested, and were now on trial. From May to October 1969 they had all been held incommunicado in solitary confinement under the notorious Terrorism Act. There were reports that the State had some eighty witnesses lined up, the majority of whom had also been held incommunicado in solitary confinement. We knew only too well what methods the Security Forces used to obtain their evidence. We also knew that fourteen people who had entered prison fit and healthy had already died at the hands of their interrogators.

A sinister figure, a Major Swanepoel, figured in many of the worst reports of torture; I wonder what has happened to him? A terrible fact of human nature is that the torturers come to enjoy their torturing. Another is that for a number of men violence is sexually stimulating, and reports from prison spoke as well of sexual assault and rape. Thanks to good legal defence, Winnie Mandela and her co-accused were all acquitted. Mrs Mandela was immediately banned and house-arrested.

We now had two new avenues for welfare assistance. Robbie Resha worked out an original idea. He went down to the Southampton docks, and met the ships arriving from South Africa. He got to know the mainly Coloured seamen, many of whom came from Cape Town, and had friends or relatives in political trouble. Robbie suggested

giving them money to take back for the political grass widows and
orphans. He insisted that those who received help must always write
letters of thanks and acknowledgement, so that we would have
receipts for the money expended. This route was never discovered.
Another volunteer who approached us was the newly appointed dean
of Johannesburg, Gonville ffrench Beytagh. He had a friend in London
with a healthy bank balance, so we arranged for IDAF money to be
sent through her for the dean to distribute. There were many families
in need in the Johannesburg area, and the dean did excellent work, but
he was too exposed. He was arrested, imprisoned, and charged under
that catch-all piece of legislation, the Suppression of Communism Act.

After ten days of interrogation, the original charges were withdrawn, and far more sinister ones were preferred under the Terrorism
Act. The dean was accused, on the evidence of a State witness, of
advocating the overthrow of the State by violence. The witness
declared that he had overheard the dean inciting a group of Black Sash
ladies to acts of violence (anything more improbable would be hard to
imagine). The clerk who operated the humanitarian Fund under the
dean's instructions testified that the money had been used solely for the
assistance of those in need; this evidence was ignored.

The dean was found guilty and sentenced to five years' imprisonment. He was given leave to appeal. John felt desperately that the
Anglican Church both in Britain and in South Africa must protest and
take action; he went to the Archbishop of Canterbury, Michael
Ramsey. 'We must pray,' said Ramsey. 'Of course,' said John, 'we
must always pray, but surely we should do something as well'. 'We
will all just have to go on praying,' said the archbishop. All John got
out of the Church was a statement by the Bishop of London, Gerald
Ellison, one of John's Westcott House pupils, that the London Diocese
would meet the cost of the dean's appeal. They did raise a certain
amount of money, the rest came from Defence and Aid.

The appeal was heard before the Chief Justice, and two appeal
judges. It was allowed, and the conviction and sentence were set aside.
The Chief Justice commented that the trial judge had erred in prefer-
ring the evidence of the State witness who was unsatisfactory and
contradictory. After this ordeal, the dean left South Africa and became
rector of a London City church.

At the end of 1970, I decided to give up editing the *Journal*; I felt I was
getting stale, and it was time for new voices to be heard. As I look
through the back numbers, I am impressed by all we did, and all the
topics that we aired. Specialists, public figures, and distinguished

writers were generous in producing first-class articles for us. We discussed problems of ecology, animal welfare, an increasingly automated society, over-population, the UN, a possible UN police force, as well as our more obvious concerns, housing, racial prejudice, Vietnam, problems of immigration, the National Health Service etc. These are only a few, and I can only touch on the numerous activities in which Christian Action found itself involved. Freda's log-book was always full; in fact she continued to run a one-woman welfare department, as well as organising our public meetings and weekend conferences, and – perhaps most difficult of all – trying to organise John.

One of the last things I did for the *Journal* was to report on an evening I spent just before Christmas at the Lambeth Shelter. Social workers have had a bad Press lately; those who worked at the Shelter were beyond praise. The fourteen beds were full every night, vagrant women came and went, but more and more the social workers found themselves taking in women and girls who were so mentally disturbed, so difficult or so helpless, that nobody else would have them.

The Lambeth Shelter was not some kind of human rubbish dump. There was an atmosphere in their modest downstairs kitchen – friendly, homely and compassionate, not just the compassion shown by the social workers, but the compassion and care shown by the inmates to one another. If anyone was in trouble, they would give readily and generously, from the depths of their own deprivation. These people were valuable as well as pitiable, many of them could be salvaged, some were already improving, and that could give hope and opportunity to their pathetic, otherwise doomed, children.

John now had more work to do in the cathedral. When the general turn-around of the various offices took place, Martin Sullivan proposed that John should take over the position of chapter treasurer. This was a friendly act on Martin's part; in the days before Martin became dean, and they were all canons together, John had told him about the time when the chapter had failed to appoint him. That little affair must have left a small hurt inside John, so Martin did something to repair it. John, of course, accepted, but in many ways he missed the precentorship, the choir was his real love, and he missed the contact with the choirmen. John eventually gave up being chapter treasurer, and became the cathedral treasurer, which meant responsibility for the 'treasures', not the finances, of the cathedral, as well as for the work of the virgers and the wandsmen.

In his time as a canon, John held all the greater offices. He was happy as cathedral treasurer, and he enjoyed once more the human contact with the virgers and the wandsmen, and they, I think, enjoyed John.

45

Sunshine and Shadow

THE problems and demands of Christian Action, Defence and Aid, St Paul's, could all be refreshingly thrown aside by even the briefest visit to Mill House. Some of my happiest hours were spent in silent but real companionship with John in the garden. I was content just to know that he was there. He attacked the weeds with ferocious energy; he hadn't had much success with the evils of the world – they went on flourishing in their wicked old way – the evils of the garden might be easier to eradicate. Personally I have a fairly tolerant attitude towards weeds except for one or two thugs – some weeds I positively like. John was against the lot; we never could agree about cow parsley.

Much love and affection, not only John's and mine, went into the making of Mill House. As I look around, I see so many presents from friends and family, pictures from our painting friends, delightful Dutch tiles in the kitchen, tapestry-covered chairs and cushions, objects beautifully crafted by the cathedral workmen – it was like getting married all over again. And in every room I see Millie Gleave's expert and imaginative sewing.

For many years Millie had come once a week to sew for the family, now she spent time at Mill House as well. During the war, when working voluntarily with the St John's Ambulance Brigade in Italy, she had married a charming ne'er-do-well officer who had soon abandoned her, leaving her to support, unaided, two little boys. As both her parents died within a short time, she had only what she could earn. Her working day began around four a.m., office cleaning, and continued often until around ten or ten-thirty p.m. with intervals to look after the boys. 'She's loving and giving,' or 'She's got fairies at the bottom of her garden': Millie's words of praise for people she liked, and a good description of Millie herself. She reckoned she had had a splendid life, she laughed at hardship and poverty, she laughed at herself, she made others laugh.

Once Mill House was in order, we could have friends and family to stay. I had a sandpit made, hoping optimistically that grandchildren might one day enjoy it. By 1974 three of the boys were married, and grandchildren did begin to appear. I used to think that women were ridiculously and boringly soppy about their grandchildren, but now I too have to plead guilty, though I do try not to be too boring about them. But when I saw my first grandchild, Andrew's son David, I was quite unprepared for the strength of the emotion that swept over me, I went about in a kind of daze, nursing this amazing secret joy.

So we worked in London, and at a very different kind of work in the country. There were signs of strain in John, his memory was beginning to fail, the *idées fixes* became more noticeable, his decisions were less reliable. For many years he had had to take pills for blood pressure. For some time, we had tried to find a director for IDAF, who would relieve John of some of the travelling and money-raising, I think it was I who pushed this hardest, and I was mistaken. Whoever was appointed – at least three took their turn – was in an impossible position, trapped between John who was unwilling to delegate, and Phyllis, whose detailed knowledge of South Africa and of all the intricacies of IDAF was unrivalled. We had to keep finding things for these unfortunate men to do, and Phyllis, with some justification, thought John was a male chauvinist, because the men were paid more than the women.

In September 1974 we were at Mill House enjoying a delicious end of summer, when, early one morning, John had a coronary. The local doctor arrived within minutes, and in less than half an hour, had a consultant out from Colchester. They looked at the beautiful and peaceful view from our bedroom window, and said that if I felt I could manage, they would prefer to leave him where he was rather than bundle him off into intensive care in Colchester. Of course I could manage, it wasn't such a bad attack, though it was serious enough.

John was a good and uncomplaining patient, and neighbours were unfailingly helpful; I never had to do any household shopping. Dr Brown was an old-fashioned country doctor, his patients loved him, he knew not only them, but their families and circumstances, he would come out at any time of the day or night. He visited John daily.

It was at this time that John's elder brother Ted died suddenly from a coronary. John was very fond of his brother, and was just well enough to attend, though not to take, the funeral.

After Christmas we were back at Amen Court, and John was back in Defence and Aid, and Christian Action. A number of people who had worked with Colin stayed on with Christian Action, and the new space in our basement soon became occupied, at first by RAP (Radical Alternative to Prison) and then by CHAR (Campaign for the Homeless and Rootless), two small projects that had attached themselves to Christian Action. Earnest long-haired young men were to be seen about in the basement. RAP held meetings and discussion groups and produced literature. The recognition that prison life is destructive of human personality becomes increasingly prevalent, and discussion about alternatives, especially for young offenders, is mounting. Some of the RAP's literature was factual, instructive and forward-looking, some was over-combative and aggressive in tone, and tended therefore to be counterproductive. CHAR was an attempt to co-ordinate the various voluntary agencies concerned with homelessness, in order to mount a concerted campaign of pressure upon the government. Many of its proposals are still being discussed, and – very tentatively – supported by authority, but it is all too evident that, twenty years later, the situation has done nothing but deteriorate.

On 23 March John reached the age of 'three score years and ten'. Although many of us live much longer, this is still thought of as a climacteric, to be specially observed and celebrated, after that it is 'borrowed time', 'downhill all the way'. So various celebrations for John were planned. Our good friend, John Morrison, with my help, organised a dinner to take place in the Stationers Hall, just opposite Amen Court. It was a splendid occasion, with about seventy people present. Frank Longford took the chair, Jack Priestley, Edward Carpenter and Kadar Asmal spoke, and since Oliver Tambo was unable to come to London his wife Adelaide Tambo spoke in his place; a group of St Paul's choirmen came and sang to us. The boys and I had given John a green velvet smoking jacket for evening wear, and with his wavy and whitening hair worn rather longer in deference to fashion he looked handsome.

It was the spirit of the evening that gave us the greatest pleasure, something felt by all present and remarked upon by many. I wrote to Jacquetta, 'We did feel that there was a rather marvellous spirit about it, and I think it really did something for John. As I saw him stand up and reply to all his friends I suddenly felt – as I hadn't quite felt before – that he was completely better again.'

There was more to come, Adelaide Tambo organised a special extra party for John from all our anti-apartheid South African friends. It was a magnificent affair – Adelaide does everything with style and a care for detail. There was a fine birthday cake with seventy candles on it, tributes to John, singing and dancing, excellent food and drink, a great

bouquet of flowers for me, and presents for John that included a very
fine wristwatch – how did she know that was exactly what he needed?
It was a wonderfully happy and jolly evening.

The AGMs of IDAF took place in turn in countries where there
were active committees, this year, 1975, it was Dublin. The situation
in Southern Africa was changing dramatically with the collapse of
the Portuguese colonial empire, and the liberation of Angola,
Mozambique and Guinea-Bissau. This alarmed the South African
government and its white supporters, especially as the newly independent governments were Socialist and mildly Marxist-orientated. Mr
Vorster feared that they might be used as bases from which to attack
South-West Africa (Namibia) and South Africa itself. The ANC
armed by the Russians might escalate its armed incursions into the
Republic. So Mr Vorster made visits to African states, and began to
talk about peace and détente, and a progress towards democracy inside
South Africa.

John was not impressed by this talk of détente: he knew that the
South African government had a record of promising one thing and
doing the opposite, he made a conference speech to that effect. Soon
the Vorster government proceeded to foment bitter, bloody and
destructive civil wars in both Mozambique and Angola. They armed,
trained and built up Renamo in Mozambique, and with the assistance
of the USA did the same with Unita in Angola. These tactics of
duplicity remain unchanged. This was a sober meeting, but it was
followed by another happy party for John, laid on by Kadar and Louise
Asmal in their home, with Irish folksongs and Irish dances, and the
presentation to John of a beautiful facsimile of *The Book of Kells*.

The period of celebration was not yet ended. In December there was
a public announcement: 'By decree of 18 December 1975, His Majesty
the King of Sweden has appointed Canon L. John Collins a Commander of the Northern Star (Sweden) in recognition of his services as
President of the International Defence and Aid Fund for Southern
Africa.' John got quite a lot of honour outside his own country which
was pleasant and gratifying, but incomparably more important and
rewarding was the friendship and affection that he inspired in so many
different people around the world, and there was plenty of that from
within his own country too.

By the end of 1975, Ian Henderson, John Morrison and I had put
together a seventieth birthday Festschrift, *Man of Christian Action*. John
Morrison arranged for the publication, Ian Henderson was the official
editor and wrote an article about the housing work, and I saw to the

rest. I impressed upon those invited to write that it was to be a serious examination and critique of the work, its mistakes as well as its value, so that this could be a tribute to all that Christian Action had done and had initiated, as well as a tribute to John. There were a number of thoughtful and perceptive articles, and Jack Priestley provided a characteristically brilliant introduction.

'Canon Collins,' he wrote, 'is not only an unusual man but also he is an *unusual* unusual man. What do I mean by this? . . . most unusual men are going to prove it at first sight. They will show you at once that they are extraordinary fellows, far removed from the common run. The *unusual* unusual man (very rare) makes no such effort . . . He just goes on being himself, leaving you to discover gradually his unique and rewarding quality . . .

'He was, I began to realise, no ordinary rebellious cleric . . . To begin with he was not really an ideologue. Instead of referring people and their needs, hopes and fears to a system . . . he saw them as fellow human beings. To see people in these terms and then to be at their disposal demands not only good feeling but also enormous patience . . . I soon discovered that he had one important ally. This was a notable sense of humour . . .

'Nevertheless, he too is a parson . . . sustaining everything this man has done and does, the whole wide range of his activities, his rich response to every human appeal, is a deep living faith . . . I rarely meet a real Christian. We have one here, one secure in his belief, and prepared to put it into practice.'

Nineteen seventy-six was the year of the children's uprising in Soweto. The government gave notice of a new restriction upon African education. Under the Bantu Education Act, elementary instruction had to be in one of the tribal languages; from then on, said the new decree, it was to be in Afrikaans. The teenage boys and girls understood very well that this was yet another attempt to hold them back, to ensure that they would be handicapped in making their way in the larger world. They decided to demonstrate against this new imposition; they made placards which they carried before them. These said 'We come in peace'. They began their march, hundreds of them, through the township. The response of the police was to shoot; many children and young people were killed and wounded.

One photograph was flashed around the world, a youth running away, and carrying in his arms the dead body of thirteen-year-old Hector Petersen, the first casualty of the shooting. The youth himself feared for his life, he went into hiding, and was neither seen nor heard of again. This was the beginning of what can only be described as a war against the African children waged by the Security Forces. Report after report reached us of shootings, detentions and tortures of even quite young children. There was an exodus of young refugees, mostly in their late teens and early twenties, many of whom found their way to SOMAFCO, the ANC school in Tanzania, established on land given to them by Julius Nyerere. Numbers also fled to London.

An inevitable result was a sudden and dramatic increase in the work of IDAF, as detentions and trials followed each other. There was a huge expansion of the need for family welfare. The young people who had left the country feared, with reason, for their parents, often mothers left alone to care for younger brothers and sisters.

Faced with the tear gas and the guns of police and army, the young themselves inevitably became violent. They had no tear gas and no guns, so they threw stones and set fire to cars and suspect buildings. As the situation worsened, and the bitterness increased, they discovered 'necklacing', a peculiarly horrible method of killing by fastening a burning petrol-soaked tyre round the neck of the victim; this was applied to police informers and collaborators. Killing is killing: somehow death by shooting appears cleaner, more respectable, more acceptable than death by burning. There was widespread horror at this new African tactic, but I heard little comparable horror expressed over the killing and maiming of unarmed children by the enormously powerful, well-armed and well-protected Security Forces. Necklacing was condemned by the external ANC leadership, and I certainly have no wish to justify it. It was finally stopped, at least as far as ANC supporters were concerned, by the firm personal intervention of Oliver Tambo.

More work for IDAF meant the need for more money. Our Scandinavian friends came to the rescue, and even the US Carter administration donated a modest sum. Successive British governments turned a deaf ear to UN appeals. British governments did not even contribute to the UN Trust Fund. There was one exception, under a Labour government. The Minister of Overseas Development, Judith Hart, was allocated a sum of money for distribution. She gave the bulk of this to the International University Exchange Fund (IUEF) based in Geneva. Shortly afterwards, this organisation was exposed as having been infiltrated by a top South African agent, who became its deputy director. He had tried hard, under guise of co-operation, to infiltrate IDAF, but was always prevented by Phyllis Altman.

Considerable misuse of money was also revealed, and IUEF was disbanded. We at IDAF were furious.

It was towards the end of 1977 that we lost another South African friend, Robbie Resha. Robbie had been going downhill for some time, and John had been unhappy at the rift between Robbie and the ANC, I don't think he ever quite understood it. The night that Robbie was dying, he wanted to see John, so our doctor son, Mark, drove him to the hospital. They stayed until Robbie lost consciousness, but just before that he began drowsily to recite 'The Lord is my Shepherd,' and he and John finished it together. The next day John received an urgent telephone call from Robbie's daughter, Chabe: she had something from Robbie that she must deliver to John immediately. This was an envelope containing a sum of money that Robbie had been unable to deliver to his seamen friends at Southampton. Robbie was faithful to the end.

John seemed physically fit, though naturally he tired more easily, but I knew that he ought to be thinking about retirement. I dared not let him travel alone, he might have forgotten important things, including his heart and blood pressure pills. But the last thing John wanted to think about was retirement. He was happy to be at Mill House – 'This really is a lovely place,' he often said to me – but he didn't want to live there. 'We have created an earthly paradise. Won't you come and live in it with me?' I pleaded, but I got nowhere. John's bulldog tenacity, his need to respond actively to any kind of challenge, and to give everything in him to the cause were what made his work and his campaigning so successful. But these same qualities became an obstinate determination to soldier on: he could never see retirement as another, if very different kind of challenge; it remained to him an abdication. However, John did agree that some new arrangement should be made for the continuation of IDAF.

So the next few years were spent in working out a new constitution, and in setting up an International Board of Trustees, people of experience and standing who would oversee the Fund, and who would inspire the necessary confidence in our donors. This took a long time, and involved many meetings and discussions. A new constitution was finally accepted, and provision made for the National Committees to have a say in policy and the election of Trustees. We only lost the Swiss who didn't like the new arrangements, the Dutch had been vocally critical all along, but they decided to stay, and have been one of the most successful and co-operative of IDAF committees.

The International Board of Trustees came at long last into being on

14 May 1982, with John as chairman, Ernst Michanek as vice-chairman, and Archbishop Trevor Huddleston; Thorvald Stoltenberg from Norway was soon added.

October 1978 found John and me once more at the UN in New York. This time it was a meeting with a difference. Mr Reddy was always coming up with new ideas for the promotion of the anti-apartheid cause. His latest was the institution of a UN Gold Medal for work against apartheid, and, along with a number of others, John was to be presented with one of these medals at a special session of the General Assembly. As John would have to speak to the General Assembly, Reddy asked me to give the customary annual IDAF speech to the Special Committee against Apartheid. Speaking at the UN is not so much alarming as frustrating: the audiences have to listen to so many speeches, that they have become almost incapable of response – it is like trying to punch an extremely soft pillow. I have never spoken to an audience from which I felt no kind of comeback, either of agreement or disagreement, it wasn't an experience I enjoyed. I was given a tape of the speech, which I played to my father when I got home; he began to cry and said in a very shaky voice, 'I am very proud of my daughter', that nearly made me cry.

John wisely decided not to make a proper speech to the General Assembly. He said a few spontaneous words of genuine gratitude, and gratitude for all the people who had shared his work. This unusual freshness and reality was enough of a surprise to stir this great world-weary gathering into truly appreciative applause.

46

Last Years

OCTOBER 21, 1979 – our Ruby Wedding – forty years of marriage. We decided to spoil ourselves. I had never been to the Lake District, so we selected one of the best hotels, Sharrow Bay, and booked in for a week. We were very lucky, only one wet day out of the seven, and that we devoted to culture and Wordsworthiana. The day of our anniversary was a Sunday. We got up in a thick white mist and went to find a local church, which, to our delight, still used Cranmer's version of the Eucharist. The hotel assured us it would be fine, packed us a picnic lunch, and we set off to climb up out of the mist, and were soon in glorious sunshine. It was a perfect day, and we were rather proud of ourselves by the time we got to the summit of a not too demanding mountain. Fell walkers are notoriously friendly, and in our exaltation we were inclined to tell everyone who greeted us that it was our fortieth wedding anniversary; they congratulated us indulgently. The evening was just as good; the hotel faced west, and looked over the wide expanse of Ullswater to mountains at the far end. As we sat over our pre-dinner drinks, nature presented us with a magnificent sunset display. Dinner was rather too good, as was most of the food at Sharrow Bay, and our dear son Andrew had been in touch with the hotel and ordered for us, at his expense, a selection of their very best wines.

I had been thinking seriously about women and men in marriage and in the Church. I was actively involved in the movement for the ordination of women (MOW), another campaign that had originated in the basement at 2 Amen Court. The Church seemed to me to be stuck with the secular social attitudes of its early centuries. It ignored the liberation in Jesus's treatment of women as children of God equal with men. He broke taboo after taboo, talked with the Samaritan woman, commended the woman with the issue of blood, though under Judaic law she was ritually unclean, and no one would have dared to touch her; he refused to uphold the sentence of the law in regard to the woman taken in adultery, and welcomed the woman 'who was a sinner'. What had gone wrong? Much of it, I thought, was due to the elevation of virginity as being higher up on the scale of sanctity, than living a normal sexual life. A hatred of the flesh developed, which seems strange in a religion of incarnation. All this was as damaging to men as it was to women.

I was appalled by some of the clerical objections that I heard voiced. 'You might as well ordain a dog as ordain a woman,' and, in tones of horror, 'But you *couldn't* have a woman celebrating the Eucharist when she was menstruating'. Old taboos die hard.

As for tradition, Jesus chose only men to be his close disciples and lead his wandering life; anything else would have been impractical. But these were all circumcised Jews, not a Gentile among them. We cannot *literally* follow tradition. The Anglican Synod has already decided by a large majority that there are no valid theological objections to ordaining women. So why are they waiting so fearfully?

John's and my marriage began in a traditional way. I accepted that my role would be to support John in all that he did; that was what I wanted to do, and what I would want to do again. It might have been different had I already had or had wanted a professional career; as it was, I was exceptionally fortunate. Of course there is no formula for a happy marriage, only an endless variety of different personal adjustments. Anything can be worked out, anything can be survived, if you love each other. On another wedding anniversary a few years earlier, I was in hospital for some minor operation, and John wrote me a letter: 'Despite modest ups and downs on the road the journey has been a wonderful and a happy one all the way. . . . I love and adore you as much, and much more, than ever I did on that glorious day when the spindleberries (and he who put them there) were the symbol of so much love and affection and goodwill that have aided us on our way.

'You are and always have been a lovely, a beautiful and an inspiring companion in love.'

I wish I could have found something similar from me, all I could discover among John's papers was a rather dull birthday card. Inside it I apologised for its pedestrian appearance, and wrote 'the love that comes with it is not at all pedestrian, that goes on wings, and never wears out'. And that was, and remained, nothing less than the truth.

Nineteen-eighty and 1981 were in many ways not easy, though, as always, we had good holidays, and good times together. But John was unwilling to admit to his failing faculties, or to face the prospect of retirement. I wish that I had been more sympathetic, more understanding, more consistently patient; there are things I wish I had never said. If he would only accept, I thought, how much easier it would all be.

While we were debating the future of IDAF we spent time consulting with our Scandinavian friends. Per and Annalena had separated and Per was now with Margaretta Ekstrom and their two children. We spent a midsummer in a wild and lovely place on the edge of a forest, with a separate little wooden house for visitors. There we were joined by Abdul and Kari from Norway. As well as consulting, we observed the traditional Swedish midsummer ritual. We rose early to collect wild flowers from the forest, with which we decorated a maypole and made wreaths for ourselves. Revived by alcohol, and to the accompaniment of a traditional band, we all danced round the maypole which is, I suppose, an ancient fertility symbol. There was more alcohol, and delicious food served 'à l'herbe'. Abdul looked like a faun out of the forest, while John's floral wreath sat askew on his thick hair; I suspect he was a little intoxicated.

In 1978 John and I had been invited to celebrate the independence of Zimbabwe. Sadly, I was in hospital, I was bitterly disappointed. There was a muddle over John's accommodation, and he was eventually rescued by his old friend Joshua Nkomo, who took him to his own home. John came back very tired.

As for me, St Bartholomew's Hospital saved my life. I had all kinds of afflictions, an alarmingly racing heart, blood pressure, overactive thyroid; it took some time, and various hospital sessions, before they got me right. I owe an enormous debt to the National Health Service. Apart from the fact that it is difficult to get enough sleep, I rather enjoy life on the wards. A great camaraderie develops among the patients, and you meet all kinds of interesting people, usually far worse off than yourself. In a big teaching hospital, I think, you see human nature at its best, certainly at its multi-racial best – the health service would collapse without the work of the immigrant community.

Our last years in Amen Court were made rewarding by friendship with Evan and Puck Pilkington who came to live next door to us. I am often critical of the Anglican hierarchy, but we have known many fine priests. Evan Pilkington was one of the best, a wonderfully understanding priest and pastor.

By 1981 it was time to go. John at last succumbed to pressure, from people other than me. He agreed that he would retire from St Paul's at the end of November 1981. Even so, whenever I made some reference to it, he countered with, '*If* we retire'. We began to give 'goodbye' parties. Our only sizeable one was a celebration of Millie Gleave's seventieth birthday. I asked her if she minded it being combined with a farewell party. 'I've always shared the good things in my life,' she said.

So there we all were, Millie and her friends and family, my family including my brothers and sister, people from the office, Freda, that backbone of our thirty-three tumultuous years in Amen Court, plenty of children around, and our indispensable helpers, smiling and undefeated by life's hardships and problems: Mrs Miles, plump and jolly, making a joke out of any misfortune; Mrs McShane, a tough dour Scot crippled by arthritis and with a hard life behind her; Mrs Parkins who cleaned the office, and her sister Rosie Claridge, who took over and then asked if she might come upstairs and work for us.

It took me more than six months to clear out 2 Amen Court, with all its large cupboards into which it had been so easy to store things, and then forget about them. I got no help from John. He so hated the whole process that he tried to pretend that it wasn't really happening. By the end I felt that I would like to be an anchorite living in a bare cell, so cluttered up were we with things. When the time came for John to sign the letter of resignation, Freda and I had to stand over him to make sure that he did it.

July was John's last month in residence. He took part in two special services that seemed to symbolise the two poles of his ministry at St Paul's. The first was the fairy-tale royal wedding of Prince Charles and Lady Diana. The weather suddenly cleared and became fine and warm, people slept out on the streets, there was no trouble or disturbance, the whole of England was on holiday, problems of poverty, homelessness, racism, drugs, violence, all were laid aside and forgotten. John, ever loyal to his own, was critical of the singing in the service. He said that Kiri te Kanawa sang flat, she didn't understand the St Paul's echo, it should have been left to our own choir. My unattuned ears couldn't recognise flat or sharp. I thought it all splendid, and I particularly liked Kiri's rainbow-coloured clothes. After the service we had a champagne party in Amen Court, presided over by John.

A week later John officiated at another wedding. Down in the crypt, he married Oliver Tambo's elder daughter Tembi to Martin, a young Hungarian, who had been brought up in England. This too was a special occasion, beautifully organised by Adelaide who, as always, made all her own clothes and looked gorgeous. The reception was held at the Reform Club. It was not only a multi-racial party, it was a united South Africa party. Oliver had invited people from across the whole political spectrum. He made one of the loveliest wedding speeches I have ever heard; it was a glimpse of an ideal, peaceful non-racial South Africa.

Leaving St Paul's was a terrible wrench, and the kinder and nicer everyone was, the harder it was to go. Of course, our sons were sad at the loss of the family home, but I was unprepared for the distress of our older grandchildren. They couldn't at all understand why we had to go: it was very wrong of us, no more family Christmas parties, no more sliding down the banisters, no more special seats for the Lord Mayor's Show, no more little privileges in St Paul's. I felt quite guilty at having so shattered their confidence in life.

Abdul Minty had suggested that IDAF should buy a flat, and our treasurer, Reg Gore, approved. Property prices were rising steadily, and in the event of a cash crisis, the flat could be sold. Meanwhile, John and I could have the use of it, and John could continue his work for the Fund.

I found a flat in a rather horrible concrete block on the south side of Blackfriars Bridge, and within easy walking distance of the Defence and Aid office in Newgate Street, where Freda, with her assistant secretary Jean, would have two small rooms and would continue to look after John and his affairs. The flat was comfortable, and its main room large enough for IDAF meetings. I soon began to enjoy the South Bank, and John was happy not to have to cut his links with IDAF.

Since John was finally leaving St Paul's, the media suddenly became more interested in us than was their habit. They were unusually sympathetic too, though one particular journalist did refer to me as John's 'bustling wife'. John and our sons thought this very funny, I naturally preferred the friend who wrote of John's 'sparkling wife'.

On 1 December we said a final goodbye. I, who had been so reluctant to move to Amen Court, wept as we left. What an amazing, unexpected, exciting thirty-three years it had been.

Two days after our move, my father died. He was old, he was ill, he was irascible and could be very difficult. My stepmother had died in 1977, and finding housekeepers and carers for my father had been something of a nightmare, but he was my father and I loved him.

47

Love is the Only Reality

E ARLY in February John and I were invited to spend the weekend
with the provost of Oriel and his wife; John was to preach in the
college chapel. We were always happy to revisit Oxford, and on our
first morning we went for a nostalgic walk round Christ Church
meadows, in a sparkling dance of frost and sunlight. Suddenly quite
distinctly and recognisably I heard Victor's voice. 'Love *is* the only
reality,' he said. This was not something I imagined, I was not, and had
not been, thinking about Victor, but it is impossible not to recognise
a unique human voice that you have heard and have known well over
many years. You can explain this as you will, an hallucination, a
psycho-sensorial phenomenon welling up from the depths of the
unconscious, whatever it was, to me it was authentically real. It was as
if Victor were saying, 'All we believed and talked about so often really
is true.'

Unfortunately, during our last night, John had a fall in the
bathroom, and hurt his right arm sufficiently for me to take him to
have it X-rayed. No bones were broken, but it was badly bruised and
twisted, it pained him for several weeks.

In a calm and sunlit autumn we went to Vienna on behalf of IDAF.
John hoped to persuade the Austrian government to contribute
directly to the Fund, or perhaps to award it the annual Kreisky human
rights prize. Although we had a friendly session with the ailing Bruno
Kreisky, our hopes did not materialise. But we had an exceptionally
pleasant few days, including a visit to the opera for a special
performance of *La Bohème*. Everyone was in evening dress, long and
elegant for the ladies, and in that beautiful, historic ambience, all was
magical and romantic.

It was after Vienna that John began to accept that the time was
approaching when he would have to leave Defence and Aid. He finally
agreed that he would resign the chairmanship at the end of the year.
IDAF was changing; with a board of trustees, it would become more

bureaucratic, and John would not have the freedom of decision and action to which he was accustomed. Once this decision was taken, John became calmer and easier. It was, I suppose, about the beginning of December that he began to complain about pain down his right arm. His mind went back to Oxford. 'I must have done more damage than we thought to this arm,' he said. Foolishly I accepted this, but the pain had a far more sinister origin.

Over the years we had had a number of reunions with the Fellowship of the Transfiguration, and they were much in John's thoughts. So together we composed one of his Christmas pastoral letters. It has a strangely, perhaps not so strangely, elegiac note. John wrote: 'Christmas and Easter – the great festivals of the Christian year – reflect the rhythms of nature, the natural rhythms of birth and death to which we, with the whole material world are all subject. But through our faith we see this rhythm as a sacrament of the true, the spiritual life. We know that in every death there is the seed of a new life, and in every loss and sorrow there is the seed of hope.

'We belong to the Fellowship of the Transfiguration, and our hope is that our human nature with all its weaknesses, its failures, its ignorance, and its sin will not only be redeemed, but will ultimately be transfigured in a manner that we cannot possibly imagine. All we know is that the only possible instrument of such a transfiguration is the power of love. And that love is something that we can begin – however inadequately – to learn and to practise in our life on earth. To quote William Blake:

> "And we are put on earth a little while
> That we may learn to bear the beams of love." '

We spent Christmas in London, as we had always done, so we were able to go to the services at St Paul's and listen to the choir that John loved. Midday Christmas dinner we had with Andrew and Nikki in their Dulwich home. Their two children David aged seven and Emma aged four were the perfect age for Christmas. Our bachelor son Peter was with us. Nikki is an excellent and imaginative cook, and Andrew, in his selection and appreciation of wine, is a true son of his father.

Richard had spent Christmas with his wife Diana and their two children in their country cottage near Newark. He was now back in London doing something with the Festival Ballet, so on the evening of 30 December he came to dinner in the flat. Richard is always a life-enhancer, and what with Christmas drinks and Christmas cigars, we had an exceptionally happy and jolly evening. John was in splendid form. As we went to bed, he made me a little speech, saying what a lovely marriage we had had, and how happy and exciting it had all been.

We woke early as we usually did, and John got up and brought me a cup of tea in bed. Then suddenly he said, 'I feel rather awful'. He looked as he had done on the morning of that first coronary. I got him back to bed and dressed quickly. 'I think its subsiding a bit,' he said. I didn't know what to do, it was still early, and in this holiday period so many doctors, including John's consultant, would be away; our doctor son, Mark, was also away. I thought I would see how John was, and would ring the hospital a little later. I went out and got a newspaper, John picked it up, and began to look at it. He didn't feel like any breakfast, but said I should go along to the kitchen to get some for myself.

After a few minutes, something made me go back to our bedroom. John had tossed the paper aside. 'I'm going this time,' he said, and within seconds he was – unbelievably – dead.

I rang 999, cherishing an unrealistic flicker of hope. It took a little time, and then two men appeared. The senior one was very tall and very black. 'How long has it been since you called?' he asked anxiously. 'About ten minutes,' I said. He shook his head, and put away his life-support machine. 'Even if we could get his heart going again,' he said, 'there would be too much brain damage'. He and his white colleague were immensely kind. I felt nothing at all, as if I had been turned into a block of ice. The black man held my hand. 'It's shock,' he said, 'but you will feel it later. You must be careful with yourself.'

As no doctor had been in charge or present at the death, no official could sign the necessary certificate. John would have to have an autopsy. They sent me briefly out of the room while they got him ready, and then left me on my own to say 'goodbye'. I kissed John for the last time. Then they took him away.

When Phyllis Altman heard the news she said: 'He met death just as he met life – head on.'

48

Bereavement, Consolation

I telephoned Andrew, who came at once, and took all the formalities off my shoulders. I asked him to telephone friends and relatives. Then Richard and Peter came, and we telephoned Mark, who was desperately distressed and guilty that he – the doctor – was not able to be there; I felt sorriest of all for him. We had the support of each other. By then the Press were clamouring at the doors; I had forgotten about them.

I had a sense of total unreality; I reacted like an automaton, did everything that I had to do and was asked to do; I felt nothing. John's death was announced on the one o'clock news, and immediately the telephone rang: it was Evan Pilkington, I was so glad to hear his voice. So many English people tend to flee in embarrassment from death and grief, as if they were something contagious.

Andrew took me home with him. I mustn't attempt to drive for several weeks, he said, not after such a shock. We could come back to the flat tomorrow for letters and messages. When our seven-year-old grandson, David, saw me, he rushed sobbing into my arms: 'I want to *see* Grandpa, I want to kiss him goodbye,' he kept pleading. That was when the ice began to crack. There is much wisdom in the worldwide custom of summoning relatives and friends to 'view the body' and take a last, almost formal farewell; it seems a deeply felt need, in children as much as in adults.

On Sunday morning, Andrew took me to St Paul's. That was painful and consoling, as were so many things. Bishop Kenneth Woollcombe who had succeeded John in the canonry preached about him. People came up to me in tears.

It was as well that there was so much to do, so many things to be decided. The avalanche of letters began to arrive from all over the world. I was determined to answer them all, and in the end I did, though I doubt if I could have managed it without the help of Freda and Jean.

Adelaide Tambo was one of my earliest visitors. She held me in her large comforting arms; Adelaide, among her other talents, is a first-class nurse. Africans have a custom when somebody dies: they come to the family to talk about the person who has gone, to extol his or her virtues. In the case of a great man there must be long speeches, and this can take many days. Africans regard our Western attitude to death as extraordinarily casual. African friends brought me much consolation, some of them wanted to speak about John in St Paul's, they couldn't understand our strict Anglican formality.

Then Oliver Tambo came, and that is something I shall remember always with tremendous gratitude. The South Africans had carried out a bombing raid on Maseru, the capital of independent Lesotho, and a number of ANC refugees had been killed. Oliver, at great personal risk, went to Maseru to bury his comrades. He had hardly returned, exhausted, to Lusaka, when he heard of John's death. He wrote me a sweet letter and came at once, travelling across Africa day and night without sleep. 'It is African custom,' he said. 'The eldest son must always come to bury his father. I regard myself as John's African eldest son.'

The evening before John's funeral service in St Paul's, his coffin was brought into the cathedral and placed in the choir, with four large and lighted candles, one at each corner. There were a few brief prayers, and silence. It was very quiet, very peaceful. Subdued lighting was left on all night in the choir, and the candles were left burning.

John's old pupil, Bishop Mervyn Stockwood, conducted the funeral service and James Fisher preached. Two very old friends – in James's case a friendship of more than fifty years. John had, said James, 'An energy of the spirit towards justice, righteousness and the protection of the weak, and towards his embracing friendship . . . He was a man resolute to see justice and freedom established, and more than most men he was successful in that seemingly endless endeavour.

'He was a priest under God who achieved his own kind of priesthood, a priesthood not to a parish, but to the world.'

It was all, as I had wished, very simple and personal, and there were a great many people in the cathedral. Oliver Tambo read the parable of the Good Samaritan more beautifully than I have ever heard it read, before or since. And then an African choir sang a lovely and haunting Zulu lament. The hymns I had chosen were, 'Once to every man and nation', which could have been written for John, and one of our wedding hymns, 'Immortal, invisible, God only wise'. The marvellous St Paul's choir sang the Russian Contakion of the Departed.

I was overwhelmed by all the hundreds of letters. I quote one or two: 'A deeply consoling priest, wise and yet without pomposity or self-importance, a very human, even stumbling, channel for the Holy Spirit.' 'John was a great man, but he was also a very loving one . . . that, I suspect, was why he was great.' 'He was so kind and understanding, and he had such an abundance of love in his heart for people, an inspiration, a special kind of prophet.' 'I look back with delight and pride to the time when he and I toured the country on behalf of CND. He was . . . a marvellous leader, tactful and firm at the same time. I worked more happily with John than with any other leader I have followed. He leaves behind him a noble memory which is itself an inspiration.' (A.J.P. Taylor)

Africans wrote me beautiful and often poetic letters. John had been given an African name, Mlamlankunzi, 'one who stands in between two fighting bulls'. Several of them said how much they appreciated the fact that John never tried to dictate to them, impose his own ideas, or tell them how to run their affairs. 'He always made us walk tall,' they said.

Raymond Kunene wrote a poem for John:

> I saw your arms flung against their night like
>   streaks of lightning
> I heard your echoes of friendliness like peals
>   of thunder.
> You planted green mushrooms in the bowels of a cave
> To be reaped in the quiet season;
> Like the moon-flower that is born a thousand years
>   in secret,
> To feed and nourish each new generation with
>   the ancestral dream.
> There are those who come with every season
> Whose vision bursts into the wombs of the universe
> Like time – infinite, their cycles like the twilight
>   children of the sun.

In Central African mythologies, Raymond explained, the green mushrooms are symbols of growth and cleansing, while 'children of the sun' are very special people. 'Their greatest suffering comes from the suffering of others. They are often pained by the present, since they live far beyond their time. It is this quality that makes them beautiful in the sense of an inner excellence and serenity'.

Some five or six weeks later, St Paul's held a Service of

Thanksgiving for John. I spent a long time planning and thinking about it, and I drew up a service. Looking back, I am not surprised that the chapter jibbed: I was not a professional, not ordained, only a woman. They said it was much too long. 'The City only allows three-quarters of an hour,' pronounced the new archdeacon. 'The City didn't love John, they needn't come,' I said. The dean, Alan Webster, was helpful and supportive and in the end I got what I wanted: the prayers, the readings, the music, all with special relevance to John's life and work, and a time of silence for our Quaker friends.

Rather diffidently, I asked Trevor Huddleston, then Archbishop of the Indian Ocean, to preach. He put everything aside, and faced the exhausting plane journey. It was, Trevor realised, not the place for the intimate personal note of a funeral, nor even a national occasion, it was international: 'We are remembering,' he said, 'a man who, in all his public ministry, dedicated himself to world issues, and pleaded with his fellow countrymen to recognise before it was too late, that "patriotism is not enough" . . . John's monument . . . is not of stone, however magnificent . . . His monument is the lives of hundreds of thousands, perhaps of millions, in Africa who have never seen him, but who, because of him and his life's work, still live in hope of that day which surely must come soon when: "The mountain of the Lord's house shall be set over all other mountains lifted high above the hills. Peoples shall come streaming to it. And many nations shall say: 'Come. Let us climb up.' " That is the message of John Collins' life'.

There is a monument to John in the crypt of St Paul's, inscribed on a piece of slate which came from Canon Alexander's old larder in 2 Amen Court. It reads:

> He worked for reconciliation between races and nations, and helped those who were deprived, persecuted, imprisoned or exiled. He founded and directed Christian Action, International Defence and Aid for Southern Africa, and with others the Campaign for Nuclear Disarmament.
> 'In as much as ye have done it unto the least of these my brethren, ye have done it unto me.'

The UN remembered John, they held a special memorial meeting, at which representatives of governments, and of the South African liberation movements, and of various humanitarian organisations spoke. The deputy permanent representative for Britain spoke. He said that he was proud to be a compatriot of such a man as John. By the end, you might have imagined that John, if not actually a member of the Establishment, at least had their wholehearted approval!

I had somehow to get used to living alone, not something I thought I would ever be able to do. At first, in the flat it was easier. Mark was back home; he had left a broken marriage, and divorce proceedings behind him in America. For a few months he came to live with me in 11 Rennie Court, and I hoped that I might be able to help him back on his feet; he certainly helped me.

I still had to face Mill House. I took Millie Gleave with me. Millie knew about bereavement and grief, she had seen plenty of it. She was the right companion, never fussed me, just helped. The bulbs that John and I had planted in the autumn were a blaze of glory, just as we had planned and hoped; it was hard to see it all looking so lovely, without John to share it.

But there was a touching surprise for me at Mount Bures. When the news of John's death spread, there was a whip-round in the village for money to put up a memorial to him in our beautiful little church. I was much moved by this.

In affectionate memory of Canon L. John Collins. He lived in Mount Bures for twelve years, and worshipped and preached in this Church.

Going Onwards

AT the conclusion of *Faith under Fire*, John wrote: 'It is the very essence of my faith that I must never stand anywhere. The life of faith is a pilgrimage, a going onwards in trust, a searching towards an end that is hoped for but unknown.'

For forty-four years, John and I journeyed together, influencing, sharing, changing, but never submerging our unique personal experience. For this last part of my journey, that I have to make without the comfort of his physical presence, I do not feel separated from him. In that sudden moment of his death, the idea that this was the obliteration of his life and of our relationship seemed an impossible absurdity; it was far harder to believe that there was nothing more than to believe in some kind of continuing reality of all that we had shared.

It is here that words fail; anything beyond our earthly existence is unimaginable. But spiritual reality is not bounded by the time and space to which we are subject. Whatever form of consciousness may or may not exist beyond the grave, whether or how personal identity survives, I hope that there may be further growth and further understanding. The Roman Catholic doctrine of purgatory reflects this hope. Eastern religions see it in terms of successive reincarnations. As to its form, I remain agnostic, that is, I neither believe nor disbelieve.

Death undams a great flood of love and concern. That was my experience, and I have had much to help me, public as well as private recognition. Now, in an immediate way, I have been able to play a part in some of the continuing aspects of John's work. I remain on the Council of Christian Action. With Trevor Beeson, dean of Winchester, as chairman, and Eric James as full-time director, the organisation has concentrated upon home affairs, in particular, the plight of the poor in our inner cities. It was Eric who, with the support of the council, suggested to Robert Runcie that the Church might carry out its own investigation. The result was *Faith in the City*, to which Eric made a tireless contribution. The report attracted immediate attention and controversy, partly through the helpful comments of one or two MPs who described it as 'Marxist rubbish'. It is now on the political agenda.

There have been nine years of work for IDAF, during which we have seen the independence of Namibia. On John's death the Trustees invited me to join them, and this has been for me a help and a privilege. Soon the ever-expanding organisation moved to Canon Collins House in Islington, with all departments now under one roof. When Phyllis Altman retired, another South African exile, Horst Kleinschmidt, became director. This was a good appointment, and in the end it was Horst who, deservedly, was given the Kreisky prize. At one time IDAF employed around fifty people, and handled £9–10 million a year – a far cry from the basement of 2 Amen Court.

One of the worst aspects of these years of repression was the onslaught upon the children of the African townships. Witnesses described it as 'an indiscriminate but systematic campaign of terror against all black children'. I prepared a report to be used publicly and sent to donor governments, the UN, and the British government. It was a harrowing experience to read through all those affidavits from children, some under ten years old, at least one aged only seven. They had been shot, beaten, imprisoned, tortured and sexually abused. There was copious supporting evidence from parents, lawyers, doctors, Church-men, social workers and psychiatrists; more than 18,000 children and young people were affected.

IDAF planned an international conference to draw world attention to the plight of these children. With the co-operation of the Zimbabwe government, we held the conference in Harare in September 1987. IDAF was still a banned organisation, so for security reasons, the conference was announced under the aegis of the Bishop Ambrose Reeves Trust. In fact it was initiated, funded and organised by IDAF, and Archbishop Huddleston took the chair.

To me, the conference was a devastating, but also an inspiring experience. The inspiration came from the spirit and courage of the South African contingent who came to Harare, men and women of all races who had worked with and for the children, mothers of those who had suffered as well as the children themselves, all were brave enough to stand up and testify. It required courage to come and speak openly, but they were prepared to risk anything to tell their terrible story to the world.

As well as many representatives of governments and of the international community, leaders of the exiled ANC and other organisations were there. Most of the people from inside had never seen Trevor Huddleston or Oliver Tambo and his colleagues in the flesh. There was singing and dancing and jubilation. But when the buses came to take the South Africans back to the airport for their return, we stood around in tears, wondering fearfully what awaited them.

The conference did have an effect: the savagery against the children abated, and by degrees large numbers of those in prison were released. We felt that this was one of our most worthwhile efforts.

With the release of Nelson Mandela, and the unbanning of so many organisations including IDAF, much, though not enough, has changed. Nevertheless, the Trustees decided that the time had come to wind up IDAF as an external organisation, and transfer its operations to bodies inside South Africa. I believed that this was premature, and argued against it, but I was out-voted. So at the end of May 1991 we held our final AGM in London. For me, and I think not only for me, this was an emotional occasion.

British Defence and Aid with John Prevett as chairman, and its dynamo of a director Ethel de Keyser, continues to raise money for the new bodies in South Africa. It also runs and raises money for the Canon Collins Education Fund for Southern Africa, and I continue to serve on both these bodies.

One of the sadder experiences of growing old is the loss of friends; too many of mine have slipped away. Jack Priestley died in the summer of 1984. He was one of my closest friends, and one who influenced me a great deal, I could talk to him about anything and everything. Jack too was always going onward: 'I search for wisdom,' he wrote, 'as other people search for rare birds'. I couldn't follow all his speculations, though I found them fascinating, as I did his rich, life-enhancing personality. I miss his understanding, his kindly humour and his affection: but I still have the friendship of Jacquetta which is equally precious, and we have had happy holidays abroad together.

In the writing of this book I have had to delve back into John's and my lives. So much that at the time appeared accidental and coincidental seems to fall into place, and has what I can only describe as an inevitable rightness. As to the value of John's work, time and others must judge. I have to confess to a smile when I hear bishops and archbishops talking about religion and politics in much the same way as John spoke in the early 1950s. One man sows and another man reaps: that is how things are, and will always be.

Many people were amazed by John's development, and rather surprised by mine – such an unsuitable candidate for a clerical marriage.

Yet in both of us, in our childhood and growing up, I find the seeds of future development. I like to believe that our marriage helped to bring those seeds to fruition. Of course, we had failures, misunderstandings and inadequacies, I am conscious of plenty of mine, I am not claiming perfection. But any clouds that there might have been were soon blown away.

With experience of life, beliefs develop and change. For John the dynamism of his faith sprang from the question-mark at its heart. 'I have become more and more doubtful,' he wrote, 'about an increasing number of the formularies of the Christian Gospel – but more and more convinced of the basic truth of the Gospel those formularies are intended to preserve . . . Once an intellectual formulary is given authoritative status it cramps rather than liberates the human spirit.'

Like John, I have less and less belief in dogmatic formulations, unless they are seen as symbols of a deeper truth. I have wrestled with theology in a dilettante manner – dilettantism is the story of my life. But I no longer find theology helpful. I return to poetry and to a search for that inner light, cultivated by the Quakers. I am no longer 'hot for certainties', but I know that the person, who or whatever he was or is, that I want to try to follow is the man of Galilee, Jesus of Nazareth. It is his teaching, the drama of his life and death, the paradox of worldly defeat and spiritual triumph, of death and resurrection that speak to me most powerfully.

My agnosticism goes further than John's. His heart was open to any human being, whatever his or her belief or lack of belief, but he did not share my interest in Eastern religions. I fear that I am that of which the orthodox most disapprove, a syncretist and a pantheist. Christianity embodies *a* truth, it is *my* truth, but I cannot believe that it is *the* only and exclusive truth. The one immanent and transcendent God is to be found in all the great world religions, and in many of the beliefs and rituals of those we patronisingly refer to as primitive people. But the truth of God is beyond and inexpressibly greater than all these.

During my lifetime we have witnessed the worst and the best of human nature. When I first grew up, if anyone had predicted the horror of the holocaust, the return to torture as an instrument of government, I wouldn't have believed them; torture was a medieval relic, now it is everywhere. Is it that we are only made more aware of horror and cruelty? Perhaps, rightly, the media doesn't let us escape.

Yet our corrupt and terrible century has its heroes and martyrs, and I have spent much of my life among people who work, often tirelessly, for others, and ask for no personal reward. I have seen and experienced kindness, generosity, courage and endurance. Yes, I have worked among 'do-gooders', and I get angry when that word is used in pejorative dismissal. My experience teaches me that the human spirit will always reassert itself; it cannot be destroyed.

When our son, Richard, was five or six years old, it was his turn to come with me on our annual pre-Christmas foraging expedition into Suffolk. We stayed with an aunt on her dairy farm near Ipswich. Richard had a wonderful time, as well as all the excitements of the farm, he shared in a birthday party for a young cousin. 'Why are we so lucky in our lives, Mummy?' he asked. I had no answer then, I have no answer now. I cannot imagine why I should have been so extraordinarily fortunate. I can only record my heartfelt thankfulness.

Author's note

I delivered the completed manuscript of *Partners in Protest* at the end of August 1991. On 11 September our artistically talented son, Richard, had a serious motor accident, as a result of which, on 19 September, he died.

After much thought, I felt that it would be too difficult to write of this tragedy; it would change and might unbalance the book and its conclusion.

This is the story of the life and work that John and I shared; we could not share in Richard's earthly death.

> Joy and woe are woven fine
> A clothing for the soul divine,
> It is right it should be so
> Man was made for joy and woe,
> And when this we rightly know,
> Safely through the world we go.
> William Blake

Index